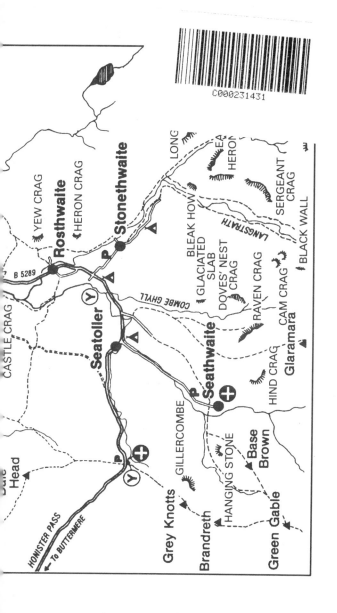

CASTLE CRAG

YEW CRAG

Rosthwaite

HERON CRAG

B 5289

Stonethwaite

LONG

HERON

EA

SERGEANT
CRAG

BLEAK HOW

GLACIATED
SLAB

DOVES' NEST
CRAG

LANGSTRATH

BLACK WALL

COMBE GHYLL

Seatoller

Y

RAVEN CRAG

CAM CRAG

Glaramara

Seathwaite

P

HIND CRAG

GILLERCOMBE

Base
Brown

Dale
Head

P

Y

HONISTER PASS

To BUTTERMERE

Grey Knotts

Brandreth

HANGING STONE

Green Gable

C000231431

The F&RCC and Rock Climbing Guides to the English Lake District

The Fell and Rock Climbing Club, founded at Coniston in 1906, published its first rock climbing guidebook in 1922 and since that date has produced a continuous series of guidebooks which are accepted as the definitive guidebooks to Lake District rock climbing.

These guidebooks are written and published by volunteers who update the text and check new climbs, many of which have been, and continue to be, pioneered by Club members.

Enquiries regarding the F&RCC and its guidebooks should be addressed to the current Club Secretary or Guidebooks Editor, whose addresses are available from the Club's website at http://www.FRCC.co.uk or from the BMC.

BORROWDALE

Above: A. Abrahams and N. Van Zuylen peer cautiously over the
Belvedere on Shepherds Crag

Ron Kenyon

Overleaf: Derwentwater from Castle Head

Ron Kenyon

Climbing Guides to climbing in the
English Lake District

Borrowdale

by G.R. Baum and A.P. Hewison

Illustrated by

A. Phizacklea, T. Wood and A.P. Hewison

Edited by S. J. H. Reid

Published by the Fell and Rock Climbing Club
of the English Lake District

© ISBN 0 85028 043 5

DEDICATION

This guidebook is dedicated to Ray MacHaffie – the original 'Jaws of Borrowdale' – and without whose efforts this guide would not be half the volume that it is.

Great Gable and Borrowdale:
1925   H.S Gross and A.R. Thompson

Great Gable, Borrowdale and Buttermere:
1937   C.J. Astley Cooper, E. Wood-Johnson and L.H. Pollitt

Borrowdale:
1953   Bentley Beetham
1960   Bentley Beetham (Reprint)
1966   Bentley Beetham (Reprint)
1968   P.J. Nunn and O. Woolcock
1978   S. Clark
1986   D. Armstrong and R. Kenyon
1990   R.J. Kenyon

Present edition: 2000

British Library Cataloguing in Publication Data

Baum, G.

Borrowdale. — [8th ed.] — (Climbing guides to the English Lake District) —
(F & RCC guide)
1. Cumbria. Borrowdale. Rock climbing
I. Title II. Reid, S. (Stephen), 1953– III. Fell and Rock Climbing Club of the Engli
Lake District IV. Series
796.52230942787   GV199.44.G7

ISBN 0-85028-043-5

Prepared for printing by Synergy, Royal Oak Barn, The Square, Cartmel, Cumbria, LA11 6QB.
Printed by The Ernest Press, Glasgow, G44 5QD.
Distributed by Cordee, 3a De Montfort Street, Leicester, LE1 7HD.

CONTENTS

Photographs

A chip off the old block – *Front Cover*
James McHaffie on The Grasp (E1),
Shepherd's Crag
Photo – David Simmonite

Adam Hocking making *Rear Cover*
the long sought after second
ascent of Bleed in Hell (E8),
Bowderstone Crag
Photo – David Simmonite

First Frontispiece
The Belvedere, Shepherd's Crag

Second Frontispiece
Derwentwater from Castle Head

	Opposite Page
Mouse Ghyll (D), Blea Crag	32
Little Chamonix (VD), Shepherd's	33
The Dangler (E2), Lower Falcon	64
The Joke (E3), Lower Falcon	65
Finger Flake Finish to the Rack (E2), Reecastle	80
Mort (E1), Goats Crag	80
Daylight Robbery (E5), Reecastle	81
Penal Servitude (E5), Reecastle	96
Guillotine (E2), Reecastle	97

	Opposite Page
The Niche (HVS), Lower Goats	112
Fisher's Folly (VS), Shepherd's Crag	112
Battering Ram (E2), Shepherd's	113
Kransic Crack Direct (HVS)	113
Chamonix Girdle (HVS)	128
MGC (E2), Shepherd's Crag	129
Finale (HVS), Shepherd's Crag	144
Conclusion (E1), Shepherd's Crag	144
Prana (E3), Black Crag	145

6 CONTENTS

Tracking down good climbing photographs for guidebooks is always a difficult task. The Guidebooks Committee of the F&RCC would like to express their gratitude to all those who submitted photographs for consideration, together with Nick Wharton (Photographs Sub-Editor), Alice Pearson of Abbot Hall Museum, Iain Whitmey (F&RCC Archivist) and Malcolm Ibbertson (F&RCC Slides Archivist) for their assistance. To those whose photographs were not selected this time, please do not be discouraged, and please keep up the flow of new material. Anyone interested in supporting this aspect of guidebook work should contact the Guidebook Photographs Sub-Editor whose address, together with details of current guidebook work being undertaken, is available from the Club's website at http://www.FRCC.co.uk

INTRODUCTION

This volume is the fifth in the Eighth Series of definitive climbing guidebooks to the Lake District produced by the Fell and Rock Climbing Club of the English Lake District. It is proposed that this series will comprise six volumes as follows:

1. Eastern Crags
2. Dow, Duddon and Slate
3. Scafell, Wasdale and Eskdale
4. Langdale
5. Borrowdale
6. Gable, Pillar and Buttermere

This guidebook covers the entire valley of Borrowdale which remains one of the most popular climbing areas in the Lake District. Ease of access and the quick-drying nature of the rock, in particular that of Shepherd's Crag, provide the explanation. The popularity of the valley has, no doubt, contributed to the enormous number of new routes recorded in the decade since the last guidebook. This has presented a difficult problem for the guidebook writers, Gary Baum and Al Hewison, who have had their work cut out in attempting to repeat all the new climbs not to mention checking up on comments made on the previous edition. Needless to say it has not been possible to repeat (or even locate!) everything, but they have, it is fair to say, grappled with so much more than their fair share of grotty, vegetated and uninspiring rock over the last five years that only the occasional well deserved holiday in Calpe could atone for it. Despite this they have been surprised to find that many of the new routes recorded are actually very good. I hope that you may enjoy them too, and in doing so, come to appreciate the incredible amount of voluntary time and effort the writers have put into producing this guide.

Stephen Reid, March 2000

General Notes

Grades

Every new edition of a guidebook gives the opportunity to review both technical and adjectival grades in the hope that the inevitable existing anomalies will be resolved and not too many new ones created. However, caution should still reign and total reliance on a given grade avoided. The current condition of a route can greatly affect its grade. What was a pleasant, generally clean route when checked for the guide can become unattractively dirty or overgrown surprisingly quickly.

Adjectival Grades
These give the overall grade of the climb in good weather conditions, taking into account such factors as technical difficulty, rock quality and protection. The grades are: Moderate, Difficult, Very Difficult, Mild Severe, Severe, Hard Severe, Mild Very Severe, Very Severe, Hard Very Severe, Extremely Severe, with the standard abbreviations being used in the text. The Extremely Severe grade is divided into E1, E2, through to E9. The system is open-ended but see the note below regarding routes of E6 and above.

Grades are very personal, being influenced by an individual's stature and physique, their ability to climb above protection, and their preference for a particular style of climbing.

Technical Grades
Included for each pitch of 4a and above on routes from VS, and others where known. This grade is an attempt to assess the problems to be encountered on each pitch and once again is open-ended. The grades to date are: 4a, 4b, 4c, 5a, 5b, 5c, 6a, 6b, 6c, 7a.

French Grades
Bolt-protected "sport" routes are given French grades overall, plus a British technical grade. These grades, prefixed with an "F", are comparable with the standard French/Spanish grades of 4, 5, 6a, 6b, 6c, 7a, 7b, 7c, and 8a. They are further subdivided with a (+) symbol.

It is considered by some of those climbing at the highest standards that French grades provide information not currently available from the normal British grade. Therefore, traditional routes of E6 and above have also been given a French grade in the Graded List, in addition to their British E-grade.

> Important Note: This French grade is applicable in a top-roping context only. It does **not** signify that the route is a sport climb, or that there are bolts on the route, or that there is any intention to place bolts on it. This step represents perhaps the beginning of an overhaul of the grading system at this level, based on the emerging thoughts of some of those most qualified to comment. It will be interesting to see how the debate develops.

Aid
Only a few routes still require the use of artificial assistance and this is indicated in the description where appropriate. Aid reductions continue to be made; routes are described and graded according to the most free style in which they are known to have been climbed.

Stars and Quality
Many more stars have been used in this guide than in previous editions and they are intended to indicate quality on a broad scale. Three stars mean good climbing, on good clean rock, with purpose to the line. Two stars indicate mainly the above, whilst a one star route will have some good climbing and a permutation of the other two factors. Routes having no stars will be those of interest to only a minority of climbers, but should not be written-off completely.

This represents a change in the starring policy adopted in earlier F&RCC guides. Its purpose is to give a wider and more balanced assessment of route quality, helping climbers to easily identify routes worth looking at, and avoiding the situation where many interesting climbs with attractive descriptions are being ignored.

When selecting a route from the huge range now available, it is worth remembering that stars are only a means of narrowing down the choice, particularly for the infrequent or first-time visitor. No matter how many stars a route may have, if it sounds attractive in the guide, be prepared to go to its start and see what it looks like. It is then up to that route to "sell" itself. Many good climbs are missed for the lack of this.

All routes have been allocated stars in good faith (no hidden agendas!) but the condition of a climb can deteriorate quite quickly and make a mockery of its stars. If this has happened to your route, sorry. No system is perfect and it is only meant to be a "guide".

It is particularly difficult to rate new or unrepeated routes. Therefore, these have been given "empty" stars as a provisional assessment. Feedback would be welcome – thank you.

Unrepeated Routes
Climbs that are not known to have been repeated, have their grades suffixed by a (?).

Location of Crags
The location of each crag is indicated by its Ordnance Survey grid reference. Beware those crags where the name on the map may be some way from the grid reference shown. The aspect of the main

faces have been included to aid the choice of crags. The altitude given
is based on the Ordnance Survey datum, which gives mean sea level
as zero. The terms 'true left' and 'true right' are used to describe the
position of a crag in a valley or gill relative to the direction of flow
of the stream. The terms 'left' and 'right', unless otherwise stated,
mean as the climber faces the climb.

New Routes and Corrections
To aid writers of future New Routes Supplements and guidebooks,
please post comments and details of all new climbs on the F&RCC
website, at the following address: **http://www.frcc.co.uk**
Traditionalists can still avail themselves of the New Routes Books at
either *Rock and Run*, Ambleside or *Needle Sports*, Keswick.

Many other New Routes books exist in the area, including the Log
Books in F&RCC huts. However, these may not be checked regularly
and first ascentionists are urged to also record their route at one of
the main sources listed above, or it may be missed.

Please provide all relevant details in the usual format including
grades, dates, first ascentionists and style of ascent, if relevant.

Bolts
The placing of bolts is a subject which has aroused much emotive
discussion during recent years.

In the interest of care and concern for crags and the mountain
environment and a belief that British climbing in general should
continue with the principle of leader-placed removable protection, the
F&RCC are generally in accord with the guidelines on the use of
bolts for the protection of routes as set out by the BMC. It is agreed
that in the Lake District bolts are only acceptable on certain quarried
crags. Only a few quarries which utilize bolts are referred to in this
guidebook. Climbers are asked to adhere to this policy and refrain
from the temptation to place bolts on any natural crags.

Retro-bolting has taken place on a number of routes in the Lake
District but only after consultation with the first ascensionist of that
route. In order to avoid any conflict, please ensure that this policy is
maintained.

In-situ Protection
A number of route descriptions in this guide contain references to
in-situ protection including pegs, slings, bolts and wires. The history
of these frequently dates back to the first ascent. There can be no
guarantee that the fixed gear mentioned will still be in place when

you climb the route or, more importantly, if it is there, that it will be of any use. It is well known that in-situ gear will deteriorate to a fraction of its original holding power due to the elements. This can occur in a matter of months rather than years, particularly where wires or hard steel blade pegs are concerned. Therefore, it is for the individual climber to assess the reliability of any in-situ protection encountered.

Fixed abseil points have been found around some of the crags over the years. They should be thoroughly inspected before use and, if found to be doubtful, backed up with new equipment.

All prospective first ascentionists are asked to consider carefully the life span of any piece of protection they choose to place if it is to be left in-situ.

This thought must also be carefully weighed when using bolts as the principle means of protection. It is essential that only the best available bolts and hangers are fixed. Climbers in the South Lakes have found it necessary to set up a fund for the replacement of unsuitable bolts in the area. It is intended that this will also be used to replace ageing bolts in future years. The support of, and contribution to, this fund is expected of all bolt users!

Safety Advice

Climbing is a dangerous pastime that can seriously damage your health! Details of climbs recorded in this guidebook, together with their grades, reference to in-situ or natural protection and locations, are made in good faith having been compiled from first ascent or past descriptions, checked and substantiated where possible with consensus comments.

Unfortunately, climbs can change; holds fall off, rock becomes dirty, in-situ gear deteriorates or disappears. Even a minor alteration can have a dramatic effect on the grade or seriousness of a route. It is, therefore, essential that climbers judge the condition of any route before committing themselves.

The contents of this guidebook are believed to be correct. However, neither the F&RCC nor its members and their friends involved with its production can be held responsible for any omissions or mistakes, nor liable for any personal or third party injuries or damage, howsoever caused, arising from its use. In this claims-conscious age, climbers are recommended to obtain suitable insurance cover. The BMC now provides third party liability cover for members and members of affiliated clubs.

CRAG GUIDE

The following guide summarises the number of routes to be found in each grade at most of the traditional climbing venues in the valley. Note that the maximum route length indicated does not include routes that are basically traverses.

Crag	Aspect	Alt (m)	Route Lengths (m)	Approach time (min)	Up to D
Castle Head Outcrops	SW	130	6-15	10	
Castle Head Quarry	E	100	20-22	10	
Rakefoot Buttress	W	300	12-24	20	
Walla Crag	NW	250	35-70	20	
Upper Falcon Crag	W	240	58-94	15	
Lower Falcon Crag	W	180	25-60	10	1
Powterhow Buttress	W	300	10-15	15	
Reecastle Crag	NW	300	22-40	10	
Reecastle South	W	300	26-36	10	
Goats Crag	SW	400	13-16	20	1
Lower Goats Crag	SW	360	25-40	20	1
Garotte Buttress	E	260	35-46	5	
Caffell Side Crag	E	260	21-26	5	
Brown Dodd	E/NE	300	30-40	15	
Cat Ghyll Bluffs	W	170	15-70	5	
Gowder Crag	W	200	36-113	10	2
Lodore Crag	E	120	54-82	10	
Shepherd's Crag	W	140	20-86	5	5
Ladder Brow Crag	W	140	12-23	10	
Green Bank Crags	W	160	16-33	15	
Black Crag	W/NW	260	36-110	20	2
Aard Crag	E	250	10-12	20	
Christmas Crag	W	340	10-16	30	
Grange Crags	NW	120	10-15	1-15	
Great End Crag	NW	225	25-100	20	1

The crags are listed in the order that they appear in the main text – i.e. geographically. Approach times may vary according to availability of parking and, of course, your fitness!

VD/MS	S/MVS	VS	HVS	E1	E2	E3	E4	E5	E6/E8
2	1		2	1	1				
				1		1			
		5	7	3	1				
1		8	3	1	7	7	4	2	
			3	1		2	3		
	2	5	6	5	8	9	9	4	
							1		
	2	2	2	3	6	5	2	4	10
1	1				3		1		
	5	1	3	5	3	2	2		
	1	2	1	2	1				
			1	1					
			2		5	1			
	1	2	3	4					
1	3	5	2	5	4	2	1		
3	4	13	5	5	1	1			
			1	1		1			
12	12	24	23	19	19	18	2	5	3
2	1	3	3		1	3			
	2	2		2	1	1			
2	5	21	8	11	8	4	4		
	1	1	1	1	1		1	1	
2	3	4	3						
	5	6	8	13	9	6			1
1			10	1	5		5	2	

Crag	Aspect	Alt (m)	Route Lengths (m)	Approach time (min)	Up to D
King's How	NW	270	28-43	15	
Quayfoot Buttress	N/NW	135	25-45	5	
Woden's Face	W	90	16-30	5	
Bowderstone Crag	SW	220	9-73	20	5
Yew Crag	W	250	20-50	15	3
Long Band Crag	W	430	30-35	30	
Lining Crag	W	460	30-73	45	2
Long Crag	NW	600	8-25	65	
Lower Eagle Crag	NE	420	22-50	40	
Eagle Crag	ENE	500	30-78	40	
Bleak How	NW	270	20-42	25	
Fat Charlie's Buttress	W	100	11-15	15	
Heron Crag	W	360	60-103	30	1
Upper Heron Crag	NW	440	22-30	35	
Sergeant Crag	NW	360	22-157	30	2
Sergeant Crag Slabs	W	400	20-50	40	
Blackmoss Pot Slab	W	350	15-27	50	
Cam Crag/Black Wall	E	400	10-30	50	1
Bull Crag	W	170	35	10	
Paper Crag	NE	220	30	15	
Glaciated Slab	NW	300	16-30	20	7
Twa Hummocks	W	360	25-68	30	4
Doves' Nest Crag	W	360	34-80	40	1
Raven Crag	NE	360	13-184	40	3
Thornythwaite Knotts	E	330	30	30	
Capell Crag	W	360	136	10	1
Hind Crag	W/SW	350	64-187	25	
Grains Ghyll	NW	360	26-40	60	
Aaron Crag	NE/E	500	35-40	45	

VD/MS	S/MVS	VS	HVS	E1	E2	E3	E4	E5	E6/E8
			1	1	1				
2	3	4	7	2	3	1	2	1	
2	6	2		1	2				
5	4	6	9	1	2	2	1	2	6
	2			2					
		1			1		3	2	
	5	3	3	2					
1	1	1		1	3	1			2
		1		3	1	2	2		
	1	8	3	2	7	2	1	5	2
	2	3	6	6	3	3	1	1	
1	1	1	2	3	1				
1	2	2	1						
		1	1	3	6				
1	5	1	3	3		1			
		5	4	5	5	1			
			2		1		1		
1		1	5	1	2	2	2		3
		2							
				2		1		1	2
3	1				1	1			
3	1	2							
2	7		5	2					
7	11	5		1	3	1			
		1	1			1			
2	2		1	2					
1	2	2							
		2							

Crag	Aspect	Alt (m)	Route Lengths (m)	Approach time (min)	Up to D
Black Waugh Crag	NE	300	25-35	35	
Hanging Stone	NE	470	20-26	35	
Gillercombe	SE/NE	480	20-140	30	1
Castle Crag	W	175	8-13	25	
Hows Crag	E	195	25-55	25	
Mac's Wall	NW	150	10-12	25	
Millican's Buttress	NE	160	10-27	25	
Southern Buttress	E	300	20-86	35	
Steel Knotts	SE	240	23-40	30	
Goat Crag	NE	350	23-116	25	
Knitting Needle Gully	NNE	325	45-100	30	
Knitting How	NE/SE	255	25-40	20	2

VD/MS	S/MVS	VS	HVS	E1	E2	E3	E4	E5	E6/E8
1				2	1				
		1	3	1	1				
3	4	1	4	2	2	3	1	1	1
	3	2	10	2		2	1		
1			4	1	1		2		1
		1		1		3			
	2	2	3	3	5				2
	1		3	2	1	1			
	3	1	4		2	1			
1	2	15	13	6	8	7	4	5	2
1			1	1	1	2		2	

ACKNOWLEDGEMENTS

This guide is the product of many peoples' hard work and commitment, not the least of whom are the writers of previous Borrowdale Guides. We have simply built upon their hard work and are greatly indebted to Archer Thompson, Eden Wood-Johnson, Bentley Beetham, Paul Ross, Paul Nunn, Oliver Woolcock, Sid Clark, Dave Armstrong and Ron Kenyon.

Behind the scenes the unsung FRCC guidebook committee does a great voluntary job and we are particularly grateful to Stephen Reid, the series editor, for his guidance, encouragement and enthusiasm during this project.

Specific thanks must go to Tim Wood for the new diagrams of Shepherd's Crag and to Al Phizacklea for updating his previous work and adding Hell's Wall. We are indebted to Nick Wharton for his efforts in searching out photographs. Grateful thanks also go to Neil Thompson and Mark Johnson for their work and comments on The Bowderstone, to John Rodgers for his geological notes and to Karen Sampson of English Nature for her conservation section.

Since the last guide there has been considerable development in Borrowdale and we have tried very hard to ensure that this guide has taken into account the ideas and opinions of as many people as possible. It would be impossible to list everyone who has provided useful comments but we would like to mention the following who have contributed through looking at graded lists, checking text or accompanying us on visits to check routes, Anyone who feels left out from this list, please accept our apologies.

Martin Armitage, Dave Armstrong, Jim and Kate Arnold, Bob Bennet, Dave Birkett, Phil Blanshard, Dave Bodecott, Andy Cannon, Paul Cornforth, Andy Crofts, Al Davis, Dave Douglas, Colin Downer, Alex Heron, Ron Kenyon, Chris King, Rick Graham, Mark Greenbank, Pete Greenwood, Craig Harwood, Mark Hetherington, Adam Hocking, Chris Hope, Alan Greig, Dave Harris, Wesley Hunter, Bob Johnson, Tony Lywood, Jane Meeks, Stuart Miller, Ray and James MacHaffie, James Moore, David Nichol, Soo Redshaw, Angela and Jack Soper, Toby Spence, Steve Stout, Colin Read, Stephen and Jilly Reid, Phil Rigby, Cam Robinson, Paul Ross, John Shepherd, David Stringfellow, Trevor Suddaby, Nick Tudor, Iain Turnbull, Nick Wharton, Adam Wilde, Roger Wilkinson, Alan Wilson.

Yet again, Les and Jean Ainsworth of Synergy have carried out the typesetting. We would like to thank them for altering and re-altering the script as our ideas changed and the manuscript developed – particularly when we decided to completely re-order the routes on Black, Shepherd's and Bowderstone Crags!

Alan would like to thank Gary for doing most of the work, Maurice and Vivienne Hewison for providing their impecunious son with his first climbing rope (little did they know what they had started!) and particularly Stephanie for her love and understanding while he has pursued his ridiculous obsessions.

Gary would like to thank Alan for doing so many second ascents but especially Jane for her encouragement, hours of text checking and days of company on some of the greenest crags in Borrowdale.

Gary Baum, Alan Hewison, May 2000

GEOLOGICAL NOTES

The rocks around Derwentwater and the Borrowdale valley belong to the oldest formations of the Lake District. To the north and west of the lake are the dark blue-grey slates of the so-called *Skiddaw Group*. These were originally deep-sea muds and have since been strongly compressed and distorted. One effect of this compression was to impose on the hardened sediment a tendency to split into thin sheets. This slaty cleavage is imperfectly developed in the *Skiddaw Group*, and as slates they are inferior to the green slate that occurs to the south. The *Skiddaw Group* actually forms most of the northern fells from Blencathra in the east to Ennerdale in the west. The slopes in this area, though steep, are relatively smooth and those crags that are present, are generally quite unsuitable for climbing. This is in stark contrast to the rugged terrain further south.

Most of the central area of the Lakes is composed of hard, resistant rocks which are collectively called the *Borrowdale Volcanic Group*. These formations were produced during an extended period of volcanic activity (perhaps ten million years) which ended around 450 million years ago. By this time a thickness of several thousand metres of erupted material had been produced. The volcano responsible was large and complex, and many of the eruptions would have been violently explosive. The resulting rocks show great variety, being the products of many quite different processes, and the following description is intended to indicate the main types.

Lava Flows
Many of the major climbing areas are composed of *andesites* (a rock commonly found in many of the great volcanoes of the Andes – hence the name). When freshly exposed it is usually a greyish-green colour and most of the crystals are too small to be seen, but typically it also contains visible pale crystals which give a mottled appearance (the polished top of the *Bowderstone* is a good example). Many of the lava flows consist of a top and bottom zone of broken fragments, formed as the upper crust fractured during movement, and then these broken fragments were carried to the front of the advancing flow, where they cascaded down and were subsequently buried as the lava continued downslope.

Pyroclastic Rocks
The molten material that was the source for the lava flows was highly viscous and tended to solidify in the various vents preventing any

further eruption – at least, for a time. The effect of this was to allow gas pressure to build up until it finally exploded, blowing out vast volumes of material which were then deposited as fragments of various kinds on the flanks of the volcano. Such deposits are collectively called *pyroclastics*. Some of these fell as small stones, ash or dust and where they landed in the water of lakes in and around the volcano a distinctive layered pattern has resulted. These finer-grained rocks are known as *tuffs*. One thick sequence of these had been altered into the famous green slate, and disused workings can be traced from *Quayfoot Quarry* through *Castle Crag* right up to Honister and beyond.

Some *pyroclastic* rocks consist of much larger angular blocks separated by finer-grained material and these represent deposits which lay much closed to an exploding vent. Geologists call such coarse-grained material *agglomerate*.

A third type of *pyroclastic* deposit is *ignimbrite*. This is highly distinctive and quite easily recognised. The bulk of the rock is pale; green, cream or pink are common colours. Scattered throughout are dark discontinuous streaks with a roughly parallel alignment. *Ignimbrites* are the solidified remains of *pyroclastic* flows, a particularly violent type of eruption which occurs as a dense, hot cloud of gas, lava droplets and solid particles accelerates downslope after erupting from an elevated vent. Modern *pyroclastic* flows have been highly destructive (Mount St. Helens and Montserrat). The lava flows and *pyroclastic* deposits tend to be interbedded and occur within the same crags. *Ignimbrites* are more common at the south end of Borrowdale, and all of these rock types can be examined in the clean water-worn rocks of the River Derwent. To confuse the picture even further, the flanks of this huge volcano were constantly being eroded by fast flowing torrents which carried loose ash away in thick mud flows, dense enough to transport great blocks along as well. In the later stages of its existence, the volcano was cut by major fractures (faults) and a large area is believed to have subsided leaving a much enlarged crater, a caldera.

A period of major earth movement that was the result of continental collision around four hundred million years ago further deformed and tilted the whole volcanic structure. These hard rocks are also cut by many minor fractures (joints) and the erosion along these together with the inclined surfaces produced by earth movements has resulted in a great range of opportunities for climbers.

J Rodgers

CONSERVATION NOTES

The crags of the Lake District, many of which are within Sites of Special Scientific Interest, provide an important habitat for wild plants. Where undisturbed, this unique environment supports several rare species. Many of the crags in Borrowdale are within woodlands which are not only nationally important SSSIs, but internationally important for nature conservation. Indeed, they have been selected as candidate Special Areas of Conservation under European legislation. These woodlands are dominated by Oak or Birch and often incorporate a luxuriant carpet of mosses and ferns in the ground flora. Many of the mosses and liverworts are rare and of special interest. They are found both on the crags, and the rocks and boulders beneath them. Many species are found only in Borrowdale or other wet woodlands on the western coast of Britain. Rare flowers are also found on crags and in some of the ghylls. Once damaged, such species may not return.

In addition, some of the crags provide regular nesting sites for Peregrine Falcons, a protected species. It may be noticeable to the older generation of climbers that the regular citizen of the crag, the Raven, is experiencing an alarming population decline. In 1995 there were only 60 nesting pairs in the whole of Cumbria and the Raven is now rarer than the Peregrine Falcon. Several factors are contributing to the decline of the Raven and disturbance by climbers is cited as one of these. Please respect the Ravens – they are having a rough time.

To protect the natural environment, the Wildlife and Countryside Act 1981 makes it illegal to disturb nesting birds, such as Peregrine Falcons, and to uproot any plant without the landowner's permission. In Sites of Special Scientific Interest, the landowner is committing an offense if permission is given for any activity that damages important vegetation. In order to avoid future restrictions on access, it is therefore important that climbers respect the natural environment and cause minimum disturbance to crags.

Many of the undeveloped crags are still havens for the flora and fauna mentioned above. On no account should "gardening" destroy these important habitats. To avoid disturbance to the Peregrines, climbers should retreat from that area. Details of restrictions are advertised in the climbing press and displayed locally in climbing shops, climbing walls and on signs positioned on the approach routes to relevant crags. Currently there are restrictions relating to Peregrines at Falcon

Crag. Although, at present, there are no voluntary restrictions relating to Ravens in this guide book area, this situation may change. On established routes, climbing can occur without conflict if wildlife is respected. There should be no gardening of new routes on crags that have significant cliff ledge vegetation and are therefore of nature conservation interest. This is especially important in Borrowdale and such crags are highlighted in this guide. Before developing new crags, environmental considerations must be taken into account. English Nature or other wildlife organisations may be contacted to find out the importance of the vegetation at a specific location.

The following Borrowdale crags and their surroundings have been highlighted as being especially important to nature conservation:-

Walla Crag, Reecastle Crag, Reecastle South Crag, Garotte Buttress, Caffel Side Crag, Torquemada Buttress, Brown Dodd, Cat Ghyll Bluffs, Surprise View Buttress, Gowder Crag, Lodore Crag, Black Crag, Grange Crags, Greatend Crag, King's How, Heron Crag, Upper Heron Crag, Sergeant Crag, Cam Crags, Stanger Ghyll Crag, Grains Ghyll Crag, Aaron's Crag, Black Waugh Crag.

K Sampson

HISTORICAL

The first recorded rock climbs in Borrowdale were made in the 1890's. The Abraham brothers, who did a great deal of exploring of the lesser crags near Keswick, were concerned in many of these. From this period come three excellent gully climbs of difficult to severe standard: Mouse Ghyll, Raven Gully on Glaramara, and Sergeant Crag Gully, led by Cecil Slingsby, W.A. Wilson, and O.G. Jones respectively. After this there is nothing noteworthy till the years just before the 1914 war when H.B. Lyon climbed Gillercombe Buttress, and F. Mallinson and R. Mayson of Keswick; Black Crag Buttress and Bowderstone Pinnacle.

In 1921 and 1922 Bentley Beetham and C. D. Frankland made a number of short climbs in the valley, including Brown Slabs Arête on Shepherd's Crag, which led to a succession of discoveries fifteen years later. In 1924 A. R. Thomson of Portinscale, with the Dolomite guide Angelo Dibona, investigating unconventional rocks in the north-western fells, added some pleasant moderates to the list. Ten years after this came the discovery of the possibilities of Lining Crag by Heaton Cooper.

Then began the serious exploitation of Borrowdale climbing by Bentley Beetham. For and with the Goldsborough Club of Barnard Castle School, he surveyed every sizable crag in the valley, working out very well over a hundred routes with a wide range of difficulty and interest. This exploration went on all through the war years: and in 1946 he turned his attention to Shepherd's Crag, hitherto neglected except by casual scramblers. The convenience of these rocks to the road – and the hotels – added to the quality of the best climbs and the beauty of the surroundings, immediately made this a favourite exercise ground. New and harder routes have been added since, it may yet prove that Finale of 1965 was misnamed.

The pioneers then began to look further north, to Gowder, National Trust and Falcon Crags. Notable leads were done during the Beetham period by W. Peascod, V. Veevers, L. Muscroft, P. W. Vaughan and G. B. Fisher.

The work of Fisher and his friends who later formed the Keswick Mountaineering Club led to a series of extremely hard climbs by Peter Greenwood, Peter Lockey, and Paul Ross in the later 1950's. Many of these were on faces of forbidding steepness and a quality of rock that in earlier times would never have been attempted; pitons were sometimes needed, as belays or for aid. As a result, two imposing precipices – Walla Crag and the north end of Goat Crag – previously admired from respectful distances have provided fine new routes. Leaders in these developments, and in others of the past few years, included R. McHaffie, A. Liddell, J.J.S. Allison, P. Nunn, O. Woolcock, L Brown and B Henderson.

Necessarily, the emphasis in this guide is on the newer, harder routes. But the invitation to climbers of all grades conveyed in Beetham's 1953 introduction, which should be read by all whose interest is other that gymnastic, is still open. Most of the Borrowdale crags are on the lower slopes; they may seem to lead to nothing in particular, and in such rich surroundings their character is often obscured till you come to close quarters. Yet they have more to offer than accessibility and difficulty. The all-round walker who likes a scramble will not be wasting his time if he goes with a friend or two, a good rope and an elementary knowledge of climbing technique to Intake Ridge on a fine winter noon, or to Ashness Ghyll for a summer sunset – preferably not after heavy rain. The moderate climber who enjoys following a good leader up something out of his usual range will find a pleasure no less deep, if different, and a sense of achievement no less flattering on Black Crag Buttress than on Moss Ghyll. Those who hold that Borrowdale is the most beautiful of Lakeland valleys will learn that familiarity with its intimate detail only strengthens their conviction.

Morley Dobson, June 1968

1968–1977

During the nine years since the last guide was published, over one hundred new routes have been climbed. The quality and standards of the climbs have increased steadily, due largely to improved protection techniques, which has resulted in many very hard new routes, and in the reduction or elimination of aid from existing routes. The advent of indoor climbing walls has also played a large part in developing the 'steel claw' necessary for today's top performers.

The latter end of 1968 saw the intermediate development of Goat Crag with the ascent in September of Athanor by J. Adams and C. Read, whilst on Lining Crag, The Ring, The Weaver and The Limit were climbed by McHaffie, Henderson and Freelands.

The ascent of Greatend Pillar in 1969 by a combined team re-awakened interest in Greatend Crag. Meanwhile on Black Crag, boulders were being trundled by B Thompson and W A Barnes to produce The Mortician, a surprisingly good climb.

From 1970 to 1973, over thirty new routes were climbed. Notable amongst these was Nagasaki Grooves, climbed in 1972 by C. Read and J. Adams using pitons for aid.

McHaffie was again active with a trio of routes on Reecastle Crag and Heron Crag. P. Livesey and J. Sheard climbed Raindrop, and made all but one peg redundant on Vertigo (subsequently climbed free by P. Whillance).

1974 was a vintage year when P. Livesey's free ascents of Footless Crow, Bitter Oasis, Nagasaki Grooves and Dry Grasp, left all gasping in his wake – but not for long. These routes have since gained a reputation for excellence and difficulty. Local climbers with fingers stiffened on Armathwaite sandstone had been steadily eliminating aid from old routes and indulging in new ones. Notable amongst these were J. Lamb, S Clegg, P Botterill and P Whillance.

In 1975 this team opened up with Blondin, Slack Alice and Juicy Lucy for 'afters', all on Caffell Side Crag. April saw the grand unveiling of Greatend Crag after a winter of secret activity: Greatend Grooves, Earthstrip and the excellent Corner, all at Hard Very Severe, were a taste of things to come from D. Nicols, C. Downer, I. Conway, D Hellier and R. Wilson. J. Lamb, alias 'The Jackal', free climbed the previously aided first pitch of Aragorn.

On Eagle Crag, P. Botterill and R. Clegg climbed The Cleft Direct, dispensing with Ross's aid pegs, the Direct start being added by J. Lamb and P. Whillance. This was followed by Autopsy, climbed by Clegg and Botterill. August saw the heatwave continue, and taking advantage of a bone dry Eagle Crag, P. Whillance and S. Clegg climbed Where Eagles Dare, and shortly after S. Clegg in the company of P. Botterill climbed Verdict; both are excellent routes on the very steep central section of the crag. September found T.W. Birkett and R. McHaffie hanging from Savage Messiah on Shepherd's Crag, and a little while later, they discovered the improbable Gleaned Grooves on Black Crag.

1976 saw the creation of Tumbleweed Connection by P. Botterill and D. Rawcliffe, a 'last problem' on the buttress to the left of Praying Mantis on Goat Crag. On the same crag, S. Clegg and P. Botterill completed The Voyage, a rising traverse of Great Buttress. Meanwhile R. Matheson and E. Cleasby were cementing the bold Grand Alliance on Black Crag.

In 1977, Black Crag was again the scene of new route activity. This time it was W. Freelands and R. McHaffie with their aptly named Jubilee Grooves. This was shortly followed by a high level girdle –

High Plains Drifter by W. Freelands, J Lamb and S Clark. C. Downer and D Nicols found Point Blank on Goat Crag. Returning to Greatend Crag, the same pair climbed Banzai Pipeline, Punk Rock and New Wave. On Eagle Crag J. Lamb and W. Freelands climbed the hanging groove below Inquest to give Inquest Direct. Back on Black Crag a route was worked out to the right of Grand Alliance and was named Prana by P. Gomersall. Meanwhile to the left of Vertigo, Livesey was busy putting up Tristar.

Such is the pace of exploration in Borrowdale that a guide book may well be out of date by the time it is published.

S. Clark, December 1977

1978–1985

As is usual with the arrival of a new guide, the following year (1978) saw an onslaught on the remaining gaps which had become apparent; and a few eliminates which were not.

Falcon Crag received much early attention; the best of the bunch being Kidnapped, which linked old variations on Dedication, Plagiarism, climbed by Pete Botterill and Jeff Lamb, and Cyclotron, a bold and difficult problem by Ken Forsythe and Bill Birkett.

A race for lines on Greatend Crag resulted in Pete Whillance and Dave Armstrong climbing Trouble Shooter, and Pete Livesey and Pete Gomersall the contrived eliminate Hiroshima. Goat Crag saw the addition of several lines, Fear of Flying and High Flyer proving most popular, both by Colin Downer and friends.

A major event was the opening up of the quiet Watendlath Valley as a popular climbing area. A trio of excellent routes on Reecastle: White Noise (named as a reminder of the verbal banter from the second), Thumbscrew and Guillotine, all by Jeff Lamb showed the potential of this neglected crag.

The final route of 1978 was Could be the Last on Shepherd's Crag. Unfortunately this was wishful thinking!

After the previous year, 1979 was an anti-climax, both in terms of weather and new routes. Some additions were made to the Watendlath Crags; and a visit to Walla Crag, a justifiably neglected crag, resulted in three routes for Dave Cronshaw and Dave Knighton, together with a pile of loose blocks. The most spectacular routes were the result of free climbing two old artificial climbs. The formidable Hell's Wall on Bowder Crag (still the hardest route in Borrowdale, if not the Lakes) eventually fell to Ron Fawcett after a concerted effort and the use of some Yorkshire tactics! His attempt the previous year employed two points of aid. Exclamation, a ridiculously steep route on Shepherd's Crag, was free-climbed by Bob and Martin Berzins. Unfortunately, this was flawed by the pre-placing of wires and a high runner in the adjoining Shepherd's Chimney.

The following year saw only five new routes recorded, none of which merit any further comments.

After this rest period, 1981 saw a major increase in development with both grades and the quality of routes taking a significant leap forward.

Locals were shaken from their winter slumbers by the addition of three hard routes to Falcon Crag by Jeff Lamb and Pete Botterill during a dry spell in February. Three months later the South Lakes team of Rick Graham and Dave Lyle climbed a first pitch to The Mirage Finish of Bitter Oasis. When combined, these pitches give an excellent route and a fitting companion to the adjacent Footless Crow.

Action continued with the difficult, and potentially dangerous, Devil's Alternative on Shepherd's Crag being climbed by Jeff Lamb and Pete Whillance; the excellent Penal Servitude on Reecastle Crag by Dave Armstrong and Pete Whillance and three good hard routes being added to Bowder Crag.

July and August saw nine new lines added to Eagle Crag by Pete Whillance and Dave Armstrong, updating the development of 1975 and transforming it into a 'modern' crag, with some fine and difficult routes. The roofs at the left end of Shepherd's Crag also received some attention. An ascent of the much eyed problem roof direct to Vesper's traverse was made by Mark Wilford and Kevin Lindhorne. Parting Shot, to its right, was climbed by Jeff Lamb, immediately prior to his departure for Australia, where a climbing accident robbed us of a friend and the Lakes of one of its most active climbers. Once again the pace of development slowed and apart from two pleasant routes by Colin Downer and Sue Kysow on Greatend Crag, Exclusion Zone and No Holds Barred, 1982 will be best remembered as the year when Footless Crow was re-cleaned by some Peak climbers. (Who else would abseil – inspect an existing route!). It then received several ascents, the first after a lapse of many years. A steady trickle of ascents followed and then a T.V. film of an ascent of the route dispelled the aura of difficulty and released the floodgates, opening up a superb route to – everybody?

Pete Kirton, living in the adjacent climbing hut, set to work cleaning the Bowderstone and together with Jerry Moffatt produced a number of extremely difficult boulder problems on the steep north side of this block. On a day off, Jerry Moffatt snatched the soaring arête to the left of Hell's Wall to produce the bold and technical De Quincy.

Goat Crag once again came in for some attention in 1983 with the addition of several routes, the hardest being Wild Times, captured by Pete Botterill and Phil Rigby after considerable effort. Yet more uninspiring routes were squeezed out of Shepherd's Crag, then during the closing months of the year the development started which was to dominate 1984 – the excavation of Bleak How Buttress and Grange Crags.

Dave Hellier sparked off interest in Bleak How Buttress while the Keswick teams of Colin Downer and Chris Bacon, and Ray McHaffie and Pete Taylor led the enterprise on Grange Crags, in various combinations and with others co-opted to help. The Keswick teams then turned their attention to Bleak How Buttress and unearthed yet more hidden gems of all grades. A Penrith group, led by Ron Kenyon and Chris Dale, keen to get in on the action, were banished to the nearby Upper Heron Crag and there produced several pleasant climbs. The development of these crags in 1984 produced many new lines and resulted in the largest number of new routes being climbed in Borrowdale in any single year. Many proved to be quite worthwhile, and a considerable number of easier grade routes were provided, a rare event these days.

Chris Sowden and Martin Berzins stole the impressive line on Reecastle to the right of Executioner, then to 'rub salt in the wounds' called it Daylight Robbery. Later in the year the crag was to receive a further batch of routes, some proving to be very good; finally Ray McHaffie stepped in to sweep up the dregs producing three poor routes at the right-hand end.

Shepherd's Crag was once again scoured in the hope of finding some unclimbed rock and several mediocre eliminates and variations were added. As each year passes and another variation is added it becomes more and more apparent that there are no worthwhile routes left to be found on this already over developed piece of rock.

1985 dawned with great expectations of a last minute crop of new routes to add to the forthcoming guide. Alas, the weather had other ideas; after a brief fine spell in spring the desperately wet summer allowed only a few of the potential lines to become a reality. Most of those climbed were in the easier grades (for modern routes) and pioneered by the locals Colin Downer, Pete Hirst and the indefatigable Ray McHaffie, who were able to snatch routes on the odd dry days. They chose such obscure crags as Hanging Stones, National Trust Crags, Raven Crag and Thornythwaite Knotts for these routes, with only a handful being discovered on the more popular crags.

Eight years and over two hundred and fifty new routes later the new Borrowdale guide has become essential to bring the record up to date. During this period, ethics and protection have changed radically.

Yo-yoing has become an almost accepted method of ascending the hardest routes, and regrettably, the more dubious technique of 'dogging' (hanging on rope and runners, checking holds and runners above), has become more widespread. Prior top roping of new routes has also been carried out, another unnecessary practice imported from the outcrop climbing scene. 'Micro nuts', 'Rocks' and 'Friends', together with the latest 'sticky boots' have now become required equipment for the modern climber, helping to make routes safer and coupled with the increase in training, make the ascent of more difficult and sustained routes possible.

What of the future? Protection equipment will, I'm sure, continue to be developed and improved. The placing of bolts on new routes, – surely the ultimate cheat in the art of protecting climbs, has not yet spread to the Lakes, and it is hoped that this will remain the case. (That's not a challenge!)

Strength and above all, stamina, are becoming essential for one to succeed on the hardest routes and training programmes to increase fitness, are being extended and improved every year by the leading activists in an attempt to stay ahead.

Alas, virgin rock is a finite material which is becoming more and more scarce each year, particularly on the lower crags. Eliminates and variations will continue to be added – and there are one or two good hard lines left, though no hint of their whereabouts! Walking may once again have to become an accepted part of the climbing day and the more remote crags be inspected. It is evident that the acceptable route length has reduced over the years; the quality and sustained nature of the climb now being more important than footage. It is possible that this process will continue and that 'routes' will be claimed on the more isolated crags and outcrops scattered around the fellside, ultimately diminishing to boulder problems status. Time and the next generation of climbers will no doubt have an answer for this dilemma.

D Armstrong, December 1985

1986–1989

The pace of development prior to the publication of the last guide has continued with over 130 new routes appearing.

New crags have been discovered or in some cases unearthed; old fashioned crags such as Sergeant Crag and Gillercombe have been re-examined and modern routes discovered and finally, crags previously considered worked out or too blank have yielded some top quality routes.

Borrowdale still attracts many climbers; it has one of the three Lake District crags of international repute – Goat Crag, it also has many other excellent popular and easily accessible crags along its length.

Many of the new discoveries are on small crags, it is too early to assess the importance of these micro-routes though many are on good rock and give good lines. It is all too easy to be dismissive of this type of route however they are a welcome addition as they provide a stimulus to further exploration and prevent local climbers becoming jaded.

Shortly after the publication of the last guide in 1986, Paul Ingham was to be found battling up a previous top roped problem on Shepherd's Crag to give the desperate Geronimo. On Falcon Crag a number of hard serious eliminates were worked out by Andy Jones though are unlikely to prove popular.

The most significant routes of 1987 are amongst the five fine routes climbed by Paul Ingham and Paul Cornforth on one of yesteryears micro crags – Reecastle Crag. These climbs and the dedication, preparation and skill required to produce them typifies the direction in which modern climbing is moving. Walls previously thought unclimbable will eventually fall to those with the 'eye of faith' – and necessary talent. Most other routes of 1987 were eclipsed by those on Reecastle though once again Andy Jones was active, finding two hard routes on the neglected Long Band Crag.

The development of smaller crags accelerated in 1988. Kit Wilkinson was at the forefront of development on the more solid lower tier of National Trust Crags and the newly developed Cam Crag while Stuart Miller instigated development of Perched Block Buttress on Goat Crag. More significantly Tom Walkington accepted the hints given in the last guide and blitzed the steep Pedestal Wall area of Gillercombe Buttress to produce several excellent short routes. About the same time Bob Smith and John Earl climbed three short but hard routes on the left-hand side of Greatend Crag.

Pete Hirst and friends carried out some extensive gardening of the areas right of Raven Crag in Combe Ghyll. Easy Street is by far the best route produced, and the most extensively gardened – gardening which would appear in this instance to have got out of hand and be the sort of thing likey to annoy conservationists.

New Years Day for most would be a day spent recovering from the night before; not however for Kit Wilkinson, Ray McHaffie and Pete Hirst who started 1989 with a search for new routes. They climbed a new traverse on Mac's Wall then started developments of Troutbeck Gully Wall. Perhaps they should have stayed at home! Kit continued his assault on all rock below 15 metres, developing a small buttress left of Castle Crag. Shortly afterwards he initiated investigations of Goats Crag in Watendlath though left Karl Telfer and friends to complete its development later in the year.

The 1990s are now with us and no doubt the development of climbing styles, ethics and new routes will continue. The move to climbs on shorter crags will continue, by necessity, although there are still one or two good lines to be found on the established crags.

Hype and greed for glory leads people to use dubious tactics and get carried away with gardening, chipping, etc. The cleaning and pre-checking of new routes is now accepted and on the hardest is in fact essential. This must however be restrained to avoid spoiling lines for others. Protection; its type, placing and use has been a popular subject for debate in recent times, particularly the ubiquitous bolt. This method of protection has not been and should not be accepted on Lakeland Crags. The use of other modern, albeit at times marginal, protection is to be advocated, provided it does not cause permanent disfiguration of the rock. This will no doubt sort out the more adventurous from the sports climber.

As for the quality of new routes; when developing a new line climbers are encouraged to think ahead and ponder the future of the 'gem' which they are unearthing from the hillside and denuding of vegetation. Will it become popular or even climbed by someone other than the next guide writer or will it get left for nature to reclaim? Is it worth the destruction!? It must be remembered that Borrowdale is a sensitive conservation zone and a thoughtless attitude is likely to produce even more conflict with authorities, landowners and conservation groups.

Opposite: An early ascent of **Mouse Ghyll** (D), Blea Crag.

Abrahams' collection

The people pressure on the Lakes is now very great. Borrowdale, one of the most popular areas is suffering with erosion of many paths and hillsides. It has a varied collection of crags and climbs, the valley crags being extremely popular, however there are many fine though less crowded crags a short walk away. It is hoped this guide will help climbers find and enjoy their chosen routes and hopefully savour some of the lesser known areas, thus spreading and easing the pressure on overused areas.

R Kenyon, D Armstrong, 1990

1990 – 2000

It has been said that The Lake District has become something of a backwater of British climbing in recent years. The evidence of this latest edition of the Borrowdale guide suggests, however, that there is still much activity in this popular valley with over 350 new routes being recorded since 1990. Amongst the discoveries has been a small number of extremely hard and bold routes which have been continued the valley's tradition as a forcing ground for climbs of the highest calibre. In addition, many good routes at more modest grades have come to light, as exemplified by the discovery and development of the superb Sergeant Crag Slabs.

As predicted by the writers of the previous historical section, much recent development has focused on smaller crags. Unfortunately, at times, the amount of gardening required to unearth routes has caused people to raise environmental concerns. Many areas in Borrowdale are highly sensitive and are designated SSSIs (see separate section). Even if they are not, it is sometimes debatable as to whether it is worth extensive gardening to produce a route that is unlikely to be popular. It is, after all, a fact of Borrowdale life that most routes will revert to their natural pre-cleaned state unless they are regularly climbed. The guide book writers have encountered many new routes that have probably received only one or two ascents and look unlikely to receive many, or indeed any, more. Rick Graham's maxim 'if it takes longer to clean it than to climb it, then it's not worth doing' is one to which new routers might sensibly adhere, and it is to be hoped they will consider the likely end result of their efforts a little more carefully in the future before reaching for their wire brush.

Opposite: Prolific Borrowdale explorer, Bentley Beetham leading the top pitch of one of his best known routes, **Little Chamonix** (VD), Shepherd's Crag   *FRCC Collection*

It also seems that climbers in general are focusing their activities on a relatively small number of the more accessible crags. As a result of this some excellent lines on less popular crags are becoming greener and less attractive. Thanks to the efforts of some selfless individuals a few crags have experienced something of a spring clean recently. If, however, more climbers were prepared to go a little further afield and put up with some less than perfectly clean rock then maybe some of the classics of the past would regain their former status.

Another trend noticed by these writers is for new routes to be squeezed in between already very close lines and for sections of existing routes to be linked up in new ways. This is an inevitable result of people wanting to create something new when there is only a finite amount of rock available. Some of these lines are really only variations or eliminates at best and have been described as such. It must be said, however, that some surprisingly good and independent lines have been created in this way and have been duly given credit.

And so to the last ten years...

The first major discovery was the work of the indefatigable Ray McHaffie, with the development of Sergeant Crag Slabs in Langstrath during the summer of 1991. This has already proved to be a mecca for the middle grade climber, offering delightful climbing on perfect rock. Just a few hundred metres further up the valley Kit Wilkinson and Ray McHaffie found the excellent Slab Happy (E2 5c) on the fine but short Blackmoss Pot Slab. Meanwhile, Malcolm Lowerson and Nick Steen were working hard on the right hand side of Walla Crag to produce a string of harder climbs. The nature of the rock here coupled with the boldness of these climbs may, perhaps, explain why they have not become more popular. Maybe this will change with time. At the end of 1991, Don Greenop with various partners revisited Ladderbrow and Green Bank Crags and began the opening up of numerous lines that may appeal to those who have 'done it all' at the nearby Shepherd's Crag.

Ray McHaffie and Terry Richardson began the New Year in 1992 with A Fistful of Dollars (HVS 5a) on Shepherd's Crag. It is more likely, however, that this year will mainly be remembered for Dave Birkett making his mark on the valley with a series of outstanding hard routes – The Whipping Post (E7 7a), Bleed in Hell (E8 6c), Hellish (E8 6c) and Caution (E8 6c). At Reecastle, Paul Cornforth was also responsible for the powerful and technical Burn at the Stake (E7 7a). The summer of 1992 saw Ray McHaffie returning to Sergeant Crag Slabs. This time he was with Colin Downer who put up one of the best slab routes in the Lake District, Aphasia (E2 5b). A week later Stuart Miller removed one of the last aid points in Borrowdale by freeing Excalibur (E3 5c) at Lodore Crag, but how many will want to repeat it is open to question!

Over the New Year period 1992/93 Ray McHaffie worked on the previously little visited Christmas Crag. In a delightful setting and offering some fine short low grade routes, this ought to become a popular venue in the future. Also in 1993 he was hard at work on Rakefoot Buttress. Meanwhile, Dave and Alistair Nicol had been busy developing Dalt Quarry into Borrowdale's first 'sport' crag although the odd bolted route had also appeared in the remains of Bowderstone Quarry. Since then, Dalt Quarry has enjoyed a period of popularity quite out of scale to its size!

1994 saw Colin Downer and others blitzing the rock to the left of Millican Dalton's Cave to produce a number of good lines on Millican's Buttress while the Ross family took to the well hidden but worthwhile Aard Crag. In 1995, Tom Walkington took time off from new-routing in Langdale to put up a couple of further lines on the by now well established and popular Sergeant Crag Slabs. Also in this year a new local climber appeared on the scene. Adam Hocking, after honing his skills on the recently opened Keswick Climbing Wall, added the Direct Start to Penal Servitude (E5 6c). Stephen and Jilly Reid, meanwhile, put up the very pleasant Horizontal Pleasure (HVS 4c) on Doves' Nest Crag thus rekindling an interest in this traditional venue that has continued throughout the decade.

In 1996 the guide book writers were guilty of following the trend for developing small outcrops with a handful of lines at Fat Charlie's Buttress. Of much greater significance were the routes on Long Crag by Paul Cornforth and Mark Greenbank – the bold and difficult Rock Lobster (E7 6b) and Borrowdale Volcanic (E6 6b). Colin Read and Graham Swainbank bucked the small outcrops trend and showed what is still possible if you keep your eyes open by producing the excellent String of Pearls (E2 5b) at Gillercombe and the enjoyable Manhattan Project (E2 5b) at Great End Crag, a venue that had otherwise been thought of as growing back to nature. In June, Ray McHaffie climbed Final Act (E2 5c) – a new route that he declared would be his last. Over 15 more have followed since!

The poor summers of 1997 and 1998 saw less activity and only a few worthwhile routes. Amongst these were, however, Adam Hocking's Disorderly Conduct (E8 6c) at Reecastle, Duncan Booth and Ian Turnbull's Satan's Little Helper (E7 6b) on Black Wall Langstrath and Martin Dale's Camouflage (E7 6b) on Cam Crags.

Adam (then aged only 17) also astounded some by his solo of Ker Plunk (E5 6a). The McHaffie family continued their development of Hows Crag. The better weather of 1999 saw a revival of interest, no doubt enhanced by the imminent production of this very guide, and activity was spread over a wide variety of crags. Karl Telfer and others added several lines to Green Bank Crags and Ladder Brow Crag, Dave Bodecott and Paul Bunting created Supercrack (E1 5b) at the almost forgotten Garotte Buttress and others managed to prove that there is still room for more development (just) at Shepherd's Crag. Finally, Phil Rigby and John Williams ended the nineties with the obvious line of Terrierman (E4, 6a) on Lower Falcon Crag.

With Borrowdale currently being home to talented young climbers of the likes of Adam Hocking, who in 1999 made the long awaited second ascent of Bleed in Hell (E8 6c), and James McHaffie, who in April 2000 on-sighted Camouflage (E7 6b), the near future surely looks healthy for climbing in the valley. There are undoubtedly good lines still unclimbed but who can really predict what developments the next few years will bring? Whatever happens, the valley will always continue to offer the climber first class routes at all grades in the unique and beautiful setting that is Borrowdale.

Gary Baum, Alan Hewison, May 2000

Postscript, July 2000

Just as the guide is about to go to print, three major new routes have been put up on Eagle Crag. The first, Guns of Navarone (E6), involving 6b climbing protected by a skyhook runner, was the work of Adam Hocking and Alan Wilson, accompanied by Borrowdale veteran Colin Downer. The second, The Ego Has Landed (E8), is possibly the most outrageous ascent in the valley to date, with total commitment being required to tackle its 20m of sustained 6b climbing, most of it above the only protection, a peg at 3 metres. It is fitting that such a breath-taking route should be pioneered by James McHaffie, son of Borrowdale's most prolific new route activist. He was accompanied by Stuart Wood. Finally Downer enlisted Wesley Hunter to lead The Restraint of Beasts (E5 6b, 5c) aptly described as "the line of the crag" and a climb that has already attracted several repeats. It is a sobering thought that Hocking, Hunter and McHaffie are all still in their teens. One can only wonder, what will they, and their generation, get up to next?

BORROWDALE NORTH

BORROWDALE NORTH

Key

P	Parking
⚠	Youth Hostel
⚠	Camping
Ⓒ	Public Conveniences

Castle Head

Just above the east side of the Borrowdale valley road, about 200 metres from the roundabout on the outskirts of Keswick, is the hillock of *Castle Head*. This is an excellent viewpoint over Derwentwater and Borrowdale. It is a volcanic plug made of dolerite, not the Borrowdale volcanic series more usual of the area.

Castle Head provides two climbing areas. Firstly, in the trees overlooking the road, is a series of outcrops containing a number of short climbs and, secondly, on the east side of *Castle Head*, is a quarry giving serious longer routes.

Castle Head Outcrops   (269 227)   Alt. 130 m   South West
Facing

These short problems have been used for many years with first details of routes being given in "Crag and Hound in Lakeland", a book by C.E. Benson published in 1902.

The outcrops are best approached from the Borrowdale valley road and are located about 50 metres south west of the summit of *Castle Head*. They comprise a short polished slab with an overhanging right wall and a short pinnacle just in front of the slab up which the first route starts.

Tommy's Crack   6 m   VD
    Climb the delightful crack up the front of the pinnacle.

Stubble   13 m   HVS   1992
Start at the left-hand side of the crag.
    (4c). Climb a groove to a tree and move out right onto the main slab. Continue to the top.

Fiddle About   10 m   MS
    Ascend the *Polished Slab* starting up the slanting ledge, from the left. Finish directly up the slab, on some doubtful flakes, to gain tree roots at the top.

The Who   15 m   E1?   1999
    (5b). From the top of the step, 3 metres left of the corner of *Pinball Wizard*, ascend delicately to dubious flakes. Make an awkward move and continue to a tree and then the top.

★ **Pinball Wizard** 15 m HVS
Start on the right of the *Polished Slab* below a leftward-slanting corner.
(5a). Gain the corner with interest and follow it with difficulty in a rising curve to finish as for *Fiddle About*.

Unforeseen Danger 15 m E2
This route ascends the gangway in the overhanging right wall. Start just right of *Pinball Wizard* in a pit below a short overhanging wall.
(6a). Overcome the wall and gain the base of the slanting gangway (peg runner). Follow this to below an inverted-V overhang and struggle over this.

15 metres to the right of the *Polished Slab Area* is a short buttress with a fine view over Derwentwater.

I'm Free 15 m MVS
(4b). Climb the groove towards the left of the buttress and either gain holds on the right and finish awkwardly or, more easily, climb up a short rib on the left.

Castle Head Quarry (272 227) Alt. 100 m   East Facing

This intimidating quarry is hidden away in the trees adjacent to the footpath which runs from Springs Road to the Borrowdale valley road around the east side of *Castle Head*. Recent rockfall (1998) confirms the dubious solidity of some of the crag, and no guarantee is given about the state of any old pegs! **This quarry can no longer be recommended as an abseiling venue**.

Jolly Joker (E5 6b, 1997) took the curving thin crackline on the left side of the buttress but rockfall has removed its final section.

Amazing Journey 22 m E1
A varied experience taking the obvious wide crack which splits the centre of the crag.
(5b). Start in the large corner and gain a small ledge. Ascend the steep crack rightwards on good holds to below the obvious chimney-crack. Enter and climb the crack until forced out near its top for a precarious finish.

The groove between *Amazing Journey* and *Miracle Cure* has been climbed at 6b to join and finish up *Amazing Journey*.

Miracle Cure   20 m   E3
A forceful line up the centre of the quarry wall.
> (5c). Start directly below the top of *Amazing Journey* and climb the wall to finish just right of the crack of *Amazing Journey*.

Rakefoot Buttress   (277 216)   Alt. 300 m   West Facing

This very small buttress of rock is about 20 minutes walk from Rakefoot Farm (signposted off the A591). Walk as if going to *Walla Crag* up the left-hand side of the stone wall. Continue past the obvious yew trees and go through the gate where the wall turns to fence for a short distance. Follow the track a little way until you are about 30 metres beyond a solitary birch tree on the left (look out for a very small old tree stump by the path). Now head down directly towards the lake via rocky steps to a small grassy spur and pine trees. The crag is now on the right (facing out) with a cave being an obvious feature. The rock has a flaky, fractured look to it and the writers provide no guarantee as to its solidity. Belays are difficult to arrange above several of the routes. In its favour, the crag provides excellent views over the lake. The routes are described from right to left.

Life Guard   17 m   E2   1993
This takes the steep wall to the left of the cave.
> (5b). Climb the steep wall then make a short traverse left. Climb the groove to the overhang and pull over with care.

The Straits of Despair   17 m   HVS   1993
Seven metres left of the cave is a step up. Immediately above this is a groove.
> (5a). Gain the groove and move right, with difficulty, onto the rib and a good handhold. Easier climbing up the rib leads to an overhang. Climb this with care.

White Dwarf   17 m   HVS   1993
Start as for *Straits of Despair*.
> (5a). Climb the groove which is difficult to start.

Salamanders   12 m   VS   1993
Four metres left of *White Dwarf* is a prow of rock with a deep groove immediately to its left.
> (4c). Climb the short steep groove to the top.

Ultramarines 14 m VS   1993
   (4c). Climb into the foot of the deep groove, as for *Salamanders*.
Step left and climb the steep wall on small holds to the top.

Unknown Warriors 34 m E1   1993
A right-to-left traverse.
   (5b). Climb the deep groove of *Salamanders* to a ledge on the
left then descend a steep crack in a groove for 3 metres. Traverse
left across a steep wall into a corner and move round the rib on
the left. Make an awkward descending traverse into a steep
groove. Just above the overhang, step left into another groove, go
round the nose and finish up the steep wall.

Death Guard 14 m VS   1993
Start just left of the deep groove of *Salamanders*.
   (4c). Move up a short way, traverse left to an undercling and then
climb a steep wall on good holds.

Night Lords 14 m VS   1993
Four metres left of *Salamanders* is a bad step. *Night Lords* starts 3
metres further left at a groove just before a small oak tree.
   (4c). Climb the narrow groove all the way to the top.

World Eaters 20 m VS   1993
   (4c). Start as for *Night Lords*. Climb the groove for 4 metres.
Step left onto the rib and climb steeply up the groove above.

White Scars 20 m HVS   1993
Start just left of *Night Lords* above the small oak tree.
   (5a). Climb the fin (more difficult than it looks), move up and
right round the overhang and go up a deep groove.

Dark Angels 20 m HVS   1993
Start 2 metres left of *White Scars*.
   (5a). Climb the steep groove, traverse right to an overhang and
move left onto a ledge. Climb up and traverse right into a
chimney/groove which is followed to the top.

The following three routes start at the lowest point of the buttress,
just to the left of *Dark Angels*.

Lunar Wolves   24 m   HVS   1993
  (5a). Climb to the overhang, swing right then climb the groove
  above.

Space Wolves   24 m   E1   1993
  (5a). Climb to the overhang and move right a couple of metres.
  Step left round the arête and follow the groove to the top.

Iron Warriors   24 m   E1   1993
  (5a). Climb the corner to the overhang, move steeply left and
  climb the wall above, past a dead tree, finishing up a short groove.

The guidebook writers could not locate the following routes and they
are included to provide you with a challenge in identification.

Phantoms of Fear   17 m   HVS   ?   1993
Start at the second groove left of *Death Guard*.
  (5a). Climb to the overhang (awkward). Easier climbing leads to
  a small tree belay.

Beneath Nightmare Castle   17 m   HVS   ?   1994
Start 3 metres left of *Phantoms of Fear*.
  (5a). Climb onto a ledge at the foot of a crack. Swing out right
  onto the steep face and climb the right side of the pillar.

Walla Crag   (274 212)   Alt. 250 m   North West Facing

This is the first large crag on the left of the Borrowdale road, after
leaving Keswick. The light-coloured buttress is plainly visible rising
out of the steep wooded hillside. Approach either direct from the
National Trust car park, below the crag, or from the stile, below
Falcon Crag, going diagonally northwards along the hillside, across
a beck and a scree fan, to the foot of the crag.

The crag is split by the narrow vegetated *Walla Crag Gully*, which
has the merit of being the first recorded route in Borrowdale. The
climbing is similar to that on *Falcon Crag* but the routes are rather
vegetated in places. The best descent is down *Walla Crag Gully*, by
abseil if necessary.

The climbs are described from left to right.

Walla's Nose 70 m E1   1986
Start behind the large beech tree at the left-hand end of the crag as
for *Ichor*.
1 43 m (5b). Move right to an orange coloured groove. Ascend this
   groove to a bulge at 6 metres, step left onto a sloping shelf and
   move up to undercut holds. Move up right and follow the groove
   to an overhang at 23 metres. Move up, step right, then back left
   to a niche and a small tree. Step up behind it and pull right onto
   the nose, where the angle eases. Climb 6 metres to a small ledge.
   Friend belay.
2 27 m (4b). Climb the groove behind the belay for 10 metres then
   exit right onto interesting vegetation. A botanical wander leads to
   the top.

Ichor 67 m HVS   1965
Start 25 metres left of *White Buttress*, to the left of the overhung base
penetrated by *Blazing Apostles*, behind a large beech tree.
1 32 m (5a). A rising traverse is made to the right above the
   overhangs, to a small ledge on the arête. Move right, along the
   ledge to join *Thanks*; then follow a corner, and traverse diagonally
   right over loose rock to the end of pitch 1 on *White Buttress*.
2 35 m (4c). Climb leftwards to a ledge below the loose
   overhanging wall. Climb up with difficulty to a ledge. Move left
   round a corner into a groove and climb this to the top.

★ **Blazing Apostles** 52 m E2   1979
A steep route with some interesting climbing. Start midway between
Ichor and *Thanks*, below a blank, rightward-slanting groove, through
the overhang.
1 22 m (5c). Climb the groove and the easier groove above to join
   Ichor; continue as for *Ichor* to belay on *White Buttress*.
2 30 m (5b). Climb the overhanging corner above to a ledge.
   Continue up the wall above an overlap and more easily up an
   obvious groove.

Thanks 43 m HVS   1962
Start at the large oak growing from the foot of the crag, about 8
metres left of *White Buttress*.
1 33 m (5a). Scramble up to behind the oak from the right and gain
   the groove on the left. Continue up for 5 metres; then traverse
   left and round a corner on a doubtful block. Move up left to a
   small ledge with a sapling, below a steep wall. Move up and
   swing right, with difficulty, onto the arête. Continue up steep rock
   to a square ledge (peg belay).

2   10 m (4b). Climb the shallow groove above, on poor holds, to finish on vegetation.

Crumble   50 m   VS?   1973
1   21 m. First pitch of *White Buttress*.
2   29 m. Climb diagonally left to a steep brown wall. Go up this to a flake. Move right then climb the groove to the overhang. Step left and climb up to belay. A loose pitch with a vertical heather exit.

** **White Buttress**   59 m   VS   1957
An airy route, which starts behind a large beech tree directly below the centre of the buttress, 25 metres left of *Walla Crag Gully*.
1   21 m. Climb straight up for about 10 metres to a grassy ledge. Move left up a sloping slab to a small stance below spiky blocks and an obvious steep corner.
2   20 m (4b). Climb up left then move back right across the spiky blocks. Move round the arête on the right to a niche. Move up and make for an oak up to the right.
3   18 m (4b). Climb the steep broken groove above and move up the left wall, finishing up a short wall.

Necrosis   50 m   VS   1973
A more direct version of *White Buttress*, starting as for that route.
1   35 m (4c). Climb up, as for *White Buttress*, to the ledge at 10 metres. Ascend the bulge and rock above to a niche with a small sapling. Climb the short crack stepping right to a ledge. Move slightly right and climb a steep wall direct to the oak tree at the top of pitch 2 on *White Buttress*.
2   15 m (4c). Move right and climb to the top of a pinnacle. Gain a rock ledge and climb the shallow groove above, passing an overhang, to the top.

Obsession   42 m   VS   1958
A rather pointless route. Start behind an oak, 10 metres left of *Walla Crag Gully* and about 10 metres below bulging rock, reached by 10 metres of scrambling
1   16 m. Climb small steep gangways slanting up to the left until an easy traverse leads to the end of pitch 1 on *White Buttress*.
2   26 m (5a). Climb a bulge, just left of the belay, and head towards some broken cracks. Step left to the top of a good flake and climb the steep loose-looking wall above. Finish up a grassy gangway running up rightwards.

About 22 metres up *Walla Crag Gully* is a steep wall on the left, below which is a grassy ledge with a yew tree to its left.

Snow Storm 48 m VS   196?

An interesting route starting at the yew tree.

1 32 m (5a). Move left and climb the rib for a short way. Traverse horizontally left into a steep groove. Move left round the rib and up strenuously to a small ledge. Move left to a small ledge and climb the steep wall above for 6 metres. Move diagonally right and climb the obvious groove to a horizontal crack on the left. Move left to a tree belay.

2 16 m (4b). Climb the rib on the right and scramble to the top.

★ **Southern Rib** 41 m VS   1957

A good and fairly direct line starting as for *Snow Storm*.

(4c). Move left onto the rib and climb this direct for 6 metres. Gain a ledge on the edge on the right. Move left a short way then climb the groove above and move up left onto the knife-edge arête, which leads to the top. Scrambling leads to a poor belay.

★ **Muscular Delinquent** 35 m E2   1979

A good steep route taking a line up the left side of the steep wall on the left of *Walla Crag Gully*. Start 6 metres up and right of *Snow Storm* at a short but deceptively steep groove.

1 22 m (5c). Climb the groove to a ledge. Continue up a thin crack in the wall to a tree belay.

2 13 m (5b). Climb up to the foot of a short overhanging wall (peg runner) and climb it, swinging left to finish.

★ **Total Mass Retain** 38 m E2   1979

Another good climb up the wall to the right of *Muscular Delinquent*. Start behind an oak tree.

1 24 m (5b). Climb the wall. Step left into a shallow groove, which leads to a ledge. Move left up a crack and gain a small niche on the right. Further steep moves lead to a tree belay.

2 14 m (4a). The easy-angled but loose ramp is followed leftwards to the top.

Girdle Traverse 97 m HVS   1962

For this fairly high level expedition, start 20 metres up *Walla Crag Gully*, just right of *Total Mass Retain*.

1 20 m (4a). Continue up the gully for 5 metres until a traverse line leads left to a belay on the arête of *Southern Rib*.

2   25 m (5a). Climb up left until an easy traverse left can be made. Descend about 5 metres to an oak at the foot of an open groove (top of pitch 2 on *White Buttress*).

3   20 m (4b). Descend leftwards for about 10 metres to a groove. Descend this. Move round an arête to some blocks and descend still further to a belay (pitch 2 of *White Buttress* in reverse).

4   22 m (4c). Move up left and follow an indefinite scoop which finishes on steep and doubtful rock at a square rock ledge. Peg belay.

5   10 m (4c). Continue slightly leftwards and finish up the open groove above (pitch 2 of *Thanks*).

★ **Walla Crag Gully**   40 m   VD   1892
This is the obvious gully which splits the crag. A once very popular route, it is rarely ascended now. The gully is fairly sound and leads to a scrambling finish. A classic of its time!

The Beast   40 m   VS   1972
Beastly! Start at an obvious crack, 12 metres right of *Walla Crag Gully*.

1   20 m. Climb the crack and easy rock above to belay below an overhanging groove.

2   20 m. Climb the overhang. Move up a short way, then right into a groove. Traverse a couple of metres right and climb a thin crack in a steep wall. Traverse left beneath a gargoyle and climb the wall on its left.

Walla Right-Hand Buttress

The following routes lie to the right of *Walla Crag Gully*. The best descent is by abseil.

The first six routes start 25 metres right of *Walla Crag Gully* at a buttress split by a central groove. Most of these six climbs end at grass ledges with a belay/abseil point under a small roof.

Wild Thing   40 m   E3   1991

1   15 m (4c). Climb the buttress on the left of the groove up between two trees and traverse left for 5 metres to below a roof.

2   25 m (5c). Climb up from the left to step on to a nose on the lip of the roof and gain a pocket. Sustained climbing leads to a rib which is followed more easily to below an arête. Follow this to the top.

☆ **Ugly Sister** 40 m E3 ?   1991
1   10 m (4c). Climb the groove to an oak belay on the left.
2   30 m (5c). Easy angled rock leads to a hanging groove left of the
    groove of *Brutally Handsome*. Climb the groove with difficulty
    and then climb a rib to the left end of a small roof. Traverse
    above the roof to a tree at the foot of a big corner and follow
    the corner to the belay/abseil point.

Brutally Handsome 40 m E2 ?   1991
1   10 m (4c). Climb the buttress to the left side of its central groove
    and up to an oak tree belay.
2   30 m (5c). Climb up easy angled rock and then climb strenuously
    up a groove in the undercut buttress to a small tree at its top.
    Traverse left across a wall to a slab bounded on it left by an arête.
    Pleasant climbing up the slab leads to a groove followed by
    moves left to reach a ledge and ash tree.

☆ **Joyrider** 40 m E5 ?   1991
1   10 m (4c). Climb the groove and belay at a yew on the right.
2   30 m (6a). Easy rock leads to a peg runner below the undercut
    buttress between the groove of *Brutally Handsome* and the open
    book corner. Strenuous climbing leads to a good hold on the lip
    of a large recess. Move into the recess with difficulty and climb
    more easily onto the slab above to a tree at the foot of a large
    corner. Climb the right wall of the corner, moving left at the top
    to the belay/abseil point.

☆ **Dangerous Corner** 40 m E3 ?   1991
1   10 m (4c). Climb the groove and belay at a yew on the right.
2   30 m (5c). Easy angled rock leads to an open book corner in the
    undercut buttress above. Bridge the corner with difficulty to gain
    a short slab leading to a wall below a twisted holly tree. Climb
    the wall, passing the holly on the left, to the top of the corner.
    Move up to the belay/abseil point.

☆☆☆ **Magical Mystery Tour** 58 m E4 ?   1991
A left-to-right girdle with an exciting high level traverse under the
overhangs. Start as for *Brutally Handsome*.
1   10 m (5a). Climb the buttress to the right side of its central groove
    and belay on a ledge at a yew.
2   20 m (5b). Climb directly up easy rock to the undercut buttress
    and traverse right to beneath a small rib, right of the overhanging
    arête. Climb up on the right of the rib to the roof and traverse

right onto a ledge beneath a groove. Step down into a niche to belay.

3   20 m (6a). Traverse right, around the arête, into an overhung groove at the level of a small ledge on its left wall. Continue rightwards and make a difficult move around the corner onto a sloping ledge below the left end of the roof. Climb up to the roof and traverse on underclings to the arête. Down climb with difficulty until able to reach a hold on the arête. Climb this to gain a small ledge beneath an overhang (hanging belay).

4   8 m (5b). Climb up the right side of the roof into a groove which leads to the top. In-situ peg belay 5 metres back.

35 metres right of *Walla Crag Gully* there is a brown rib between twin oak trees.

Spruce the Bedworm Rides Again   43 m   E2   ?   1991
1   8 m (4a). Climb the brown rib to a grass ledge and belay on the oak on the left.
2   35 m (5b). Easy angled rock leads to a bulging wall at 5 metres. Pull up the wall, moving right into a leftward trending groove. Follow the groove up left to below the overhanging arête. Climb up into a groove on the left side of the arête and follow it passing the left side of a square overhang with difficulty. Prickly belay.

Shadow Lands   43 m   E2   ?   1991
1   8 m (4a). As for *Spruce* but belay on the right-hand oak.
2   35 m (5b). Climb up past a tree stump and step right onto a sloping ledge to gain a diagonal crack above. Move left up into a diagonal groove and climb up out of it to below an overhanging arête. Pull up on its right and climb up to below the overhang. Move out on the left wall to pull over the roof. Easier climbing leads to a holly.

☆ **Sex Bomb Boogie**   43 m   E3   ?   1991
1   8 m (4a). Pitch 1 of *Shadow Lands*.
2   35 m (5c). Climb up to the right of a tree stump onto a sloping ledge to gain a diagonal crack. Make a dynamic move up to the right on a sharp flake to reach higher holds leading up to a broken groove. Climb it to the right end of the overhanging roof. Step right onto a ledge and follow the groove above to the top.

★★ **Burning Bridges**   45 m   E3   1991
Start 5 metres right of the twin oak trees, at a short slab leading to a small steep buttress.

1   10 m (5c). Climb the easy slab and continue boldly up the grooved buttress above to reach a grass ledge.

2   35 m (5c). Climb to the groove above and then go up right onto a ramp (in-situ peg and thread). Move back left onto the steep wall and climb strenuously up to a small niche. Take the groove and wall above.

Serious Omission 45 m E3 ?   1990

1   10 m. Pitch 1 of *Burning Bridges*.

2   35 m (5c). Follow *Burning Bridges* to the peg runner, then move right above the ramp and up left into a shallow groove. Follow the groove up to a small block and make a difficult move left onto a small ledge to reach the arête. Climb the arête to a ledge and go up a wall to the top. Belay at a rock outcrop above the holly.

To the right again is a sycamore growing out of the base of the crag. Three metres to its right is a groove which is the starting point for the next five routes.

✩✩ **Over the Top** 45 m E4 ?   1991

1   10 m (4b). Climb the groove to a grass ledge. Peg belay in block.

2   35 m (6a). Climb directly above the block and pull up into a groove on the left. Continue boldly to reach a peg in the edge of a ramp (junction with *Serious Omission*). Climb up onto the ramp, moving right and back left up into the groove and follow it to the block as for *Serious Omission*. Climb straight up the groove and move right onto the overhung wall. Climb the wall to a sloping ledge and follow the easy wall above. Belay above the holly.

✩✩ **High Anxiety** 45 m E5 ?   1991

1   10 m. Pitch 1 of *Over the Top*.

2   35 m (6a). Climb the slab for 3 metres and move left onto the buttress and up a groove (peg) to reach a ramp. Move up right onto the ramp and boldly back left onto a steep wall. Bold, poorly protected climbing leads to a difficult move up onto a small sloping ledge in a shallow groove below the left end of the large overhanging roof. Climb up to and over the overhang onto a sloping ledge. Follow the easier groove above. Peg belay in rock outcrop.

✩✩ **Way Out Yonder** 45 m E3 ?   1991

1   10 m. Pitch 1 of *Over the Top*.

2   35 m (5c). Climb the rightward trending slab to below the wall. Follow the leftward diagonal ramp until it is possible to move up and traverse right across the wall to gain the foot of a vertical crack in the arête. Climb the crack to a jammed flake on the arête and pull round and up onto a sloping ledge below a roof. Traverse out onto the left wall and climb up onto a sloping ledge. Move up right and follow a groove. Peg belay in rock outcrop.

Return Ticket   45 m   E4   ?   1993
1   15 m (4b). Follow *Over the Top* to the grass ledge and continue up the rightward trending slab to belay at a double-trunked hawthorn below a block.
2   30 m (6a). Climb up onto the start of the leftward diagonal ramp and take the bulging wall above directly to the foot of the crack in the left of the arête. Follow the crack and shallow recess up to the roof and traverse its underside to a weakness at the left end of the overhang. Climb up the overhang and the easier groove above to belay at pitons in the rock buttress.

☆☆ **On a Mission from God**   45 m   E4   ?   1991
1   15 m. Pitch 1 of *Return Ticket*.
2   30 m (6a). Climb up past the block onto a small ledge below the bulging wall. Difficult moves up the base of the wall lead to a good hold in the crack on the left. Continue strenuously to the overhang. Pass this on its right and finish up a groove. Peg belay in rock outcrop.

Beyond Redemption   45 m   E3   1991
1   15 m. Pitch 1 of *Return Ticket*.
2   30 m (6a). Climb up to a small ledge above a small ash and below the bulging buttress. Make difficult moves up to the right to gain the foot of the groove. Climb the groove, moving left onto the wall after a few moves and then up to a small roof. Pull into the groove above and follow it. Peg belay in rock outcrop.

Dionysius   45 m   VS   1965
A rather vegetated route, the first pitch of which has been obliterated by a rockfall. The second pitch follows a groove to the right of the overhangs on the right-hand buttress.

Falcon Crags

The two *Falcon Crags* dominate the hillside about three kilometres south of Keswick. The upper crag, a 70 metre dome in a magnificent situation, is characterized by a large smooth wall in the upper left corner. This wall is bounded on its right by a prominent corner up which *Route 1* finishes. To the right of this the crag becomes much looser and there are large areas of extremely friable rock before the crag finishes in a large open gully.

To the right of and below the upper crag is *Lower Falcon Crag*. This is a compact crag about 50 metres high, extending some 200 metres and abounding in overhangs. At the northern end, an overhanging black buttress is bounded on the left by a grey rib, merging into steeper walls, and on the right by a groove starting from a large mass of ivy shrouding the base of the crag at this point. To the right, past an area of easier routes, is a complex system of bulges with the obvious grey 'niche' in the centre. Continuing rightwards, the crag is cut first by the gangway-groove of *Dedication* and then by the slender line of *Plagiarism*. Towards the southern end, part of the base of the crag is shrouded in trees and a prominent roof caps a grey grooved wall before the crag merges with the hillside.

There is still some loose rock on the lower crag, due mainly to human factors (the loosening effect of the number of climbers), and the blocky, slaty nature of the rock. No widespread friability, however, occurs as on parts of the upper crag. The climbing is rather serious for a small crag. At every point of the crag there is an overhang at some height, all the routes are in the Very Severe category or above and some are not easy to protect even with modern devices. Please also note that the mention of a peg does not imply anything about the condition in which you will find it!

The approach to the crag is easy and obvious, taking but a few minutes from either the lay-by in the main road below the upper crag or from a car park a few metres up the Watendlath road.

Upper Falcon Crag   (272 206)   Alt. 240 m   West Facing

Descent is to the left of the crag, down the ridge and loose scree slope. The routes are described from left to right.

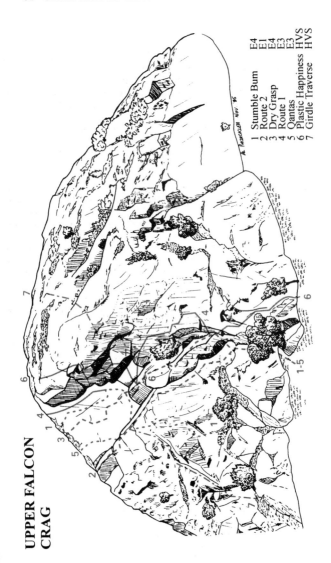

UPPER FALCON CRAG

A. PANZIEGER Nov '95

1	Stumble Bum	E4
2	Route 2	E1
3	Dry Grasp	E4
4	Route 1	E3
5	Qantas	E3
6	Plastic Happiness	HVS
7	Girdle Traverse	HVS

★ **Stumble Bum**   94 m   E4   1981

A serious second pitch leads to pleasant climbing on the upper wall.
Start as for *Route 2*.

1   32 m (4c). Follow *Route 2* to its belay, then continue to a peg
    belay at the left-hand end of a large vegetated ledge.
2   32 m (6a). Climb a groove to a triangular overhang. Pull up
    leftwards, then move right to a groove/crackline and up this to
    ledges on the *Girdle Traverse*. Up rightwards to belay below the
    corner of *Route 1*.
3   30 m (6a). Start up the corner of *Route 1* and climb diagonally
    left to a junction with *Dry Grasp*. Move straight up for 6 metres,
    step right to a sentry box just left of *Route 1* and climb the
    diagonal crack back left to the top.

★★ **Route 2**   64 m   E1   1963

The climb starts above an ash tree on a grassy hump below the centre
of the crag and gives some pleasant climbing. A popular route.

1   22 m (4c). Climb the broken groove, past an old oak tree, until
    a short groove leads up left to some broken ledges.
2   20 m (5a). Climb the rib on the left and move right into a groove.
    Climb this to a large flake. Either continue up the groove a short
    way and pull out right or move to the right round the rib and
    climb the wall. Peg belay in a grassy niche.
3   22 m (5b). Climb the easy slab to the top of a pinnacle. Step up
    onto the wall and move left to a steep crack. Climb it and the
    groove above to the top.

Variation Finish   **Qantas**   22 m   E3   1979

A good pitch up the wall left of *Dry Grasp*. Start from the top of
pitch 2 of *Route 2*.

    (6a). As *Route 2* to the top of the pinnacle. Step up onto the wall
    and climb for 3 metres to a thin crack. Climb this to a good
    pocket. Move right and climb up to the top, or finish direct with
    a long reach from the pocket.

★★★ **Dry Grasp**   60 m   E4   1974

The friable groove between *Route 2* and *Route 1* leads to an excellent
sustained pitch up the centre of the headwall. Start as for *Route 2*.

1   22 m (4a). Climb the broken groove, past an old oak tree, until
    a move right and a short right-slanting groove leads to a ledge.
    Belay below the groove on the right.
2   20 m (5b). Climb the groove, over a bulge, and up to a second
    bulge. Pull over this and up leftwards to an easy groove leading
    to a stance at the foot of the headwall (peg belay).

3   18 m (6a). Climb the crack going diagonally left (peg runner). When the crack closes, use sloping ramp holds on the wall above to gain a small ledge and in-situ thread runner. Move up to good holds leading leftwards to another ledge, then follow a break up and rightwards to a crack. Climb this and finish by stepping left.

Variation   20 m   E5?   1980
3a (6a). The small ledge can be gained from the left, but is poorly protected.

Variation finish **Dry Bum** E4   1996
    (6a). Go straight up from the in-situ thread to the top part of *Stumble Bum*.

★★★ **Route 1**   60 m   E3   1958
A stunning route finishing up the impressive corner on the right of the headwall. Start as for *Route 2*.
1   20 m (4a). Pitch 1 of *Dry Grasp*. Belay at the right-hand end of the ledge below a short wall.
2   22 m (5b). Climb the wall for 6 metres (peg runner). Move diagonally up left, then climb an overhanging crack (peg runner just right of an ivy mass). Continue straight up then left to a peg belay below the corner.
3   18 m (5c). Climb the corner direct. The final groove is entered with difficulty, then followed more easily to the top.

Plastic Happiness   75 m   HVS   1969
A rather poor route with much suspect rock. Start 12 metres down and to the right of *Route 2*, just right of a large ash tree, beside a small hawthorn.
1   22 m (4c). Climb a short corner to a gangway/slab which is ascended to a peg belay in a block niche (junction with *Dry Grasp*).
2   23 m (5b). Climb the crack system on the left to a peg belay on *Route 1*, below the steep wall, as for pitch 2 of *Dry Grasp*.
3   30 m (5b). Traverse right to a hold on the arête. Swing right into a corner and climb up to a peg runner. The twin cracks above are climbed to a large pinnacle. The shattered wall above leads to the top.

The Walk on the Wild Side   58 m   HVS ?   1995
Takes a direct line up the very centre of the crag to the left of *Hallucination*, starting above the same hawthorn bush at the start of

Plastic Happiness. The climb gives a taste of the atmosphere and exposure of *Upper Falcon Crag*.

1   30 m (4c). Boldly climb the bulges directly above the hawthorn and then follow the right-facing groove. Climb slightly up left then back diagonally right, following a broken seam to the foot of the three-step groove. Belay near its top on a small stance (very large Friend or Hex useful for belay).

2   28 m (5a). From the top of the ramp go straight up the very steep wall to a niche where the difficulties ease. Above the niche follow easier rock to the top.

Hallucination (VS 4c, 1961) starts 3 metres right of *Plastic Happiness* and **Falcon Front** (VS, 1950) traverses right out of *Plastic Happiness*. Neither can be recommended.

Girdle Traverse   80 m   HVS   1963
From a grassy alcove near the left end of the crag, 12 metres of easy scrambling leads to a tree belay. Pitch 3 crosses some rather doubtful rock and needs care.

1   30 m (4c). Traverse to the right to below the base of a gangway. Pull over a bulge and follow the gangway which trends to the right to a pinnacle (junction with *Route 2*).

2   10 m. Traverse right to a peg belay below the corner of *Route 1*.

3   18 m (5a). Descend 5 metres until it is possible to traverse right across a brown slab to a peg runner at its end. Swing right and traverse loose rock to a loose groove. Climb the groove to a stance and peg belay.

4   22 m (4c). Traverse right to easier ground and ascend to the top of the crag.

Lower Falcon Crag   (271 205)   Alt. 180 m   West Facing

Descent is down the steep loose slope on the left of the crag.

On the left end of the crag a ledge cuts across its base about 50 metres up the slope from a large ash tree. The first three routes start from this ledge below a left-slanting fault.

Meccano Man   25 m   E3   1989
(6a). Climb the faultline to the very steep groove through the bulge (peg runner). Climb this groove, exiting left at the overhang, and climb up to a small oak tree on the grassy ledge.

LOWER FALCON CRAG

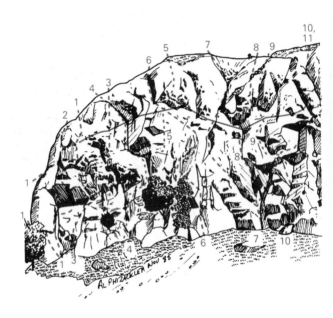

AL PHIZACKLEA NOV 88

1	Spinup	VS
2	The Raging Bull	E3
3	The Dangler	E2
4	Hedera Grooves	MVS
5	Cyclotron	E4
6	Stretch	HVS
7	Funeral Way	HVS
8	Masquerade	E2
9	Close Encounters	E3
10	The Niche	E2
11	Interloper	E1
12	Premonition	E4

13	Dedication	E1
14	Kidnapped	E2
15	Illusion	HVS
16	Plagiarism	E2
17	Usurper	E1
18	Joke	E3
19	Lamplighter Eliminate	E4
20	Lamplighter	VS
21	Extrapolation	E2
22	The Riddler	MVS
23	Girdle Traverse	E1

★ **The Push**   25 m   HVS   1989
   (5a). Start up the faultline then step right and climb up to the
   left-slanting overhang. Overcome this, on unbelievable holds, to
   gain a ledge on the right. Move up left and up a groove until a
   traverse right is made to a large oak tree.

Who is this Lakeland Activist?   25 m   HVS   1989
   Climbs the wall just right of *The Push*. Start as for *The Push*.
   (5a). Move up a short wall on the right to gain a ledge then move
   up right to gain a niche. Climb the wall above and continue
   leftwards up steep broken ledges to finish at the large oak tree.

★ **Autobahn**   50 m   HVS   1970
   Start at the bottom left corner of the crag, below and left of the large
   ash tree.
   1   30 m (4c). Climb up and follow a left-slanting gangway to an
      overhang. Move left then up and right to belay on *Spinup* (top of
      pitch 1).
   2   20 m (5a). Climb onto a small rock ledge on the left, then up the
      overhanging wall above and continue up to the top.

The next four routes start in the first grassy bay reached by
scrambling up and right from the large ash tree.

★★ **Spinup**   45 m   VS   1957
   A very popular and exciting climb starting at the back left corner of
   the grassy bay.
   1   20 m (4c). Follow a small slab leftwards and step left around a
      rib to a ledge. Climb straight up from the left end to a gangway
      leading left for 3 metres, then up right to a small stance just left
      of a black groove. A bold pitch.
   2   25 m (4c). Move up slightly, step right and climb the black
      groove for about 5 metres. Step right and down to gain an
      exposed traverse line above the overhangs. Follow this to its end
      then climb up to a pillar of rock. Step left onto a narrow slab and
      follow an airy fingery wall to the top.

   Variation   **The Original Finish**   25 m   VS   1975
   (4c). As for pitch 2, but from the end of the traverse right climb
   directly up to the top.

★ **Alternator**   30 m   VS   1967
   Start just right of the back left corner of the grassy bay.

1   18 m (4c). Climb the open groove, stepping left over a bulge, and move up to a slab and belay on *Spinup*.
2   12 m (4c). Move right and climb the black groove of *Spinup*. Move left and up to the top.

Variation   1995
2a 12 m (4c). Climb the black groove of *Spinup* for 5 metres and step right. Go straight up the wall, bearing right at the top.

The Raging Bull 36 m   E3   1981
Attacks the hanging groove right of *Alternator*. Start as for *Alternator*.
    (6b). Climb easily up the back left-hand corner of the bay to a ledge. Climb the groove (peg runner) to the traverse of *Wuthering Heights*. Climb the bulge directly above, step right and finish up the rib above.

★★★ **The Dangler** 42 m   E2   1963
A very good route giving steep and exciting climbing. Start 2 metres left of the back right-hand corner of the grassy bay.
1   12 m (5a). Climb a wall and small bulge. Move diagonally right past a small rose bush, then straight up to a block belay.
2   30 m (5c). Climb a steep groove past an ancient and rather dubious bolt runner and pull out left onto a ledge (peg runner). Pull up right to a peg runner and traverse right on large flat holds. Move up and right into a grooveline just right of the nose. Climb this and continue direct to the top.

Variations.
1a 10 m. The original start was the easy first pitch of *Graviter*.
2a 30 m (5c). An easier alternative to pitch 2. Follow pitch 2 to the peg runner over the bulge, climb up and follow a grooveline leftwards, and then more easily straight up to the top.

To the right is an easy-angled rib.

Graviter 52 m   VS   1956
A rather unsatisfactory and wandering route. Start just right of the easy rib below the groove of *The Dangler*.
1   10 m. Climb the rib, past a sycamore tree, to a block belay.
2   18 m (4a). Traverse left along a narrow break below the overhangs to a belay on *Spinup* (top of pitch 1).
3   24 m (4c). Step down, follow a narrow ledge left, then climb up a short wall to a groove which is followed by a steep juggy wall.

★ **Wuthering Heights**   50 m   E2   1978
Pleasant climbing with an airy traverse between the overhangs. Start
as for *Graviter*.
1   10 m. Pitch 1 of *Graviter*.
2   40 m (5c). Climb the groove and pull out left to a ledge and peg
    runner as for *The Dangler*. Traverse horizontally left for 6 metres
    to gain a short crack and climb it to a resting place. Move right,
    then up left onto a steep wall which is climbed on good small
    holds to the top.

To the right again is a second grassy bay. The next four routes share
the same first pitch, that of the very popular *Hedera Grooves*.

Nothing by Chance   50 m   E5?   1989
1   10 m (4a). Pitch 1 of *Hedera Grooves* to the niche.
2   40 m (6b). Step left and climb the cracked overhanging groove
    to the large overhang. Using a large undercut hold reach out left
    and climb the overhang and wall to a ledge. Move left onto the
    steep black wall and climb this to easier ground and the top.

★★ **Hedera Grooves**   40 m   MVS   1956
The easiest route at *Falcon Crag* giving a good introduction to the
crag. It climbs the groove with a holly tree, above the left edge of
an ivy mass. Start in a small bay, left of the ivy, 15 metres left of
The Niche.
1   24 m (4a). Gain a grass ledge, then climb the short groove above
    to a niche. A traverse line leading rightwards is followed to a
    groove. Climb this, then step left to the holly tree.
2   16 m (4b). Climb the groove above the holly, then follow the
    ramp leading leftwards to the top of the crag. A brilliant pitch.

Variations
1a 30 m (5a). The original route started up *Funeral Way*, then
    traversed left to the holly belay. A pointless unprotected route.
2a 16 m (4b). From the holly, step out left onto the arête and climb
    straight up to the top.

★ **Inarticulate Speech**   50 m   E4   1983
This eliminate line, based on *Hedera Grooves*, is rather short of
protection when most needed.
1   10 m (4a). Follow pitch 1 of *Hedera Grooves* up to a belay beside
    the niche.

2   10 m (6a). Climb the cracked overhanging groove on the left of
    the niche or the wall on the right to the same point. Move up to
    a holly belay at the top of pitch 1 of *Hedera Grooves*.
3   30 m (6a). Climb the overhanging groove in the right wall and
    follow the crackline above to the top. Serious.

★ **Cyclotron** 52 m E4   1978
A steep route with a bold and poorly protected crux up the black wall
right of *Hedera Grooves*.
1   16 m (4a). Pitch 1 of *Hedera Grooves* to a belay in the groove
    after the traverse right.
2   36 m (6a). Climb the steep groove until it is possible to pull up
    right to a small ledge on the black wall. Traverse right to a niche
    in the arête, pull up and left, then move back right to better holds
    in a slim groove. Follow this, then go left above the overhang for
    5 metres and straight up to the girdle ledge (possible belay).
    Climb directly up the bulging wall above.

Direct Variation **Atomiser** E3   1978
    (6a). From the small ledge on pitch 2, climb direct to rejoin the
    original route below the top bulges.

To the right is an oak tree and a mass of ivy.

★ **Stretch** 52 m HVS   1965
A good climb starting up the clean corner immediately right of the
ivy.
1   18 m (5a). Bridge up the corner, then move left to below another
    corner.
2   16 m (4c). Ascend the corner and move up right onto the large
    flake. Step left and bridge up the groove to a junction with the
    Girdle Traverse. Traverse left across a slab to a small stance
    below a large detached block.
3   18 m (4c). Climb the broken crack in a bulge above and finish
    up the slab.

★★ Variation **Direct Finish** 24 m E2   1980
A serious and poorly protected pitch.
    (5c). Climb up as for pitch 2. From the top of the groove (junction
    with the *Girdle Traverse*) move right to a block. Climb the
    overhanging groove, exit left and climb to the top past a sapling.

★ **Funeral Way** 46 m HVS   1956
A deceptively difficult route. 10 metres right of the ivy mass is a
slender beech tree. The route climbs the short undercut groove 3
metres to its left and finishes up a groove through the left end of the
final bulges. Note that there is a worrying, large loose flake on pitch
2. Avoidance of this increases the difficulty of the pitch significantly.
1   24 m (5a). Climb up left and make an awkward move up onto
    the gangway, which is followed for 3 metres, then traverse left
    to a prominent flake crack. Climb this, then move left onto a
    ledge. Move up to a smaller stance a few metres higher.
2   22 m (4c). Gain the groove and follow it for 6 metres until good
    holds lead to a left-trending gangway, which is followed to the
    top.

Deruptus 45 m VS   1956
Starts as for *Funeral Way* but turns the bulges above on the right.
1   15 m (5a). Follow *Funeral Way* onto the gangway and, as soon
    as possible, climb the wall on the right to a small ledge and peg
    belay.
2   30 m (4c). Straight up for 6 metres, then step right and continue
    traversing right across a groove to two small ledges (possible
    belay on second). From the end of the second ledge, ascend a
    groove direct until a slightly overhanging wall is reached. Climb
    this and easier rock to the top.

Variation Finish 18 m VS   1978
    (5a). From the possible belay on the ledge below the overhanging
    wall, make a rising traverse left for 7 metres and step left across
    the top of a groove (above the thread belay on *Masquerade*).
    Finish straight up to the big ash at the top.

★★ **Masquerade** 44 m E2   1969
A good route with a strenuous start up a rust-coloured groove, just
left of the small beech tree at the start of *Funeral Way*.
1   22 m (5b). Climb the groove direct, moving left at the top, then
    move up and left to some large blocks and saplings. Thread belay.
2   22 m (5c). Step down and traverse right for 3 metres to a steep
    crack. Climb this to a ledge. Ascend a steep crack in the bulge
    above and continue direct to the top.

Variation **Original Pitch 2** 25 m   1978
    (5b). Step down and traverse right for 7 metres. Move up, then
    back left, to below the crack in the bulge. Continue as for pitch
    2.

★★ **Close Encounters**   50 m   E3   1978

Starts as for *Masquerade* and ascends the groove on its right behind
the slim beech tree.

1   30 m (6a). Climb the groove to an overhang; then move right and
    up to the peg runner at the start of the traverse on *The Niche*.
    Traverse left to a groove and climb this over a bulge to a junction
    with the *Girdle Traverse*. Peg belay on the right.
2   20 m (5c). Move left for 6 metres and climb the overhanging
    groove some 3 metres right of *Masquerade's* final crack,
    continuing more easily to the top.

The large niche of the route of that name can be seen 20 metres up
and to the right.

☆ **Vicky**   60 m   E5   ?   1990

Good exciting open climbing starting just left of *The Niche*.

1   (6b). Pull over the overhang, move up to the wall with a crack
    in it and go up this to the peg on *The Niche*. Desperate climbing
    leads, via a leap for a finger jug, first left from the peg then back
    right to a runner on the lip of the overhanging nose above the
    peg. Move up and left to a stance.
2   (6a). Climb up to the overhang on the left then go over it with
    difficulty via a groove on the right. Climb more easily to the top.

★★★ **The Niche**   60 m   E2   1962

A classic route, giving good, sustained climbing in excellent
positions. Start in the centre of the crag directly below the obvious
niche.

1   26 m (5c). Climb the bulging wall for 10 metres, step left onto
    a rib and climb to a peg runner 3 metres left of the niche.
    Traverse right with difficulty and pull up to a peg belay in the
    niche.
2   12 m (5b). Climb the back of the niche and exit on the right.
    Traverse right to a break in the overhang. Pull over this into a
    short groove, then step right to a small ledge and peg belay.
3   22 m (4c). Step back left and climb the gangway/groove. Pull
    over a slight bulge on the right and finish up the slabby wall.

★ Variation   **The Left Exit**   34 m   E4   1966

2a 12 m (6a). Climb the left wall of the niche and up to a small
    ledge and peg belay.
3a 22 m (4c). Move left to a groove which is followed to a junction
    with *Deruptus*. Finish up this.

☆☆ **Terrierman**   42 m   E4?   1999

A bold and exciting route taking the large open corner immediately right of *The Niche*. Start at a small hawthorn bush at a groove below the corner.

(6a). Climb straight up the broken groove to a narrow ledge below the green coloured corner. Move left carefully past a small spike and make bold moves up the wall. Enter the fine V-groove above and follow it to a slabby wall on the right. Finish easily rightwards.

★★ **Star Wars**   52 m   E3   1978

A steep route, requiring bold climbing, over the bulges below and above the niche. Start 2 metres right of *The Niche* at a slim groove in the bulging grey wall, beside a small hawthorn bush.

1   22 m (5c). Climb straight up to a bulge (peg runner high in the corner on the right). Step left and climb the bulge, into the right side of the niche, using a hollow flake with trepidation!
2   30 m (5b). Climb the back of the niche. Traverse right to a nose, as for *The Niche*, and pull directly over the bulge to a groove. Climb the groove slightly leftwards to finish up a short crack/slab, 5 metres left of the top pitch of *The Niche*.

★★ **Interloper**   50 m   E1   1962

An enjoyable route which takes the steep grooveline starting 6 metres right of *The Niche*.

1   29 m (5c). Climb easily up to a ledge on the right, with a small tree, then go left for 5 metres to a sloping ledge. Step right and ascend to a large ledge. On the left is the steep groove. After an awkward start, continue on good holds past two peg runners to a small stance and peg belay on the left (top of pitch 2 *The Niche*).
2   21 m (4c). Climb the bulge above the belay and follow the gangway/slab leftwards to a bulge (junction with *The Niche*). Move right and up the slabby wall to the top.

Variation   **Defy Gravity**   15 m   E5?   1986

Takes the overhanging rock between *The Niche* and *Interloper*. Start from the old peg at the left end of the large ledge of pitch 1 of *Interloper*.

2a (6b). Gain an undercut under the roof (Friend 3 and nut protection). Make devious undercut moves right then pull over the

Opposite: Mark Hetherington on **The Dangler** (E2), Lower Falcon
Mike Hetherington

roof at its narrowest point to join *Interloper*. Swing out leftwards and up an overhang to belay on *The Niche*.

Variation Finish 22 m E2

2a (5c). Climb up rightwards to below an overlap. Pull over and climb the slabby wall above, leftwards to the top.

★★ Premonition 45 m E4
1981

Bold and exciting climbing up the wall and overhang between *Interloper* and *Dedication*.

1 15 m (4b). Pitch 1 of *Interloper* to the large ledge.
2 30 m (6a). Climb easily up left, until it is possible to pull onto the wall above, just right of a slim, green groove. Boldly climb the wall to a peg runner beneath the roof. Pull over (in-situ thread runner) and up to join *Dedication*. Follow this and finish up the right-hand groove above.

★★★ Dedication 48 m E1
1957

A fine popular climb. Start as for *Interloper*.

1 18 m (4a). Follow *Interloper* to a ledge then go up right to another ledge and easily to a large ledge and block belay.
2 30 m (5a). Pull over a small overhang and enter an open groove. Climb it, and either step right onto the edge and up a metre, then back left or climb directly (harder) into a fine slanting corner, which is followed until it is possible to traverse left. Finish up the groove on the left.

Variation **Original Start** 24 m VS
1957

1a (4c). Starting as *The Niche*, climb up rightwards to a small ledge, then mantelshelf onto a ledge below the overhangs (peg runner) and traverse right and down to the block belay at the top of the first pitch.

Variation Start 18 m VS

1b (4b). Climb the dirty wall behind a large ash, left of *Kidnapped*, direct to the top of pitch 1.

Two large trees can now be seen to the right at the foot of the crag.

Opposite: No laughing matter – Cavel Greg on **The Joke** (E3), Lower Falcon
Dave Kells

★★★ **Kidnapped** 42 m E2   1978
Tremendous and sustained climbing, linking the old direct start to
Dedication and variation finish to *Plagiarism*. Start below a groove
between two large trees.
    (5c). Climb the groove and continue to reach some small spikes
on *Dedication* after 16 metres. Climb into the overhung niche
(junction with *Plagiarism*). Move up to the roof (peg runner),
traverse left to the arête and follow the groove above to the top.

☆ **Canna Do It?** 45 m E4?   1986
Start behind the right-hand large tree. A 'faith in runners to come' is
useful on both pitches.
1   30 m (5c). Climb the overhanging rib to a ledge. Move up for
    runners on *Plagiarism* then swing left and over an overhang into
    a scoop between *Kidnapped* and *Plagiarism* – bold and thin.
    Climb up and left to a yellow slab and go up to the flake on
    Plagiarism. Continue up this and traverse right under the
    overhang to an old ring peg and belay.
2   15 m (6a). Climb up to the roof, traverse left to good nuts on
    Plagiarism and climb straight up the black wall. Move right on
    jugs to the middle of a green wall. Move up to a horizontal crack
    and then make a hard finishing move to a rest. Climb the slab
    leftwards to a tree belay.

To the right is a wall capped by a large overhang. Below and left of
the overhang is a large tree at the foot of the crag. The following
five routes start at a block just right of the tree, and share the same
first pitch.

★★★ **Plagiarism** 48 m E2   1962
A justifiably popular route up the rust coloured groove just left of
Illusion.
1   8 m (4b). Climb straight up to a stance at a large block on the
    right.
2   30 m (5c). Move left and climb the slanting groove, finishing up
    its left rib to gain a small ledge. Traverse left across a steep wall
    (peg runner) to a shallow groove, which is followed up to a roof
    (peg runner). Surmount this on the right and move left to reach
    a small stance and peg belay in a groove.
3   10 m. The groove above is followed to the top.

★★★ Variation **Direct Finish** 9 m E3   1986
   3a (5c). Make bold moves rightwards to gain the hanging flake and
    continue up steeply to a tree belay.

★★★ **Usurper**   50 m   E1   1975

Enjoyable steep climbing with fine, open and improbable positions. Care required with some hollow flakes near the top of pitch 2.

1   8 m (4b). Climb straight up to a stance at a large block on the right, as for *Plagiarism*.

2   26 m (5a). Continue up Illusion until it moves to the right. Move left on a steep gangway to a ledge on the left (peg runner). Move right and up to a roof then pull up round the rib on the right to a small niche. Go up left through the overhang onto the wall above and continue up rightwards to a tree belay.

3   16 m. Follow the groove above to the top.

★ **Sunset Cruise**   45 m   E4   1986

(6b). Follow pitch 1 of *Plagiarism* then climb the corner on the left of the arête and swing right onto a yellow slab. Climb the left edge of this, then go up leftwards on black rock until a hard move gains a hold in the middle of the wall above the bulge. Move up to a ledge on *Usurper*. Climb over the large overhang above, left of *Usurper*, using some hollow undercuts to start. From above the overhang move up left to a small niche, then climb straight up the steep wall on the right to easy ground.

★★★ **Illusion**   44 m   HVS   1956

Pleasant climbing across the wall below the large overhang.

1   8 m (4b). Straight up to a stance at a large block on the right as for *Plagiarism*.

2   30 m (5a). Climb the steep groove above until it is possible to gain a large flake on the right. Traverse to the right, past several grooves, into the corner groove. Climb up this for a couple of metres then swing out right round the arête and move up to a ledge.

3   6 m. Climb up the wall above to finish beside a holly.

Variation Start   **Good Times Bad Times**   24 m   E1   1978

Start up the shallow groove between Illusion and Joke. A dirty unpleasant pitch.

1a (5a). Climb the vegetated groove to a small tree and go up behind this, slightly rightwards, to below the overhangs. Pull over (peg runner) to a niche. Bridge up, then left to better holds. Continue to a junction with *Illusion* and follow this to the top.

☆ **Vanishing Act**   45 m   E3   ?   1991

A good route in a spectacular position taking the hanging groove/crack left of *Joke*.

1   8 m (4b). Climb straight up to a stance at a large block on the right as for *Plagiarism*.
2   37 m (5c). Climb *Illusion* to the top of the large flake. Continue up the wall to the overhang and bottomless crack/groove on the left. Climb the superb crack and short wall above to the tree.

★★ Joke   46 m   E3   1965
An impressive route which takes the large overhang on its left side. A long reach helps! Start 10 metres to the right of *Illusion* at a white rib below and right of a groove.
1   22 m (5b). The rib leads up to an obvious groove, which is followed to a poor stance near its top.
2   24 m (6a). Climb up leftwards to the roof. Move left to the corner and up to an old peg runner on the left. Make a hard move left (especially for dwarfs), then go up and back right to a hanging groove above the roof. (Possible belay on the tree on the left). Finish up the groove on good holds. It is also possible to gain the groove above the roof direct, though slightly harder.

★ Lamplighter Eliminate   42 m   E4   1981
This free climbs the original aided start to *Lamplighter*, then the bulging wall left of *Extrapolation*. Thin and fingery. Start as for *Joke*.
1   14 m (6a). Climb a blunt rib for 5 metres. Step right, and pull over a bulge at a hairline crack (peg runner) or, easier, pull up and traverse right to the peg. Move up and right to belay at the foot of a groove.
2   18 m (6b). Follow *Lamplighter* until just above the old peg runner. Pull up the bulging wall above to a ledge, step right and use a high side hold next to a thin crack to reach tiny holds above. Climb up the short wall to a ledge and tree belay.
3   10 m (5a). Climb up left to a small holly in the corner. Make an airy traverse left (thread runner) across the wall above the big roof. Finish easily up the wall above.

☆☆ Variation Breakin' in Space   12 m   E5   ?   1985
An alternative finish in a spectacular position but with some dangerously loose rock. Belay 3 metres below the top of pitch 2, just right of the top groove of *Illusion*.
3a (6b). Swing down left into the groove. Climb it (peg runner where it steepens) and up past a large loose block to the obvious traverse line. Step right to rest and for runners. Traverse left over loose blocks to a peg runner with a long sling, in a short groove. Pull up (peg runner), and exit on the right. Finish up the slabs as for the normal route.

★★ **Lamplighter** 40 m VS 1964

An interesting route up the obvious slanting groove. Start 3 metres right of the white rib of *Joke*.

1 16 m (4b). Ascend the short steep crack past a vegetated niche on the right and pull up into a short steep groove above. Step left and up to a stance at the foot of a left slanting groove.

2 18 m (4c). Follow the groove to a small ledge at 8 metres. Continue straight up the groove with a smooth slab on the left to join *Illusion*. Follow this to the top of pitch 2.

3 6 m. Up the wall above to finish beside a holly.

★★ **Extrapolation** 42 m E2 1975

A good route up the right side of the buttress with an awkward crux bulge. Start as for *Lamplighter*.

1 36 m (5c). Follow *Lamplighter* into the short groove. Make a delicate step right, then the steep slabs are followed to below a red groove. Climb this and pull left over an overhang onto a ledge below a steep wall. Climb this at its weakest point and continue up the short wall above to belay at the top of pitch 2 of *Illusion*.

2 6 m. Climb up the wall above to finish beside a holly.

Right-Hand Variation E4 1999

(5c). Follow *Extrapolation* to the top of the crack but, instead of moving left to the ledge, make a bold traverse right to gain a groove up and right. Follow this to *Extrapolation's* belay.

The Riddler 40 m MVS 1966

A scrappy climb which starts about 10 metres right of *Extrapolation*.

1 18 m (4b). Climb the shallow chimney to a grass ledge. Move up to a deep chimney then swing out to the right, on doubtful holds, and up to a ledge and tree belay.

2 22 m (4c). Return to the chimney, move left to a steep groove and climb it to a small ledge. A short difficult wall leads to the belay ledge on *Illusion*. Climb up the wall above to finish beside a holly.

★★ **Girdle Traverse** 132 m E1 1962

A good girdle with excellent positions and climbing. Start as for *Spinup*.

1 20 m (4c). Pitch 1 of *Spinup*.

2 24 m (4c). Follow pitch 2 of *Spinup* to the end of the traverse right. Climb up until it is possible to move down a gangway on the right to a stance on *Hedera Grooves*.

3   22 m (5a). Traverse to the right, across a steep wall, and follow
    the obvious traverse line to a small ledge. Continue the traverse
    across *Funeral Way* to a stance on a small vegetated ledge (on
    the left of pitch 1 of *Deruptus*).
4   24 m (4b). Follow the traverse of *Deruptus* and continue
    traversing until the groove of *The Niche* is reached. Move to the
    right to a peg belay (at the top of pitch 2 of *The Niche* and
    Interloper).
5   36 m (5b). Climb up and right across a steep wall, to join the
    groove of *Dedication*. Reverse this until just above the initial
    bulge on pitch 2. Move out right onto *Plagiarism* and descend a
    short way to a small ledge at the top of a groove. Move right
    (peg runner) round a steep rib and step right to a groove (junction
    with *Illusion*). Climb the groove until it is possible to gain a large
    flake on the right. Traverse right past several grooves into the
    corner groove. Move up it for a metre and swing out right round
    the arête and up to a ledge and belay (all as for *Illusion*).
6   6 m. Ascend the wall above to finish beside a holly.

Variation **Original pitches 5 and 6** HVS
5a 15 m. Abseil down the second pitch of *Interloper* and pendule
    into the rock. Traverse right to belay as for *Dedication*.
6a 23 m (5b). Follow *Dedication* over the initial bulge then move
    right onto *Plagiarism*. Pitch 5 is then followed to the stance on
    Illusion.

Variation **Extension to the Girdle** 76 m E1   1975
5b 36 m (5b). Pitch 5 is followed as described to the corner groove
    on *Illusion*. Step down and move right around an arête to a small
    stance of the top of the groove of *Lamplighter*.
6b 16 m (5b). Traverse right on the lip of a bulge to its right-hand
    end. Climb down the overhang and red groove below
    (*Extrapolation* in reverse) until possible to move right to *The
    Riddler* and belay.
7b 24 m (4c). Climb the chimney above, then move to the right and
    ascend a wall rightwards to the top.

★★ **Five Nations of the Iroquois** 182 m E3   1978
    A right to left girdle of the crag. Little new climbing but an enjoyable
    expedition. Start as for *The Riddler*.
1   22 m (4b). Climb the shallow chimney and continue for 3 metres
    to a tree. Traverse left for 6 metres to a belay at the foot of the
    groove of *Lamplighter*, or follow pitch 1 of *Lamplighter* to the
    same point.

2   15 m (5b). Step down and traverse leftwards, passing below the grooves of *Joke* and *Good Times Bad Times*, to a stance at the top of pitch 1 of *Illusion*.

3   24 m (5b). Climb the groove of *Plagiarism* for 5 metres, traverse leftwards and descend *Dedication* to its stance at the top of the first pitch.

4   33 m (5c). Traverse left for 10 metres (peg runner). Step down and then ascend into the niche as for *Star Wars* (peg runner). Reverse *The Niche* traverse (peg runner) and continue leftwards to the corner on *Close Encounters*. Step left and across to a stance and belay beside a large flake.

5   24 m (5a). Traverse leftwards, descend the corner and then move left and up to the holly belay on *Hedera Grooves*.

6   36 m (5c). Step down and traverse left round the arête to a junction with *Dangler*. Descend this past several peg runners to the top of its initial groove (peg runner). Traverse left, as for *Wuthering Heights*, and continue traversing to a belay on *Spinup*.

7   28 m (5a). Up to grass ledges and traverse left on these for 6 metres. Climb leftwards up the pocketed wall to a belay on a large oak tree.

Variation   20 m   E3   1980
5a (6a). Traverse left and pull up left, to the small niche in the arête (junction with *Cyclotron*). Traverse leftwards to a small ledge round the corner, then move down and left (*Cyclotron* in reverse) and up to the holly belay on *Hedera Grooves*.

Horizontally left of *Lower Falcon* and directly below *Upper Falcon* are some small crags,

Falcon Pinnacle   17 m   D   1992
A detached pinnacle with a crack on its right-hand side stands out from the lowest wall. Start at the crack. Climb the crack to a shoulder on the right and then gain the summit block. Step onto the wall behind and finish easily.

A gently angled slab midway between *Falcon Crag* and Ashness Bridge is usually wet, but can give a good easy ice climb in a hard winter.

Ashness Ghyll (278 193)

★★ **Ashness Ghyll** D   1924

This is an interesting and usually wet expedition, which takes the right-branch of the ghyll. It is reached in about 10 minutes from Ashness Bridge. The Ghyll is crossed and recrossed several times but the way is obvious. A historical curiosity, recommended to everyone, but take care with the poor protection. In a hard winter it can provide a pleasant ice climb.

Watendlath

In the small Watendlath valley there is a large amount of rock, though none of it is of any great height. The Watendlath road, which branches from the main Borrowdale road about three kilometres out of Keswick, is followed for three kilometres. On emerging from the woods a long, low, black crag appears on the left (east side of the valley), a few hundred metres from the road; this is *Reecastle Crag*. *Reecastle South Crag* is some 200 metres to the right of this, round the corner, and *Goats Crag* is further up the valley.

The other crags are on the opposite (west) side of the valley and they can all be seen from the road. These crags are reached from the footpath which crosses the river at a bridge, below the point where the road emerges from the woods, and follows the river to Watendlath village. The river can be crossed on stepping stones below Caffell Side during dry weather.

The lack of suitable parking facilities presents a problem in Watendlath, particularly during the busy summer months. Care should be taken to avoid blocking passing places on the narrow road.

Powterhow Buttress (274 178)   Alt. 300 m   West Facing

Of the small crags that lie up and left (N) of *Reecastle*, this is the one closest to the prominent Thwaitehouse Beck, roughly 300 metres from *Reecastle*. A small niche is easily located at the foot of the crag.

The Emigrant 15 m   E4   1990

(6a). From the niche climb the thin, parallel, left-slanting cracks to the top.

Reecastle Crag (273 176) Alt. 300 m   North West Facing

A long, low crag which can be reached in ten minutes from the road. The left half of the crag is smooth and barrel-shaped; the right split by slim grooves and ramps. The rock is of good quality and fairly clean. All the routes give strenuous climbing. An excellent crag where strong fingers are a considerable asset.

The most obvious faultline in the centre of the crag is taken by *The Rack Direct* with *White Noise* following the leftwards-slanting crack just to its left.

The routes are described from left to right. Descent can be made at either end.

The Axe 22 m S   1972
A rather wandering route up slabs at the left end of the crag. Start at a huge split block just left of an ash tree.
   Climb the front of the block, step across a gap onto the slabs behind and move up to a ledge. Climb up the leftward-slanting groove to a tree belay.

Ador 24 m VS   1979
A fine little route giving steep juggy climbing. Start as for *The Axe*.
   (4c). Climb the block and slabs as for *The Axe* to below a steep wall. Go up this on long reaches, finishing up a short groove to a spike belay.

★ **Bold Warrior** 24 m E1   1979
A good, steep route with an awkward start from the grass ledges behind the ash tree, 3 metres right of *The Axe*.
   (5b). Climb the short square-cut groove to a foothold on the left. Layaway moves gain a spike on the left, then go straight up to a shallow V-chimney which leads to the top.

The Executioner 26 m E4   1979
Short, technical and very serious climbing up the left side of the bulging wall. Start 5 metres right of *Bold Warrior* below an overhanging layback flake.
   (6a). Steep moves lead up and left to a shallow green scoop. Move rightwards and climb the easier wall above.

REECASTLE CRAG

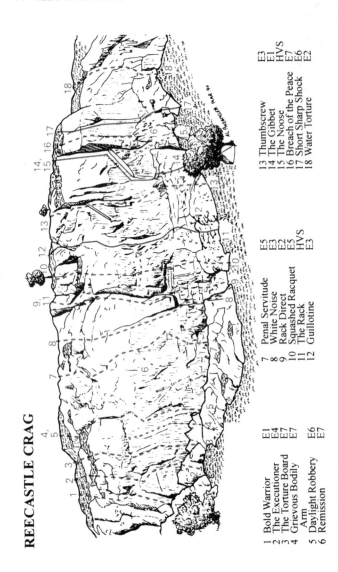

AL Phillips MAR 94

1 Bold Warrior — E1
2 The Executioner — E4
3 The Torture Board — E7
4 Grievous Bodily Arm — E7
5 Daylight Robbery — E6
6 Remission — E7

7 Penal Servitude — E5
8 White Noise — E3
9 Rack Direct — E2
10 Squashed Racquet — E5
11 The Rack — HVS
12 Guillotine — E3

13 Thumbscrew — E3
14 The Gibbet — E1
15 The Noose — HVS
16 Breach of the Peace — E7
17 Short Sharp Shock — E6
18 Water Torture — E2

★★ **The Torture Board** 26 m E7 {F7c+} 1987
A desperate modern testpiece which climbs the obvious twin cracks
2 metres right of *The Executioner*.
(6c). Climb the steep rock to gain the base of the twin cracks
(peg runner). Make hard moves up the crack to the horizontal
break. Continue directly up the steep wall with less difficulty.

★★ **Grievous Bodily Arm** 26 m E7 {F7c} 1987
Climbs the right-hand of the two crack systems between *The
Executioner* and *Daylight Robbery*.
(6c). Start up the wall passing a small spike to gain the crack.
Climb the crack to a good fingerlock (wire in-situ) then straight
up to a good jug on the right (crux). Move diagonally right to a
good spike and continue up to the top.

☆☆ **Last Request** 26 m E6 {F7c} ? 1998
Steep climbing up the middle of the bulging wall. Start as for
Daylight Robbery.
(7a). Climb to the peg and make desperate moves left and up on
very small holds to a large spike. Climb the easy slab above.

★★★ **Daylight Robbery** 26 m E6 {F7b+} 1984
Steep, finger-searing climbing up the red streak near the middle of
the bulging wall.
(6c). The crack is followed to a peg runner at its top. Move right
and make desperate moves up to a good hold. Continue up the
easy crack/groove, then slabs above to the top.

★★ **Disorderly Conduct** 26 m E8 {F7b} 1997
A good, hard and sparsely protected route up the red wall to the left
of *Burn at the Stake*.
(6c). Climb up to a small break (good Rock 3). Pull up right and
make some hard and bold moves to poor RPs and then pull up
left to a large hold and good gear. Follow the red wall to the top.

★★★ **Burn at the Stake** 26 m E7 {F8a} 1992
(7a). The oft tried central crackline right of *Daylight Robbery* is
bold, powerful and technical. (Peg runner and preplaced wire
should be in-situ.)

★★ **The Whipping Post** 26 m E7 {F8a} 1992
(7a). Climb directly to the peg on *Remission* with hard moves
past a Friend 1 in the break.

★ **Remission**   25 m   E7   {F8a}   1987
Takes a desperate line left of *Penal Servitude*.
   (6c). Start as for *Penal Servitude* and gain the obvious quartz
   break. Follow this left to below a thin crack. Using a side-pull
   on the left move past a peg runner (crux) using an obvious
   undercut on the left and a slap up right. Use a hidden edge straight
   above and step up right to finish up *Penal Servitude*.

★★★ **Penal Servitude**   30 m   E5   1981
Brilliant climbing up the overhanging wall, starting 5 metres left of
White Noise below three horizontal quartz breaks.
   (6b). Climb up rightwards to a peg runner in the top break. Pull
   up, then leftwards on tiny finger pockets and up to a resting place.
   Step left into a slight groove and follow it more easily to the top.

Direct Start   E5   ?   1994
   (6c). Climb the wall to the peg, and missing out the RP 2, go up
   the wall to the left on small holds to the big side-pull.

Sentenced to Hang   30 m   E5   1990
   (6b). Start up *White Noise* to place gear in the crack and move
   left up an obvious flaky rising traverse. This leads to the RP2
   placement on *Penal Servitude*. From here (crux) go directly and
   boldly up the wall for about 6 metres until it is possible, and
   advisable, to move right back on to *White Noise*.

★★★ **White Noise**   30 m   E3   1978
Superb climbing up the left-slanting crack, immediately left of *Rack
Direct*. Start at the right-hand end of a ledge running below the left
side of the crag.
   (5c). Climb up to a small overhang; pull up left to gain the crack
   and follow this up the wall to a bulge. Go over this to a nut belay
   at the top.

Variation   1999
   (5c). Climb the overhang as for the normal route but finish direct
   up the wall.

★★ **Rack Direct**   30 m   E2   1977
A very direct route up the obvious faultline in the centre of the crag.
Poorly protected initially but the difficulties soon diminish.
   (5b). Up the steep wall to a break in the bulges. Pull over and
   climb the crack, as for *The Rack*, to the top.

★★ Squashed Racquet   30 m   E5   1984

An eliminate, squashed between *The Rack Direct* and *The Finger Flake Finish*. Start just left of *The Rack*.

(6a). Climb the smooth scoop (peg runner) and pull over the overlap and up to the traverse of *The Rack*. Continue up the wall above (bold to start), moving rightwards to the top.

★★★ The Rack   40 m   HVS   1973

A good route which gains the classic central crack from the steep walls on its right. Start 6 metres right of *Rack Direct* in a small grassy bay below a short black bulging wall.

(5a). Climb the short wall, past a sloping ledge, to a better ledge on the right. Climb the wall to a resting place on the left. Move up left to a sloping ledge. Descend and traverse left boldly to the obvious crack. Go up this, and a short groove, to a flake and ledge on the right. A rib leads to a tree belay.

★★★ The Rack – Finger Flake Finish   30 m   E2   1981

Fine steep climbing.

(5c). *The Rack* is followed to where it traverses left to the crack. Step up right into a white scoop and follow a thin flake crack. At its top, move left onto a wall and pull up to a large sloping ledge. Straight up to a large birch tree on the top.

★★★ Guillotine   30 m   E3   1978

A superb route giving sustained climbing on small holds. Start 2 metres right of *The Rack* below a bulging black wall.

(5c). Climb the black wall to a ledge. Continue up a thin groove to a bulge, and pull over to a thin hollow flake on the wall. Step right and up to a second bulge. Surmount this, step left, and continue up to the top.

★★★ Inquisition   30 m   E4   1984

A bold eliminate line, trying to avoid *Guillotine* and *Thumbscrew* and giving excellent climbing. Start just right of a small hawthorn.

(6a). Climb easily up to a ledge. Layaway moves up a slight rib lead to a good hold on the left. Move up to a niche above. Move right and climb steeply over a bulge to gain a rightwards-sloping ramp. Follow this to a junction with *Thumbscrew* and up to the top.

★★★ **Thumbscrew**   30 m   E3   1978
A fine steep route, fingery and sustained, up the bubbly wall. Start
behind the sprawling silver birch below the right-hand half of the
crag.
    (5c). Take the easy wall to a ledge. Go up the steep wall to a
    flat hold below a tiny overhang, between two parallel cracks.
    Climb the left-hand crack and groove above direct.

★★ **The Gibbet Direct**   30 m   E2   1984
Fine fingery climbing. The problem is staying on line! Start behind
the silver birch.
    (5c). As for *The Gibbet* to the gangway. Pull out steeply left onto
    the wall. Climb this and the central crack above, just right of
    Thumbscrew, to the top.

★ **The Gibbet**   32 m   E1   1964
Follows the obvious right-slanting gangway, after an awkward start.
Start behind the silver birch.
    (5c). Climb diagonally left, then right, to below the short wall at
    the foot of the gangway. Gain the gangway, with difficulty, and
    follow it to the right to a steep groove, which is climbed until it
    is possible to move out right and up to the top.

★ **The Gauntlet**   30 m   E1   1984
An eliminate. Start as for *The Noose*.
    (5b). Follow *The Noose* to a block 3 metres up in the corner
    crack. Finger traverse left across the steep wall to gain the
    gangway of *The Gibbet*. Climb the wall above, directly, on
    improving holds.

Direct Start   **Off the Cuff**   E3?   1995
    (5c). Start below the centre of the gangway and climb up to join
    The Gauntlet at the gangway. Combined with *In the Neck* this
    gives a good sustained route.

★★ **The Noose**   30 m   HVS   1972
Follows the prominent crack and corner right of and behind the silver
birch.
    (4c). Easy slabs lead up rightwards to a short corner. Climb the
    corner crack above to a junction with *The Gibbet* at the top of
    the gangway. Follow this to the top.

Alternative finish **In the Neck** E2 ?   1995
(5c). From the top of the gangway move out right to a good hold
on the arête. Continue up the wall just right of the arête to the
top.

★ **Breach of the Peace** 17 m E7 {F7b+}   1987
Climbs the overhanging wall 3 metres right of *The Noose*.
(6b). Climb up to a spike runner. Move up left, then right. Move
up again (crux), and continue to the top to finish up the slab.

★ **Short Sharp Shock** 12 m E6 {F7b+}   1987
The name says it all!
(6c). Climb the obvious crack right of *Breach of the Peace*. The
crux is passing the peg runner.

★ **Water Torture** 26 m E2   1981
Short but very fingery.
(5c). Scramble up to spikes below thin, twin cracks in a bulging
wall. Climb the cracks then continue more easily up slabs trending
leftwards to the top.

The right-hand end of the crag is split at half height by a left-slanting
slab. This section is climbed by three rather poor routes.

Skewered 26 m VS   1984
Start 3 metres left of *Crucified*.
(4c). The groove is climbed on doubtful spikes to a slab. Continue
direct to the top.

Crucified 26 m MVS   1984
Rather short and forgettable. Start 3 metres left of *Gyves*.
(4b). Climb the steep wall to the left-slanting slab, then up the
short wall behind.

Gyves 26 m E2   1984
A boulder problem start, then not much else of interest. Very dirty.
Starts at the extreme right-hand end of the crag, 3 metres left of a
fallen silver birch.
(5b). Climb a shallow, clean-looking groove. From a large
foothold, move left across a bulge to gain a rightward-slanting
ramp. Go up to the overhanging wall and climb the crack, or,
more easily, go up the wall on its right.

★★★ **Crime and Punishment**   62 m   E3   1984
A left to right girdle giving excellent climbing throughout. Start from
the ledge 6 metres up the easy slabs of *The Axe*.
1   36 m (5c). Follow the obvious break right to *Bold Warrior*.
    Descend a little and cross into the shallow green niche on *The
    Executioner*. Hand-traverse strenuously right to a rest on *Daylight
    Robbery*. Large flakes lead horizontally to a shallow groove on
    Penal Servitude. Descend slightly to a line of holds leading to
    White Noise then continue to the crack of *The Rack* and arrange
    a hanging belay.
2   26 m (5c). Reverse the traverse of *The Rack* to a tiny ledge on
    the rib. Move across, past the groove of *Guillotine*, then up
    rightwards to *Thumbscrew* arriving at foot level on the 'flat hold'.
    Move right to a thin crack on *Gibbet Direct*, then cross the wall
    on the right on small holds into the corner of *The Noose*. Finish
    up this.

Reecastle South Crag   (273 174)   Alt. 300 m   West Facing

About 200 metres right from *Reecastle*, this steep little crag is
characterized by its smooth domed top and overhangs along the
bottom.

Scrape   36 m   MS   1964
A rather dirty direct start to *Scratch*. Start at the left end of the crag
behind an ash tree.
    Climb the groove and continue up for 10 metres. Move diagonally
right to the left end of the smooth bulge which runs across the
crag. Step left, pull up, and climb a slab rightwards to the top.

★★ **Ricochet**   26 m   E2   1979
A steep route which attacks the upper bulge at its left end. Start from
behind a tree in the centre of the crag, below the overhangs.
    (5c). Climb through the block overhangs on the left into a twisting
groove which is followed to the steep, blank bulge. Overcome
this via a crack in its left-hand side and continue to a spike belay.

Opposite: Superb evening climbing on the **Finger Flake Finish** to
The Rack (E2), Reecastle   *Stephen Reid*
Overleaf: Jane Meeks climbing **Mort** (E1), on the pleasant, secluded
Goats Crag, Watendlath   *Al Hewison*

★★ Scratch 33 m S   196

A pleasant route which starts at the foot of the rib on the right of the crag.

Climb the rib to the bulge and traverse to its left end. Step left and finish up the slabs on the right, as for *Scrape*.

Blonde Ambition 30 m E4   199

(6a). Climb *Scratch* (or the airy groove to its left) to the leftward traverse. From a broken spike halfway across the traverse climb the bulging headwall, via a vague groove between the top parts of *Ricochet* and *Widowmaker*. Make a long move to a fingerlock and continue with awkward pinching above. (A wire was pre-placed in the fingerlock for the first ascent.)

★★ Widowmaker 33 m E2   1973

A beautiful and interesting route but not too well protected taking the old aided finish to *Scratch*. Start as for *Scratch*.

(5b). Climb the rib to the bulge. Step up right and follow thin cracks in the rounded arête to the top.

Lost Boys 24 m E2   1984

Climbs the short steep buttress right of *Widowmaker*. Best lost!

(5c). Scramble up to a large block behind a silver birch. Gain the ramp above the overhang, then up right to the rib. Climb the rib and continue to small trees at the top.

Goats Crag (277 170) Alt. 400 m   South West Facing

Goats Crag is in an idyllic setting affording splendid views of the Central Lakes. It is quick drying, faces the evening sun and offers a selection of good routes only twenty minutes from the road. Well worth a visit.

It is the last buttress on the east side of the valley before the hamlet of Watendlath. Drive past *Reecastle South Crag* and park on the right immediately before the point where the walls begin on both sides of the road. The crag can be seen above the trees on the left, being the leftmost and higher of two buttresses, with a drystone wall running up to its base.

Opposite: Nick Wharton steals up tiny crimps on the bulging wall of **Daylight Robbery** (E5), Reecastle   *John Fletcher*

GOATS CRAG

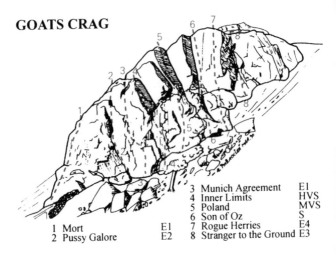

	3 Munich Agreement	E1
	4 Inner Limits	HVS
	5 Poland	MVS
	6 Son of Oz	S
1 Mort	E1	7 Rogue Herries	E4
2 Pussy Galore	E2	8 Stranger to the Ground	E3

The best approach is to go through the gate, opposite the lay-by, and then another gate, just to the right, into a field. Go up the left side of the field then cross the fence along its top. Continue directly up the fellside, passing the right-hand buttress (*Lower Goats Crag*) and follow a drystone wall directly up to the base of the crag. Great care should be taken not to damage the drystone wall.

Kid Gloves   15 m   HS   1996
   Takes the obvious slanting corner on the left of the crag.

Littlejohn   15 m   VS   1996
   (5a). To the right of *Kid Gloves* there is a short overhanging wall. Climb this and then go up the easier slab.

★ **Mort**   15 m   E1   1989
   Start at the lowest point of the crag to the left of the drystone wall.
   (5b). Climb up easy rocks to a triangular overhang. Move over this then go right, with difficulty, to gain a small ledge. Finish up slightly easier rock above.

Balancing Act   14 m   E1   1996

(5b). Climb up easy rock right of *Mort* to a small flake. Climb left of this on incuts to a good hold. Move right to a short crack and use this to make further progress.

Light Fantastic   14 m   E2   1989

(5c). Start above where the drystone wall meets the crag and climb the bulge and easier rocks above.

★★ **Pussy Galore**   13 m   E2   1989

(5c). Climb the obvious leftward-slanting crack. Moving left to leave the niche is the crux but the upper crack maintains one's interest.

Lucky Luke   14 m   E3   ?   1993

The leaning wall to the right of *Pussy Galore*.

(6a). Climb past a Friend slot, finishing between *Munich Agreement* and *Optional Omission* (side runner on *Munich*).

★ **Munich Agreement**   15 m   E1   1989

Start 3 metres right of *Pussy Galore*.

(5b). Climb the awkward steep wall leftwards to a ledge. Finish up the thin crack just right of the corner at the left end of the ledge.

★ **Optional Omission**   14 m   E1   1989

(5a). Start just left of a blunt arête and climb the wall leftwards to a ledge. Climb the steep wall on the right of *Munich Agreement* to the top.

★ **Inner Limits**   14 m   HVS   1989

(5a). Start as for *Optional Omission*. Climb the steep corner, step slightly left, then move right onto a slab. Continue up the gangway on the left of the slab, in a fine position.

The Slab   13 m   D   1989

Climb the obvious slab just right of the blunt arête.

★ **Nightmare Zone**   14 m   E1   1989

Start as *The Slab*.

(5b). Climb up past the rowan to the overhanging groove avoided by *Poland*. Climb this groove awkwardly and finish up the arête on the left.

Poland   15 m   MVS   1989
>   (4b). Start as for *The Slab* then move right under the overhang to a corner. Move right slightly and climb up for 2 metres. Ascend the slab on the right.

Everybody's Dream   15 m   S   1989
>   Climb the centre of the slab to the right of *Poland*.

★ **Berlin Wall**   15 m   E2   1989
>   (5b). Climb up to the slab taken by *Poland* to below its steep right wall. Climb this wall awkwardly, with a small spike runner on the right arête, taken by *Emma Line*.

★★ **Emma Line**   16 m   HVS   1989
>   (5a). Start up *Son of Oz* then move left and climb the sharp arête in a fine position.

★ **Son of Oz**   15 m   S   1989
>   Climb the obvious corner-crack, which is reached by awkward scrambling.

★ **Rogue Herries**   15 m   E4   1989
>   A poorly protected route.
>   (6a). Climb the steep wall right of *Son of Oz*, which thankfully relents after mid-height.

The Colour of Magic   15 m   E4   1989
>   A bold, strenuous and committing route.
>   (6a). Climb the arête on the right of *Rogue Herries*.

Stranger to the Ground   12 m   E3   1989
>   (5c). Climb a short groove to a sloping ledge, just above a small tree. Step left and climb the wall directly and boldly on holds which never seem to go the right way.

★ **Mull Wait**   12 m   S   1999
>   Climb the leftward-rising wide crack. Short but sweet.

Route 8   15 m   HVS   1996
>   (5a). On the far right of the crag, climb the short leftward-slanting arête, not using the slab.

Lower Goats Crag

The hummock seen on the right when walking up to Goats Crag has a bay with a short steep wall hidden round to the right. The routes are described from right to left.

Black Moss Groove 25 m VS   1990
Start under the vertical marsh in the corner on the right of the crag.
   (4c). Climb the corner, move right to avoid the overhang and finish up the V-groove.

The Trick 25 m E1   1993
   (5c). From the overhang on *Black Moss Groove*, move left past the groove on *The Witch* and step into a slabby overhung groove. Move right to finish. (This groove can be climbed at 4c from *The Niche*.)

★ **The Witch** 25 m E2   1993
   (5c). Step off the large block left of *Black Moss Groove* and climb the wall into a groove. Reach left from the overhang and climb the steep groove to the top.

★ **The Niche** 25 m HVS   1990
Start under the lowest overhang just left of the large block.
   (5a). Climb up into a groove on the left of the overhang. At its top, swing right onto a narrow slab. Move up this until it is possible to traverse left on good holds and finish up a groove.

★★ **Mackanory** 25 m E1   1993
   (5b). Follow *The Niche* to the top of the narrow slab. Move right into the corner using a good handhold high up. Pull round right and continue straight to the top.

Left-Hand Route 25 m S   1990
   Climb the slab and vague groove to the left of *The Niche* moving right near the top.

Down to the left of the bay is an obvious short chimney.

Gone for a Pizza 25 m VS   1991
   (4c). Climb directly up to the chimney on improving holds and thrutch up it (or through it). Either walk off right or climb choss to the foot of a solid wall, which is climbed.

The area to the immediate left is climbable virtually anywhere at an easy standard and is devoid of obvious lines. It is also somewhat loose. The following route lies well to the left and is on sound rock.

Copperhead 40 m M   1991
  At the left-hand, lowest point of the crag is a shallow cave. Start at a blunt rib to the left of this. Climb a right-slanting groove, then a left-slanting one, then move up right and back left to a terrace. Climb the scoop on the left or, better, the short crack in its right (D). Scrambling remains.

Garrotte Buttress (271 171) Alt. 260 m   East Facing

This is the small crag on the west side of the valley, nearest to the hamlet of Watendlath. It can be identified by an obvious fin of rock in the upper part of the crag and the dirty slabby groove on its left.

Park as for *Goats Crag*. Follow the farm track to the stream which is crossed on stepping stones, take the track rightwards for 50 metres or so and then strike up towards the crag. (10 minutes.)

★ **Supercrack** 35 m E1   1999
  A worthwhile route with a well protected but quite hard crux. Start at the left-hand end of the crag at a scoop below a slanting layback crack.
  (5b). Climb the scoop, crack and wall above (beware loose rock) to the base of the right-slanting upper crack. Follow the crack, jam awkwardly where it flares, and pull up to the terrace.

★ **The Garrotte** 46 m HVS   1975
  A pleasant route making the best of the rock available. Start at the lowest point of the crag just left of a small ash tree.
  1   20 m (4c). Climb the impending wall boldly to a ledge on the left. Go up left onto a grass ledge, move onto the rock rib then go up to a good crack above the detached block. Make an awkward traverse right to a small ledge on the arête. Traverse diagonally right under a bulge and climb the arête on the right to a large block belay.
  2   13 m (5a). From the block, step onto the steep wall. Climb round the corner to the right and up the obvious left-slanting groove which forms the right side of the fin. Belay at the foot of a crack.
  3   13 m (5a). Climb the crack to the top.

Caffell Side Crag (269 175) Alt. 260 m

East Facing

On the west side of the valley, almost opposite *Reecastle Crag*, is the small buttress of *Caffell Side Crag*. It is clearly visible from the road, the vertical nature of the features and routes being very obvious. The rock is rather slaty and care is required with some of the holds. Protection can also be rather difficult to arrange on some routes. At the left end of the crag a chimney-crack separates the crag from a small buttress. The first route takes the arête right of the chimney. It is best to descend by abseil, though it is possible to scramble down either end.

Juicy Lucy 26 m HVS   1975
A good route up the arête.
    (5a). Start up the left side of the arête and follow it direct to the top. Alternatively (5b), start up the wall 2 metres to the right and climb the groove and crack to rejoin the arête after 10 metres.

Slack Alice 26 m E2   1975
Rather loose and poorly protected, but a good line. Start at the groove 5 metres right of *Juicy Lucy*.
    (5b). Climb the groove to an overhang. Pull left and up over suspect blocks to below a smooth curving groove. Go up this and pull out right at the top.

Variation Finish **Dogma** E1   1976
    (5a). From below the curving groove, move right below an overhanging rib and finish up the broken wall to a tree on top of an arête on the right.

★ **Blondin** 26 m HVS   1975
Pleasant climbing with reasonable protection. Start 3 metres right of *Slack Alice* below a curving crack.
    (5a). Starting in a groove, follow the crack past a small tree at 6 metres and finish up the groove on the right.

★ **Apricot Lil** 26 m E2   1978
A good climb with a delicate crux section. Start 6 metres right of *Blondin*, just right of a silver birch.
    (5b). Ascend the square groove for 5 metres and move left onto the wall. Climb up this, passing a pinnacle, and finish up an obvious groove on the right.

Everard 26 m E3   1978

A strenuous route up the thin crack above the start of *Apricot Lil*.
(5c). Ascend the square groove, traverse right to a hollow flake
and then pull up left to the crack, which is followed to a painful
holly-filled groove below the top.

Hairy Mary 24 m E2   1985

A variation on the right of *Everard*.
(5c). Follow *Everard* to the hollow flake and continue direct up
the wall to rejoin *Everard* at a small tree after 6 metres. Finish
direct up the wall above.

Street Walker 21 m E2   1985

Follows the shattered wall, just right of the vegetated gully in the
centre of the crag.
(5c). Climb a groove until a step left can be made onto the arête.
Go up this and the left wall and then move back into the top of
the groove. Surmount the overhang and continue up the steep wall
until a mantelshelf move leads to easier climbing to the top.

Miss O'Gynist 21 m E2   1990

Takes a fine obvious crackline to the right of *Street Walker*. Scramble
beneath bushes to a comfortable platform.
(5c). Initial hard moves lead rightwards to the crack which is
followed directly or by a slightly easier diversion to the left at
half-height. Finish leftwards on good holds to a tree.

Torquemada Buttress (268 177) lies about 300 metres up and right
of *Caffell Side Crag*. It is a small, dirty crag with two poor routes.
A stone wall runs up to the foot of the crag after crossing the river
below *Caffell Side Crag*. **Torquemada** (HVS 1974) starts up the dirty
groove 5 metres left of the wall, **Iron Maiden** (VS 1973) takes
another dirty groove 3 metres right of the wall.

Brown Dodd (268 178) Alt. 300 m   East and North Facing
East Face

Some 150 metres further right (north) of the *Torquemada Buttress* is
a larger slabby wall with an overhanging wall at the bottom. Once
again this is rather dirty and lichenous, though the main upper wall
is more compact and, therefore, less vegetated. Many routes have
been claimed and counter-claimed on this wall. Only the best have
been included. Descend with care down a loose gully on the left.

The Rib   36 m   VS   1979
This route takes the rib at the left end of the crag, just left of a large heather-choked crack. Start below the rib.

 (4c). Vegetated rock leads to the rib. Zig-zag up this on good holds to the top.

The slanting groove has been climbed but it is dirty and always escapable to the grass-filled groove.

The Rift   36 m   HVS   1973
This route takes the groove system left of the upper wall, below a small tree overhanging the top. Start at a rock ledge 13 metres right of *The Rib*.

 (5b). Move left and up into a groove, which is followed for 6 metres to a ledge. Go up to another ledge. Step right and go up the steep wall to mantelshelf onto a ledge. Step left, and climb the steep groove to the top.

Variation   **Alternative Finish**   HVS
 (5a). From the second ledge climb the groove above, then the left-hand groove, to a tree belay at the top.

Anyone For Tennis   30 m   E1   1985
A good direct line up the wall. Start at the flat ledge, as for *The Rift*.
 (5b). Ascend the groove past two suspect blocks. Exit right and go up to a ledge. Amble up easy ledges to a crack. Follow this, over a bulge, to a groove and finish on the left.

Boiling Point   40 m   HVS   1979
Start at the right-hand end of the crag.
 (4c). Gain the overhang and move onto a gangway on the right. Move left across the steep wall and follow ledges to the foot of a groove, which is climbed to a tree belay.

North Face

Situated some 50 metres round the vegetated corner to the right of the *East Face*, this is the most northerly crag on the west side of Watendlath Valley and overlooks Derwentwater. A dry stone wall runs up to the rock face. (This should not be confused with the wall running up to the foot of the *Torquemada Buttress*). Descend well to the right.

Hawkwing 33 m E1   1981
A pleasant route which climbs a groove and rib at the left-hand end
of the crag. Start 3 metres left of the dry stone wall at a groove.
(5b). Climb the groove. Pull up left at the top to ledges and move
up to another groove. Climb this to a ledge with a large block.
Pull up left and climb the blunt nose to the top.

Poxy Brown Crows 40 m S   1981
Start at a large holly 10 metres right of the stone wall.
Climb up behind the holly and follow ledges leading diagonally
leftwards to reach the base of a prominent groove. Climb up this
to two small trees and exit leftwards.

Kes 36 m HVS   1981
Follows the right-hand of three shallow grooves above a large holly
at the foot of the crag. Start as for *Poxy Brown Crows* at the holly.
(5a). Climb up behind the holly and step left into the groove.
Climb this, then go leftwards up the slab to a small tree. Step
right and continue to the top.

The Buzzard 40 m VS   1969
A rather dirty, vegetated route which starts 10 metres right of *Kes*,
just right of a rib.
1 27 m (4b). Climb a short wall over heather ledges onto the slab
   above. Go up leftwards on good holds to a small tree. Move round
   left into a corner. Climb up onto a ledge on the left wall and then
   climb the vegetated corner to a tree belay.
2 13 m (4b). Move left into a groove and climb it to the overhang.
   Traverse to a ledge left of the overhangs and continue to the top,
   as for *Kes*.

In addition to these routes, two others of Very Difficult standard
called **Orchard Slabs** and **Babylon** have been climbed on the slabs
on the left end and diagonally across the centre of the crag
respectively. These areas are very dirty and the routes not worth
re-excavating.

Bird Brain 33 m E1   1985
Follows the pillar and loose overhanging headwall at the right end of
the crag. Start behind a silver birch on a ledge up and right of the
start of *The Buzzard*.
(5b). Step left and climb a groove to the left side of a tree,
containing a large nest, below the headwall. Climb this, moving

first left then right, to a block overhang above the tree. Straight up to the top. Belay 10 metres back.

Bird's Nest Buttress   33 m   E1   1985
A companion to *Bird Brain*; also loose at the top. Start as for *Bird Brain*.

(5b). Climb straight up the front of the pillar to the right side of the tree. Climb the headwall, moving left above the tree, to a block overhang. Straight up to the top as for *Bird Brain*. Belay 10 metres back.

National Trust Crags

These comprise the series of crags on the hillside between Barrow House and *Gowder Crag*. In the main the rock in this area is less than perfect but there are a few routes that are worth seeking out. Two main buttresses emerge from the thick shroud of trees.

Cat Ghyll Bluffs   (268 196)   Alt. 170 m   West Facing

This is the northerly crag which can be approached in about 10 minutes uphill from the car-park near Mary Mount Hotel, or, much more easily, in 5 minutes from the car-park in the woods just above Ashness Bridge, where a path leads to the edge overlooking Derwentwater. Follow a narrow gully down past the right (facing out) edge of the upper crag. Continue down until a path leads off left and skirts the lower crag. Twenty metres up from the lowest point of the crag is a large triangular boulder, providing an obvious gearing up point. In front of this is the smooth slab and crack of *Wild Boys*. The crag is composed of two tiers and the first routes described are at the left end of the upper tier, just right of the descent gully.

Upper Tier

The *Upper Tier* is split into two separate sections with very different characteristics. The Smaller *Northern Buttress* is just to the right of the descent gully. The routes here are shorter and generally solid. The much bigger, more impressive and looser *Southern Buttress* is some 100 metres south of the gully and is clearly visible from Kettlewell car park. It can be approached via routes on the *Lower Tier* or by a traverse right from the routes on the *Northern Buttress* across steep rubbish-strewn hillside, or an abseil is possible from above.

Spider Wall 15 m VS 1985

A pleasant climb with limited protection.

(4c). Start just left of *Spiderman*, in the descent gully, and climb the wall above, direct, on excellent holds.

★ **Spiderman** 18 m HVS 1984

(5a). Start near the base of the descent gully, 5 metres left of *Holly Tree Corner* below an obvious left-slanting gangway. Gain the gangway and climb it to its top.

★ **Single to Cemetery Gates** 20 m E3 1992

A good route which takes the arête just to the right of *Spiderman*.

(5c). Climb the arête passing the small, dark, loose (but mechanically sound!) *Flake of Temptation*. Continue steeply up until it is possible to move diagonally up and right for 2 metres then straight up to jugs. It is possible to continue in the same line, rather than traverse right, at E3 5b, (**The Body Variation** 1993).

Holly Tree Corner 18 m HVS 1984

An easy start leads to an awkward finish. Despite the name, there is no holly!

(5a). Start at a large oak, below the obvious square-cut corner, just right of the descent gully. Climb the groove and go up the corner to finish up the crack on the left.

Batman 20 m HS 1984

Start 5 metres right of *Holly Tree Corner* below a holly. Climb into a niche and ascend a steep crack to gain a slab on the right. Continue up to the top.

Rave Night at the Mortuary 18 m E1 ? 1993

(5a). Climb the obvious wall 3 metres right of *Batman*.

In the centre of the *Upper Tier* is an obvious corner (*One-In-Six*) which can be reached by traversing right from *Holly Tree Corner*, descending slightly initially, to just above the lower tier. Alternatively it is possible to climb the first pitch of *Cat Ghyll Grooves* directly up to the corner, or to abseil from the top.

One-In-Six 30 m E1 1985

This route's name was derived from the fact that on the first ascent one in six of the holds fell off (or was it stayed in place?), and one block actually bounced over the road! Start below the obvious groove.

(5b). Climb the groove (loose) and step left under an overhang into a hanging groove. Climb this to gain a large ledge. Climb the faultline to the right of a tree, then step left and finish up a wide groove.

Dicing With Death 40 m E2 ?   1989
This takes the impressive steep wall between the *Naked Edge* and *One-in-Six*.

(5c). Climb the bulge into the groove of *One-In-Six*. Climb to the large overhang using a dubious block. Traverse strenuously 3 metres right across the bulging wall. Climb the wall above, with difficulty, moving slightly right then back left to the obvious groove. Climb the final overhang to a tree belay.

The Naked Edge 30 m E2   1985
Start below the impressive arête right of *One-In-Six*, at a large block, just left of pitch 2 of *Cat Ghyll Grooves*. The first runner is above the crux.

(5b). From the right-hand end of the block, pull up onto a sloping ledge and move left to the arête proper. Climb the overhang, strenuously, to a resting point 8 metres above on the left. Move back right onto the arête and climb directly to the top.

Lower Tier

The *Lower Tier* is reached by following the descent gully and scree slope until it is possible to traverse under the crag. *Vicissitude* is the obvious 'V' corner.

★ **Vicissitude** 64 m S   1949
A pleasant, clean route ascending both tiers which starts at the lowest point below a prominent V-corner.
1 18 m. Climb a 5 metre groove, then a cleaned slab rightwards to a tree root. Move up left to a tree below and left of the V-corner.
2 18 m. Gain the corner and follow it to the overhang. Traverse right to the edge, and climb up to a tree belay.
3 28 m. Broken slabs lead up left to a rock buttress. Climb its arête to the top.

Variation **Vicissitude Regained** 12 m VS   1985
2a (4c). Gain and climb the corner above, then finish directly up the overhanging crack.

Ivor the Boneless   25 m   VS   1985
A steep route taking the cleaned rock and overlaps, starting as for *Vicissitude*.

(4c). Climb the cleaned ramp rightwards to the tree root and the overlapping wall above, on good holds, to a steep slab. Finish up the right arête as for *Vicissitude*.

Blood Axe   23 m   HS   1985
A good little route starting 3 metres left of *Wild Boys* at a tree on top of a shattered pillar.

Climb the wall to a perched block. Move leftwards and climb the groove to a tree belay.

★ **Charlie the Chicken Farmer**   20 m   E2   1988
(5c). From the large tree at the base of *Wild Boys* climb directly up a fine thin crack to the roof. Surmount the roof at the obvious central crack to good holds above.

★ **Wild Boys**   20 m   E1   1984
A solid pitch. Start just left of *Cat Ghyll Grooves* below a slab with a right-slanting crack.

(5b). Gain and follow the crack to a small tree under an overhang. Using the tree, pull onto the slab above and move up a corner to a tree covered ledge.

An easier upper pitch was completed but this is out of keeping with the lower pitch.

Beer and Sex and Chips and Gravy   23 m   E1   1988
An interesting traverse.

(5c). Gain the crack of *Wild Boys* from the right and follow that route to the tree below the overhang. Traverse left beneath the roof until hard moves up the wall, at the left end of the roof, lead to good holds round an overhang and the top.

My Mam's Rockery   51 m   E1?   1987
Start as for *Wild Boys*.
1   17 m. Follow the diagonal crack up right to a sound tree belay at the top of the initial gully of *Cat Ghyll Grooves*.
2   8m. Traverse right on a grass ledge to the second tier and standing block belay.
3   26 m. Traverse out left from the block towards an obvious pinnacle. Continue on for 22 metres to the top.

★ **Tina Turner** 22 m MS   1985
A good route starting at the obvious clean slab to the right of *Wild Boys*.
 Climb the corner of the slab to its top. Pull up the rib, move left
 and climb a groove to a tree belay.

Cat Ghyll Grooves 70 m VS   1963
A rather scrappy start leads to better climbing above. Start below the
grassy gully splitting the lower tier, 5 metres right of *Wild Boys*.
1   37 m. Ascend a short slab to gain and climb the earthy gully.
    Scramble up right to belay below an ivy groove, right of *The
    Naked Edge*.
2   33 m (4c). Climb up to and over the overhang (loose). Continue
    up the groove and over a bulge, then up a short crack and better
    holds to a ledge. Finish up the slabs and short wall on the right.

Bat Out of Hell 12 m E2   1985
An awkward route lacking in protection in the upper crack. Start just
right of *Cat Ghyll Grooves* and just left of a large boulder, at a holly
tree.
 (5b). Climb the steep smooth wall to a good jug under a bulge.
 (No. 3 Friend in bulge). Move up left over the bulge and finish
 up the steep crack above.

I Need A Hero 12 m E1   1985
A deceptively awkward climb starting on top of the boulder, 6 metres
right of *Cat Ghyll Grooves*.
 (5b). Climb a leftward-slanting crack, on side pulls, to a bulge.
 Make an awkward move left and pull up the wall above. Move
 right into the bottom of a groove which leads past a tree to the
 top.

★ **This Little Piggy** 12 m E2   1988
Start 3 metres right of *I Need a Hero* below a leftward-slanting crack.
 (5c). Climb the initial groove with difficulty and gain the crack
 which is followed to the top.

The Sheep's Apprentice 12 m E4   1988
An interesting, technical, steep wall climb with just adequate
protection.
 (6a). Start just right of *This Little Piggy* and climb up to a
 protection peg at 6 metres. Continue steeply up, on good but
 spaced holds, to the top.

Marijuana   60 m   VS   1960
Starts 13 metres right of *Cat Ghyll Grooves* below a loose groove.
1   15 m (4b). Climb up the groove to a yew tree belay.
2   10 m. Scramble up to a large three-stemmed tree.
3   35 m (4c). Bear left up a wall to amazing quartz formations, man.
     Pull over the overhang and climb the flake crack above to a tree.
     Traverse delicately right to the edge. Move awkwardly into a
     groove and finish up easier rock.

Variation   **Direct Finish**   24 m   VS   1965
A much better line.
3a (4c). Climb up to the left for 5 metres then climb straight up to
     the top.

Variation   **Strawberry Fields**   33 m   VS   1970
3b (4c). Climb the wall behind the tree to the bulge. Move right and
     climb the arête to the overhang. Move right, below the overhang,
     and climb the steep, loose wall. Pull back left and follow the
     groove to the top.

Speed Kills   80 m   E2   ?   1989
A girdle of the upper tier starting on the right of the lower tier.
1   35 m (4c). Climb the easy rock behind the yew tree to the tree
     belay on *Marijuana*. Traverse right to another tree and climb a
     groove and traverse left 6 metres to belay on *Marijuana*.
2   13 m (5c). Move down a metre or so to the lip of the overhang.
     Make a thin traverse left and then make an awkward move into
     a narrow groove. Climb this to a ledge and peg belay.
3   32 (4c). Traverse left onto the *Naked Edge*. Move down and
     traverse left under the overhang to the top of *One-in-Six*. Finish
     up this to a tree belay.

The Hemp Road   70 m   HVS   ?   1989
Start at the same place as *Speed Kills*.
1   37 m. Climb the slab behind the yew tree until the wall steepens.
     Move right on good holds to a ledge at the foot of a groove. Tree
     belay.

Opposite: Stuart Wood pulling through the crux of **Penal Servitude**
(E5), Reecastle, anxiously watched by John Hydson, Eddie Wright,
and belayer Steven Whitall   *Dave Kells*

2   33 m (5a). Climb the groove and reverse the traverse of *Marijuana* for 3 metres to a steep crack. Climb this and traverse left, then climb cracked blocks to the top.

Two unsatisfactory routes ascend the rock to the right, but do not warrant description.

Surprise View Buttress   (268 192) Alt. 170 m   West Facing

This is a collection of crags situated just below and north of Surprise View on the Watendlath road. From here the crags can be reached by abseil, or by scrambling down one of the gullies. The whole area is inherently unstable with poor loose rock, much vegetation and a very large and active giant ant population. For those who like this sort of thing there is undoutedly much scope here. Everyone else is strongly recommended to admire the view and then find somewhere else to climb.

A number of routes have been climbed on the lower leftmost buttress, identified by the large red corner left by a recent rockfall! To the left of this and down a little is the infamous **Horrible Arête** (45m VS 1987). In the last guide it was given the ultimate accolade of three black spots. A full description is given below for those climbers bored with life. The wall to the right is taken by **Top Rope** (45m E2 1989). The red streak is taken by **Nervous Shakedown** (45m E2, 5c 1990), the arête to the right of this route being **On Edge** (VS 4c 1986). **Dream Warriors** (45m E2, 5c 1990) takes the overhanging corner/groove just right again. The first ascensionist described the second pitch as "nerve-racking"! **Slide Show** (38m HVS 1986) takes the wall and gangway 15 metres to the right. Finally, **1990** (26m E1, 5b 1989) takes the right-hand side of the top of the gully from which the other routes start.

●●● **Horrible Arête** 45 m   VS   1987

The ultimate in Borrowdale tot routes. Start at the left end of the buttress just left of a steep wall. A scary route with the outcome uncertain until the belay!
>   Climb the short slab leading left under an overhang. Move out left on to the rib, climb up past a tree on the rib and up to the next tree. Step right and worry your way up on doubtful holds to the next curving rib above. Continue up on good holds to the top and tree belay.

Opposite: George Rea lost in a sun-kissed sea of rock on **Guillotine** (E2), Reecastle   Dave Simmonite

BORROWDALE EAST

Gowder Crag (266 187) Alt. 200 m   West Facing

This is the steep imposing buttress rising out of the trees on the east bank of Lodore Falls. It gives a number of good routes on variable rock. Keep an eye out for the amazing anthills to be found around this crag.

The main sweep of the buttress is clean but its left side is now vegetated. To the right of the buttress the crag diminishes in height and further right there is a vegetated ridge, *The Hog's Back*, with an isolated vegetated buttress to its right.

The crag can be approached either by a private footpath from beside the Lodore Hotel, or by a footpath starting at a small lay-by at a bend in the road 200 metres north of the hotel. The crag dries quickly after rain and is only a few minutes walk from the road. It must be remembered that a popular path passes the foot of the crag and that any stones dislodged inevitably rake this tourist-frequented path. It is at its best during the winter months when the vegetation, ants and tourists are at a minimum.
Descents can be made either well along to the right of the right-hand buttress or by the open wooded gully to its left.
The routes are described from left to right.

Warlock 80 m VS   197

A now rather vegetated climb starting about 12 metres up and to the left of the toe of the main buttress at a tree.
1 12 m. Climb a short corner and a broken slab to a double stemmed tree below a cleaned groove.
2 16 m (4a). Move right and up vegetated rock to a ledge, below and right of a square-cut groove.
3 24 m (4c). Climb the groove and the arête on its left. Finish up the rib to a tree belay (top of pitch 3 *Lodore Groove*).
4 28 m (4b). Traverse right to the prominent rib on the skyline, which is climbed to the top.

Side Line (HVS 1981) is an unpleasant direct variation of pitches 2 and 3 of *Warlock* and **Ragged Crow** (VS 1971) takes the vegetated line right of *Warlock*.

Gowder Buttress 80 m VS   1947

A varied route taking the prow of the buttress. The route description has been altered over the years but this description appears to fit the original line. Start to the left of *Fool's Paradise* at a vegetated groove.

1   30 m (4c). Climb the groove and a short corner above and then move right to the arête to join *Fool's Paradise*. Follow it to the tree belay.

2   16 m. Move up slabs on the right then work left on better holds to an oak belay.

3   34 m (4c). Traverse right and follow the prominent rib to the top.

★★★ **Fool's Paradise** 113 m VS   1951

A varied and popular climb. Start at the toe of the main buttress, just above the path.

1   15 m. Climb the short buttress, past a tree, and go up ledges to a tree at the foot of the clean buttress.

2   24 m (4c). Gain the groove just above the tree, move left onto the arête and reach a hidden hold. Climb up just left of the arête to a tree belay on *Lodore Groove*.

3   22 m (4c). Descend the groove on the right for 5 metres and traverse right to a small tree. Climb up, then move right, awkwardly, to belay beside a large block of doubtful stability.

4   22 m (4b). Move back left and climb a steep groove, leaning left slightly, to a stance.

5   10 m. Traverse easily right to a large yew below a deep chimney.

6   20 m (4b). Climb the chimney direct to the top.

Variation 30 m VS

Start as for *Lodore Groove*. Frequently used to get to the meat of the climb more quickly.

1b   12 m. Ascend to a ledge (pitch 1 of *Lodore Groove*).

2b   18 m (4c). Climb the groove on the left, then traverse right to the small tree and continue as for pitch 3.

Variation 20 m VS

Start just right of the toe of the buttress and scramble up the vegetated groove to the highest of two trees, just above the belay above the first pitch.

2c   (4c). Traverse awkwardly left to gain the arête. Join pitch 2 *Fool's Paradise* and climb up to the tree belay. The thin crack above the belay can be climbed direct to the tree belay.

GOWDER CRAG

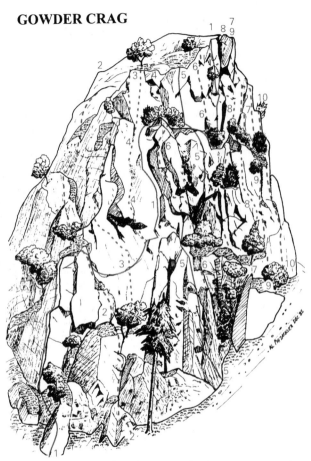

1	Fool's Paradise	VS	6	Voodoo	HVS
2	Lodore Groove	VD	7	Lodore Buttress	VS
3	Kaleidoscope	HVS	8	The Neb	HVS
4	First Offence	E3	9	Hog's Earth	VS
5	Paradise Lost	HVS	10	Little Pig	VS

** **Revenge of the Giant Climbing Ants**   104 m   VS   1992
Start as for *Fool's Paradise*.
1   15 m. As for *Fool's Paradise*.
2   26 m (4c). Climb the groove above the trees and continue up until
    a small ledge is reached at a break. Continue up the bulging
    groove above, pull over onto the broken wall and climb the wide
    crack on the right to a grassy ledge. (Or step left from the break
    to the arête and climb it to the ledge.)
3   43 m (4c). Descend the groove on the right for 5 metres and
    traverse right to a small tree. Climb the wall and go directly up
    the groove above. Pull over some large blocks to a belay.
4   10 m. Move left to a wide ledge and up a grassy ramp to a tree
    belay below a short wall.
5   10 m (4a). Climb the cracked groove up the wall to the top.

Last of the Summer Wine   62 m   E1   1989
A direct line up the left side of the crag. The main difficulties on the
second pitch are short but committing. Scramble up easy ledges, just
right of the start of *Fool's Paradise*, to the foot of the clean buttress.
Oak tree belay.
1   22 m (4c). Climb the groove on the right, as for *Fool's Paradise*
    (pitch 2b) then continue up the steep crack to an oak tree belay.
2   20 m (5b). Climb directly up broken cracks above the belay to
    the large block at 8 metres. From the top of the block committing
    moves are made straight over the bulge, then pleasant climbing
    leads to a small oak tree on a triangular ledge.
3   20 m (4c). From the belay ledge, traverse a metre or so right,
    passing under the final arête of *Kaleidoscope*, to a holly tree in
    the corner. Climb straight up from the holly using broken cracks
    to a bulge which is climbed on the left. Easier ground leads to
    the top.

* **Lodore Groove**   58 m   VD   1947
This route has some good positions and starts about 10 metres up to
the right of the toe of the buttress at a narrow ridge. Not
recommended in wet conditions.
1   12 m. Ascend to a ledge and belay on a yew tree.
2   14 m. Climb the groove up to the left to a large ledge.
3   12 m. Climb the groove above to a tree belay on the left.
4   20 m. Move up to the right and continue up vegetated rock to
    the top.

First Offence   70 m   E3   1978

Takes the overhang and slab between *Kaleidoscope* and *Fool's Paradise*. A problematic roof with mediocre protection. Start as for *Lodore Groove*.

1   30 m (4c). Climb pitch 1 of *Lodore Groove* and then follow pitch 2a of *Fool's Paradise* to belay on a small ledge at the end of its traverse.

2   30 m (6a). Step left and climb the wall above the traverse on *Fool's Paradise* to a bulge. Step up left, climb the hanging groove at the right side of the overhang and gain the slab above. Climb the crack on the left and step right and up the middle of the slab and short wall to a belay.

3   10 m (4b). Step down right and climb the crack in the wall and slab above to the top.

★★ **Kaleidoscope**   76 m   HVS   1971

Start as for *Lodore Groove*.

1   12 m. Ascend to a ledge and belay on a yew tree.

2   24 m (5a). Move right, then climb up and pass to the left of a small tree on *Fool's Paradise*. Ascend the wall above to a sloping ledge, beneath the large overhang. Move left and climb the black groove to a block belay on the left.

3   18 m (4b). Move right up a shallow groove and the wall above to a ledge.

4   22 m (4b). Move right and climb a thin crack and the arête above to the top.

Anthill   77 m   E1   1978

This route takes in some good pitches but is now superseded by the harder *First Offence*. Start as for *Voodoo*.

1   24 m (4c). Gain the small block and climb the arête on the left to belay as for *Voodoo* (as for Pitch 1 – *Paradise Lost*).

2   30 m (5b). Move left to the bottom of the groove of *Fool's Paradise*. Make a difficult move left to a line of holds leading to a bottomless groove in the overhang. Climb the crack above. Go up the left edge of the slab until it is possible to traverse right across a short corner to the tree belay of *Fool's Paradise*.

3   23 m (4a). Climb up to a yew and rib where easy climbing leads to the top.

★ **Paradise Lost** 70 m HVS   1972

Starts as for *Voodoo* and as with that route the rock should be treated with suspicion.

1 24 m (4c). Gain the small block then climb the arête on the left to belay as for *Voodoo*.
2 24 m (5a). Climb to the overhang at 5 metres. Traverse right and climb up *Voodoo* to the grassy bay. Traverse right, go up to a tree (possible belay) and continue up the chimney/groove to a hollow. Move up left to a good ledge.
3 22 m (4b). Walk 5 metres left and climb the wall and overhang to easy ground.

★ **Voodoo** 76 m HVS   1962

A scary experience. Start 26 metres up to the right of *Fool's Paradise*, at a small block below a shallow groove which slants up the left wall of the open gully. This is a serious route on suspect rock.

1 24 m (4c). Step up left onto the small block at the foot of the groove and climb the groove to a stance beside the large block belay on *Fool's Paradise*.
2 24 m (4c). Move 5 metres right and climb a thin crack to a tree. Move up left to a grassy scoop and continue up left, via a rib, to a tree belay.
3 6 m. Move easily right to a belay at a large block.
4 22 m (5a). Move right and climb a crack up the front of the block. Climb the groove above, past a tree, and the crack above to the top.

The shorter, steeper, right-hand section of crag, on which there are three yews forming a triangle, is reached by scrambling up to the right of the vegetated rib to the right of *Voodoo*.

★★ **Lodore Buttress** 54 m VS   1952

A worthwhile climb. Start below the left-hand yew.

1 24 m (4c). Climb straight up to a rib and then go left to below a steep undercut groove. Climb this, with difficulty, to easier ground and then move rightwards to a narrow terrace.
2 20 m (4a). From a pile of blocks, climb the steep wall to a niche with a withered tree. Climb the groove above and go up easily to beside a tall pinnacle.
3 10 m (4b). Finish up the wide chimney on the left.

Gowder Face 52 m VS   1948
Start at the same point as *Lodore Buttress*.
1   24 m (4b). Climb up the right-hand groove to the yew. Go
    diagonally right to a narrow terrace and move left to the foot of
    the final chimney of *Fool's Paradise*.
2   18 m (4a). Climb the chimney until it is possible to move right
    and up, easily, to the final chimney of *Lodore Buttress*.
3   10 m (4b). Climb the chimney on the left.

★ **Polymer** 50 m E1   1981
Two short problem pitches, linked by broken and easy rocks. Start
behind the oak tree 2 metres right of *Lodore Buttress*.
1   22 m (5b). Climb the wall to a scoop and go up this with
    difficulty. Keep right of the first yew tree and continue to the
    next one, just right of the foot of the final chimney of *Fool's
    Paradise*.
2   18 m (4c). Climb the broken chimney to an old tree. Traverse up
    leftwards to a block belay below the right-hand side of a large
    pinnacle at the top of pitch 2 of *Lodore Buttress*.
3   10 m (5b). Gain and climb the ramp on the right side of the
    pinnacle, finishing up the arête on the left.

★★ **The Neb** 50 m HVS   1975
This good route takes a steep and fairly direct line up the crag. Start
as for *Hog's Earth*.
1   28 m (5a). Climb the wall. Move left to gain a prominent crack
    which is followed, past a gnarled oak, to the middle yew.
2   22 m (5a). From the top of the yew, climb the steep wall to a
    ledge. Move up left across the chimney, past a holly tree. Move
    to the right, onto the nose, and climb this to the top.

★ **Hog's Earth** 46 m VS   1967
This route deteriorates after the first pitch. Start below the right-hand
yew.
1   18 m (4b). Climb easy rock and the groove, strenuously, to the
    yew.
2   18 m. Climb the wall above to a smaller yew and move up left
    to a large ledge.
3   10 m (4b). Climb the chimney on the left.

★ **Little Pig** 54 m VS   1982

Start at the tree 3 metres right of *Hog's Earth* for this good though poorly protected route.

1 42 m (4c). Climb the wall above, via a square cut niche and ancient piton, to a small tree branch (possible belay). Climb the wall rightwards, past the yew, to the grooved arête. Follow this to a blocky ledge.

2 12 m (4b). Either climb over the overhang above a large spike, or move right, and up a crack through the overhang, to a pleasant slab to finish.

Although the crag does not lend itself to traversing, two girdles have been made.

The Old Girdle Traverse 52 m VD   1949

Start from the upper reaches of the earth gully, right of the main buttress.

1 16 m. Climb up the wall to a corner level with, and right of, a yew.

2 18 m. Follow the ledge leftwards, past the bottom of the chimney of the final pitch of *Fool's Paradise*, to a corner just right of *Kaleidoscope*.

3 18 m. Move left round the arête and finish up leftwards.

★ **The New Girdle Traverse** 120 m VS   1963

An extension of *Fool's Paradise* which traverses right from pitch 3 of *Fool's Paradise* to follow pitch 1 of *Lodore Buttress* and pitches 2 and 3 of *Hog's Earth*.

To the right of the large vegetated gully bounding the right side of the main buttress, the rock again steepens.

★★ **Gosh** 54 m E1   1971

A good climb, meandering up the centre of the buttress. Start at a large slabby groove, just right of the lowest point of the buttress.

1 28 m (5a). Climb the slabs on the left, or the back of the groove, to gain the obvious V-groove above. Exit onto the right arête and move up rightwards to a ledge of stacked blocks.

2 19 m (5b). Pull over the bulge above the belay at the obvious break (peg runner) to a ledge. Traverse right and climb a groove, pulling out left to a ledge at its top.

3 7 m (5a). Move right and climb the crack in the wall above, trending right to a niche. Climb up left to the top.

★ **The Hog's Back**   90 m   D   1948
    This is the long ridge which runs down almost to the path. It is
    gained by an easy rising traverse from a short way up the right
    side of the ridge and followed direct to the top of the crag.

Variation   **The Antiman**   72 m   VS   1974
    A wandering route starting just left of *Fool's Gambol*. Climb the
    left-hand groove, then the diagonal crack in the slab on the right
    and finish up the wall above.

Variation   **Fool's Gambol**   72 m   D   1951
    Start on the right of the ridge, about 35 metres above the path,
    and gain the ridge by an easy chimney.

Variation   **Masochism**   55 m   VS   1976
    Climb the slab just left of the *Slab Start* to *The Hog's Back*, to
    a yew tree, then finish up the rib and corner on the right, to join
    The Hog's Back.

Variation   **Slab Start**   54 m   VS   1958
A loose route starting at the rib 5 metres right of *Fool's Gambol*.
1   27 m (4b). Climb the rib and the slab above, moving left up a
    prominent wide crack. Make a semi-hand-traverse right to a tree
    belay.
2   27 m (4a). Climb up left (loose) and traverse left to the ridge.
    Follow this to the top.

The following two routes start from the bay up and to the right of
The Hog's Back.

Cold Sweat   48 m   E1   ?   1989
Start below the obvious groove on the left side of the bay.
1   30 m. Climb the cleaned groove and a slab to an obvious crack.
    This leads to a yew tree belay.
2   18 m (5b). Climb steeply into a corner on the right. Move
    awkwardly right for 5 metres under an overhang and climb the
    obvious left-hand corner, moving onto the left rib. Finish over the
    overhang.

Dangerous Assignment   40 m   E2   ?   1989
This intimidating route takes the obvious hanging groove to the right
of *Cold Sweat*. Start below the groove at a tree.

(5c). Climb cleaned rock up a short chimney onto a slab below the hanging groove. Bridge up the groove to finish on some very dubious holds to reach a tree belay.

About 50 metres to the right of *The Hog's Back* and to the left of the right-hand descent path is a buttress about 40 metres high, containing the following routes.

The Adze   36 m   MVS   1976
  Climb the vegetated slab and arête, left of the tree-filled gully – not recommended.

Jennipod   34 m   S   1976
Start at the foot of the buttress, right of the tree-filled gully.
  Climb the slab and leftward sloping groove to a block just below the top. Move right and climb the overhang.

Heather Groove   36 m   VS   1976
Start as for *Jennipod*.
  (4b). Climb the slab, moving right, and climb a shallow groove to gain a corner below the main overhang. Climb the corner then traverse right under the overhang to a ledge.

★ **The Rib**   30 m   HVS   1976
  A poorly protected route in a good position.
  (4c). Follow the leftward-slanting fault, past an oak, to below an obvious rib. Climb the left wall to gain the rib and follow this to the top.

Tempo   40 m   S   1976
Start as for *Jennipod*.
  Climb the slab to the shallow groove. Traverse right below *The Rib* into a groove and follow this to the top.

The Gardener   30 m   VD   1976
A mossy start leads to an awkward mantelshelf. Start 6 metres right of the base of the buttress at a slab.
  Climb the slab and wall above until a mantelshelf move leads left into the groove of *Tempo*. Follow this to the top.

The Groove   36 m   S   1976
   Climb the groove right of *The Gardener*, past a birch, to an oak,
   and climb the groove above to the top.

Lodore Crag   (265 187)   Alt. 120 m   East Facing

This is the large, impressive but extremely vegetated crag opposite
Gowder Crag on the true left bank of the Lodore Falls.

Excalibur   84 m   E3   ?   1970/1992
A much neglected adventure (and rightly so), which follows the
cleanest and most obvious line up the crag. It was originally climbed
with some points of aid at HVS. Start by jumping across the stream
to a jumble of boulders on the true left bank of the stream below the
main waterfall.
1   27 m. Move up and traverse left along a narrow ledge, passing
    two iron spikes, to the foot of a steep, very vegetated groove.
    Climb this with difficulty (usually wet) to an oak belay.
2   8 m. Climb the overhanging crack in the corner above to gain a
    ledge.
3   18 m (5c). Climb the thin corner crack. Move right on a dubious
    flake. Continue moving right under the overhang to a larch tree
    belay.
4   31 m. Climb the overhanging groove which leads to a better
    groove. Tree belay at the top.

Lancelot Start   20 m   E1   ?   1992
A variation start to *Excalibur* that avoids the 50 metres of grass shrub
climbing. Start at the top of the main waterfall.
   (5b). Step off a rock wedged in the lip of the fall into the bottom
   of a corner. Break out right from the corner after 3 metres and
   follow two thin cracks direct to the oak tree belay.

Merlin   54 m   HVS   ?   1983
This route could not be located and as the description indicated that
this was a route to conjure with – perhaps it has vanished. The
description is given here for you to conjure with. Start on the
right-hand end of the crag at an obvious rib.
1   24 m. Climb the rib to a tree ledge and the gross choss behind
    to another tree.
2   30 m. Follow the wall up right to a tree.

Shepherd's Crag (263 185) Alt. 140 m West Facing

Without doubt the best known and most frequented crag in the valley. A wide selection of quality routes across the grades, ease of access, good quick-drying rock, not to mention the cafe at the bottom, all combine to ensure its popularity.

Situated 5 kilometres from Keswick between the Lodore and Borrowdale Hotels, this crag can be approached in a few minutes from the road. Unfortunately, cars may not be parked on the roadside below the crag. The nearest car-park lies 1 kilometre away on the Keswick side of the crag. **N.B. The limited parking at High Lodore Farm is for customers of the cafe.** Parking may be possible at the side of the road beyond the Borrowdale Hotel but beware of further restrictions.

The crag runs roughly north to south and is bounded at each end by an old stone wall extending from the road to the foot of the cliff. Working from the north, or left-hand end, the crag can be divided into three main sections: *Brown Crag*, *North Buttress Area* and the *Chamonix Area*, the last being separated from the others by a wide scree fan.

An important and intriguing characteristic of the place is the difference in rock types between these areas. *Brown Crag* is solid and compact, whilst *North Buttress* is rougher and has some loose areas, particularly towards the steeper right-hand end. *The Chamonix Area* is composed of smooth green slaty rock with many large flakes and spikes reminiscent of the Chamonix Aiguilles, which give the area its name.

The trees which surround many parts of the crag prevent an adequate view of the buttresses as a whole and can cause problems with identification of some routes, though there is generally someone there who knows it all!

In contrast to previous editions, the crag is described as if approaching from the south, from the track leading from High Lodore Farm. In general routes are ordered from right to left.

Chamonix Area

This is the first area of crag reached when crossing the stile on the path from High Lodore Farm. It extends from the boundary wall to the steep *Fisher's Folly Buttress* containing the prominent feature of *Kransic Crack* 100 metres to the north. Nearly all the climbs end on *The Belvedere*, the flat, platform-like top of the crag. The Main

SHEPHERD'S CRAG
General View

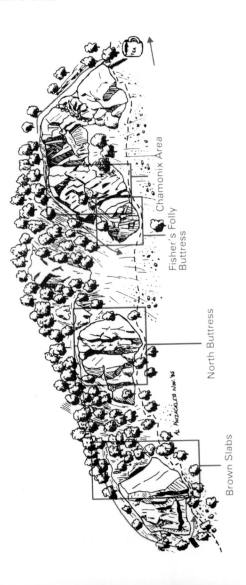

Chamonix Area

Fisher's Folly
Buttress

North Buttress

Brown Slabs

AL PHIZACKLEA Nov. '86

descent is to traverse rightwards from here, descend slightly into the top of a gully (this gully is a possible but unpleasant descent) and reascend the other side to a good path that leads back down to the stile. Alternatively, locate the top of the easy variation of *Donkey's Ears* and scramble down it to the ledge that runs under *Monolith Crack* etc.

Why Not   20 m   MVS   197

Start 2 metres left of the stile at the south end of the crag.

(4b). Climb the obvious leftward-slanting crack and finish up rightwards to easier rock.

Plug   23 m   E1   199

Start 2 metres left of *Why Not*.

(5b). Take the overhanging wall directly.

★ **Jackdaw Ridge**   76 m   D   1946

Start 10 metres left of the dry stone boundary wall at a prominent rib.

1   26 m. Climb the rib for 10 metres. Traverse 3 metres right to an oak, ascend a scoop and then move left to a ridge, belaying above. Alternatively continue above the lower rib passing a yew stump to reach the belay.

2   24 m. Continue directly to a ledge then climb a short rib and awkward corner to *Jackdaw Terrace*.

3   26 m. Easy rocks lead up to the *Belvedere* along the crest of the ridge.

★★ Variation   **Jackdaw Ridge Direct**   26 m   VD   1946

More properly called Indirect Start.

1a   Climb the rightward-slanting groove, 8 metres left of *Jackdaw Ridge* at the lowest point of this part of the crag. Continue past a yew stump to belay in the groove above.

Variation   **Jackdaw Promenade**   20 m   VD   1946

1b   Climb the less pronounced rib 3 metres left of the ordinary start.

Ethelred   24 m   HVS   1983

The interest is mainly in pitch 1 followed by scrambling to the top. An inferior variation on *Odds 'n' Sods*. Start at the lowest point of the crag.

(5a). Follow the groove of *Jackdaw Ridge Direct* for 5 metres to a leftward-slanting crack. Follow this to the large doubtful looking block on *Odds 'n' Sods*. Surmount this then go up the wall to the arête. Follow the arête to tree belays.

Odds 'n' Sods   24 m   E2   1980
Takes the prominent nose at the lowest point of the crag. Care is
needed with some suspect holds. Start at a steep groove in the nose
behind a large tree.

   (5c). Climb the groove to a ledge with difficulty and move right
   to a large doubtful looking block. Surmount this and go up the
   wall onto the arête. Cross the easy slab of *Ant Highway* and climb
   the right side of the wall above direct.

★ **Ant Highway**   48 m   MVS   1947
An intriguing little route with an awkward start. Start 5 metres up
and left of the toe of the buttress on a ledge below a wall featuring
a rightward-rising crackline.
1   26 m (4b). Climb the wall to gain a slab on the right. Climb this
    until a move can be made to the left. Go up to a belay.
2   22 m. Climb easily up to a tree ledge then move left to ascend
    the left-hand of two sharp ridges to gain *Jackdaw Terrace*. Either
    continue up *Jackdaw Ridge* or descend to the left, below *Monolith
    Crack*.

Human Racing   28 m   E3   1984
Start just left of *Ant Highway*.
   (5c). Climb the slanting crack and easy slab for 10 metres. Climb
   up left. Pull straight over a bulge to a hidden jug then over
   another bulge to finish on a slab.

★ **Bits 'n' Pieces**   21 m   VS   1976
The steep wall left of *Ant Highway*. Start just left of *Human Racing*.
   (4c). Climb straight up the wall on good holds to a ledge. Step
   up left and ascend the wall above to tree belays at the top, or
   climb the short groove above the ledge directly to the top.

Mule Train   18 m   E2   1976
A steep climb with an unprotected boulder problem wall to start. Start
3 metres right of the chimney start to *Donkey's Ears*.
   (5c). Climb straight up the wall to a shallow niche. Follow the
   small grooveline on the left to a tree belay on the ledge above.

Opposite: Andrew Slattery making the second ascent of **The Niche**
(HVS), Lower Goats Crag   *Stephen Reid*
Overleaf: Helen Brownlee on the classic VS, **Fisher's Folly**,
Shepherd's Crag   *Stephen Reid*

Variation   HVS   1976
(5a) The niche can be gained by following the slanting break from the right.

★★ **Donkey's Ears** 80 m S (VD if pitch 4 omitted)   1947
A popular climb. Start 5 metres round to the left of the obvious chimney where an ash tree is guarded by a slim flake.
1   28 m. An easy wall leads to a short chimney which is ascended. Walk 6 metres left to a small cave below a cannon stone.
2   8 m. Crawl into the cave and climb up onto an outward-pointing spike. Either hand-traverse left and up to a ledge or fight up between the 'two ears' to the ledge.
3   22 m. Ascend the pile of blocks above on the left side of *Jackdaw Terrace* to below an overhanging block. There is a tree belay midway up and on the right of the wall, to the right of *Monolith Crack*.
4   16 m. Traverse left into a corner and along an obvious traverse line to V-cracks. Climb these precariously and continue up right to an oak.
5   6 m. Continue up to the *Belvedere*.

Variation **Chimney Start** 12 m MVS
1a Climb the chimney to the right. It is more awkward than it looks.

4a. **VD Variation** Follow the jumbled ridge to the top.

The crag now forms a tree-filled bay above a cone of scree. Follow the base of the crag for about 35 metres up and left until scrambling leads you to the high point of the bay beneath a smooth, gently overhanging orange/brown wall. This wall is taken by *The Devil's Alternative*. The next route starts just to the left of *Shepherd's Gully* which is the prominent dirty gully situated over to the left behind a large tree. **Routes are subsequently described left to right**.

NB. Traversing directly across the scree below the bay leads more directly to the area around *Little Chamonix*.

Previous Page: One of the most photographed views of Shepherd's Crag, but this time it is David Stringfellow on **Battering Ram** (E2)
Al Hewison
Opposite: Adam Hocking cruising **Kransic Crack Direct** (HVS), Shepherd's Crag
Dave Simmonite

The Fou 32 m E2   1955
A poor climb, now superseded by the next two routes described. Start
at a large flake below the prominent inverted-V-overhang to the left
of the dirty gully on the left of the bay.
1   18 m (5c). Follow a right-slanting line across the wall to a spike
    below the right side of the overhang. Move round to a slab on
    the right and go up this to the *Saddle* of *Little Chamonix*.
2   14 m (5a). Climb straight up the wall, just left of the oak tree on
    the right, to join the finish of *Little Chamonix*.

★ Variation Finish **Entertainment Traverse** 18 m E2   1958
An outcrop style eliminate beginning from the *Saddle*.
2a (5c). Move up leftwards to a junction with *Stone Tape*, just right
    of an overhanging rib. Swing left and descend a steep groove to
    an overhanging niche, just right of the pinnacle of *The Bludgeon*.
    Finish up the pinnacle and crack above, as for *The Bludgeon*.

★★ **Stone Tape** 34 m E3   1964/1978
A better first pitch than *The Fou* with good steep climbing and an
airy finish above pitch 3 of *Little Chamonix*. Start as for *The Fou*.
1   12 m (6a). Follow the right-slanting break across the wall to a
    spike below the right side of the overhang (as for *The Fou*). Step
    left and up to below the top of the overhang (peg runner). Swing
    out left and up to belay on the *Saddle* of *Little Chamonix*.
2   22 m (5b). Descend a slab on the left and stand on a large block
    below an overhanging groove. Climb this, past a large, dubious
    spike to a ledge. Continue up the groove above to a sloping ledge
    and finish up the short wall.

★★ **Battering Ram** 33 m E3   1984
An eliminate up the right side of the arching overhang, finishing up
a fine, steep finger crack. Start to the left of *Shepherd's Gully* directly
below the upper pitch of *Little Chamonix* below a large flake.
1   18 m (5c). From the flake, climb directly up the wall to the right
    end of the overhang. Follow the overhanging diagonal groove
    above the overhang to a ledge and traverse right to belay at an
    oak tree.
2   15 m (5c). Climb the thin right-hand crack directly behind the
    oak to a groove which is followed to the top.

★★ **Shepherd's Gully** 45 m MVS   1947
Start behind a large tree at the base of the earthy gully.
1   17 m. Scramble up the back of the gully. Swing out and climb
    the ridge on the right then move back left to a tree in the gully.

2   28 m (4b). Continue up the loose gully and move right to finish
     on better rock, as for *Derision Groove*. A looser and less pleasant
     left-hand finish is possible.

★ **Thin Air**   40 m   HVS   1978
An airy variant with the main interest on pitch 2. Start at the rib to
the right of *Shepherd's Gully*, behind a large tree.
1   12 m (4b). Climb directly up the rib to a good ledge.
2   28 m (5a). Climb the rib above to a ledge. Pass the rib above on
     the right. Cross *Derision Groove*, after 3 metres, and make an
     awkward traverse past a tree stump to the foot of a hanging
     groove which is ascended to the *Belvedere*.

★★ **Shepherd's Chimney**   44 m   VS   1946
Noted for its pitch 3! Start just right of *Shepherd's Gully* and below
a stepped corner.
1   10 m (4a). Climb the corner to belay as for *Derision Groove*.
2   10 m. Traverse to the right and down to a recess.
3   10 m (5a). Go up the corner on the left, past a spike, to a very
     awkward finish.
4   14 m (4a). Continue up the slanting chimney/corner, which is
     steep initially but is followed by easier climbing on the left wall.

Variations
There are three short but very difficult problems above pitch 4 of
Shepherd's Chimney. The first two of these were originally climbed
on pegs. All give extremely strenuous free climbs in sensational
positions.

★ **Exclamation**   18 m   E6   {F7b+}   1962/1979
4a (6b). Climb the corner to the right of the belay (peg runner) to a
     second peg runner at its top. Alternatively, and harder, traverse
     right across the slab to gain them from *Shepherd's Chimney*.
     Climb the very overhanging groove on the left, past a peg runner,
     by long dynamic reaches. On the first ascent a runner was placed
     in the chimney to protect the last move.

★★ **Inclination**   18 m   E4   1960/1979
4b (6b). Climb the corner to the right of the belay (peg runner) to
     the second peg runner at its top, as for *Exclamation*. Make an
     airy traverse right and gain an easy groove which leads to the
     top.

★ **Ker Plunk** 17 m E5   1985
The overhanging arête right of *Inclination*. A technically precocious
and strenuous 'little' pitch.
  (6a). Start on the belay of *Shepherd's Chimney* and move out
  rightwards to a small slab, via a small tree. Follow its left arête
  to a rest by a dubious block. Now take two deep gasps and test
  your mental faculties on the tremendous arête.

★★ **Derision Groove** 32 m MVS   1955
A popular route with some tricky moves which follows the obvious
gangway 8 metres to the right of *Shepherd's Gully*. Its first pitch,
illogically, ascends the diagonal flaw to the right of the stepped corner
of *Shepherd's Chimney*.
1   8 m (4a). Ascend the flaw to belay below the upper gangway.
2   24 m (4b). Continue up the steep gangway until a traverse left
    can be made to the *Belvedere*.

★★ **Black Sheep** 34 m E2   1977
A good but very bold route up the overhanging arête to the left of
the final section of *Shepherd's Chimney*. A small bush grows at the
bottom right-hand side of the arête. Start directly below this.
  (5b). Climb directly up easy ramps and corners to a ledge. An
  awkward groove leads to the bush. Step left onto the overhanging
  side of the arête. Climb onto a pedestal, then gain and climb the
  right side of the arête to the top.

★★★ Variation **Wild Sheep** E2   1989
Takes the arête of *Black Sheep* on the left in its entirety and is more
sustained than *Black Sheep*.
  (5b). Gain the pedestal as for *Black Sheep* and continue up
  steeply, just left of the arête, on superb incut holds.

★ Variation **Wild Side** E3   1985
  (6a). From the top of the flake left of the bush move left across
  the steep wall, past a peg runner, to finish up the final corner of
  Thin Air.

Rob's Route 33 m E3   1984
A disjointed series of poor variations. Start at a large pinnacle ledge
just to the left of the left bounding corner of the smooth overhanging
wall.
1   10 m (6a). Climb a slight groove past a peg runner and ascend
    the wall above to a ledge.

2   10 m (5c). Climb the left-hand side of the arête, left of pitch 3
     of *Shepherd's Chimney*, gained from the right, to the bush on
     Black Sheep.
3   13 m (5c). Climb the right-hand side of the arête, to a junction
     with *Black Sheep* after 5 metres. Follow this to the top.

Variation Start   **Rob's Cafe**   10 m   E3   1984
     (6a). Gain the peg runner from the ramp on the left. Traverse up
     left to a quartz pocket and make a long reach to gain the ledge
     above.

★ **Rogues' Gallery**   72 m   VS   1954
This entertaining traverse of the buttress takes in some good climbing.
Start at the head of the scree slope, below a short steep corner on
the left of the gently overhanging wall taken by *The Devil's
Alternative*.
1   6 m (4c). Climb the corner to below pitch 3 of *Shepherd's
     Chimney*.
2   10 m (5a). Climb the awkward, polished corner above (pitch 3 of
     Shepherd's Chimney).
3   18 m (4b). Move down left and traverse left, using a large flake,
     into a corner at 6 metres. Climb up and left a metre to gain
     Shepherd's Gully, with difficulty. Continue left to an oak belay.
4   18 m. Traverse left to the *Saddle* of *Little Chamonix* and descend
     pitch 3 of that climb.
5   20 m (4b). Climb pitch 3 of *Scorpion*.

★ **Bob Martins**   28 m   E2   1978
A poorly protected eliminate with a very exposed top section. Start
at the corner at the left end of the smooth wall.
1   10 m (4c). Climb the corner. Belay on the right.
2   18 m (5b). Climb a flake which curves leftwards to a holly bush.
     Move right along a gangway onto a slab and climb this to the
     foot of the final groove of *Devil's Wedge*. Traverse low down on
     the left wall to gain the arête and climb this on pockets to the
     top.

★ **The Devil's Alternative**   12 m   E6   {F7a+}   1981
A finger tearing and intriguing technical climb with poor protection
which is difficult to arrange. Start below the centre of the wall, just
right of *Rogues' Gallery*.
     (6b). Step up onto a ledge and use a layaway hold to reach a
     good ledge. Move left a metre or so and then move back up right

to good pockets. Pull straight up to a large oak and a yew tree on the large ledge above.

Variation **Woody's Alternative**   12 m   E6   1999
Start as for *Devil's Alternative*.
   (6b). Follow *Devil's Alternative* to the small ledge, make a rockover right to small holds and span right from these to the big sidehold on *Geronimo* (RP 2). From this span right again to crimpy sidepulls which lead to the arête which is followed to a tree belay at the top.

★★ **Geronimo**   12 m   E6   {F7c+}   1986
A technical and very serious problem starting 2 metres left of the right arête.
   (6c). Climb small pockets leading up left and then go straight up past a peg runner to a good hold. Pull left to an obvious layaway and climb straight up the wall above on small holds to the trees at the top of *The Devil's Alternative*.

The Witness   12 m   E6   1987
A committing and protectionless boulder problem. Start below the right-hand arête.
   (6b). Climb the arête on its overhanging left side.

★★ **Devil's Wedge**   34 m   HVS   1948
A rather fearsome little climb starting at an obvious left slanting V-groove.
1   12 m   (5a). Climb the leftward slanting groove to belay on the right, below *Monolith Chimney*.
2   22 m   (5a). Step up onto a rib and traverse left into a V-groove which is ascended directly to the top.

★★ **The Black Icicle**   30 m   E1   1958
Although well protected, the blocks at the foot of this climb give this route a serious feel. Start at the large spikes just to the right of *Devil's Wedge*.
1   14 m   (5b). Climb the thin, black quartz crack running up the steep wall and move up to a yew tree belay.
2   16 m   (5a). With or without the use of the tree, gain and climb the blunt arête above. Finish airily up the wall above, slightly on the left, using a good but suspect hold.

★★ **Porcupine**   28 m   E3   1955/1977

A pleasant first pitch leads to a short difficult final corner. Start as for *The Black Icicle* at the large spikes. Combining pitch 1 with pitch 2 of *Devil's Wedge* makes for a good outing at a more consistent grade.

1   18m (5a). From the spikes, pull directly up the overhanging rib on the right, and follow the groove and wide crack above to the large ledge and tree belay of *Monolith Crack*.

2   10 m (6a). Ascend the prominent short corner, past a ledge on the right, pulling up rightwards to finish.

Exasperation   60 m   E3   1981

Two totally disjointed pitches linked to form a route. An eliminate first pitch, a walk, then a contrived start to pitch 2 which gradually improves to a fine finishing crack. Start 3 metres right of *Porcupine* at a right-slanting line leading to a small niche on *Monolith Crack*.

1   16 m (5b). Climb up the right-slanting fault for a metre or so then follow a thin crack left to a niche on *Porcupine*. Pull up right and follow a layaway crack up left to another smaller niche. Move out left and climb directly to a large ledge.

2   12 m. Stroll down ledges, leftwards, past a large yew tree, to a short corner just right of pitch 2 of *Bob Martins*.

3   32 m (6a). Climb the corner for a metre or so. Hand-traverse right to a rib and pull up onto the slab above. Start again if you touch the tree! Climb the slab to an obvious overhanging crack and finish up this direct.

Variations

A number of variations to pitch 3 have been claimed, pulling directly over the bulge above the traverse right from the in-situ wire. All are very contrived requiring one to avoid using available holds on the right. The further left the harder the grade.

★★ **Monolith Crack**   32 m   HVS   1947

An interesting and popular route up the centre of the wall. Start below the oak stump, sporting a single branch. A tricky and poorly protected first pitch leads to an awkward finishing crack.

1   12 m (4c). Gain a small slanting niche at 3 metres and then move up using a small slanting foot-ledge on the left. Pass the oak stump and gain the ledge above, with interest, and ascend a short chimney to a tree belay.

2   20 m (4b). To the left is the *Monolith*. Climb the crack, just to its right, then ascend a short corner and finish up the wall above.

Variation **Monolith Chimney** 23 m S   1948
2a For those not wishing to battle with the crack, it is possible to
move to the left of the *Monolith* and ascend the chimney. Finish
up the short corner and wall above.

★ **Hippos Might Fly** 26 m E1   1983
A poorly protected route starting 3 metres right and slightly higher
than *Monolith Crack*.
    (5a). Gain a small triangular niche and continue precariously up
the leftwards-sloping crackline to the oak stump. Move right and
climb the crack rightwards to join and climb *Donkey's Ears*.

★★ **Straight and Narrow** 16 m E3   1983
If you keep to this "straight and narrow" you could be in trouble! An
eliminate with a poorly protected crux, pulling over the overlap. Start
as for *Hippos Might Fly*.
    (6a). Climb straight up the wall to a small triangular niche. Step
immediately right and pull directly over an overlap on small holds
to gain a small pocket in the slab above. Go straight up to the
horizontal break and finish up a triangular wall on the left.

Hee-Haw 16 m VS   1983
A short and pleasant in-filler. Start a metre right of *Hippos Might Fly*
and 4 metres left of a corner.
    (5a). Climb a faint cracked groove to gain the traverse of
Donkey's Ears. Above is an obvious crack slanting left, with a
faint crack on its right. Climb the right-hand crack to gain a ledge
and continue to the *Belvedere*.

Following the crag 40 metres or so down to the left leads you out of
the trees to the final, more open section of the *Chamonix Area*.

It is the most extensive but also the most broken area of the crag,
characterized by its spiky, aiguille-like nature. The crag consists of
many small buttresses interlinked with large boulders and tree covered
ledges. It is topped by a series of impressive overhanging walls below
the flat top area which is known as the *Belvedere*.

Descents can be made either down the path on the extreme right of
the crag, the gully just right of *Jackdaw Ridge*, or the sloping shelf
below *Monolith Crack*, called *Jackdaw Terrace*. All are gained from
the right end of the *Belvedere*. Alternatively it is possible to descend
to the left of the crag by a steep path heading from just left of the
finish of *Crescendo* to just above the finish of *Kransic Crack*,

traversing to the left behind a large block to gain the scree on the left of the crag.

The right-hand end is marked by a prominent outcrop sporting two stunted trees and at the far northern end, beyond the very large central pinnacle, lies *Fisher's Folly Buttress*.

The following routes are described from right to left.

★ **Scorpion** 50 m VS   1952
This climb has suffered a rockfall which has affected the final moves: care should be taken, but it is still a worthwhile route. Start behind a small yew which is a few metres left of a large oak and a few metres up and right of the start of *Little Chamonix*.

1   18 m. Climb the mossy wall, first left then right to a narrow terrace. Easy but brambly and poorly protected.
2   12 m. Climb the wall above passing just right of a small oak and drop down to a belay below the twin ribs on *Little Chamonix*.
3   20 m (4b). Ascend the left-hand groove of *Little Chamonix* for 3 metres; then move left below a projecting rock and up into a V-scoop. Head diagonally left to a large platform below a rock scar groove. Spooky moves up this gain good holds – eventually, and the top.

3a (5b). Alternatively, from the large platform, climb diagonally leftwards to gain the spiky arête on the left.

★★★ **Little Chamonix** 71 m VD   1946
A well photographed final pitch has made this a justifiably popular route. Start below a polished open groove just left of the outcrop in a small bay with a crack on its left side.

1   30 m. Climb the crack and continue upwards right into a groove slanting up to the left. Follow this, finishing up the flake crack on the left to gain a tree root belay.
2   12 m. Scramble up right through a wood to below the left-hand of two conspicuous V-corners.
3   16 m. Ascend the left-hand corner to an overhang. Use the block under the overhang (best done sitting down) to gain and cross the slab on the right. Climb its right arête to a belay on the *Saddle*.
4   13 m. Ascend to the pinnacle above. Step right and continue directly to the top in a superb position.

Variation 15 m
3a Ascend the right-hand groove then cross the slab as for the ordinary route.

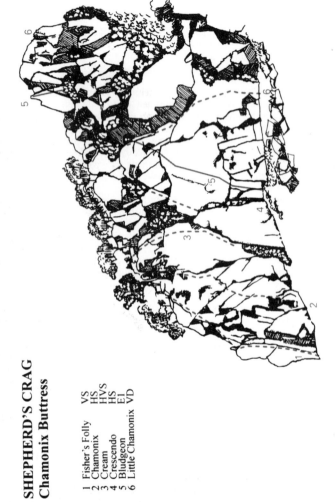

SHEPHERD'S CRAG
Chamonix Buttress

1 Fisher's Folly   VS
2 Chamonix   HS
3 Cream   HVS
4 Crescendo   HS
5 Bludgeon   E1
6 Little Chamonix   VD

Immediately left of the start of *Little Chamonix* is a large semi-detached pinnacle.

★★★ **The Bludgeon**   54 m   E1   1957
A strenuous and spectacular final pitch up the steep wall below the left side of the *Belvedere*. Start just right of the chimney at the back of the large pinnacle.
1   30 m (4c). Climb the blunt arête to a ledge and go straight up the wall above, just left of a large spike on *Little Chamonix*. Scramble up to belay at a 3 stemmed oak tree on the right-hand side of the large tree covered terrace.
2   24 m (5b). Move left and climb the left side of the easy angled rib up the right side of the large dirty central groove. Step right around the rib and go up a short groove to its top, below and right of a large overhanging pinnacle. Climb the crack on the right of the pinnacle and manoeuvre onto its top. Finish directly using the crack above and/or the flake holds on the right wall.

Variation Finish   **Shepherd's Pie**   24 m   E3   1984
A very contrived set of boulder problems up the overlaps to the left of the normal finish.
2a   (6a). Follow *The Bludgeon* pitch 2 to the top of the rib. Climb the overhanging scoop on the left, past a peg runner, and pull up right onto a slab. Climb straight over the bulge above onto another slab, step left and climb the final bulge, at twin thin cracks, passing a tiny sapling.

Variation Finish   **Missing Link**   24 m   E3   1982
Originally climbed with much aid this now gives an exciting free climb.
2b   (5c). Follow pitch 2 of *The Bludgeon* to the overhung niche right of the large pinnacle. Climb the groove on the right and pull round a corner to a junction with *Stone Tape* (*Entertainment Traverse* in reverse). From the ledge, move left and climb a crack in the wall to the *Belvedere*.

★ **Crescendo**   66 m   HS   1948
This is a good route starting just right of the large pinnacle at a chimney/crack.
1   26 m. Climb the chimney to a platform behind the pinnacle. Climb boldly up the polished wall on the right and exit to the tree covered ledge using cracks on the left.
2   40 m. Scramble directly up to a large triangular block below a small ridge. Ascend the ridge, or the rock to its left, and then

move left to an oak. Climb easily up the ridge on the right to the *Belvedere*. (Original finish: Just before reaching the *Belvedere* traverse slightly down and right across a wall to gain and climb the obvious groove above a sapling – rather contrived.)

The steep slab between *Crescendo* and *Chamonix* has had several claimants over the years; these routes make the best of the rock. Both start just left of *Crescendo's* pinnacle.

★ **Cream** 25 m HVS   1997
  (5a). Scramble up into the bay behind the pinnacle and climb a scoop, moving right to gain a crack in the right-hand side of the wall. Climb the wall to the left of this (with or without the crack) and continue straight up to a break. Either follow the crack above with a hard move to finish, or step right and climb the chimney, or make a bold step right to finish through some big blocks of dubious stability.

Variation **Milk** 25 m E2   1997
  (5c). Start as for *Cream*, but from the scoop, climb directly up the wall just left of *Cream* to the break. Take the crack to finish.

Fisher's Folly Buttress

Down and left of the pinnacle is a small compact buttress containing a prominent wide crack in its centre (*Kransic Crack*) and a rightward facing corner just to its left (*Fisher's Folly*). This is *Fisher's Folly Buttress*. Descent is easy from this crag and takes less time than rigging up an abseil: just traverse horizontally leftwards and then scramble up slightly to a notch from whence a path leads down to the foot of the crag. **Please do not abseil off, or top rope directly, from the trees!** They are required for belays and have suffered from needless abuse in recent years.

On the right-hand side of the buttress (just down and left of the pinnacle) is a very large boulder.

★★ **True Cross** 30 m VS   1996
An obvious rising traverse across *Fisher's Folly Buttress* giving steep, well protected climbing. Start on the large boulder.
  (4c). Step onto the blunt arête and follow parallel cracks to gain the almost horizontal juggy break that cuts across the crag. Traverse along this leftwards, with difficulty, and step down into the top of the scoop of *Creeping Jesus*. Pull out left again onto

Fisher's Folly. Move up to the roof and traverse left under it to its left-hand end. Keep moving diagonally leftwards to finish at the top of *M.G.C.*

★★ **Chamonix**   26 m   HS   1946
A rather devious route, starting at the right-hand end of the huge flake that dominates the buttress.
1   16 m. Climb the wall rightwards, using parallel flakes, to gain the arête. Climb this then go rightwards to belay behind a pinnacle.
2   10 m. Either climb the corner above direct or, slightly more easily, use the right wall to gain a ledge.

Two eliminates have been squeezed in to the rock between *Chamonix* and *The Grasp*, (**Poop and Scoop** E2 5c and **Thrutch and Clutch** E2 5c 1998). It is probably more worthwhile to combine the best of both routes as follows.

Poop and Clutch   23 m   E2   1998
(5c). Start up *The Grasp* (flake crack) and continue up the corner where *The Grasp* moves left. Move right and head for the shallow scoop above, climb this direct using high holds on the right.

★★ **The Grasp**   24 m   E1   1978
Good but bold climbing on excellent rock. Don't grasp – snatch it gently! Start just left of *Chamonix*, behind a sprawling oak.
(5b). Climb the left-hand side of the large flake and move up to the scoop to the right of the black overhang. Make a committing move left over the overhang to gain a good hold. Continue up the wall above, crossing *Kransic Crack*, to gain a leftwards-slanting gangway which is followed to the top.

★★ **Creeping Jesus**   24 m   HVS   1978
A direct pitch of continuing interest, without use of the arête! Start just right of the obvious hand-crack forming the left side of the flake.
(5a). Climb the front of the flake to its top. Move up the scoop above then go right to finish up the wall above.

★★ **Kransic Crack**   22 m   VS   1952
Start at the obvious hand-crack forming the left of the flake.
(4c). Climb the crack to the top of the flake, traverse to the right along the flake and make an awkward move onto the wall. Traverse rightwards and then move up to the top.

SHEPHERD'S CRAG
Fisher's Folly Buttress

1 CDM   VS
2 MGC   E2
3 Shanna   E2
4 Fisher's Folly   VS
5 Kransic Crack   HVS
   Direct
6 Kransic Crack   VS
7 Creeping Jesus   HVS
8 The Grasp   E1
9 True Cross   VS

Tim Wood
Oct 99

Variation **Right-Hand Start**   10 m   MVS   1978
   (4b). Climb the right-hand crack of the enormous flake to gain
   its top.

Lower Girdle of Fisher's Folly Buttress   30 m   MVS   1996
Another very obvious rising traverse across *Fisher's Folly Buttress*,
taking a lower line than *True Cross*. Rather scrappy. Start at the
off-width crack of *Kransic Crack Right-Hand*.
   (4b). Climb the off-width crack and traverse left along the top of
   the flake. Step down off the flake, traverse left across the wall
   into the groove of *Fisher's Folly* and climb up left to the ledge
   (possible belay. From the left-hand end of the ledge climb the
   juggy wall to a tree belay.

★★★ **Kransic Crack Direct**   20 m   HVS   1956
Start as for *Kransic Crack*.
   (5a). Struggle up the crack to the top of a huge flake. Traverse
   along the top of the flake. Move right off the flake and below a
   bulge, for a metre or so. Climb up and leftwards until excellent
   holds are gained to finish up the wall above.

★ **Twittering Heights**   25 m   E4   1993
This route takes the centre of the wall between *Fisher's Folly* and
Kransic Crack.
   (6a). Climb the centre of the wall to the centre of the bulge.
   Surmount the overhang using a hidden slot for the left hand.
   Climb directly up to the next overhang on good holds and climb
   this on the left.

★★★ **Fisher's Folly**   24 m   VS   1955
A fine little climb starting at the obvious corner, just left of *Kransic
Crack*.
1   13 m (4c). Climb the corner to a ledge on the left.
2   13 m (4c). Move delicately rightwards for 5 metres. Climb up to
    the overhang, pass it on the right, and continue to the top.

★ Variation **Direct Finish**   10 m   1955
2a (5a). Follow the traverse of pitch 2 but climb directly over the
    overhang to the top.

Shanna 22 m E2   1981
An exciting route taking the arête just left of *Fisher's Folly*.
1   13 m (5c). Climb the left side of the arête to gain the belay ledge
of *Fisher's Folly*. Move left along the ledge and climb a wall to
a tree belay.

★★ **M.G.C.** 20 m E2   1957/1958
A popular problem that attracts many failures. To the left of the
corner of *Fisher's Folly* is a steep wall split by a thin peg-scarred
crack. Hard for the short.
     (5c). Ascend the overhung base and the short crack to gain a
flake. Attack the crack on the left to gain a ledge. Have a rest,
then continue up the wall above.

The bulging wall left of *M.G.C.* goes at E2, if you must.

★★ **C.D.M** 18 m VS   1975
The steep little crack sporting a small oak tree at its foot just left of
M.G.C.
     (4c). Climb the crack past the small oak tree and finish directly
up the blunt juggy arête, just right of another small tree.

T.D.M. 12 m HVS   1995
The short groove left of *C.D.M.*
     (5a). Climb the groove direct.

North Ridge 15 m VD   1946
This route has an interesting first pitch but degenerates after that.
Only the first pitch is described although broken rocks can be
followed above.
     Start at the twin-stemmed tree and climb the wall rightwards to
its top.

Hollow Stones 114 m VD   1946
A rambling climb starting 3 metres left of the twin-stemmed tree.
1   18 m. Climb the wall and move across left to a pinnacle. Climb
the front of this to a ledge.
2   14 m. Amble up the ridge above to an oak.
3   8 m. Move right 3 metres into a recess and climb the steep narrow
chimney. Walk 6 metres left to the next buttress.

Opposite: Pure enjoyment – Jo Grinbergs having a great time on
Chamonix Girdle (HVS), Shepherd's Crag   *Stephen Reid*

4   14 m. Climb the left side of the pinnacle. Move right and climb
     to, and cross, a huge perched block.
5   68 m. Scramble up an easy ridge and finish up a broken
     promontory and cracks to the left.

Stony Silence   15 m   HVS   1989
     (5b). Enter the short overhanging crack just left of *Hollow Stones*
     and layback this to join *Stoned Again*, finishing up the arête.

Stoned Again   15 m   HVS   1988
A short boulder problem up the front of the rib just left of *Hollow
Stones*.
     (5b). Climb the short steep wall to gain a ledge then follow the
     sharp arête on the right of the easy groove.

★★ **Chamonix Girdle**   100 m   HVS   1972
This traverses the crag from left to right giving a more complete
girdle than *Rogues' Gallery*.
1   20 m (4c). Climb *Kransic Crack* to the flake. Move right but
     instead of climbing to the top, move right to belay beside the
     pinnacle on *Chamonix*.
2   18m (4b). Move up rightwards and cross *Crescendo* to join and
     follow *The Bludgeon* (pitch 1) to belay on *Little Chamonix*.
3   28m. Scramble up right to below the gangway pitch of *Little
     Chamonix*. Gain and climb the arête on the extreme right to the
     oak belay on the *Saddle*.
4   20 m (4b). Move right over suspect rock into *Shepherd's Gully*
     and hand-traverse right, across a wall and round a corner, into
     Shepherd's Chimney (reverse of pitch 3, *Rogues' Gallery*).
5   14 m (4a). Finish up *Shepherd's Chimney*.

North Buttress Area

The crag base now again rises leftwards to form another tree-filled
bay above a cone of scree. The prominent tower of *North Buttress*
can soon be seen across this bay. This area stretches north to the
routes just left of the *Ardus* corner. Descent can be made either to
the left or right of the area.

The following routes can be reached by striking directly up into the
back of the bay but it is probably easier to traverse across the scree
path to *North Buttress* and then head back up right along a path
following the crag edge.

Opposite: Matt Perier solos **MGC** (E2), Shepherd's Crag   *Dave Parton*

Attic Stairs   52 m   M   1947
Start at the top right-hand point of the bay. Go up a broken scoop and then past two yews to discontinuous rocks above.

Bluebell Wall   67 m   VD   1946
This climb improves in the middle, but not much. Starts at the back of the bay, below a tree, by a short corner.
1   24 m. Climb past the tree up ledges, first right, then left to an oak, just right of a rocky buttress.
2   15 m. Follow a ramp leading leftwards then climb the wall to its top.
3   28 m. Climb the wall above to the top.

Symbiosis   68 m   HVS   1995
Starts 14 metres up right of *Shepherd's Delight* and 16 metres down left from *Bluebell Wall* at a smooth, recessed triangular slab.
1   11 m (5a). Climb the centre of the slab then the impending corner above to a ledge and oak.
2   23 m (4b). Another corner straight ahead leads to pleasant mossy slabs. Climb these directly to a ledge below a clean wall and corner.
3   23 m. Climb the corner and steep steps above to a gentle, left-slanting stony rake. Oak tree belay at the top of this. Now scramble up 8 metres to a pinnacle below a smooth wide wall.
4   11 m (5b). Climb the thin ramp behind the pinnacle, left of the easy ridge. An alternative, more strenuous, finish takes the straight line of pockets 5 metres to the left.

Shepherd's Delight   86 m   MS   1946
This route has a number of interesting pitches. It starts above the highest point of the scree at the prominent right arête of a buttress, behind a large tree and directly below a many-stemmed oak.
1   18 m. Climb the buttress and shattered rocks to the many-stemmed oak.
2   20 m. Turn the small overhang above on the right and climb the right arête of the buttress above.
3   20 m. Scramble up to a steep wall and climb this, using a crack just above a small block. Move up rightwards, then back left up an aspen shelf.
4   15 m. Either make an awkward hand-traverse right to a difficult finish or, more easily, move up leftwards and then scramble up to below a ridge with a square groove in it.
5   13 m. Climb the ridge to the top. Descend to the left to the top of *North Buttress*.

Variation **Shepherd's Warning** VD   1947

1a 15 m. Climb the centre of the buttress, 6 metres left of *Shepherd's Delight*. Scramble up to a wall with an oak in its upper part.

2a 15 m. Climb the nose, past the oak, to join *Shepherd's Delight* above pitch 2.

North Buttress

This lies down and left of the previous route and is the next major buttress encountered when traversing horizontally across the scree from the base of *Fisher's Folly Buttress* (about 100 metres to the left). It contains a host of justifiably popular routes. Descents are possible to the left or the right of the crag – both require care, particularly the one down *North Gully* to the right where a greasy holdless slab must be down-climbed and a large dubious block circumnavigated. **A much better and safer descent that is very quick is to walk up the hill behind the crag a few metres to a path that leads leftwards to the top of Brown Slabs from whence an easy descent can be made to the left.** Due to the dangerous state of *North Gully*, many parties have been tempted into abseiling over the years and this has resulted in damage to the trees which are often an important part of the belay. There have also been numerous incidents of climbers at the base of the crag, or even worse, on routes, being hit by dislodged stones and/or thrown ropes. **Please do not abseil from this crag.**

⋆ **Turning the North** 70 m VD   1946

Start below the prominent left facing corner/groove at the right-hand side of the buttress. The route crosses the descent path and can be abandoned at this point.

1 18 m. Climb the groove and move right to an oak stump. Continue up the ridge to a tree belay.

2 19 m. Move left and climb to the top of the buttress. The descent gully to the right is spanned at the top by a block.

3 15 m. Pass under the block and climb the wall, just to the left, on good holds.

4 18 m. Climb the steep wall on the left, with interest, to the ridge above.

⋆ **Gemma** 40 m HVS   1993

(5b). Climb the crack in the left of the corner of *Turning the North* to a resting place, make a delicate step left onto a small slab and then another delicate move upwards (crux) to a small tree. Climb the groove above and step left onto the arête. Swing round boldly onto the face and climb easily on good holds to the top. Belay at the birch tree.

P.P.S. 38 m E2   1978
A direct route up the right-hand side of the buttress with a short, steep, difficult section. Start below the thin cracks in the wall 3 metres left of *Turning the North*.

(5c). Ascend the cracks to a slab below an overhang. Move right and gain a short hanging arête. Go up this to a junction with *P.S.* and climb easily up the arête above to the top.

★★ **P.S.** 38 m E1   1959
An awkward climb starting at the broken groove left of the corner of *Turning the North*.
1   18 m (5a). Climb the groove to a stance on *North Buttress*.
2   20 m (5b). Continue up the fault above then swing right, with difficulty, and follow the easy arête to the top.

Variation **Direct Finish** 15 m E3   1981
2a (6a). Climb the crack, as for pitch 2 of *P.S.*, for a metre or so. Step onto the wall on the left and climb straight up past a short crack, finishing directly up the easier rock above.

At the foot of the buttress, a few metres right of its true lowest point is a large flake.

★★ **North Buttress** 45 m E1   1954
An impressive climb whose second pitch up the steep buttress has stopped many. Start on the left side of the large flake.
1   30 m (4c). Climb the flake and the bulge above. Continue up until a short traverse left gives access to a gangway trending back right. Follow this to a stance.
2   15 m (5b). Step left and ascend the overhanging groove with difficulty, followed by easier climbing to the top.

Variation **Slab Finish** 18 m VS   1954
2a From the belay traverse rightwards below the overhang then make a long reach to gain a ledge. Easier climbing leads to the top.

★★ **Central Girdle** 62 m VS   1955
A traverse which links some of the best climbing on the buttress. Begin at the same point as *North Buttress*.
1   20 m (4b). Ascend the flake and the bulge above. Continue until a short traverse left and down leads to a belay on *Eve*.

SHEPHERD'S CRAG
North Buttress - Right Side

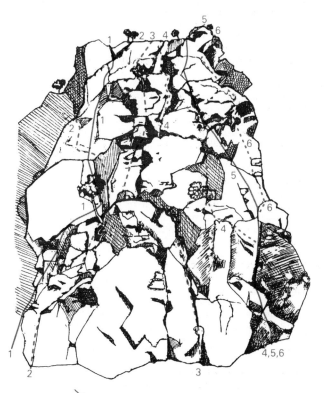

1	Delight Maker	HVS
2	Eve	VS
3	Adam	VS
4	Crunchy Frog	HVS
5	True North	E2
6	North Buttress	E1

2 20 m (4c). Ascend the groove for a metre or so and step left to gain a slab. Work across the slab then go straight up to a stance overlooking *Ardus* (pitch 2 of *Eve*).

3 8 m. Move left into the groove and climb up to a belay, under an overhanging corner on *Ardus*.

4 14 m (4a). Traverse left across the steep slab and finish up the left-hand of two cracks (pitch 3 of *Ardus*).

★★ **True North** 40 m E2   1981

A good pitch giving a direct variation on *Crunchy Frog* with thin fingery climbing up the hanging slab. Start at the blunt arête to the left of the left bounding crack of the flake.

(5b). Climb the blunt arête and groove above to a broken ledge. Continue straight up the crack in the wall above to a ledge, just right of a hanging slab. Gain this from the right and climb it to a broken ledge. Finish up the steep rib above on the right.

★★ **Crunchy Frog** 40 m HVS   1975

An exciting and quite bold climb up friable rock taking a fairly direct line up the buttress. Start as for *True North* just left of the crack of *North Buttress*.

(5a). Climb the arête on the left (or the crack) and the broken groove above to a broken ledge, just below the gangway on *North Buttress*. Move left slightly, to near *Adam*, and ascend the groove above, with difficulty, to gain holds at its top on *Adam*. Move up right on magnificent holds to reach a ledge and continue direct to the top.

★★★ **Adam** 40 m VS   1955

A varied and harder companion to *Eve*. Start in the corner immediately right of the lowest point of the crag.

1 12 m (4c). Ascend the corner to a ledge shared with *Eve*.

2 28 m (5a). Climb up right then back left and up a short crack to a holly tree. Either climb the wall above the tree or move right, climb an overhanging arête to a ledge, and traverse left. Climb a fine steep wall to finish.

★ **Katherine** 50 m HVS   1999

Little new climbing but takes a fairly direct right to left line up the buttress. Start at the lowest point of the buttress, left of *Adam*.

1 12 m (4c). Climb straight up the centre of the buttress to belay on the ledge shared by *Adam* and *Eve*.

2   38 m (5a). Climb the groove to its top and exit onto the wall above *Eve* on the left. Climb directly up for 5 metres to a ledge (3 metres left of the holly tree on *Adam*). Move left along thin, rather grassy parallel cracks to an obvious crack in the wall above. Climb this crack (crux) and continue to the top, trending slightly left.

★★★ Eve   50 m   VS   1951

A popular route which weaves up the buttress. Start 8 metres left of the lowest point of the crag behind a large ash tree and beside a split block. Poor protection for both leader and second on pitch 2.
1   13 m (4b). Climb the short slab and steep crack to a ledge.
2   22 m (4c). Ascend the groove for a metre or so and step left to gain a slab. Work across the slab then go straight up to a stance overlooking *Ardus*.
3   15 m (4b). Climb the short rib above until it abuts the overhang. Move right onto the face and continue to the top using a good crack.

★★ Magnetic North   42 m   E1   1995

1   12 m. Pitch 1 of *Adam* or *Eve*.
2   30 m (5b). Climb up *Adam* and into the corner of *Crunchy Frog*. At the obvious break, pull right on flat hand and foot holds to the base of the hanging slab on *True North*. Go up the hanging slab and traverse right under a nose into the base of the *North Buttress* groove and climb to the top.

★★ Delight Maker   40 m   HVS   1982

A fairly direct line up the buttress, starting just left of *Eve*.
1   10 m (4c). Climb the shallow groove to belay on *Eve*.
2   30 m (5a). Move down left onto the arête and follow this in an improbable position. Climb a steep wall and slab to a shallow depression. Climb its right-hand side, move left and cross *Eve* to finish up the groove above. Quite a bold pitch at times.

Golden Delicious   40 m   E2   1983

A poor eliminate up the steep wall between *Sin* and *Eve*. Start behind the split block at a pointed flake.
    (5c). Climb up the right side of the wall above, passing a thin crack. Go diagonally left into the centre of the wall and up to a junction with *Eve*. Continue straight up and climb the wall above, just left of the scoop of *Sin*. Finish straight up, crossing the top traverse of *Eve*.

★ **Sin** 40 m VS   1971

Start at the wide, dirty, left-slanting crack.

1   10 m. Climb up to a tree.
2   30 m (4c). Move awkwardly right to the arête and follow this to
    the mantelshelf on *Eve*. Move right to the overlap and climb the
    slab and depression above, on the left, to join *Eve*.

10 metres to the left, a line of four large trees marks the foot of the
slabby ramp start of *Ardus*, which takes the obvious left-facing corner
line. Several other routes share this start.

★ **Savage Messiah** 42 m E3   1975

A strenuous and intimidating route which takes the hanging gangway
in the overhangs right of *Ardus*. Care is required with some dubious
flakes. Start as for *Ardus*.

1   28 m. Follow the right side of the slabby gangway of *Ardus* to
    the main corner. Follow this then move right slightly to belay as
    for *Eve*, below its top pitch.
2   14 m (6a). Climb the rib above to the overhang, pull up left, and
    follow the steep, left-slanting gangway to gain the slab above with
    difficulty. Continue more easily to the top.

★★★ **Ardus** 42 m MVS   1946

This is a varied and very popular climb up the slabby recessed corner.
Start at the foot of slabby rocks leading right to the central corner.

1   18m (4a). Ascend rightwards and up to a block belay at the foot
    of the main corner.
2   12m (4a). Ascend the block and the corner above to a ledge with
    a block belay.
3   12m (4b). Traverse left across the exposed slab for 5 metres and
    climb a crack to the top. Another crack, 3 metres left, is slightly
    easier.

★ Variation **Short Notice** VS   1960

Often overlooked but worth the diversion.

2a (4b). Ascend the block above the belay. Move leftwards then
    ascend, in an exposed position, to finish up the final crack of
    Ardus.

★★ Variation **Direct Finish** 8 m VS   1956

3b (4c). Climb the corner above the belay.

★ **Saturday Night Beaver**   40 m   E3   1997
   (6a). Follow *Ardus* to the foot of the corner, move left onto the
   wall and arrange a clutch of runners. Hard moves on crimps and
   layaways, lead to a standing position on a good hold above the
   crux. Continue straight up to a bulge and pull over to join the
   traverse of *Ardus*. Climb the wall between *Aaros* and *Ardus* on
   small but good holds.

★★★ **Aaros**   40 m   E1   1978
   Fine, fingery climbing up the steep wall with the crux saved until the
   end. Initially poorly protected. Start as for *Ardus*.
   (5b). Move up the ramp for 3 metres then follow the narrow right
   -slanting gangway, just left of *Ardus*, for about 4 metres. Gain a
   shallow V-shaped sentry box in the wall on the left. Climb
   straight up the steep wall on the right to a junction with *Short
   Notice*, which leads to the traverse of *Ardus*. Follow this right
   (*Ardus* in reverse) and finish up a thin slanting crack in the
   headwall, 2 metres left of the corner of *Ardus Direct Finish*.

★★ **Ovation**   40 m   E1   1992
   This takes the bulges between *Evel Kneivel* and *Aaros*. Start as for
   Ardus. A bold approach helps but the gear is good when most needed.
   (5b). Step from Ardus onto the narrow gangway of *Aaros*. From
   below and just left of the short corner on *Aaros*, pull over a shield
   of grey rock and climb straight up to the bulging wall midway
   between *Evel Kneivel* and *Aaros*. Climb the wall to a blunt
   pinnacle and finish up the overhanging wall on the left or the rib.

★★ **Evel Kneivel**   46 m   HVS   1975
   This route takes the cracked groove right of the prominent crack of
   Finale. Start as for *Ardus*.
   1   30 m (5a). Climb up, as for *Aaros*, until moves can be made left
      to below the cracked groove. Ascend to a tree belay.
   2   16 m (4a). Finish up the open groove and crack in the slab on
      the right.

★★ Variation **Encore**   HVS   1983
   (5a). Follow *Slings* to a spike below a small roof. Pull over and
   climb straight up to a small nose. Step right and up the groove
   to the tree belay.

SHEPHERD'S CRAG
North Buttress - Left Side

Tim Woal
Nov '89

1	Imago	E1
2	Finale	HVS
3	Jaws	E1
4	Aaros	E1
5	Evel Kneivel	HVS
6	Ardus	MVS

Variation **Long Notice** HVS   1996
    (5a). Follow *Encore* to the foot of the cracked groove of *Evel Kneivel* but continue the traverse rightwards into *Ardus* (possible belay). Finish up *Short Notice*.

★ **Slings** 40 m VS   1948
The meat of this route is on the first pitch which requires competence of both leader and second. Start as for *Ardus*.
1   12 m (4b). Climb the ramp rightwards for a short distance to a gangway leading left. Move up this until an awkward step round a nose gives access to a tree belay.
2   12 m (4a). Climb the steep crack above and move right along a grassy ledge.
3   16 m (4a). Final pitch of *Evel Kneivel*.

★★ **Jaws** 39 m E1   1975
A good first pitch with some pleasant steep climbing. Start below the blunt steep arête above the start of *Ardus*.
1   24 m (5b). Climb the blunt arête on its right side to join *Finale*. Go up this for a metre or so and follow a line of stepped grooves on the left to a small overhang. Climb this, using a thin crack on the right, and continue up the wall to a tree belay.
2   15 m. Climb the wall behind the tree and go directly up the arête above.

Scallywag 40 m E3   1997
    (6a). Start as for *Finale* but continue up the steep groove via a loose block and attempt to climb the wall between *Jaws* and *Finale* without recourse to runners and holds on either route!

★★★ **Finale** 40 m HVS   1965
A good route giving strenuous and sustained climbing. Protection is good but only if you can hang around to place it. Start at a steep groove just left of the blunt arête of *Jaws*.
1   24 m (5a). Climb the groove for 6 metres then step right and climb the bulge and crack above to a tree belay.
2   16 m (4a). Move right and finish up the open groove and crack in the slab on the right.

Imago 26 m E1   1974
A short steep problem starting just left of *Finale*.
1   12 m (5c). Climb up the thin overhanging groove to a tree belay.
2   14 m (5a). Continue up the open corner and broken rocks to the top.

Scare the Tourist (E2? 6a 1999) takes the central crackline in the overhanging wall just left of *Imago*.

Tarzan   27 m   E2   1998
A pumpy route with protection awkward to arrange. Start behind the large tree left of *Imago*.
   (5c). Climb up the wall (with or without use of the tree) until a big swing right around the arête leaves you dangling on the overhanging wall. Pull up the wall on good but spaced holds. Climb the overhang and wall above on good holds, slightly right of centre.

★ **Desperation**   50 m   S   1948
Start behind a large tree to the left of *Imago*.
1   25 m. Ascend directly up to below an overhang and possible belay. Traverse left under the overhang and climb a corner to a ledge.
2   25 m. Climb the wall above to gain a narrow chimney. Climb this with difficulty and follow broken rocks to the top.

★ **North Buttress Girdle**   82 m   E1   1971
Although there is not much new climbing, this route links some very good pitches. Start as for *Desperation*.
1   12 m. Either climb the corner of the first pitch of *Desperation* or, (5a) much more strenuously, climb the overhanging crack of *Imago* to a ledge with a tree belay.
2   15 m (5a). Traverse right and move down to join *Finale* and climb the crack to a tree belay.
3   15 m (4b). Go along the ledge to the right and reverse *Short Notice* onto *Ardus*. Climb past the holly tree onto the smooth slab. Continue right and belay at the small belay on *Eve*.
4   20 m (5b). From the belay descend slightly then traverse right to the tree on *Adam*. Move rightwards, with difficulty, to belay on *North Buttress*.
5   20 m (5b). Last pitch of *P.S.*

★ **A Fistful of Dollars**   35 m   VS   1992
1   25 m (4c). Climb the slab, moving left to a short black crack and climb this for a metre or two before moving left onto the left arête.
2   10 m (4c). Climb black rock behind the belay and veer left up a short crack.

A Few Dollars More 35 m VS   1991
Start as for *A Fistful of Dollars*.
1   25 m (4c). Climb the slab into the chimney of *Desperation* and
     move right into a black shallow groove. Swing onto the right arête
     and climb it steeply to a tree belay.
2   10 m (4c). Climb black rock to a small overhang and pull right
     up a crack.

A few metres left of the *North Buttress* area and just above the path
there is an obvious narrow mossy slab featuring a leftward rising
crack.

Sylvan Way 77 m MS   1946
1   18 m. Climb the slab, following the crack, until a move right can
     be made to a vegetated ledge below an oak.
2   24 m. Move right slightly then ascend a mossy slab and crack in
     the wall above to gain and climb easy vegetated rock, until a
     traverse can be made right, below steep rock, to a rowan.
3   15 m. Ascend the short groove above. Move slightly right and up
     an awkward scooped wall.
4   20 m. Walk left for 6 metres under some blocks. Climb the lower
     of two steeply sloping shelves to reach a gnarled stump. Gain the
     higher shelf and climb leftwards to the top.

Further left again, just before reaching the popular slabs at the
right-hand end of the *Brown Crag* area is a rib with a massive root
boss 6 metres up it.

100-Foot Slab 52 m M   1946
1   22 m. Climb the rib then go easily rightwards to below a large
     block.
2   30 m. Either climb the block, or the corner on the left, to gain
     and climb a vegetated slab.

★ **Gibbon Variation** 13 m HVS   1983
Out of character with *100-Foot Slab* but worth doing on its own.
     (5b). Ascend the obvious overhanging layback crack, 5 metres
     right of the start of *100-Foot Slab*, to gain a belay at the large
     block. Either continue up *100-Foot Slab* or abseil off.

Brown Crag

The is the most northerly crag and can be easily reached through the trees from the road 100 metres south of the Lodore Hotel. The right-hand section contains the *Brown Slabs* area which is very popular with novices and with groups. It is climbable virtually anywhere and only the main routes are described. Further left is the steep *Brown Crag Wall* which faces west through the trees. Descent is to the left and a return to the foot of the routes is made by crossing the stile over the northern bounding stone wall.

The routes are described right to left starting in the corner at the right side of *Brown Slabs*.

Brown Slabs

This is an extremely popular area for beginners and groups under instruction. Descent is simple, just scramble down the easy sloping ground behind the slabs and walk back round under *Brown Crag*. **Please do not abseil off, or top rope directly from the trees!** They are required for belays and have suffered from needless abuse in recent years.

★★ **Brown Slabs Crack**   30 m   VS   1947
1   20 m (4c). Climb the corner/groove on the right of the slab which leads, in 10 metres, to a tree stump. Ascend the corner above, with difficulty, to a tree belay.
2   10 m. Either move left onto the slab and follow it to the top, or climb the corner direct.

  Variation   **The Original Way**   MS
    Just above the tree stump, leave the corner and ascend diagonally left to a scoop, which is climbed until a traverse can be made back right to the tree belay.

★★ **Brown Slabs**   36 m   D   1946
The climb takes the well worn faultline 5 metres left of *Brown Slabs Crack*. Start just left of *Brown Slabs Crack* and move up and left to an oak. Alternatively climb directly to the oak. From here follow the obvious line to the top. A belay is possible on a second oak just to the left of the faultline.

SHEPHERD'S CRAG
Brown Slabs

Tim West
August 93

1	Brown Slabs Face	VD
2	Brown Slabs Arête	D
3	Brown Slabs Direct	VD
4	Brown Slabs	D
5	Brown Slabs Crack	VS

★★★ **Brown Slabs Direct**   38 m   VD   1948
A popular and now well worn route. Start about halfway between two
obvious trees at the base of the slabs where a smooth line leads
diagonally left.
1   26 m. Climb straight up then rightwards and ascend a scoop to a
    good tree belay.
2   12 m. Climb the wall above, moving left slightly to finish.

★★★ **Brown Slabs Arête**   44 m   D   1922
A very popular route. Start as for *Brown Slabs Direct*.
1   16 m. Ascend the scratched line to a conspicuous notch in the
    arête.
2   10 m. Climb the crest of the arête.
3   18 m. Continue up the pleasantly exposed ridge.

★★ **Brown Slabs Face**   42 m   VD   1947
A fine open route which starts at the oak at the bottom of the slab.
    Climb up, crossing *Brown Slabs Arête*, and ascend the apparently
    smooth slab, on excellent holds, to finish just left of *Brown Slabs
    Direct*.

Down and left of *Brown Slabs* lies the obvious dark right-facing
corner of *Conclusion*.

P.T.O.   24 m   VS   1959
    (4c). This route climbs the arête just right of *Conclusion* starting
    on the right of the arête and eventually joining *Brown Slabs Arête*.

Rattle   20 m   MVS   1964
    A rather poor variant on *P.T.O.* which moves right from it at 13
    metres and follows a loose groove to *Brown Slabs Arête*.

Evolution   34 m   E2   1988
Start just right of *Conclusion*.
    (5c). Climb directly up the wall. Step right to the arête for a
    couple of moves until it is possible to move back left to the centre
    of the wall, below a small overlap. Climb up to and finish up the
    final groove of *Conclusion*.

Opposite: Cam Robinson on the strenuous crack of **Finale** (HVS),
Shepherd's Crag   *Al Hewison*
Overleaf: Ryan Dempsey on the crux of **Conclusion** (E1), Shepherd's
Crag   *Ron Kenyon*

☆ **Jenny Wren**   34 m   E3   ?   1997
  (6a). Climb the centre of the wall without using the arête on the
  right. Good gear, though hard to place on sight.

★★ **Conclusion**   42 m   E1   1955
  A striking and strenuous route up the prominent right-facing corner.
  Low in the grade.
  1   24 m (5b). Climb the steep corner and follow the easier corner
      until it curves right to gain a V-groove. This leads to a junction
      with *Brown Slabs Arête*.
  2   18 m. Climb easily up slabs above to the top.

  Could Be The Last   30 m   E1   1978
  Start 2 metres left of *Conclusion*.
    (5b). Climb to below the groove then climb the arête on good
    holds, passing an overhang, to a small tree. Traverse right, round
    the corner, to a flake. Move up left to regain the arête which leads
    to a block belay.

  Theseus   36 m   E1   1960
  An eliminate, with very poor protection starting 2 metres left of
  Conclusion.
  1   14 m. (5b). Climb to the overhang and into a groove on the right,
      with difficulty. Climb this to belay as for *Brown Crag Wall*.
  2   22 m (5a). Traverse right into a groove. Ascend it then climb
      direct to the top.

★ **Frontline**   52 m   HVS   1979
  Serious climbing in good positions between *Brown Crag Wall* and
  Theseus starting at a flat triangular block 3 metres left of *Conclusion*.
  1   12 m (5a). Climb up and over a bulge. Move right and up a small
      groove to a belay ledge on *Brown Crag Wall*.
  2   18 m (5a). Climb the wall above, trending right over overlaps,
      until a leftward-rising traverse leads to a tree belay.
  3   22 m (4b). Finish up the mossy wall above.

Previous Page: Roger Newall alone on the amazing upper wall of
Prana (E3), Black Crag   *Stephen Reid*
Opposite: Steve Frame in a fine position at the end of the day on
Mortician (HVS), Black Crag   *Stephen Reid*

★★ **Brown Crag Wall**   45 m   VS   1950

A classic route, varied and interesting, though it is now rather polished, especially on the first pitch. Start at a weakness in the wall at the twin stemmed oak tree 8 metres left of *Conclusion*.

1   15 m (4b). Gain and climb the scoop for 3 metres and step right onto an arête. Move up boldly into a corner and onto a ledge.

2   15 m (4a). Move up, traverse left for 3 metres and ascend the slab to a sloping ledge. Continue up the slab and scoop then traverse right to a tree belay.

3   15 m (4a). Climb straight up a shallow corner and continue to the top.

★ **Seamus**   42 m   HVS   1967

An interesting direct route starting at the groove of the variation start to *Brown Crag Grooves* behind the twin stemmed oak.

1   18 m (5b). Climb the groove, then the overlap and steep wall above, to a ledge to the left of *Brown Crag Wall*.

2   24 m (4c). Step left onto a hanging block and climb directly to the top.

★★ **Brown Crag Grooves**   57 m   E1   1959

A fine climb taking the grooveline just right of the undercut wall with two crux sections on pitch one. The pegs are old but can be backed up with good gear. Start at a smooth corner just left of the twin stemmed oak.

1   24 m (5b). Climb the steep wall for 3 metres and move right and ascend a steep corner leftwards to the wall above. Move left to the base of the upper groove and climb this with interest to a ledge.

2   33 m (4b). Climb delicately onto the block above and move left to climb a groove for 10 metres. Finish up to the right.

Variation Start

(5b). Climb the groove to the right of the start and traverse left to join the original route.

Variation   **Direct Start**   E3   1979

A boulder problem with a very hard move. Start as for the original route.

(6a). Climb straight up the steep smooth wall to the roof. Go up left using undercuts to gain a thin crack in the lip and pull over into the groove above. Step up right to rejoin the original route at the large groove.

Parting Shot 15 m
1981

(6b). A problem over the roof 3 metres left of *Brown Crag Grooves* and immediately behind a large oak tree, using a runner placed high in the tree.

Rough Boys 12 m E5
1981

The boulder problem roof to the right of *Dire Straits*. There are two alternative methods, the left-hand way being easier. Start 2 metres right of a pointed block.

(6b). Climb up past an undercut to an obvious fist jam slot in the roof. Either pull leftwards to gain a standing position, then back right, or (6c) pull up the layback crack on the right and gain the wall above. Continue up the wall to the traverse of *Vesper*. Either reverse this or follow it to the top.

★ **Dire Straits** 33 m E3
1979

A good route up the grooves to the right of the black overhangs, with a problematic start at a pointed block a few metres from the left end of the undercut wall.

(6a). Pull over the overhang above the block to gain the traverse of *Vesper*. Follow the grooveline above to a ledge then climb the short corner to a tree belay.

American Beauty 23 m E5
1981

An interesting problem over the black roof above the traverse of *Vesper*. Start 3 metres to the right of the tree at the left end of the undercut wall.

(6b). Climb directly up to the traverse of *Vesper*. Step right then back up left above a small nose, to below the overhangs. Gain a good hold above the lip, pull over onto the arête and climb straight up to a tree belay.

Parlophone 36 m E2
1971

A rather dirty and unpleasant route with a poorly protected crux. Start at a small block at the left end of the undercut wall, just right of the tree.

1   24 m (5c). Climb direct to the traverse of *Vesper*. Climb the groove on the left of the large overhang and pull over a small overhang into a groove. Climb up rightwards to a heather ledge. Pull over a nose and up to a belay ledge.

2   12 m. Climb the wall behind the belay, first on the right, then up to the top.

★★ Vesper 48 m   VS   1955
An interesting excursion, starting just left of the overhanging base of
the crag at a rib. The first pitch is quite serious for leader and second.
1   18 m (4c). Ascend the rib to below an overhang then make a
    short traverse right until stopped by a bulge. Move below this and
    into a corner. Move up rightwards across the wall to a scoop.
    Climb up the wall above to a tree on a narrow ledge on the right.
2   30 m (4b). Move right along the ledge and up above an old oak.
    Climb the overhang on the left and continue right to below a
    bulging wall. Ascend it leftwards and finish up a steep groove.

Downer's Delight 36 m   E1   1999
Start 3 metres left of *Vesper*.
    (5b). Climb the crack until a very awkward move gives access to
    the wall above (peg runner). Climb up and right on good rock to
    a possible belay. Climb the wall above to a tree belay.

★★ Just Another Expedition 500 m   HVS   1989
A complete girdle of *Shepherd's Crag*, not recommended on bank
holiday weekends! The line is infinitely variable and brief details only
are given. Start as for *Vesper*.
    Follow pitch 1 of *Vesper* and follow *Brown Crag Traverse* to
    mid-height on *Brown Slabs Crack*. Move out right to a broken
    groove and recess. Leave the recess with VS moves to ledges.
    Follow these and walls, crossing *100 Foot Slab Route* and *Sylvan
    Way*, to the *North Buttress* area and link up with the last pitch
    of *Slings* and *Finale*. Climb this to the *Ardus* traverse and descend
    Ardus to a belay on the rib on the right below the third pitch of
    Eve. Traverse right to the holly on *Adam* and descend the crack
    until it is possible to traverse right onto *North Buttress* and follow
    the slab finish of this. Follow more ledges upwards crossing
    Bluebell Wall and *Attic Stairs*. From *Attic Stairs* descend
    rightwards and descend a steep crack to the *Fisher's Folly* belay.
    Follow pitch 2 of *Fisher's Folly* and traverse right onto *Little
    Chamonix* which is followed to the *Saddle*. Reverse pitch 3 of
    Rogues' Gallery to *Shepherd's Chimney* and then reverse pitch 3
    of *Shepherd's Chimney*. Move up ledges on the right to where it
    is possible to descend the V-cracks of *Donkey's Ears* and then
    reverse the traverse (pitch 4) and finish up *Jackdaw Ridge*.

★ **Brown Crag Traverse**   86 m   VS   1955
A pleasant outing, starting as for *Vesper*.
1   18 m (4c). Climb pitch 1 of *Vesper* to the narrow ledge.
2   24 m (4b). Move right and up onto a heathery ledge below the
    overhang. Continue rightwards onto *Brown Crag Wall* and follow
    this to the tree belay.
3   8 m. Climb up rightwards to a large rock ledge below the last
    pitch of *Brown Slabs Arête*.
4   24 m (4a). Traverse right across the slabs to *Brown Slabs Crack*.
5   12 m. Climb the slab above on the left to finish.

Meet on the Ledge   54 m   HVS   1978
Traverses the faultline starting at *Vesper* and gradually rises
rightwards.
1   32 m. Move round a bulge and continue right across the mossy
    wall to good holds on the right arête. Step right and cross two
    bays to *Brown Crag Grooves*.
2   22 m. Cross the open groove and finish up *Conclusion*.

Groove and Crack   30 m   VS   1971
This is the vegetated corner just right of the stile. Not recommended.
1   18 m (4b). Climb the left-hand groove to near its top. Move into
    the right-hand groove and climb this and the slabs above to a tree
    belay below an overhanging crack.
2   12 m (4a). Climb the crack.

Final Act   12 m   E2   1996
As you come over the stile to the left of *Brown Crag*, this is a very
steep arête (the second one from the stile). This short route starts to
the left of the arête and moves onto it at the top. On the first ascent,
the top runner was placed on abseil.
    (5c). Climb up the groove to good runners. Make very awkward
moves onto the ledge above. A rest can be taken on a foothold
on the left edge. Reach up the overhanging wall to the right for
a hidden jug. Swing across and up to easier climbing and tree
belay.

For completeness only, the following route is included. It is at the
right-hand end of *Shepherd's Crag*.

Free 'n' Easy   15 m   HS   1980
A route on the 'best forgotten' area of rock right of the descent gully,
right of *Jackdaw Ridge*. Start 70 metres up the scree, 20 metres right

of the boundary wall at the top of a small gully and right of a yew tree.

Hand traverse right up a diagonal crack to a block. Surmount the block, move right to a slab and continue up to a large spike belay.

Ladder Brow Crag   (262 181)   Alt. 140 m   West Facing

Also known as Borrowdale Hotel Crag. From High Lodore Farm, briefly follow the track for *Shepherd's Crag* and then take the right branch up to a bench seat. From just above here follow a slightly rising traverse rightwards through the rough woodland, skirting just below the base of some crags. After about 200 metres you emerge from the wood at a faint track across the top of the scree. Follow the track until you see a prominent, steep, clean looking wall through a break in the trees above you. This is before you reach a point above the wide clearing in the trees at the foot of the scree slope. The first routes are to be found on the compact rock to the left. You should note that there is a large amount of loose rock on the ledge at the top of the first few routes. Be mindful of this when wandering around at the foot of the crag. Those with an ant phobia should also avoid this crag! Descent is to the left.

Scramble up to the left of the clean wall until you are below a hanging triangular boulder.

The Look   12 m   E2   1999
Start 3 metres down and right of the triangular boulder at a thin crack.
(5c). Climb the crack to where it steepens and then make a long reach rightwards to join *The Smile*.

A few metres down and right of *The Look* is an obvious left-sloping ramp. The next three routes start at the foot of this ramp.

The Smile   18 m   HVS   1999
(5a). Follow the ramp to steeper rock, then follow the left-sloping groove to its top.

★ **Track of a Tear**   18 m   E3   1999
(5c). Follow the ramp to where it steepens then move right onto the ledge on the wall. Move up into a crack and follow it to the top.

The Touch   18 m   E3   ?   1999
   (6a). Climb the wall steeply rightwards to a ledge. Step left onto
   the wall and climb the steep groove and wall on its left to good
   finishing holds.

The Kiss   18 m   E3   ?   1999
Start 2 metres right of *The Touch*, at the right edge of the wall.
   (6a). Climb to a ledge beneath an open groove. Back and foot up
   the groove to good holds at the top.

Countermure   18 m   S   1991
A faulted flake-blocked wall bars entrance to a large recess to the
right of *The Kiss*.
1   9m. Climb up to an overhung niche and pull strenuously into the
    recess.
2   9m. The ramp on the left leads to a bad finish right of an oak
    tree. Alternatively climb the wall at the back of the bay.

Renaissance of the Retired   18 m   VS   1991
A contrived start leads to a good finish. Start below a left-inclining
black edged flake crack which leads up to the recess.
1   9m (4b). Climb flakes and the black flake to the recess.
2   9m (5a). Follow the prow on the right to a slabby finish.

30 metres further along to the right there is a bay below a slabby
groove system. On the left of the bay there is an oak tree 3 metres
up the crag, just left of a groove.

Flamboyant Decay   23 m   VD   1991
   Start just right of the oak tree. Climb 5 metres then step right
   across the groove to a spiky rib. Climb past the large gnarled oak
   ahead to a wide flake-strewn chimney. Leave this by pulling up
   the right wall and finish up a pleasant ridge.

10 metres up and right at the back of the bay is another large oak
tree.

Fight with a Beech Tree   18 m   HVS   1985
   (5a). Climb the groove behind the central oak and move up to a
   small beech tree. Climb through this, go over the overhang on the
   right and finish up a mossy slab.

Revenant's Groove   19 m   MS   1991
Start behind the large oak and climb the slabby corner to an overhang. Take the wall on the right to join the cracked slab of *Cosmetic Artifice*. Continue up the broken groove above, moving right below a beech sapling, to gain the left edge of the finishing slab.

Cosmetic Artifice   18 m   VS   1991
Start 3 metres up and right of the large oak.
   (4c). Climb the cracked slab left of the groove for 5 metres then pull up onto the overhanging right wall. Step delicately round to the right onto a slab until an awkward move up the adjoining right wall is made to join another slab. This is climbed on the right.

Some 30 metres up right from the southerly bounding spur of the bay containing *Cosmetic Artifice* is a prominent 3 metre high needle.

Restless Ecstasy   15 m   VS   1995
Start just left of the needle.
   (5a). Easy broken rocks lead to a vegetated bay. Climb the obvious groove, avoiding its continuation crack by moving up left to the slab edge. Small holds lead up right.

Four metres right of the above route is a snouted sharp-edged pinnacle preceded by a subsidiary rib.

Moral Narcosis   14 m   HVS   1995
   (4c). A serious little problem because of no protection on the fin section. Climb up the subsidiary rib to a ledge. Belay here if needed. Mantelshelf to a small ledge on the right side of the arête, then step up left to finish excitingly up the steep knife edge.

Green Bank Crags

150 metres to the right of *Ladder Brow Crag* (and slightly further up the hillside) lie two sheltered outcrops.

North Crag

Dramatically quarried and the more impressive of the two outcrops. There is a large shallow cave on the left and a smooth rampline on the right. It is best to descend to the right of the crag continuing down to the gap in the wall about 50 metres below the crag.

The Late Remorse of Love 33 m VS   1991
Start at a groove near the left end of the crag, immediately left of the cave.
1   20 m (4b). Climb the groove for 5 metres. Step right to a wedge-shaped niche and follow a thin gangway across the lip of the cave. Gain an earthy ledge above and move up beneath an ash sapling before climbing diagonally right and steeply up to *Block Ledge*.
2   13 m. Climb the curving crack behind the birch to a small shrubbery. Traverse 3 metres left and climb a short, steep wall.

Heartbreaker 25 m E2 ?   1999
    (5c). Climb the right edge of the cave to the niche. Make awkward moves out of the niche and go up a thin crack to step left onto a glacis. Move left, avoiding loose rock, then go up to tree belays.

Auguries of Eternity 23 m E1   1991
5 metres to the left off the foot of the ramp are two inverted V-niches below a ledge with a tree. Start below the right-hand, more vaguely defined, niche.
1   17 m (5c). Climb the niche and move rightwards on shattered rock (peg runner) to join *Jaws of Sheitan* at the crux. Overcome this then bear right to *Block Ledge*.
2   6 m. An ill-defined groove.

★ **The Jaws of Sheitan** 30 m E1   1991
Start at the foot of the ramp.
1   15 m (5c). Climb the slab rightwards to a diagonal crack and go up to a roof of spiky blocks. Either squirm between these via the *Manhole*, or avoid them on the left, to belay on *Block Ledge*.
2   15 m (4b). Follow a diagonal fault up the wall behind the *Manhole* moving right at the top.

The Promise 20 m E3   1999
    (5c). Climb the arête on the right of the crag.

South Crag

This lies 80 metres to the right of, and slightly above, the *North Crag*. It is reached by initially descending to go through a break in the high stone wall. It is very sheltered and thus usually dry. It is identified by a prominent left-leaning ramp, and 5 metres to the right, a large ash growing from the foot of the crag. The routes end below a 15 metre face of shattered rock which is best avoided.

The Perishing Pleasure of Apes   19 m   VS   1991
Start at the foot of the ramp.
(4c). Climb the ramp to a V-shaped hollow with a holly. Hand-traverse a flake rightwards to an oak. Swing right under this to a little ledge below a groove. Climb the groove via its right wall and scramble up left to an oak and block.

Farewell to the Fifties   16 m   S   1991
Start 5 metres right of *The Perishing Pleasure of Apes*, just to the left of the ash. Climb up the hollow and follow a crack to a ledge with a holly. Climb the overhang.

The Chest of Ozymandias   18 m   S   1991
Start right of the ash and climb the impending wall to a V-groove, then go up right to a ledge. Bear right up slabs to a vague ridge, then move left to an oak and block.

Black Crag   (263 172)   Alt. 260 m   West to North Facing

This is one of the best and most impressive crags in Borrowdale. It has something for everyone on clean sound rock. Protection is generally good, the climbing is delightful and the situations are excellent!

The crag dominates the small valley of Troutdale and is easily visible from the road after passing *Shepherd's Crag* and the Borrowdale Hotel. Parking is found 1/2 kilometre further on just past the Derwent Hotel where the road enters a series of sharp bends. From here walk back 100 metres and take a narrow lane (no vehicles or parking please) opposite the hotel. This leads past several cottages to an open grassy meadow. *Black Crag* is now obvious. Follow the track and stream to where the valley narrows, cross the stream and take an improved track up the hillside to the crag (20 mins).

The crag has two distinct halves, split by a vegetated gully. The best climbing is to be found either side of this feature as the climbing tends to deteriorate as the crag merges into the fellside. To the left, (*North Buttress*) is a steep wall, topped by overhangs, that eases in angle towards the summit. To the right of the gully (*South Buttress*) is a series of grooves and corners and *Troutdale Pinnacle* may be seen directly above the lowest point of the crag (and is usually waymarked by climbers).

Descent from most routes is achieved by following tracks up and right across the top of the crag. A stile leads over a stone wall and a path leads down the right-hand side of the crag to its base.

The normal point of arrival is at the lowest point of the crag by an obvious fallen tree. Just to the left is the initial slab of *Obituary Grooves* that provides the start for several routes (can be a bottleneck) and just to the right is the short wide crack of *Troutdale Pinnacle*. Up and further left can be seen a vegetated gully forming the left boundary of this, the *South Buttress*.

North Buttress

The following routes are described from right to left from the vegetated gully between the *North* and *South Buttresses*.

★★★ **Prana**   72 m   E3   1977
A brilliant route with good holds and reasonable protection up the wall left of the vegetated gully. Start at the foot of the easy-angled and often wet slab below and left of the gully.
1   12 m (4b). Climb the fault leftwards up the slabs to a tree belay below the wall.
2   42 m (5c). Move right and climb up the wall, 3 metres left of the gully, pulling up left onto the slab below the overhangs of the half-way break. Pull over on small holds, usually climbed by an easier alternative 2 metres right. Climb the wall until a step left can be made to a ledge (junction with *Grand Alliance*). Climb the bulging wall above to where the angle eases and continue to a large ledge.
3   18m. Scramble up easier rocks on the left to the top.

★ **The Lastest**   75 m   HVS   1965
A rather wandering route, finding the easiest way up the *North Buttress*. Start as for *Prana*.
1   12 m (4b). Pitch 1 of *Prana*.

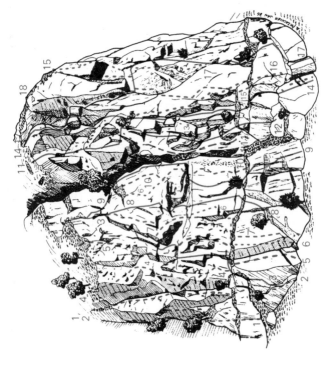

BLACK CRAG
Left-hand Side

1	Moonraker	VS
2	The Wreath	MVS
3	Jubilee Grooves	E1
4	The Coffin	VS
5	The Shroud	VS
6	Grand Alliance	E4
7	Tristar	E4
8	Vertigo	E2
9	The Lastest	HVS
10	Prana	E3
11	The Dice Man	HVS
12	Triptych	E1
13	Obituary Grooves	VS
14	The Mortician	HVS
15	Black Crag	E1
	Eliminate	
16	The Mortuary	E1
17	Troutdale Pinnacle	S
18	Wack	E4

2   24 m (5a). Climb the wall, just right of the tree, direct to a large
    slab. Traverse right along the overhung slab to a belay in the
    gully.
3   21 m (5a). Step up left onto the rib and climb a groove to a block
    at 11 metres. Step left and up to a small spike. A long reach gains
    good holds and easier climbing leads to a large ledge.
4   18 m. Scramble up easier rocks on the left to the top.

★ **Astral Weeks** 74 m E3   1982
An eliminate, squeezed between *Grand Alliance* and *Vertigo*, with a
desperate mantelshelf move over the overhang.
1   12 m (4b). Pitch 1 of *Prana*.
2   23 m (6a). Follow pitch 2 of *The Lastest* to the large slab. Make
    a very difficult pull over the weakness in the overhang, 3 metres
    right of *Vertigo*, onto the traverse of *Grand Alliance* and follow
    it right to a good block. Step up and traverse a narrow slab,
    leftwards, between the overhangs until a pull up left can be made
    onto a small stance above the overhangs on pitch 3 of *Vertigo*.
3   21 m (5b). Climb the wall behind to a bulge. Continue over this
    onto a steep wall, which leads to easier climbing and a large
    ledge. Tree belay on the right.
4   18 m. Scramble up easy rocks on the left to the top.

Another 30 metres along the crag you will arrive at a distinctive and
very symmetrically split oak tree just below the open corner of *The
Shroud*, with the blunt arête of *Grand Alliance* bounding its right side.
The next six routes start close to here.

★★ **Vertigo** 80 m E2   1958
A good, varied route up the *North Buttress*, originally climbed with
much aid. Quite strenuous. Start on the rightward-leading tree-covered
gangway, above a large holly.
1   12 m. Walk up the gangway, climb a short corner and step right
    to a yew tree.
2   14 m (4c). Step off a block into a corner on the left and climb
    it to a large slab. Move left for 5 metres to a block belay.
3   24 m (5c). Go up right, across the slab, to the left end of a long
    overhang. Mantelshelf onto a ledge on the wall on the left. Climb
    a series of short corners, trending leftwards (peg runners) to the
    final roof. Pull over, moving right to gain a small ledge. Climb
    up left for 2 metres then up the wall above to a small ledge on
    the left.

4   30 m. Climb the rib on the right and the groove above to a hanging block. Go over this and follow easy slabs above to the top.

★ **Tristar**   63 m   E4   1977
Good but contrived climbing with a serious second pitch. Start 2 metres right of the blunt arête, on the right-slanting gangway.
1   21 m (5b). Climb the wall, 2 metres right of the arête, to a ledge. Climb straight up to a small overhang up and left of the overhang on *Grand Alliance*. Pull round right (peg runner) onto the face and go up to a slab and belay on *Vertigo*.
2   30 m (6a). Climb the wall, just right of the cut-away roof on the left, to a small overhang. Traverse left, above the lip of the roof, to a resting ledge. Step up and back right on a narrow slab between the overhangs. Pull up into a groove above and climb it and the easier wall above to the large ledge. (A runner on *Vertigo* can be used to protect the traverse left).
3   12 m. Easy scrambling leads up the rib above to the top.

★★ **Up for Grabs**   60 m   E3   1965/1988
The long standing aid route of *D.T's* provides the meat of this climb which now gives a good direct free route up the crag.
1   25 m (5b). Climb the wall just to the right of the blunt arête and continue up the wall above to belay at the top of pitch 2 of *The Shroud*.
2   35 m (6b). Climb the obvious triangular roof above at its widest point, passing a peg runner, and finish up the easy rock above.

★★★ **Grand Alliance**   70 m   E4   1976
A superb route giving delicate climbing up the steep walls of the *North Buttress*. Start at the arête on the right of the corner of *The Shroud*.
1   10 m (4c). Climb the blunt arête to a ledge. (Or, more easily, climb pitch one of *The Shroud*.)
2   15 m (5b). Traverse right to twin blocks on the ledge. Climb into the overhung corner above. Pull out right and climb the wall above to a slab and belay on *Vertigo*.
3   32 m (6a). Go up right, across the slab, to the left end of a long overhang. Mantelshelf onto a ledge on the wall above, as for *Vertigo*, and traverse delicately right between the overhangs. Ascend with less difficulty to small ledges and go up the wall, trending left to some small undercuts. Step right, and make some difficult moves up the wall to better holds. Easier climbing leads to the large ledge.

4   13 m. Easy scrambling up the rib above to the top.

★★ **The Shroud**   72 m   VS   1958
A good and varied route of great interest, starting up the obvious corner.
1   12 m (4b). Ascend the corner to a stance on the right.
2   15 m (4c). Climb the groove to a peg runner under the overhang. Reach right (for the tall) or teeter right (for the short) and then enjoy steep jug-pulling to easier ground. Peg belay below the overhang.
3   21 m (4c). Cross the slab on the left for about 7 metres and then climb up left and up a short groove on the left of a nose. Continue up to the right to another small overhang which is passed on its left. Go up the short groove above and step left to a ledge.
4   24 m (4a). Move onto a rib on the right and climb a series of mossy slabs and grooves towards bulging rock up on the right. Move right at the bulge, then up easily to the top.

Romeo Error   66 m   E2   1978
An eliminate route with a difficult first pitch. Start just right of the arête that forms the left boundary of the corner of *The Shroud*.
1   15 m (5c). Climb up right, then straight up, just left of the heather-choked cracks. Keep right of a thin crack near the top, then pull up left to the arête. Traverse right and belay on *The Shroud*.
2   36 m (5a). Follow *Jubilee Grooves* to below the groove, then traverse left for 6 metres. Climb the steep wall on good holds and continue to belay below the slab above at the top of pitch 3 of *The Shroud*.
3   15 m (5a). Gain the hanging groove above on the left and follow it to the top, finishing as for *The Coffin*.

The following three routes all start at the foot of a wall just left of the left-bounding arête of the corner of *The Shroud*.

★★ **Jubilee Grooves**   114 m   E1   1977
An enjoyable and varied route requiring a bold approach on pitch 1.
1   21 m (5a). Climb straight up a scoop in the wall to a ledge. Step right and boldly up to a heather ledge. Traverse 5 metres right to belay on *The Shroud* – as no good belay can be found in the line of the route. A serious pitch.

2   33 m (4c). Move back left for 5 metres, ascend a short wall and
    continue up a groove on the left. At the top, climb back right and
    down the slab to a peg belay below the overhang.
3   36 m (5b). Climb back left for 3 metres to a groove at the end
    of the overhang. Surmount this, moving out right at the top.
    Continue up the slabby groove to a heather ledge. Walk right to
    a large block belay.
4   24 m (4a). Go back left to the top of the groove. Climb directly
    up a rib and continue to a tree belay.

★★ The Coffin   70 m   VS   1967

A good route through the grooves and walls at the left end of the
North Buttress.
1   15 m. Climb a slab leftwards then follow the corner sprouting a
    tree to a ledge. Belay on the right.
2   33 m (4b). Climb a steep wall behind the belay, passing a bulge.
    Traverse left for about 6 metres along an obvious gangway. The
    steep groove on the right is climbed on good holds to a niche,
    just left of pitch 3 of *The Shroud*. Make a steep step left to a
    short groove which leads to a ledge.
3   22 m (4b). Move right and up for 3 metres then go left past ledges
    to below a steep wall. Avoid this by a short groove round the left
    arête and go easily to tree belays.

The Wreath   67 m   MVS   1967

An entertaining route up the chimney/groove at the left end of *North
Buttress*.
1   15 m. Pitch 1 of *The Coffin*.
2   12 m (4a). Move up and left to the foot of a groove. Move up
    to belay beside an oak tree.
3   40 m (4a). Climb the bulge above the tree into a chimney/groove
    which is followed to the top.

Up and left 15 metres along the crag there is a right-slanting slabby
ledge overlooking the sprouting tree of *The Coffin*.

★ Moonraker   48 m   VS   1971

A pleasant route on quite clean rock. Worth the wander across. Start
at the left end of the slabby ledge.

Opposite: The classic route of the valley – Jilly Reid on the crux top
pitch of **Troutdale Pinnacle** (S), Black Crag   *Stephen Reid*

1   14 m (4c). Climb a steep wall and crack on the left to a heather ledge and birch tree belay.
2   34 m (4c). Traverse right and make a difficult move right to the foot of a steep groove. Climb it and the crack above. Move right into the final chimney of *The Wreath* and follow this to the top.

High Plains Drifter   172 m   E2   1977

The meat of this girdle is in pitches 4 and 5 which give good, though little new climbing. The remainder is then a rather wandering continuation to add length.

1   14 m (4c). Pitch 1 of *Moonraker*.
2   18 m (4c). Pitch 2 of *Moonraker* to a flake belay in the chimney of *The Wreath*.
3   24 m. Traverse the slabs on the right to *Jubilee Grooves*. Step across this to a belay on a ledge down on the right.
4   10 m (5c). Step down rightwards and traverse a narrow slab between the overhangs. Step down and right to a peg belay above the overhangs on pitch 3 of *Vertigo*.
5   18 m (5b). Traverse right to the small ledge on *Grand Alliance*. Descend rightwards to a lower traverse line leading right to the rib. Swing down right to belay on *The Lastest* at the top of pitch 2. It is better to finish up *The Lastest*, though one can continue:-
6   42 m (4c). Move right, crossing ribs, and reverse the 'swing-layback' moves of *Obituary Grooves*. Continue up the crack on pitch 2 of The *Mortician* and belay below the *Finger-Traverse* on *Troutdale Pinnacle Superdirect*.
7   16 m (4c). Move right, round the rib, and climb a steep groove to a block belay on *Troutdale Pinnacle* below pitch 6.
8   30 m (4b). Descend rightwards across a slab and ascend the slabby wall of *Gleaned Grooves*. Pass a holly and continue to the summit.

Some 13 metres left of *Moonraker* there is a wide open rocky gully that has seen much recent cleaning. At the right side of the gully, 4 metres up the crag, is a prominent tree growing out of a crack in the rock. The next three routes start below this tree.

The best descent from all the following routes may be by abseil.

Opposite: Black Crag – Jane Meeks starting the crux pitch of
Raindrop (E1), with the Pinnacle above   *Stephen Reid*

Waiting for God   35 m   HVS   ?   1995
   (5a). Walk along the ledge that leads rightwards. Climb the steep
groove to the overhang. A long reach for good holds on the right
leads to easier climbing. Move left and climb up the slab.
Traverse 6 metres left to easier climbing.

The Gravestone   36 m   VS   1967
Start at the groove below the tree.
   (4b). Go up the groove to the tree. Climb the corner crack to a
smaller tree. Move right then back left up a short gangway and
then over a bulge on the right onto a slab. This is followed by
vegetation to a tree belay.

Tombstone   35   VS   ?   1995
   (4b). Climb the crack up to the prominent tree. An interesting
traverse leads right into a narrow chimney. Move left onto the
arête. Traverse left into the *Gravestone*. Climb the gangway a
short distance and pull over the bulge into the groove above.
Move left to a tree belay.

One Foot in the Grave   35 m   VS   1995
   (4b). Climb the groove and tapering chimney a few metres left
of *Tombstone*. Move up to the holly then step onto the slab above.
Climb this to a short corner and step right above the overhang.
Easier climbing leads to a tree belay.

Walking round to the left side of the wide, open rocky gully reveals
the obvious chimney of the next route.

Age Concern   35 m   VS   ?   1995
   Climb the chimney, moving up and left onto the wall. Step across
the top of the chimney and traverse right onto the last section of
One Foot in the Grave.

Death Bed   40 m   VS   ?   1995
1   20 m (4c). Climb the narrow wall to the left of *Age Concern* and
   the groove above. Pull up onto the slab and move up to belay.
2   20 m (4c). Traverse left and climb the steep slab to a small flake
   belay.

To the left of the chimney is a large groove and then a steep wall.

★ **Ashes to Ashes** 45 m E1   1995

Start 3 metres up the big corner groove.

1 31 m (5b). Climb boldly up the steep wall on small holds. Climb
   up and traverse right above the groove. Continue up to the
   overhang and move up and left onto the slab. Climb up to a peg
   belay.

2 14 m. Traverse left, pull over the small overhang and climb the
   slab above. Spike belay high on right.

Original Start (VS) climbs the groove for 6 metres then traverses
left to join the direct route.

The Mole 66 m VS   1968

An extremely dirty and uninspiring route best left alone. Start below
the centre of the wall.

1 36 m (5a). Climb up for 2 metres, step left on poor holds and
   climb straight up a shallow vegetated corner beneath some
   overhangs. Move up, pull onto a heather ledge and move right to
   belay in a groove.

2 30 m (4c). Climb the groove for a couple of metres, traverse
   diagonally right to an awkward little corner and go over a bulge
   onto the slabs above. Belay well back on the right.

☆ **Dust to Dust** 52 m E1 ?   1995

Start on the left-hand end of the wall below a groove.

1 22 m (5b). Climb onto a good foothold and make a hard step up
   on a very small foot hold. Follow the steep groove on better holds
   and go over the bulge to a peg runner. Make an awkward move
   to the roof. Move out and left over the roof onto a slab and
   traverse right to a peg.

2 30 m. Pitch 2 of *Ashes to Ashes*.

Angel in the Wood 60 m E1 ?   1995

This takes the groove up the front of the buttress to the left – from
its lowest point.

1 35 m (5b). Climb onto the short slab then move right into the
   groove. Follow this to the overhang which is climbed directly into
   the groove above. Climb the groove to the next overhang and
   make a long traverse right. Peg runner (on *Dust to Dust*). Climb
   the overhang. Move left on good holds then move up right to a
   belay peg.

2 25 m. Move left and climb the fine slabby wall to peg belays.

South Buttress

The following routes are described from left to right starting from the vegetated gully in the centre of the crag near the initial point of arrival by the dead tree.

★ **Triptych** 90 m E1   1979

A meandering route with no logical line but interesting climbing. Scramble up towards the vegetated gully then traverse right along a ledge to the base of a short cleaned mossy slab 8 metres right of the gully, and overlooking the initial slab of *Obituary Grooves*.

1   15 m. Climb the steep slab to a ledge. From its left end climb a groove to a grassy ledge on the right.

2   33 m (5a). Move back left to a groove splitting the overhang and climb this to a junction with *Obituary Grooves*. Climb the overhanging corner direct to a tree belay. (Top of pitch 2 of *Obituary Grooves*).

3   15 m (5b). Above and left is a wall with an undercut groove. Bridge up to an obvious foothold on the lip (peg runner on the right) and swing round into the groove. Follow a crack across the wall to an arête and move easily up to below a holly tree.

4   12 m (4a). Continue past the holly tree. Move left across a steep wall, below the top overhang, and finish up its left arête.

5   15 m. Steep scrambling leads to the top.

★ **The Dice Man** 96 m HVS   1981

A route of similar character to *Triptych*. Start as for that route.

1   15 m. Pitch 1 of *Triptych*.

2   28 m (4a). Move left into a groove and up to below a large overhang. Belay on the right.

3   38 m (5a). Move across left under the roof and swing out onto a ramp, moving left and round a small rib. Go straight up a wall above to a small bulge. Go over this and step right into an obvious groove in the arête. Continue up this to belay on top of a pinnacle.

4   15 m. Finish easily.

Wasp 90 m E2   2000

An eliminate line giving some good climbing but with a hard and worrying finish. Start 2 metres left of *Obituary Grooves* at the left-hand side of the slab just left of the dead tree.

1   21 m (4b). Climb up the left side of the slab, to the ledge beneath the flake crack. Step left and climb a crack. Continue to a good

ledge with nut belays on the left. (Several metres below the corner of *The Mortician*).

2   24 m (5b). Climb the short clean wall on the right, which leads to beneath a hanging groove. Enter this with difficulty and continue up to an overlap. Step right and pull back left into the upper groove. Continue to a junction with *Mortuary* and *Black Crag Eliminate*. Move up the crack on the right as for *Black Crag Eliminate* for a couple of metres, until a move left leads up the wall above directly to a small stance and nut belays, beside the jamming crack of *The Mortician*.

3   18 m (5a). Move easily right for 2 metres then directly up to climb the wall left of the crack of *Troutdale Pinnacle Superdirect*, until a move up and left leads onto the slab above. Continue up to a block belay, below the *Finger-Traverse* of *Troutdale Pinnacle Superdirect*.

4   10 m (5a). Move round to the right and step into a right-slanting groove (top section of *Raindrop*) and follow this to belay 4 metres below the top of the pinnacle at a good block.

5   17 m (5c). Step up and pull rightwards onto a slab, continue up past a shattered flake, move across right, then up impending rock to a rest. Very strenuous moves then lead up and left to gain a good prominent spike and in a few more moves the top. A serious and worrying pitch.

★★ **Obituary Grooves**   100 m   VS   1955
Interesting climbing, quite sustained at its standard. Start at a steep slab, just left of the old fallen tree at the lowest point of the crag.

1   30 m (4b). Climb the steep slab to a ledge beside a flake crack. Climb the wall on the left to a ledge. Move left to ascend a vegetated corner, then left again to a birch tree.

2   34 m (4c). Climb a groove to a yew tree below an overhang. Move out to the right and up to the top of a groove where an awkward 'swing-layback' move leads left. Climb the groove above a little way, move left, then go up and out to the right to a tree belay.

3   36 m (4c). Easier rock leads to a large flake. Go up leftwards and make an awkward move into a leftward-slanting corner from which an exit is eventually made on the right. Gain the groove above, move left to a holly tree and back right via twin cracks to the top.

★ Tumbling Dice 97 m E2   1981

An eliminate route with good climbing but no real line. Start as for *Obituary Grooves*.

1 30 m (4b). Pitch 1 of *Obituary Grooves* to a birch tree belay.
2 15 m (5b). Go up a groove, past a yew tree, to below a crack splitting an overhang. Pull up and swing right to gain a groove. Traverse immediately left, across a steep wall, to the arête and go up to a ledge and junction with *Obituary Grooves*.
3 14 m (5c). Move up to below the roof above and step round right onto the front face. Climb this, trending left to a tree belay on *Obituary Grooves* (top of pitch 2).
4 26 m (5a). As for *Triptych* pitch 3 to its peg runner then continue up to a groove. Climb up this, pulling out right, and follow *Obituary Grooves* to a holly tree.
5 12 m (4c). Move back right and climb a steep wall to the top.

★★★ The Mortician 90 m HVS   1969

A very good route up a clean groove and jamming crack.

1 30 m (4b). Pitch 1 of *Obituary Grooves* to a belay just below and right of the tree belay.
2 36 m (5a). Step up right and enter an obvious clean-cut groove with difficulty. Climb this and the wide crack above to belay below the *Finger-Traverse* of *Troutdale Pinnacle Superdirect*.
3 10 m (4c). Move into a broken groove and continue directly to the top of the pinnacle on *Troutdale Pinnacle*.
4 14 m. The final pitch of *Troutdale Pinnacle*.

★★ Black Crag Eliminate 110 m E1   1964

A wandering route with some pleasant climbing. Start as for *Obituary Grooves*.

1 12 m (4b). Amble up the steep slab to a ledge below a flake crack.
2 40 m (5b). Ascend the crack to a ledge. Climb the groove just right of *Mortician* to an overhang where an awkward step right gains the arête. Climb the slab up and right until it is possible to step right to another slab which leads to a good hold and crack. Go to the right to a small ledge at the top of pitch 3 of *Troutdale Pinnacle Direct*.
3 22 m (4a). Go up the easy slab on the right and traverse right to its end. (Top of pitch 3, *Troutdale Pinnacle*.)
4 36 m (5b). Move up left to a big black corner below a break in an overhang. Step off a pointed block and climb the corner and overhang into a groove, trending to the right. Follow this and the face above to the top.

Variation Finish **Roach Clip** 35 m HVS 1980
A loose variation, requiring care.

4a 25 m (5a). Move up and left and traverse horizontally left along the lip of an overhang, above the slabs of *Troutdale Pinnacle*. Follow the obvious finger-traverse and swing onto a fin of rock. Climb this and go directly up the mossy slab above to a tree covered ledge.

5a 10 m (5b). Move up and left and then climb a vegetated corner for a metre or so until it is possible to swing left into a groove in the arête. Pull over a small bulge to finish.

★ **The Mortuary** 90 m E1 1978
An eliminate up the arête right of *The Mortician*. Rather contrived. Start as for *Obituary Grooves*.

1 21 m (5a). Climb the right edge of the steep slab to below an undercut crack, 3 metres right of the corner. Climb the crack and slab above to a ledge and belay on the right.

2 30 m (5a). Climb diagonally left, then go up a thin crack to a junction with *Black Crag Eliminate*. Cross this to enter a hanging groove in the arête on the left. Climb this to belay below the jamming crack of *The Mortician*.

3 15 m (5a). Climb cracks in the right wall until forced left at 6 metres onto *Mortician* pitch 2.

4 24 m (4c). Pitches 3 and 4 of *Mortician* to the top.

★★★ **Troutdale Pinnacle Direct** 96 m VS 1952
A fine route giving delicate slab climbing. Start as for *Obituary Grooves*.

1 24 m (4b). Climb the steep slab to a ledge. Go up the flake crack to another ledge and traverse right and then climb up 2 metres to a block belay at the top of pitch 1 of *Troutdale Pinnacle*.

2 24 m (4c). Move left a little and climb the wall direct for 10 metres. Step left and continue more easily to a small ledge.

3 24 m (4a). Move right and climb up to join *Troutdale Pinnacle* at the steep wall on pitch 4. Climb this to a small ledge and belay.

4 24 m. Pitches 5 and 6 of *Troutdale Pinnacle*.

★★★ **Troutdale Pinnacle Superdirect** 95 m HVS 1954
An enjoyable route with both delicate and strenuous climbing. Start as for *Troutdale Pinnacle Direct*.

1 24 m (4b). Pitch 1 of *Troutdale Pinnacle Direct*.

2 24 m (4c). Pitch 2 of *Troutdale Pinnacle Direct*.

3 24 m (5a). Climb the steep crack, just left of the stance, and pull out left at the top to a ledge.

BLACK CRAG
Right-hand Side

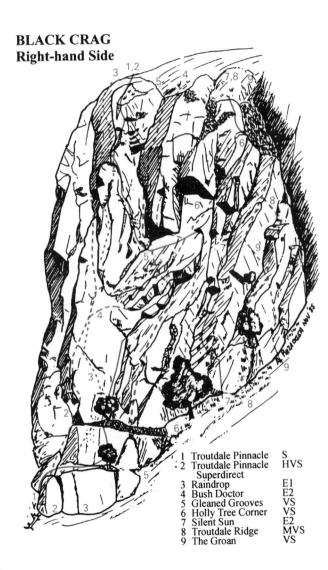

1	Troutdale Pinnacle	S
2	Troutdale Pinnacle Superdirect	HVS
3	Raindrop	E1
4	Bush Doctor	E2
5	Gleaned Grooves	VS
6	Holly Tree Corner	VS
7	Silent Sun	E2
8	Troutdale Ridge	MVS
9	The Groan	VS

4   10 m (5a). Move into a broken groove and make an awkward
    move to gain the *Finger-Traverse* (5b for fat fingers!) which leads
    rightwards. Continue up an easier groove to the top of the
    pinnacle.
5   13 m. The final pitch of *Troutdale Pinnacle*.

Variation   10 m   1959
4a (5a). It is possible to move right and up a groove (*Raindrop*) in
    the front of the pinnacle to belay on its top.

★★★ **Troutdale Pinnacle**   105 m   S   1914
Originally known as *Black Crag Buttress*, this magnificent route
winds its way up the walls and overlaps of the *South Buttress*, giving
interesting climbing right to the top. Start at the lowest point of the
crag, behind an old fallen tree at a short wide broken crack.
1   21 m. Climb the crack, past a tree stump, to a ledge. Alternatively
    climb the wide crack 5 metres to the right to the same point.
    Move to a birch tree at the right end of the ledge. Climb the wall
    behind for 6 metres to another ledge and continue up a broken
    groove to a large block belay.
2   28 m. Follow a groove on the right onto slabs. Climb these
    rightwards to a large ledge and block belay below a shattered
    corner.
3   10 m. Ascend the steep corner on good holds, then step left to a
    small stance on the right extremity of a sweep of slabs.
4   21 m. Traverse left and down the slabs below a steep wall to a
    corner. Swing across the steep left wall on polished holds and
    pull up to some ledges.
5   12 m. Continue easily up to the top of the pinnacle and an
    exposed belay.
6   13 m. Climb the steep, exposed groove above until it abuts a
    steeper wall. Pull up left across this then go more easily up the
    rocks above to finish.

Variation Finish   28 m   HS   1959
6a An unnecessary variation which climbs down and right into a
    corner, then up and right across a vegetated slab to finish up the
    rib above the overhang of *Wack*.

Variation Finish   **Anaconda**   30 m   E1   1997
    (5b). From the top of pitch 3 of *Troutdale Pinnacle* traverse left
    (at a higher level than as for that route) under the prominent roof
    until a good hold on the arête can be reached. Climb the arête,

veering slightly rightwards, onto vegetated slabs and cracks above.

Wack   82 m   E4   1959/1981
Takes the prominent roof above the slab of *Troutdale Pinnacle*. Very strenuous for a couple of moves!

1   36 m. Follow *Troutdale Pinnacle* to a belay on the slabs on pitch 2 below a slabby groove which lies parallel and to the left of pitches 2 and 3 of that route.

2   18 m (4c). Step up left into the groove as for *Gleaned Groove* and climb it, exiting right to a small stance (top of pitch 3 of *Troutdale Pinnacle*).

3   28 m (6b). Climb the slab rightwards to a steep wall. Climb this and the right-hand crack in the roof to a notch in the lip (peg runner). Move up left, then back right above the overhangs and finish up the wall above.

Variation   **High Explosion**   28 m   (Bash and Dangle and 4c)
The thin crack in the roof left of *Wack* has been climbed using pegs for aid and finishing up the wall above.

★ **Bush Doctor**   93 m   E2   1980
A wandering route linking some interesting climbing. Start at the problem arête between the alternative starts of *Troutdale Pinnacle*. Beware of loose rock on the last pitch.

1   15 m (5c). Climb the arête to the top of the block. Follow the arête directly above to a ledge at the top of pitch 2 of *Troutdale Pinnacle Direct*.

2   12 m (5a). Move up left to a crack in the arête. Climb this round a small bulge, then move diagonally right up a scoop to a small belay.

3   24 m (4c). Traverse 5 metres right and into the groove as for *Gleaned Grooves*. Follow this, exiting right to a small stance and belay at the top of pitch 3 of *Troutdale Pinnacle*.

4   42 m (5c). Traverse left until below a crack which splits the overhang and goes through a V-notch in the upper roof. Follow the crack and pull onto a rib above the upper roof. A direct line leads to the top, passing just right of a tree-covered ledge.

★★★ **Raindrop**   90 m   E1   1973
A very direct route up the pinnacle, giving good climbing and airy positions. Start 5 metres right of the arête of *Bush Doctor*, and just right of the right-hand start of *Troutdale Pinnacle* at a thin, left-slanting crack.

1   15 m (5b). Climb the crack to a ledge. Climb the slab behind, trending left to break through the moustache of heather at the left end.

2   27 m (5a). Climb straight up to the left end of a small overhang, then move left along a diagonal crack to below a shallow scoop which is followed to a stance. (Top of pitch 2 of *Troutdale Pinnacle Direct*.)

3   33 m (5b). Climb the wall on flakes, just right of the crack of *Troutdale Pinnacle Superdirect* to a good foothold on the right. Move left for 2 metres, then go straight up to gain a rightward-slanting groove. Climb this and the arête on the right to the top of the pinnacle.

4   15 m (4c). Climb a little way up the groove, taken by pitch 6 of *Troutdale Pinnacle,* swing round the arête to the left and so to the top or, like most people, finish up *Troutdale Pinnacle*.

Variation Finish   **Cloudburst**   20 m   E2   1981

4a (5c). Traverse mossy slabs, down and rightwards, to a corner below a steep wall. Pull up leftwards across the wall to a small ledge. Above and to the right is a good hold which is difficult to reach. From this pass a large loose block with care and finish on the left.

★ **Gleaned Grooves**   78 m   VS   1975

Start 8 metres up to the right of *Raindrop* at a dirty crack.

1   10 m. Climb the crack to a ledge.

2   18 m. Climb the buttress on the right, trending left to belay below the shattered corner at the top of pitch 2 of *Troutdale Pinnacle*.

3   20 m (4c). Move left and climb the groove to a junction with *Troutdale Pinnacle* on the large slab. Move leftwards and belay in a corner beneath a hanging groove.

4   30 m (4c). Climb the groove and move right onto a slabby wall. Climb this to a ledge with a holly and finish up the slabs above.

★★ **Holly Tree Corner**   82 m   VS   1937/1966

The combination of the old *Holly Tree Corner* with a direct entry gives an interesting and worthwhile climb. Start 14 metres right of *Gleaned Grooves* below a mossy slab behind a large birch tree.

1   15 m. Ascend the slab and shallow corner to a ledge.

2   15 m (4b). Traverse the slab on the right to a tree. Climb the slab in the corner above until a steep move left leads into the groove proper. Climb direct to a large ledge below a steep corner. (Top of pitch 2 of *Troutdale Pinnacle*).

3   10 m. Climb the corner and step left to a small stance (as for pitch 3 of *Troutdale Pinnacle*).
4   30 m. Ascend the slab rightwards, below the overhang of *Wack*. After a steep move, a gangway is followed rightwards to its top. Steep heather leads to an oak tree.
5   12 m (4a). Traverse left on ledges and climb an exposed corner to a good ledge but poor belay.

Grip Factor   75 m   HVS   1977
A rather disappointing route. Start just right of a holly tree, 8 metres right of *Holly Tree Corner*.
1   30 m (5a). Climb a slab, past a small sapling at 10 metres, to a small ledge. Follow a thin crack up rightwards until a vertical crack splitting a wall is reached. Climb this to the top of an overhung sweep of slabs. Traverse left across the slabs to a short wall which is climbed to a small stance at the top of pitch 3 of *Troutdale Pinnacle*.
2   45 m. Finish up the final 3 pitches of the *Girdle Traverse*.

★ **Silent Sun**   60 m   E2   1978
A good route, though care is required with horrendously loose rock on pitch 2. Start as for *Grip Factor*.
1   38 m (5b). Climb the slab, past a sapling, to a ledge. Step up and left to pull onto a slab. Climb the slab to an overhang, which is ascended via a break in the centre to a short groove. Climb the right arête to a small ledge and belay.
2   22 m (5b). Above and left is a thin groove in a steep wall. Enter the groove and climb it until it is possible to swing up left onto *Holly Tree Corner* which is followed to the top. Serious.

★ **Troutdale Ridge**   68 m   MVS   1921
Pleasant varied climbing. Start 10 metres right of *Grip Factor* at a short rib below a large oak growing from the crag.
1   26 m. Climb the easy rib and right-slanting ramp above to belay at its top below a short steep wall.
2   12 m (4b). The wall is climbed to a poor belay on the right.
3   18 m. Move left round an exposed corner onto a large slab. Go up this, step left and belay on an oak.
4   12 m. Step up left to a ledge and climb a steep little crack.

The Groan   60 m   VS   1972
Start to the right of *Troutdale Ridge*.
1   15 m. Climb the gangway, then move left across some flakes to belay on the ridge below the difficult wall of *Troutdale Ridge*.

2   15 m. Traverse the steep left wall and climb the slab above on its right-hand side to a flake belay on the ridge.
3   30 m. Step down from the ridge to the right and climb a long crack to the top.

★★ Girdle Traverse   165 m   VS   1955
An enjoyable expedition at a reasonable grade.
1   12 m (4b). Pitch 1 of *The Shroud*.
2   15 m (4c). Pitch 2 of *The Shroud*.
3   24 m (4b). Traverse the long, narrow slab to the right and go up to an oak tree belay in the gully. (Beware loose rock.)
4   26 m (4c). Ascend slabs to the right and traverse diagonally right to a tree. Continue up to a ledge and belay at the top of pitch 3 of *Troutdale Pinnacle Superdirect*.
5   10 m (5a). Pitch 4 of *Troutdale Pinnacle Superdirect*.
6   33 m (4a). Reverse pitches 5 and 4 of *Troutdale Pinnacle*.
7   18 m. Descend to the slab on the right, which is climbed to a junction with *Troutdale Ridge*.
8   15 m. Climb the slab above to a stance at an oak.
9   12 m. Traverse left and ascend the corner to a good ledge.

About 30 metres up right of *Troutdale Ridge* is a large square slabby corner which is frequently wet and generally loose.

Frenzy   63 m   E1   1979
   (4b). A poor, loose route which climbs the centre of the slabs to a tree belay on the left. The second pitch (5a) climbs the steep corner, then the slab and groove above to the top.

The following two routes are on the buttress to the right of the slabby square-cut gully.

Arthur Scargill   30 m   S   1984
Starts up the black, coal coloured wall. Not recommended.
1   Climb the groove, moving right onto the right-hand side of the slabs.
2   Climb up these to where the wall steepens. Traverse left behind a silver birch and climb the long slabby groove to the top.

Troutdale Introductory   48 m   M   1950
   A rather poor, wandering route, which meanders its way up the vegetated rock on the right of the buttress.

Troutdale Gully VD   1955
  This is the deep gully just to the right of the descent path where
  it crosses the stile before slanting down left to the main crag. The
  gully is gained by scrambling down grassy ledges to its base.

Little Black Crag

This small buttress is found on the descent from the main crag just
after crossing the wall.

Ashley Slab 12 m VD   1992
  Climb the groove onto the slab and follow it up rightwards.

Ashley Rib 12 m D   1992
  The right-hand side of the slab.

Short Slab 11 m VS ?   1992
  Climb up left to a tree, pull up onto the narrow slab and climb
  it and the rib above.

Troutdale Gully Wall

On the south (true left) side of *Troutdale Gully* is a steep wall which
provides a number of routes.

Ring In the New 20 m S   1989
  Climb the bed of the gully for a metre or so onto a boulder then
  climb the obvious groove on the right.

Wring Out the Old 20 m E1   1989
  (5b). From the base of the gully climb the groove and over a
  metre-wide roof to easier climbing above.

Holly Tree Climb 25 m HVS   1989
  Start to the right of *Wring Out the Old* and scramble up to a holly
  tree. Move left up a short groove to a good spike runner.
  Awkward layaways lead to a tree. Climb the wall above moving
  right to a small overhang and layback over this using a good
  crack.

Karakoram Experience 26 m VS   1989
  Start as for *Holly Tree Climb* from behind the holly tree. Climb
  the obvious wide crack for 3 metres then traverse left and up to
  an oak tree. Finish up the obvious groove.

Kit Kat   26 m   VS   1989
Start as for *Holly Tree Climb* from behind the holly tree. Climb the
obvious chimney/crack until a crack in the right wall can be climbed
to the top.

Black Crag Far Right-Hand

This small buttress is found by walking up the path right of *Black
Crag* to the wall at its top. Walking right for 100 metres leads to the
crag's top. Descent is easiest via the open gully on the left (facing
out). The approach to the base of the crag is rather steep and scrappy.
The routes start at a grass ledge with two small trees and a large
spike.

Ishmael   20 m   E4?   1998
Start on the left-hand side of the large spike in the centre of the wall.
A poorly protected pitch.
  (5c). Stand on the spike. Step into the groove on the left and
  climb it until moves can be made into the groove/crack on the
  right via the obvious downward-pointing fang. Continue up the
  crack until a step left can be made, 2 metres below a small tree,
  to join another crack leading to the top.

Spawn   20 m   E3?   1998
A dirty, serious climb starting on the right-hand side of the large
spike.
  (5c). Step off the right-hand side of the spike and climb the
  groove and serious wall above to a small ledge. An awkward
  move up the rib on the left leads, with a scramble, to a tree belay.
  Another uninspiring pitch!

The following routes start left of the buttress containing *Spawn* and
Ishmael.

Hazard Warning   20 m   VS?   1998
Start at the cleaned groove.
  (4c). Climb the groove, moving up and left to a black crack.
  Climb this and the awkward corner, moving left up the crack to
  tree belays.

Horn Control   20 m   VS?   1998
Start at the cleaned groove.
>   (4c). Climb the groove up the wall, just right of the block.
>   Traverse left across the top of the groove to a good ledge. Move
>   back right to a good hold and climb the tree to belay on a tree
>   at the top.

Ignition Switch   20   VS?   1998
Start up the cleaned groove.
>   (4b). Climb the groove and then follow the shattered crack
>   moving right, on good pockets, passing the tree on the right.

Aard Crag   (261 169)   Alt. 250 m   East Facing

Aard Crag is a white spur of rock easily seen from *Black Crag*.
Follow the path into Troutdale, as for *Black Crag*, but, instead of
crossing the beck, follow the path to the right that leads steeply up
a paved footpath. About a quarter mile up the path the crag will be
seen 90 metres up to the right (15–20 mins). The crag is small but
offers some good, sustained climbing up clean and slightly
overhanging rock. Descend on the left of the crag.

At the foot of the centre of the crag is a small pinnacle of rock.

Poor Man's Utah   10 m   VS   1994
About 5 metres left of the pinnacle, look up to find an obvious hand
crack.
>   (4c). Climb up to the crack and follow this directly to the top.

Cithaeron   12 m   E4   1994
>   (6a). Start about 1 metre left of the pinnacle and climb up small
>   cracks. Move right with difficulty to the upper headwall crack to
>   finish.

★ **Family Tree**   10 m   HVS   1994
>   (5a). Climb the crack behind the pinnacle and follow the groove
>   above to the tree.

★ **Nepotism**   10 m   E2   1994
Just right of the crack of *Family Tree* is a stepped wall leading to a
small but prominent groove.
>   (5c). Start in the crack, move out steeply right and then enter the
>   groove which is followed to the top.

Progeny   10 m   E5?   1994
Starts about 3 metres right of *Nepotism*.
   (6b). Make difficult moves up the very steep wall.

Parricide   10 m   E1   1994
   (5b). Climb onto the ledge at the right of the crag then go
strenuously up the thin crack.

Christmas Crag   (262 167)   Alt. 340 m   West Facing

This is a small crag in a very attractive situation lying on Broom Fell
opposite King's Howe. It is reached by following the path into
Troutdale as for *Black Crag*. Rather than crossing the beck to reach
the latter, continue straight on up a steep well-made path. Where this
levels out look out for a stile over a fence on the left. Cross the stile
and follow a path over a small col and down to a broken stone wall.

It is composed of two tiers. The lower tier is rather shattered and
broken and is topped by a prominent overhanging block – *The
Gargoyle*. The upper tier offers pleasant climbing at a moderate grade
and is best reached by walking to the right of the crag and traversing
in above the lower tier. Descent is on the right of the crag.

Upper Tier

A few metres from the right of the crag, is a small pinnacle at ground
level.

Christmas Groove   10 m   S   1993
   Climb the groove just to the left of the small pinnacle.

Christmas Rib   10 m   HVS   1992
   Climb the rib to the left of *Christmas Groove*.

There is a tall clean buttress to the left.

★ **Christmas Pudding**   13 m   VS   1993
   (4c). Climb the leftward-slanting chimney/groove on the right side
of the buttress.

★ **Happy Christmas**   13 m   VS   1992
   (4b). Climb leftwards from the foot of the buttress then go straight
up.

Jingle Bells   16 m   VS   1992
   Climb the groove left of *Happy Christmas*.

Sleigh Ride   16 m   S   1992
   Climb the groove to the left of *Jingle Bells* – which sports a small
   tree at 3 metres.

To the left is a leaning pillar.

Christmas Decoration   16 m   VS   1992
   Climb the pillar and groove above.

Left again is a wall with a rib on its left.

★ **1993**   16 m   HVS   1993
   (4c). Start below a small tree in a mossy groove to the left of the
   wall. Traverse right onto the rib and climb it on excellent rock.

Variation   **Christmas Tree Groove**   13 m   HS   1993
   Climb the mossy groove directly, move right and finish as for
   1993.

Lower Tier

Gargoyle Groove   13 m   HVS   1993
   (5a). Climb the wide left-facing groove to the *Gargoyle* and move
   right to belay. Repulsive.

Easy Ridge   13 m   VD   ?   1992
   Start 6 metres left of *Gargoyle Groove* at the lowest point of the
   crag. Climb the shattered ridge, if you must.

The original route on this crag was probably **Gunner's Climb** (VD
1944) which linked together the easiest rock on the two tiers to the
left of the overhanging boulder and may be the same as Easy Ridge.

Grange Crags   (258 177)   Alt. 120 m   North West Facing

Following frantic activity by some enthusiastic members of the
Keswick 'Horticultural Society', during the winter of 1983/84, a
number of small buttresses were extensively gardened and developed
to provide this climbing area. Some of these are now growing back
(and deservedly so) into the hillside. The best climbing is almost

exclusively on *Car Park Crag* and *Nagg's Buttress*. It is situated on the tree covered hillside above the track to *Black Crag*. Although short, many routes are of reasonable quality. The best are mainly in the higher grades but a few good easier routes do exist. All these crags form part of an SSSI and the initial gardening was at best misguided. **No retro-cleaning or further gardening please!**

The Buttresses are described from right to left. The routes on each buttress are described from left to right.

The land below the crags between the fences running up to *Car Park Crag* and *Veterans Buttress* is private, but the land above belongs to The National Trust. **Unfortunately the owner of the private land prohibits climbers from crossing his ground to gain access to the crags.**

All routes in this area are included for completeness of records **but this in no way infers a right to trespass on private land.**

The first buttress encountered is immediately behind the car-park used for parking for *Black Crag*. It is the closest crag to the road in Borrowdale!

Car Park Crag

A steep buttress with some good routes on sound rock. Descend by a path on the left. The routes are described from left to right.

First Contact 12 m VS   1984
Start 5 metres left of the fence at the left end of the crag.
　　(4c). Climb the obvious short arête.

Reliant Robin 15 m E3   1984
An eliminate. Start as for *Desmond Decker*.
　　(6a). Climb the wall just left of *Desmond Decker*.

★ **Desmond Decker** 18 m E2   1984
Good climbing up the open bottomless groove just left of the fence.
　　(5c). Pull over the overhang with difficulty and climb the groove above, mainly on its right side.

Double Decker 18 m E3?   1995
　　(6a). Start 2 metres right of *Desmond Decker* under the roof in the corner. Bridge up the corner. Using small edges in the roof, lay out to reach a hold over the lip. Make a strenuous swing to

reach/jump for two separate ledges and pull up over the roof. Reach *Desmond Decker* in a few moves.

★★ **Fender Bender**   20 m   E3   1984
Interesting climbing up the grooved arête above the fence. Start at a short wall just left of the fence.
(5c). The short wall and grooves are followed, finishing directly over the top overhang.

Lead Free   22 m   E3   1989
Takes the wall between *Mercedes* and *Fender Bender*.
(6a). Move up Mercedes a metre or so then move awkwardly left round the arête. Climb up then right to the pinnacle. Continue directly up then step right onto *Mercedes* just below the top to finish.

★★ **Mercedes**   24 m   VS   1984
A popular route.
(4c). The obvious slanting groove and chimney, starting 2 metres right of the fence.

Rush Hour   20 m   E2   1984
A variation on *Mercedes*, starting 3 metres to its right.
(5c). Climb the wall until forced onto *Mercedes* at the roof. Follow this for 5 metres to an overhang. Step right and up the gangway then swing out boldly rightwards and climb the wall to a dirty finish.

★★ **Fuel Economy**   24 m   HVS   1984
An awkward slab leads to pleasant climbing up the groove on the right of *Mercedes*. Start at a large flake below the overhung corner.
(5a). Climb the corner or the wall just to the right. Move right, pull over bulges and move up to a large spike. Climb the groove on its right.

The Bodycount   24 m   E6   {F7b+}   1991
A serious lead taking the roof and overhanging wall between *Mercedes* and *Fuel Crisis*.
(6c). Climb the 'awkward slab' of *Fuel Economy* to the obvious break in the roof above. Climb up this and go directly up the steep wall on sidepulls and small holds.

★★ **Fuel Crisis**   18 m   E2   1984

Thin climbing in good positions on the obvious upper white wall.
Start on the right side of an arête below the white wall.

(5c). Climb the cracked arête to a large spike (junction with *Fuel Economy*). Step off this and move up left across the wall to a short crack which is followed to the top.

Cross Ply   36 m   E2   1984

A poor left-to-right girdle of the left-hand half of the crag. Beware of rope drag. Start up left of *First Contact*.

(5c). Move up right to the arête, then right into the corner of *Desmond Decker*. Step round the corner to the ledge on *Fender Bender* and round into the chimney of *Mercedes*. Hand traverse then foot traverse across the ramp to the large spike on *Fuel Crisis*. Continue down and right to the large ledge below *Driving Ambition*.

The next two routes start from a large ledge above some large split blocks, near the centre of the crag.

★ **Driving Ambition**   12 m   E1   1984

A steep little route on good incuts.

(5b). Climb the steep wall above the ledge.

The Crack   12 m   MVS   1984

(4b). Climb the wide crack in the back corner above the ledge.

There is a large vegetated corner in the centre of the crag. The following three routes are on the slab to its right.

★ **Hatchback**   18 m   E1   1984

Start at a scoop in the left side of the slab.

(5a). Climb the scoop, pull over a bulge and continue up a groove above.

Plastic Pig   18 m   E1   1984

(5b). An eliminate up the centre of the slab, finishing slightly leftwards.

★ **Cavalier**   18 m   VS   1984

Enjoyable climbing up the right-hand side of the slab. Start at the toe of the buttress.

(4c). Gain and climb the crack, finishing up a short groove.

Mini Minor   20 m   S   1984
Starts in a groove just right of the slab.
    Pull up into a short V-groove. Follow this and the slab above, trending rightwards to the top.

Alvis   18 m   S   1984
Starts below a groove, 3 metres left of the pinnacle at the right-hand end of the crag.
    Dirty ledges lead to the groove with a flared crack. Follow this and the slab above to join and finish up *Mini Minor*.

Traffic Warden   20 m   E1   ?   1984
Takes the pinnacle and wall behind. Recently there has been a large rockfall just right of the pinnacle, leaving the pinnacle in its original position but looking somewhat unstable. The route is not believed to have been repeated since the rockfall. This is a public health warning.
    (5a). Climb a short wall, then the outward facing rib of the pinnacle directly to its top. Step across (or now leap across) to the wall behind and climb it via a wide crack.

Upper Car Park Crag

A small outcrop about 50 metres above *Car Park Crag*.

Millesimus   12 m   HVS   1984
    (4c). Climb the crack on the left side of the wall.

Ponticum   12 m   E1   1984
Start below a small gangway in the centre of the crag.
    (5a). Climb onto the gangway, step right and climb straight up, finishing up a short rib on the right at a tree.

The 'A' Team   12 m   E1   1984
    (5c). Climb the crack through the left side of a small cave at 6 metres.

'G' Force   12 m   HVS   1984
Start 3 metres right of *The 'A' Team*.
    (5a). Climb the wall into the right side of the cave. Go up the groove on its right and the wall above.

The 'B' Team   12 m   E1   1984
Start as for *'G' Force*.
> (5b). A rising rightward traverse leads to a bulge, which is climbed on good holds. Climb the steep wall to an overhang and exit on its left with difficulty.

Nagg's Slabs

Just round the corner to the left of *Car Park Buttress* is a sweep of slabs that have now returned back to nature. Even in its heyday the rock was dirty and friable. Going from left to right the routes were **Lilly Leek** 45 m VS, **Colin Cucumber** 42 m S (the right-facing corner), **Oliver Onion** 42 m MVS, **Casper Carrot** 36 m S, **Emma Apple** 42 m VS, **Percival Pea** 35 m HVS, **Roger Radish** 35 m VS (takes the central weakness), **Green Fingers** 40 m S, **Gardener's World** 35 m VS, **Rhubarb Patch** 35 m E1 (all done in 1984). All very appropriate names considering the gardening efforts of the first ascensionists.

Beth's Buttress

The buttress is situated some 50 metres up and left of *Nagg's Slabs* and gives some reasonably good routes on relatively solid rock. The descent route is down a gully on the left of the scree fan, left of the buttress. The routes are described from left to right.

★ **Impulse**   15 m   E1   1984
Takes a line up the short pillar at the left end of the crag. The tree and arête on the left are considered out of bounds!
> (5b). Follow the groove/crack to an awkward move up to a short wall. Step right, reach up to a hold above a slanting crack, then move left onto a ledge. Finish more easily.

Ad-Lib   15 m   E3?   1986
Start 5 metres right of *Impulse*.
> (5c). Climb the bulge and go directly up the wall to the slanting crack of *Impulse*. Finish directly above the crack.

★ **Low Profile**   20 m   E1   1984
Fine climbing up the steep wall. Start behind three straight-stemmed oak trees some 13 metres right of *Impulse*.
> (5b). Climb the wall to a ledge. Step right and up a short wall to a slim green groove. Go up this, steeply, then make a long reach for a good jug. Pull up, then easier climbing leads to a tree belay.

Rolling Thunder   20 m   E3   1984
Follows the shallow groove and wall, right of *Low Profile*. Steep and fingery. Start as for *Low Profile*.

(6a). Climb up rightwards to a ledge with a holly bush. Climb to the crack above, step out left onto the wall, then pull up and right to a good jug in the groove. Continue to another good hold, step up onto this, then climb the wall trending left near the top.

Stingray   20 m   MVS   1984
Takes the slanting groove, right of *Rolling Thunder*.

(4b). Follow *Rolling Thunder* to the holly. Step up right and follow the groove directly to a steep grassy finish.

★ **Joining Forces**   40 m   HVS   1984
Takes the prominent stepped grooves on the higher, right-hand section of the crag. Start 10 metres right of *Low Profile*. Scramble up to ledges below the grooves. Beware of loose blocks.

(5a). Climb the clean-cut groove to a small overhang. Move across into the groove on the right and follow this and the corner above to an awkward exit onto a ledge on the right.

Variation   E1   1984
(5c). It is possible to pull over the overhang at the top of the first groove then move up right to rejoin the original route.

Nagg's Buttress

About 100 metres across the hillside on the left of *Beth's Buttress* are two steep buttresses separated by a large vegetated gully. These give some of the best climbing on *Grange Crag*. Descent is down a gully to the right of the buttresses.

★ **Sleeping Partner**   32 m   HVS   1984
At the base of the left-hand side of the left buttress is a large oak tree. Start 5 metres right of the tree at a niche.

(5a). Climb into the niche. Pull out left and climb up a steep juggy wall to a pleasant slab finish.

★★ **Pressure Drop**   30 m   E2   1984
A good route which climbs the centre of the left buttress. Start 3 metres right of *Sleeping Partner* below a right-curving crack.

(6a). Climb straight up on the left of the crack for 6 metres and follow a steep, right-slanting groove to a ledge. Move back left on good holds and pull up onto a ledge. The steep corner on the right is climbed, followed by easier scrambling to the top.

★★ Variation **Direct Start** 1986
(5c). Climb the wall left of the right-slanting groove directly on small but good holds and finish as for the ordinary route.

★★ **Rough Justice** 30 m E2 1984
Start as for *Pressure Drop*.
(5c). Start at the lowest point of the left buttress. Climb up to reach a sinuous crack which is followed up and right to gain a niche. Go up the crack on the left until a traverse can be made across the wall on the right to the arête (or climb the wall direct). Climb up this to a ledge. Scrambling remains.

Intrusion 36 m VS 1983
Rather serious, on suspect rock. Start at a groove in the left corner of the right buttress.
(4c). Go up the easy groove to a ledge. Traverse 5 metres right and up to a junction with *Sudden Impact*. Follow this up the obvious corner to finish.

Crime Wave 30 m E1 1984
Rather serious in the upper section. Start 3 metres right of *Intrusion*.
(5b). An awkward start leads up and left to an easy crack which is followed to a ledge. The wall above is climbed, first on the left, then right, to a ledge. Two short walls lead more easily to the top.

★ **Sudden Impact** 30 m E2 1983
Good climbing up the steep, greenish wall in the centre of the right buttress.
(5c). Climb the wall direct to a small overhang. Pull over this and move left onto a ledge. Step left, and pull steeply over a bulge into a fine corner which leads to the top.

★★ **Red Neck** 33 m E2 1983
Follows the red streak near the right side of the buttress. A very good route with a bold start. Start 3 metres right of *Sudden Impact* behind a large larch tree.
(5b). Climb up the wall directly, until a step right can be made to the arête, just before the ledge. Climb the steep corner crack above and easy groove to finish.

Variation **The Skinhead Finish** E3   1984
> (5c). Where *Red Neck* steps right to the arête, climb straight up
> and gain the slim groove on the left. Climb this and the groove
> above, as for *Red Neck*.

Regardless 22 m HVS   1984
Start 6 metres right of *Red Neck*.
> (5a). Easy, blocky rock leads to a rightward-leaning groove.
> Continue up this and the steep wall and crack above.

Super Cool 50 m VS   1984
Follows the broken arête to the right of *Nagg's Buttress*. Pitch 2 is
very loose and unpleasant. Start from the path below the lowest part
of the arête.
1   30 m (4c). Climb up until forced left onto doubtful rock. Move
    up, step right and swing up onto the arête proper. Follow this to
    a large pinnacle belay.
2   20 m (4b). Follow the shattered arête above, trending left to an
    obvious block above a steep corner. From the block follow
    heather to a tree in a corner. Pull up right over a large flake to
    the top.

Veterans' Buttress

Continue left from *Nagg's Buttress* for approximately 30 metres to a
wire fence. The small outcrop just left of this is *Veterans' Buttress*.
The rock is still dirty and the routes loose and not very appealing.

The Crack 20 m S   1984
> Climb the obvious crack and groove in the left side of the
> buttress.

Porridge 20 m VS   1984
Start 1 metre right of *The Crack*.
> (4c). Pull over the bulge and continue straight up the wall to a
> tree belay.

Stir 20 m E1   1984
Start at the fence.
> (5a). Climb the weakness immediately above the fence to a
> triangular overhang. Move up and left to a good hold then climb
> the crack above to finish.

El Cap Buttress

A further 40 metres left of *Veterans' Buttress* at a slightly higher level is another even smaller buttress giving pleasant problems with minimal protection. Not quite in the same class as their American namesakes.

Dihedral Wall 18 m   HVS   1985
Start at a shattered crack at the left side of the buttress.
  (5a). Climb the crack onto a pinnacle. Step up and traverse the ramp rightwards below the top bulge, finishing up the arête on the right.

The Shield 15 m   E1   1985
Start 3 metres right of *Dihedral Wall*.
  (5b). Climb the wall direct to the ramp of *Dihedral Wall*. Pull round the bulge above, leftwards, to finish on good holds.

The Nose 12 m   HVS   1985
Start just right of the arête.
  (5a). Climb up left to gain the arête and follow it to the top. Alternatively the arête can be gained from the left-hand side (5c).

North America Wall 10 m   E1   1985
The wall just right of *The Nose*.
  (5b). Follow the crack for a metre or so to a good runner. Swing left onto the wall and climb it directly to the top.

BORROWDALE MIDDLE

MIDDLE BORROWDALE

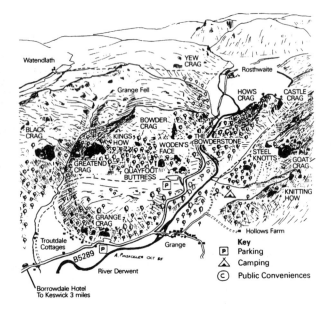

Watendlath · YEW CRAG · Rosthwaite · Grange Fell · HOWS CRAG · CASTLE CRAG · BLACK CRAG · BOWDER CRAG · KINGS HOW · WODEN'S FACE · THE BOWDERSTONE · STEEL KNOTTS · GOAT CRAG · GREATEND CRAG · QUAYFOOT BUTTRESS · KNITTING HOW · GRANGE CRAG · Hollows Farm · Troutdale Cottages · Grange · B5289 · A. PHIZACKLEA OCT 85 · River Derwent · Borrowdale Hotel To Keswick 3 miles

Key

P Parking

△ Camping

C Public Conveniences

Greatend Crag (260 170) Alt. 225 m   North West Facing

This large crag is about a kilometre south-west of *Black Crag* at the head of Troutdale. It is approached in 20 minutes from the *Bowderstone Quarry* car-park. Go over a stile on the north side of the car park. Strike up right across wet ground to reach a fence which is followed on its left side. Eventually cross a stile and 50 metres further on, at a subtle change of fence direction, bear off and up rightwards picking up a path leading to the foot of the crag.

This fine crag has had a varied history. With its northerly aspect and very vegetated drapery, it once had a dank appearance. It was brought to the attention of climbers after a fire raged there for more than a week in 1940. A number of routes were climbed but in time the vegetation returned through the remains of dead trees and ashen soil, and the popularity of the crag diminished. Amongst routes now lost completely into obscurity or vegetation are; **Vulcan's Buttress** (S 1949) at the far left-hand end of the crag; **The Undertaker** (VS 1967), **Redberry Wall** (VS 1958) and **Slime Corner** (VS 1959), all starting near the obvious black cave; **Charon** (VS 1963) and **The Styx** (VS 1950), starting close to *Great End Corner*; **The Fields** (VS) starting several metres right of the *Great End Corner*. In 1975 however, a group of local climbers "attacked" the crag with such non-conventional climbing aids as saws, ice axes and yard brushes. These "sodbusters" reclaimed the crag and a number of excellent routes were ascended. To descend, go up and rightwards to pick up fairly indistinct paths leading down the right (facing in) side of the crag. Alternatively, go down a path on the left of the crag.

The climbs are described from left to right.

Veil of Tears 64 m HVS   1979
Start 6 metres up and left of the lowest point of the arête on the left side of the crag, at a groove.
1 18 m (5a). Climb the groove. Move left at a bulging nose of rock and climb up to a ledge. A short wall then leads to below a hanging groove.
2 12 m (5a). Climb the groove using the right wall. Follow the left arête to a tree stump. Scramble 10 metres through heather to a cleaned wall.
3 34 m (5a). Climb up then right to a thin crack. Climb up on small holds to a ledge. Climb up to a ledge and move left, finishing up a wide crack and groove above.

★ **Punk Rock**   87 m   HVS   1977

Start 3 metres right of the lowest point of the arête.

1   16 m (4c). Climb up the wall to ledges and a tree belay above.
2   15 m (4c). Climb a shallow groove to a corner groove. Exit and traverse up left to below an arête.
3   10 m (4a). Climb the arête and traverse to another arête.
4   24 m (4b). Follow the arête and a long corner above. Exit left onto a slab below a V-groove.
5   22 m. Finish up the pleasant groove.

★ **New Wave**   100 m   HVS   1977

Start 6 metres right of *Punk Rock* on a small ledge below a pinnacle.

1   36 m (5a). Climb the obvious crack to the pinnacle. Follow the groove above to a small slab on the left. Traverse rightwards and pull over an overhang at an obvious niche to a tree belay above.
2   18 m (4a). Follow a break rightwards to a cleaned arête. Belay on a grass ledge.
3   16 m (5a). Climb the crack in the wall above to below a block.
4   30 m (4b). Follow the groove above, left of the dirty corner. Move right at the top, into a corner, and exit left onto a white slab to finish.

About 25 metres right is an obvious black cave which is frequently wet. There are some easy slabs below this.

The following three routes start at the tree stump at the left end of the slabs, left of *The Sorcerer*. From the stump scramble up a couple of metres to a pinnacle on the right.

The Dissident   25 m   E5   1988

(6b). Climb the smooth groove leftwards to a peg runner. Continue with difficulty to a second peg runner, then move past this, making more awkward moves. The groove is followed more easily to the top. A bold approach is needed at the top.

Perestroika   25 m   E5   1988

(6a). From the pinnacle, climb the slab just left of a small tree, to a downward-pointing flake. Step left and climb the crack to another slab. Climb this to a niche in the roof. Pull over this and continue up to the upper roof. Move left under this and finish up a groove.

Glasnost   25 m   E4   1988

(5c). Climb up as for *Perestroika* to the downward-pointing flake. Climb the dark, rightward-curving flake and move up to a hold below the roof. Pull up to the roof and a jug on the lip. Reach left to a very good slot and runner. Climb the rib and finish on the slab on the left.

The Sorcerer   78 m   HVS   (Aid)   1970

Start below the slab at the right-hand side of the obvious cave.
1   10 m. Climb diagonally left to the back of the cave. Peg belay.
2   10 m. Gain a ledge on the steep left wall. Use three points of aid to reach the overhang and gain the stance with difficulty.
3   16 m. Climb the slanting groove and surmount a bulge onto steep heather, which leads to a corner.
4   30 m. Climb the corner for 8 metres and move left into the next groove. Climb the rib, which separates the grooves and traverse left to climb an obvious flake crack. Tree belay.
5   12 m. Climb the slab above.

★ **Trouble Shooter**   80 m   E4   1978

This serious climb takes the wall and hanging rib to the left of *Nagasaki Grooves*.
1   30 m (5b). Follow pitches 1 and 2 of *Banzai Pipeline* and then move left to a tree belay.
2   20 m (6a). Go up a small slab, over a bulge, and up a groove in the slab above to an overhanging wall (peg runner on the right). Move up to undercuts and pull over to ledges above. Move up and climb a groove to a ledge on the right. Block belays.
3   30 m (6a). Climb up leftwards over blocks to below a V-groove. Climb the groove for 5 metres to a spike. Move left across the wall on undercuts to the arête. Pull up left into a hidden groove, and climb it to a sloping ledge on the right. Step right and climb the right side of the arête to the top.

★★★ **Nagasaki Grooves**   90 m   E4   1972/1974

This superb climb follows a line of interlinking grooves and corners up the steep wall left of *Banzai Pipeline*.
1   30 m (5b). Pitches 1 and 2 of *Banzai Pipeline*.
2   45 m (6b). Climb up a slab on the left to where it steepens. Climb the wall and grooves until it is possible to move up rightwards to the foot of a long smooth groove. Gain this and climb it with difficulty. Move left and up to a bulge. Surmount this on the right and continue up the thin, poorly protected, groove above to a ledge.

GREATEND CRAG

1	The Sorcerer (start)	HVS	6	Banzai Pipeline	E1
2	Trouble Shooter	E4	7	Greatend Pillar	E4
3	Hiroshima	E4	8	Greatend Corner	HVS
4	Nagasaki Grooves	E4	9	No Holds Barred	E2
5	Japanese Connection	E2			

3   15 m. Continue more easily to the top.

Variation **Hiroshima** 45 m E4   1978
A rather poor eliminate variation up the blank groove on the left of
the crux section of *Nagasaki Grooves*. Poorly protected.
2a (6b). Follow *Nagasaki Grooves* for 16 metres to where it pulls
     up right to its crucial groove. Climb the blank groove above, using
     its right rib, until a long step left can be made to gain an obvious
     foot-hold on the slab. Move up to some balanced blocks. Gain
     the undercut groove up to the right and follow it to a junction
     with *Nagasaki Grooves*. Move up leftwards to climb the face, as
     for the last moves of *Trouble Shooter*.

★★★ **Banzai Pipeline** 90 m E1   1977
A brilliant route up the left side of the buttress of *Greatend Pillar*,
giving varied and interesting climbing with quite a bold second pitch.
Start on the right-hand side of a pinnacle, 16 metres down and left
of the corner.
1   15 m (5a). Ascend the pinnacle and follow a white diedre. Move
     left over an overlap and up to a holly tree belay.
2   15 m (5b). Climb the corner above, move left, and ascend the
     next corner over a bulge to a slab. Belay below a crack.
3   30 m (5a). Climb the jamming crack to a ledge. Climb the
     chimney-crack above to a ledge and belay at the top of pitch 3
     of *Greatend Pillar*.
4   30 m (5a). Move up left to stand on a spike. Swing left round a
     rib into a slanting groove, and follow it and the walls above direct
     to the top.

Variation **Japanese Connection** 30 m E2   1980
An eliminate up the steep grooveline to the right of the main pitch
of *Nagasaki Grooves*. Now very dirty.
3a (5c). Climb the jamming crack of pitch 3 of *Banzai Pipeline* for
     a metre or so then step left and follow an open groove to a grassy
     ledge. Continue up the obvious groove above to a ledge and belay
     on the right at the top of pitch 3 of *Banzai Pipeline*.

★★ **Manhattan Project** 90 m E2   1996
A very good route taking a direct line between *Banzai Pipeline* and
Greatend Pillar. A good reach is an advantage for pitch 2. Start 4
metres right of *Banzai Pipeline*, just up and right of the toe of the
buttress.
1   20 m (5b). Climb directly and boldly to the foot of an obvious
     groove. Continue up the groove to a good ledge.

2   24 m (5b). From the left end of the ledge negotiate your way past the horizontal tree. Step left to a good foothold and move up and left to gain the arête. Go up to a hidden peg runner and move round onto the wall on the left. Continue directly up just left of the arête for about 4 metres, until a move right onto the arête leads to a flake runner on its right. Continue up, first on the right, then on the crest, to a large stance.

3   18 m (4c). Move up to a ledge on the left and follow the left edge of the groove above for about 12 metres, to gain and follow a crack to the ledge and belay at the top of pitch 3 *Greatend Pillar*.

4   28 m (5b). From the left-hand end of the ledge climb directly up a couple of metres right of a prominent downward-pointing spike of rock, until a move left can be made. Move up and left to a flake. Step down right, ascend a steep scoop and continue to the top.

★ **Greatend Pillar**   100 m   E4   1969/1977
Interesting and sustained climbing up the front of the prominent buttress to the left of the huge corner. Start 3 metres left of the corner, about 13 metres up and right of *Banzai Pipeline*.

1   15 m (4b). Climb the wall and step left to a small groove. Climb this and continue to a ledge.

2   24 m (6b). Go straight up the steep wall, past a small tree and peg runner, to gain better holds where the angle eases. Step left to a spike and continue up to a large stance.

3   28 m (5a). Climb a short wall behind the belay and the groove above to a ledge.

4   33 m (5a). Straight up a flake crack to a ledge with an embedded flake. Surmount this and climb a short groove. Step left and move up until the arête on the left is gained. Continue to the top and belay well back.

★★ **Exclusion Zone**   102 m   E2   1982
A good route up the walls and grooves, just left of the corner. Start as for *Greatend Pillar*.

1   14 m (5b). Climb up left to a tiny ledge, and climb the wall above to a large hold. Move up the leftwards-slanting crack above to a large ledge. Bold.

2   20 m (5c). From a block on the right of the ledge, gain a thin crack in the wall above and climb it to a tree. Continue up the rib behind to a short crack and ledge above.

3   38 m (5a). Step down to the right and, using undercuts, gain a
    groove above. Move right into the next groove and follow it to a
    ledge, above on the left. A bold pitch.
4   30 m (5a). Climb slabby rock diagonally up rightwards and then
    move right into a steep corner. Climb it and the gangway above
    to the top.

★★ **Greatend Corner**   72 m   HVS   1975
A striking climb which goes up the obvious long corner in the centre
of the crag. Once very popular, this route now sees less traffic than
it used to due to the encroaching vegetation. It still provides a
memorable outing.
1   15 m. Go up an easy chimney and step left onto a ledge.
2   45 m (4c). Climb up past an old tree stump to easier ground and
    an overhang. Continue up a vertical groove and either make an
    exit on the right to a tree on the rib, or continue up the groove,
    with difficulty, and move right to a pedestal and belay.
3   12 m (5a). Go up the wall, enter a corner crack on the left, and
    climb it to the top.

★★★ **No Holds Barred**   57 m   E2   1982
An excellent and direct line up the slab, just right of *Greatend
Corner*.
1   45 m (5b). Go up *Greatend Corner* for 3 metres. Step right and
    climb directly up an obvious line of slim grooves and a difficult
    crack to belay at a tree.
2   12 m (5a). Pitch 3 of *Greatend Corner* or abseil off.

★ **Earthstrip**   65 m   HVS   1975
A companion route to *Greatend Corner*, starting below a groove 3
metres to its right. The vegetation, once stripped, has returned.
1   15 m (4c). Climb the groove and crack above and move right
    onto a ledge.
2   22 m (5a). Follow the groove above to ledges on the right. Climb
    to a sapling and a small flake. Gain a niche on the left, with
    difficulty (good runners). Gain a ledge above using a loose hold.
3   28 m (4c). Climb the groove above onto a slab. Trend left, then
    right, to an arête. Finish up the short groove above.

Big Sur   90 m   HVS   1976
This route is now superseded by *No Holds Barred* and a detailed
description is not given.
    (5b). Start up the crack in the pillar between *Earthstrip* and
Greatend Grooves, then gain *Greatend Grooves* and traverse left

into *Greatend Corner*. Finish up on the right of the corner, following the line of *No Holds Barred*.

★★ Greatend Grooves   70 m   HVS   1975

Start at a short smooth groove, 16 metres right of *Greatend Corner*, below a vegetated gully and just left of a small holly tree.

1   25 m (5a). Climb the corner past a shattered flake and go up grooves to an overhang. Belay on the left.
2   45 m (5a). Move up 3 metres, then traverse right to a smooth groove. Climb the groove (crux). Move up and left to climb a steep wall to a slab, which is crossed to a fang of rock (natural thread). Continue up another slab to the top.

Aragorn   80 m   E2   1971

A difficult first pitch, then wandering leads to the top. Start 10 metres right of *Greatend Grooves* behind a large holly tree. Rarely climbed.

1   36 m (5c). Climb to the bottom of an obvious hanging groove and follow it, and the steep corner above, to a vegetated exit. Continue up to a good ledge.
2   44 m (4b). Traverse left for 5 metres and climb the wall above to the top.

★ Endless Summer   114 m   HVS   1976

A girdle traverse which starts between *Sauron* and *Aragorn* at a clean buttress.

1   28 m (4c). Climb up right and follow a short crack to a blank groove. Reach a good hold on the left arête and climb up for 5 metres. Move left and climb a slab to a tree belay.
2   18 m (4a). Go up the wall to the left and traverse to the arête. Cross a gully (loose) to a tree. Go up and left, round the arête, to belay on *Greatend Grooves*.
3   22 m (5a). Move left to *Earthstrip*. Go up for 10 metres and traverse left to join pitch 2 of *Greatend Corner* (piton belay).
4   22 m (4b). Ascend the V-groove to the overhang and then traverse left to the ledge below pitch 4 of *Greatend Pillar*.
5   24 m (5a). Ascend to the right of the last pitch of *Greatend Pillar*. Go up a narrow slab, past a tree and up to a V-groove. Follow this and a slab above to the top.

Sauron   70 m   HVS   1971

Start on the right side of the buttress, 10 metres right of *Endless Summer*. A route quickly returning to nature.

1   25 m (5a). Gain a V-groove from the right. Step up and left. Go up and across the top of the groove to the base of a gangway.

Climb this, and move right at an overhang. Move back left and follow the easy groove to an old tree belay on a ledge.
2   45 m (5a). Climb the wall behind the tree for 6 metres, move left round the blunt arête and go up a metre or so. Climb in the same line then up the prominent groove above.

Phoenix Ridge   100 m   VD   1950
Start at the foot of the buttress on the right of *Sauron*.
1   20 m. Follow the ridge on the right avoiding a difficult central section.
2   22 m. Ascend leftwards, cross a small gully and move onto the rock on the left, passing a large detached pinnacle. Climb up to a ledge on *Sauron*, with an old tree.
3   22 m. Climb a groove on the right to a stance on the right.
4   36 m. Continue easily to the top.

Open Cast   42 m   D   1950
This route climbs the ridge 10 metres right of *Phoenix Ridge*.
Initially scramble up to a corner and go up this rightwards, past a block, until moves lead back left. Climb up the ridge to the top.

King's How   (257 168)   Alt. 270 m   North West Facing

This crag lies on the rim of the valley, midway between *Greatend Crag* and *Quayfoot Buttress*. It is generally rather broken, though two pleasant routes have been climbed up the clean arêtes, each side of the large groove on the right-hand side of the crag. Approach by scrambling up the tree covered hillside, diagonally leftwards from the foot of *Quayfoot Buttress*.

The Lion Heart   43 m   E2   1979
The blunt left-hand arête. Start just left of the large central groove.
1   28 m (5c). Climb the wall leftwards to gain the arête and follow it to a good ledge and oak tree belay.
2   15 m (5a). Traverse right and follow the chimney/crack past a tree, exiting leftwards to the top.

Crack and Chimney   38 m   HVS   1971
A dirty and unsatisfactory route. Start at a short steep crack below the groove.
1   24 m (4b). Climb the crack and groove above to a pinnacle belay.

2   14 m (5a). Move into the chimney and climb it past a tree, finishing on the left.

The Black Prince   28 m   E1   1979
This takes the shorter right-hand arête. Start at a large embedded flake.
(5b). Climb the flake and then the right-hand wall of the arête until an awkward move back left gains the arête itself. Follow this to the top.

The short vegetated groove just right and the arête right again have both been climbed at Very Severe.

Quayfoot Buttress   (254 167)   Alt. 135 m   North West and
                                                    North Facing

Locally pronounced 'Whyfoot'. This is the obvious buttress above the Bowderstone Quarry car-park which gives good, very accessible and popular climbs on compact rock. It can be reached, in a few minutes, by going over a stile and striking directly up to the crag. Descent can be on either side of the crag.

The climbs are described from left to right starting well round to the left of the fence at the foot of the crag.

Meshach   36 m   VS   1970
Well up to the left of the crag is an undercut wall. Start 3 metres right of its left side where a short groove cuts through the overhang, giving a desperate problematic start.
(5c). Gain the groove with great difficulty. Move up left and follow a slabby gangway and slab above, over an overhang, to a tree belay.

Shadrach   36 m   VS   1970
Start as for *Meshach*.
(5c). Gain the groove. Traverse right beneath the upper overhang and climb up past a tree on vegetated rock, over an overhang, and up the groove above.

★★ **The Mound**   30 m   MVS   1969
Start from the grass ledge, right of *Meshach*, at a birch tree.
(4b). Climb the steep slab and move up to a V-groove. Climb this, and the narrowing gangway on the left. Pull out onto a slabby wall and climb to the top.

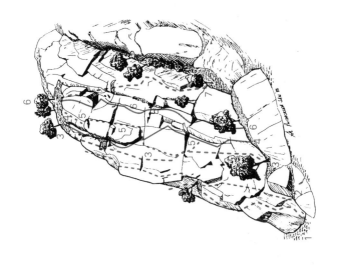

QUAYFOOT BUTTRESS

★★ **Quayfoot Buttress**   60 m   VD   1946

An enjoyable and varied route. Start 3 metres right of the fence at the foot of the crag.

1   15 m. Climb a groove rightwards to a block overhang, which is avoided by an awkward move on the left. Climb to a ledge. Poor belay on the left.

2   15 m. Move left, above a small birch, then climb a groove and arête to a ledge below a large scoop on the left.

3   30 m. Climb the scoop, moving left at its top, and follow slabs to finish.

Catafalque   48 m   HVS   1976

A poor route starting as for *Quayfoot Buttress*.

1   15 m. Pitch one *Quayfoot Buttress*.

2   15 m (5a). Move right and gain the slab above. Move up left, over an overlap, to gain and climb a mossy wall to a belay at the top of pitch 2 of *Quayfoot Buttress*.

3   18 m (4c). Climb up the scoop on the left to a flake runner. Move right onto the rib and follow this to the top.

Variation   **Loitering with Intent**   18 m   E4   1981

A short and poorly protected climb between the top pitches of *Catafalque* and *The Crypt Direct*.

3a   (5c). Enter the groove below the steep section of the rib from the left (old peg down on right). Climb the rib on pinch grips and layaways to the top.

★★ **The Crypt Direct**   40 m   E1   1971

A fine route taking the shallow groove to the left of the top pitch of *Aberration*. Start from a grass ledge above and just right of *Quayfoot Buttress*.

1   22 m (4a). Climb up rightwards to a ledge. Pull over an awkward bulge and move up to a tree belay at the top of pitch 2 of *Quayfoot Buttress*.

2   18 m (5b). Move onto the ledge on the right. Move up slightly left and climb a scoop, go over a small overlap and continue, with difficulty, to a large hold on the right wall. Use this to continue to the top.

★★ Variation   **The Crypt**   22 m   HVS   1969

2a   (5a). Follow *The Crypt Direct* to the overlap. Now move left to the rib and follow this to the top.

★ Variation **The In Between** 18 m E3   1985
Climbs the right-hand side of the arête of *Loitering with Intent*.
2b (5c). Follow *The Crypt Direct* a short way up to a good hold on
   the right, then step down and left to the arête. Pull over a small
   overlap and finish up the rib.

★★★ **The Go Between** 36 m E2   1981
An enjoyable route giving delicate climbing up the wall between
Mandrake and *The Crypt Direct*. Start on a ledge, left of *Mandrake*,
at a short crack in a steep little wall.
1 20 m (5b). Pull up the crack and continue more easily up grooves
   above to a large ledge, 5 metres right of a birch tree. If the lower
   crack is wet it is possible to gain the large ledge by climbing
   directly up to the birch tree.
2 16 m (5c). Climb up onto the wall above and follow a vague
   crackline in the middle of the wall to a horizontal break. Continue
   directly up the wall above to the top.

★ **Brain Stain** 42 m E4   1982
An eliminate line giving thin and technical climbing directly up the
wall above the traverse on *Mandrake*. Start as for *The Go Between*.
(6a). Follow *The Go Between* to a large ledge, 5 metres right of
   a birch tree. Step right and go up the delicate steep slab to the
   traverse of *Mandrake/Aberration*. Move up left, then pull up right
   over the overlap onto an oval hanging slab. Climb up right past
   a sickle-shaped flake to a second overlap (protection in horizontal
   crack). Continue over this and up the short groove above to the
   top.

★★ **Aberration** 38 m MVS   1965
A pleasant route with good positions. Start below the obtuse-angled
corner in the centre of the buttress.
1 20 m (4b). Gain the corner and climb it and the chimney above
   to a ledge on the right.
2 18 m (4c). Move left, with difficulty and then climb up a steep
   slab crossing *Mandrake* to a chimney/groove, which is climbed,
   past a tree, to the top.

★★★ **Mandrake** 44 m HVS   1964
A superb and popular climb. Start as for *Aberration*.
1 20 m (4c). Start up the corner, and almost immediately traverse
   left, and climb up to a large sloping ledge.
2 24 m (5a). Climb a crack to the bottom of the chimney/groove
   on *Aberration*. Move right for 6 metres to another crack and climb

this to an overhang. Surmount this and continue to the top in a fine position.

★★ Morceau 45 m HVS   1995

An enjoyable route but not one for a busy day. Friends are useful on the traverse of pitch 2. Start by the birch tree on the ledges just right of *Aberration*.

1 15 m (5a). Climb the groove between *Aberration* and *Irony* to an overhang. Step left, then back right into a groove above the overhang just right of *Aberration's* chimney and belay as for *Aberration*.

2 18 m (5a). Pull over a bulge and follow the crack past a horizontal break, then move rightwards across the slab to join the crack of *Irony* at the right end of the large horizontal break. Sensationally hand-traverse the break leftwards, crossing *Mandrake* and *Brain Stain* (crux) to the oak tree on *Aberration*.

3 12 m. Climb easily up the rib to the top. Oak belay.

☆☆ Dark Angel 40 m E5?   1997

Takes the main buttress between *Mandrake* and *Irony*. Start as for *Irony* below a short groove.

(6b). Climb the groove to a ledge, then go up the nose of a blunt pillar via a hard move using layaways and a foothold to the left. Continue up the pillar to join *Irony*, then traverse below overhangs to a V-groove. Pull up through the groove on surprisingly good holds to reach a good ledge. Surmount a bulge, then go up a steep wall to the right of a thin crack to the overlap right of *Mandrake*. Pull over the overlap with great difficulty, using under-clings and small holds, to a right slanting ramp. Rock over to reach a one finger pocket and continue up a shallow scoop, via a break and scant protection, to exit just right of *Mandrake*.

★★ Irony 40 m HVS   1961

A good climb with sustained interest on each pitch. Start to the right of *Aberration* below a short groove.

1 18 m (4c). Climb the groove to a grass ledge. Follow a groove and slab on the left. Move slightly rightwards to a crack which is climbed to a ledge.

2 12 m (4c). Surmount the broken overhang and the thin crack above. A swing right at the top leads to a ledge and peg belay.

3 10 m (5a). Move up left under the overhang (gnarled peg) then pull over it with great difficulty and continue to the top.

The Keek (HVS, 1993) follows the vegetation-choked crack between *Irony* and *The Creep* but cannot be recommended.

★★ **The Creep**   35 m   HVS   1965
A climb with a vicious start, taking the right edge of the crag. Start part way up the gully below a steep corner crack.
1   23 m (5b). Attack the crack. At the top move out right to a slab and ascend to a ledge on the left. Climb the mossy wall above to the peg belay on *Irony*.
2   12 m (5a). Climb the steep groove to the roof, traverse left round the arête and finish up the pleasant wall.

★★ **Sidewinder**   33 m   E2   1998
Start a few metres up the gully on the right of the crag near a wide crack above the start of *The Creep*.
    (5b). Step left from the crack and climb the wall on good holds to gain the top of the flake. Use the two cracks on the right to pull onto the slab. Continue up over a small overlap in the corner and pull up onto the top slab. Climb up to the large overhang in the corner, pull over it and move up to a good hold 2 metres above the lip. Make an exposed traverse left through the ever widening crack to the top.

★★ **The Girdle Traverse**   73 m   HVS   1969
An interesting excursion. Start as for *Shadrach*. (It may be preferable, and easier, to start up *The Mound* and take belays so as to avoid congestion.)
1   28 m (5c). Gain the groove, with difficulty, then traverse right under the overhang, as for *Shadrach*. Continue the traverse round into *The Mound*. Move across the groove, cross its right wall and join *Quayfoot Buttress* at the traverse. Belay to the right below an overhanging groove.
2   33 m (5a). Climb up the groove until moves lead rightwards to the rib. Make a descending traverse right to a shallow groove (*The Crypt Direct*). Swing across to the chimney/groove of *Aberration*. Continue the traverse across *Mandrake* to the peg belay of *Irony*.
3   12 m (5a). Pitch 3 of *The Creep*.

Variation Finish   20 m   E1   1969
3a (5b). Traverse right across the slab to the overhang. Climb the overhang and the slab above into a corner, which is climbed to a tree belay.

The following three routes are on the obvious small slab to the right of *Quayfoot Buttress*, adjacent to the descent path.

Freak Brothers   25 m   VS   1995
>   (4b). Start at the lowest point. Climb the bulge and wall above to a ledge. Climb the groove above for 3 metres and step right to the arête. Continue up the arête and step right to finish on the wall. Variations are possible.

★ **Freak Power**   15 m   E2   1995
>   (6a). Start up and right of *Freak Brothers* at a huge detached block at the centre of the slab. Climb to the right of the small roof up the slab and crack. The *Crucifix* crux is at half-height.

★ **Short Circuit**   10 m   VS   1998
>   (4b). Climb the groove to the right of *Freak Power*.

South Wing

Ascend the normal descent path to a point about 30 metres below the top of the main crag where the path veers left and turns to easy scrambling. Walk up right 7 metres to a prominent buttress behind some oaks.

The Cyclostome   25 m   MS   1992
Start behind an oak, below a black niche. Climb to the niche. Climb the groove on the left, stepping right at the top and following an exposed slab to an easy ridge. (Climbing the final slab by its easier left edge reduces the overall grade to VD.)

☆ **A Confected Persona**   32 m   VS   ?   1992
Start 1 metre right of *Cyclostome* at a short arête.
1   7 m. Climb the arête to a bulging wall, then traverse 3 metres right to a holly.
2   25 m (4c). Climb the overhang directly behind the tree for 5 metres before traversing right via easy slabs to a wide V-recess. Climb boldly up the centre of the impending headwall above. A central line up the wall slightly down and right leads to the top.

Upper Quayfoot Buttress (256 168), lies on the tree-covered hillside immediately above and left of *Quayfoot Buttress*. It consists of two tiers but is very broken and contains much vegetation and dirty, loose rock, amongst which might be found lurking, on the

Lower Tier, **Merlin** (MVS 1970) and **Tingler** (MVS 1970), and on the *Upper Tier*, **The Groove** (VS 1970).

Quayfoot Quarry (Bowderstone Quarry) (253 167)
Alt. 110 m

This disused quarry is seen on the left when approaching the *Bowderstone* via the main path shortly after leaving the National Trust Bowderstone Quarry car park. It used to be a much more impressive face complete with a large bivouac cave, a popular dossing and party spot with bikers and itinerant climbers. The cave collapsed spectacularly in the 1970s leaving the large boulder slope and a few steeper buttresses. Much of the quarry is still unstable although the climbs below are fairly solid. Towards the top of the scree slope and to its left are the following routes centred around an obvious deep groove system.

Mosquito Coast F6b 1993
A diagonal line crossing *Cleavage* from right to left. Start to the right of the main grooves.
  Climb up left to *Cleavage*, follow the arête up and left to a lower-off (5 bolts).

Cleavage 16 m F6a 1993
Start left of the main grooves below a bolt.
  Move up right to good holds and mantleshelf into the groove, go up and right into the main groove. Follow this to the top to a tree (4 bolts).

Twin Peaks 12 m S 1993
Start just left of *Cleavage*.
  Climb up into the corner until moves left lead to the left edge. Finish up the groove above.

Wombley 13 m MVS 1993
  (4a). To the left of *Twin Peaks* is a leaning wall with an offwidth corner crack. Climb this to a niche and move right and up past a jammed block. Step left and climb the blunt arête to the top.

There are other bolts suggesting a counter diagonal to *Mosquito Coast*: the writers have been unable to locate any details.

At the bottom of the quarry and to the right (looking in) is a small cave.

Quay West   16 m   F6b+   1993
Start just right of the cave.
> Climb to the first bolt and traverse left to the niche above the
> cave. Climb out of the top of the niche with difficulty and follow
> a faultline to a lower off (3 bolts).

Graveyard Fiend   E3   1993
> (6b). Climb the wall and crack 2 metres right of *Quay West* to a
> difficult finish.

Cave Quarry   (254 168)

This lies just above and slightly to the left of the main *Quayfoot
Quarry* when viewing it from the path. The easiest access is from the
National Trust Bowderstone Quarry car park. From the topmost
parking spot a short steep path leads to the quarry, the routes are on
a smooth slab to the right of the obvious cave at the bottom.

Smear Today – Gone Tomorrow   15 m   F6c+   1993
Climbs out of the deepest part of the quarry. Take a red patch up to
a good hold and follow the faultline diagonally left to the flared
corner and the top (5 bolts).

All Stopped Up   8 m   F6a   1993
Starting just right of *Smear Today*, climb straight up (3 bolts).

Woden's Face   (253 167)   Alt. 90 m   West Facing

This popular, though now well worn crag is situated just above the
Bowderstone path, about 250 metres from the Bowderstone Quarry
car-park. Descend to the left of the crag.

On the left of the main face is a short wall. A tree at the top of the
wall on a ledge provides a useful belay.

This crag is often frequented by groups under instruction.

★ **Family Outing**   16 m   MS   1989
> A pleasant clean route. Start at the left of the wall and climb the
> left-hand groove to the ledge.

Blue Riband 16 m HS   1989
  Climb the steep crack just right of *Family Outing*.

Jaffa Cake 16 m S   1989
  Climb the ramp up the centre of the wall to the ledge.

★ **Custard Cream** 16 m MVS   1989
  (4c). Start just right of *Jaffa Cake* and climb the wall which is
  more awkward than it appears.

★★ **Wimpey Way** 30 m S
  Start just left of *Woden's Face*.
  1   24 m. Ascend the slanting crackline just left of the centre of the
      crag to gain an obvious groove which is climbed to the terrace.
  2   6 m. Climb the wall above.

★★ **Woden's Face** 30 m VD   1921
  A popular and quite exposed route. Start at the centre of the crag.
  1   24 m. Teeter up the scratched wall to below an overhang at 6
      metres. Move leftwards into *Wimpey Way*. Follow this for a short
      way and step right and follow the buttress to the terrace.
  2   6 m. Climb the wall above.

★ **Woden's Face Direct** 30 m S   1921
  A well worn climb up the centre of the crag.
  1   24 m. Follow *Woden's Face* to the overhang at 6 metres and
      avoid this on the left to gain the flake above. Step off the flake,
      move right a metre or so, then gain and climb a shallow scoop.
      At its top either move left or right. Climb directly to the terrace.
  2   6 m. Climb the short wall above.

★ **Woden's Wotsit** 30 m E2   1984
  An eliminate climb starting below the wall left of *Woden's Cheek*,
  on the right of a crack leading up left.
  (5b). Climb the wall, avoiding the right arête, to a ledge. Continue
  up the wall and the slab above, between the *Direct Route* and
  Woden's Cheek.

★ **Woden's Cheek** 28 m HS   1935
  An awkward start leads to an airy finish.
  1   24 m. On the right side of the crag is a short groove above a
      small overhanging wall. Gain the groove, awkwardly, and ascend
      to a good ledge. Continue up the groove above, moving right
      slightly to finish.
  2   6 m. Climb the short wall above.

Wodentops 24 m E2   1989
   (6a). Just left of *Tantalus* is an obvious overhanging crack. Gain
   this, awkwardly, and climb it, more awkwardly, to gain good
   holds and a ledge. Continue up the groove between *Woden's
   Cheek* and *Tantalus*, past a poor spike. Move over a bulge and
   finish up twin cracks.

★ **Tantalus** 20 m VS   1969
A short but worthwhile climb starting up to the right of *Woden's
Cheek*.
   (4c). Climb up broken rocks then to the right to gain the top of
   the obvious flake. Climb the groove and crack above to the
   terrace.

Soxon 20 m E1   1992
Start up and right from *Tantalus*, and down and left of the oak tree
in the gully.
   (5a). Climb the pinnacle, passing to the left of the oak, and follow
   the arête to the top. Tree belay well back.

Girdle Traverse 50 m VS   1989
A mainly low level traverse, best done on a really busy day! Start as
for *Family Outing*.
1   20 m (4a). Climb to a ledge then traverse rightwards into *Jaffa
    Cake* and follow this to the ledge at mid-height. Move down right
    for 3 metres and traverse to the top of the flake of *Woden's Face
    Direct*.
2   30 m (5a). Descend a metre and make some awkward moves right
    (crux) to gain *Woden's Cheek*. Climb up right and finish up
    Tantalus.

Bowderstone Crag (256 165) Alt. 220 m   South West Facing

More properly called *Bowder Crag*, it is situated on the hillside above
the *Bowderstone* and is composed of a number of buttresses with
routes varying from the pleasant *Bowderstone Pinnacle* to the modern
testpieces around the *Hell's Wall* Area.

Opposite: "There must be a good hold up there somewhere" –
Climbers looking in hope on **Irony** (HVS), Quayfoot Buttress
                                                          Leslie Shore
Overleaf: Bowderstone Crag – David Birkett on **Bleed in Hell**, his
desperately thin E8 of 1992   *Bill Birkett*

It is approached from the Bowderstone Quarry car park from where a track leads to the *Bowderstone*, passing below *Woden's Face*. About 100 metres before the *Bowderstone* take a track on the left heading more or less directly up the hillside. The centrally situated *Bowderstone Pinnacle* is directly above the *Bowderstone*, with the fierce modern routes to its left. It is reached in about 20 minutes from the car park. The best descent from those routes around the *Pinnacle* is to the right of the crag, and those on the left of the crag by following a broken ramp, left of *Hell's Wall*.

Right-Hand Section

The first climbs are described left to right from the *Bowderstone Pinnacle*.

★★ **Bowderstone Pinnacle**   36 m   D   1914
The classic easy route of the crag. This route ascends the prominent buttress in the centre of the crag. Start 10 metres up the gully to the right of the buttress below the large tree.
1   12 m. Traverse diagonally left along polished ledges to a broken crack, which leads to a stance on the arête.
2   18 m. Continue up the buttress, past a holly and dead stump, into the cleft between the buttress on the left and the pinnacle on the right.
3   6 m. Either climb onto the *Pinnacle* direct, or climb the left arête of the buttress on the left, then leap across the gap onto the top of the *Pinnacle*. Finish by crossing the ridge from the buttress and climbing a short step. The obvious gully on the right is not recommended for descent.

Variation   **Direct Start**   16 m   HS   1933
1a Ascend the left arête of the *Pinnacle* for 5 metres; then move right and ascend a crack to join the ordinary route.

Variation   **Superdirect Start**   15 m   HVS   1997
1a (5a). Climb the left arête directly to join original route at the top of pitch 1.

Previous Page: Plus ça change... David Birkett on The Bowderstone
circa 1990
                                                            Dave Willis
Opposite: Plus c'est la même chose... Boulderers in the Lake District
circa 1890
                                                      Abrahams' Collection

★ **Balder's Crack** 38 m   HS

An interesting route starting at the back of the bay to the right of
Pinnacle.
1   20 m. Climb past yew and oak trees and up a V-groove to a l
    ledge.
2   18 m. Ascend the awkward crack in the line of the groove to
    top.

Angelus 35 m   HVS

An eliminate line taking the steep upper wall to the right of *Bal*
Crack. Start as for *Balder's Crack*.
1   20 m. Climb to the yew and oak trees; then move up right
    a holly and up a crack to a large ledge.
2   15 m (5b). Climb the obvious crack to a tree; then trav
    delicately 3 metres left and mantelshelf onto the ledge on to
    the *Pinnacle*.

Thor's Exit 40 m   MS

Though somewhat devious, this is an interesting climb, especiall
its second pitch.
1   24 m. Climb *Balder's Crack* to the yew and oak trees; move
    to a niche on the arête and climb the ridge to a large ledge. M
    down rightwards, with difficulty, into the gully.
2   16 m. Climb the polished crack above to the gap behind
    Pinnacle then gain its top.

The Right Wall 40 m   S

Start at the foot of the gully below (you guessed!) its right
Nothing like its Welsh namesake and not recommended.
1   30 m. Climb the wall, past a holly, to a yew. Climb the
    behind the tree and go rightwards to a tree belay below a
    groove.
2   10 m. Climb the groove.

Trundle 38 m   HVS

A now vegetated route, starting just left of *Thor's Ridge*.
1   28 m (4c). Climb the slabby wall left of the ridge, past a
    and up the steepening wall to a ledge.
2   10 m (5a). Attack the overhanging crack on the left.

Thor's Ridge 50 m   VD

This route starts 22 metres right of the *Pinnacle*.

1   24 m. Climb broken rocks; then move left to gain and climb a
    clean ridge to a holly belay.
2   26 m. Move right to an oak and climb to a block belay.

Variation Thor's Wrath   20 m   HVS   1985
2a (5a). Ascend vegetated rocks to gain and climb a chimney which
    narrows to a steep finishing crack.

Balder's Buttress   73 m   D   1945
A pleasant climb up the ridge, 20 metres right of *Thor's Ridge*.
1   24 m. Climb the lower rocks past a flake and go up the buttress
    on the left. Oak belay above.
2   15 m. Continue up the ridge, climbing two gendarmes.
3   18 m. Climb a V-chimney and twin cracks on the left. Move right
    for 6 metres and scramble 20 metres up to the right to a slabby
    outcrop.
4   16 m. Climb the centre of the slab to a square-cut niche, which
    leads to easier slabs above.

Woden's Way   50 m   D   1945
    Takes the vegetated ridge, 21 metres right of *Balder's Buttress*.

Walking the Plank   55 m   M   1949
    A rather scrappy climb, making the most of the rock just right of
    the descent path.

Far Right Buttress

This small crag of good rock is reached by following the path
rightwards from the *Pinnacle* for about 100 metres until it is possible
to scramble up and back left to the pronounced arête with a well
defined groove to its left.

★ **The Punchline**   15 m   E3   1992
    (6a). Traverse into the hanging groove from the left with difficulty
    and make a hard move to better holds. More hard moves lead to
    the top. Easier for the tall.

Die-Hard   20 m   HVS   1992
Start just left of *The Punchline*.
    (5a). Climb the strenuous but well protected groove to the left of
    The Punchline.

Left-Hand Section

The remaining routes are found to the left of the *Bowderstone Pinnacle*, and are described from **right** to **left**.

Thor's Entrance   40 m   S   1953
This climb, which is not without interest, starts behind a large tree 5 metres left of the arête of the *Pinnacle*.
1   16 m. Climb the steep crack to a ledge, and the crack above to belay on the *Pinnacle* route.
2   24 m. Climb to the rotten step, which cuts off the V-groove above. Move left round a bulge and up a steep groove. Finish up easy slabs.

Variation   **Rib Pitch**   20 m   VS
1a (4c). Follow the arête of the *Pinnacle*, passing a steep little wall to reach the ordinary route.

Frigga's Staircase   50 m   M   1945
Start just left of the *Pinnacle* and follow the inclined ridge. Continue up left and follow better rock to the top of the ridge. Various finishes are possible.

The path now rises up to the left. Where it levels out in the back of a small bay 15 metres before the prominent arête of *Hell's Wall*, there is a short crack to the left of a vegetated groove.

Abednego   36 m   HVS   1971
1   10 m (4b). Climb the crack then move up right to a yew tree.
2   26 m (4c). Step down and move up right to the foot of a chimney. Climb the chimney, finishing with a short overhanging section.

Hell's Wall

The impressively smooth *Hell's Wall* now boasts several modern testpieces.

★★★ **Hell's Wall**   30 m   E6   {F7c+}   1964/1979
The original testpiece. Previously an old artificial route, it now gives an excellent, technically very hard and sustained free climb. Well protected by in-situ pegs.
(6c). Climb the wide crack to a ledge then go up right to a ledge on the arête. Move up and right to gain a crack. Go up this then

LEFT OF THE ARETE   **HELL'S WALL**

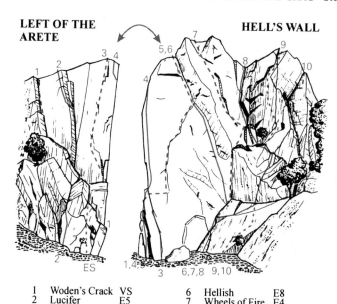

1	Woden's Crack	VS	6	Hellish	E8
2	Lucifer	E5	7	Wheels of Fire	E4
ES	Easy Start	(4a)	8	Valhalla	E1
3	DeQuincy	E7	9	The Bulger	E5
4	Bleed in Hell	E8	10	Heaven's Gate	E3
5	Hell's Wall	E6			

move out right and up rightwards to below a curving groove. This is followed boldly to the top.

★★★ Bleed in Hell   30 m   E8   {F8a+}   1992
The stunning arête.
    (6c). Start as for *Hell's Wall* but, instead of climbing its crux crack, follow the arête throughout. Much harder than *Inferno*.

★★ Inferno   30 m   E7   {F8a}   1988
A sensational line, starting up *Hell's Wall* then traversing left, up the arête and round to finish up *De Quincy*.
    (6c). Follow *Hell's Wall* past its crux crack to the first jug. Traverse left along some good handholds and move up passing a stacked peg runner to reach a good small ledge (crux) – dyno just right of the peg. Stand on the ledge awkwardly (peg runner) then pull round left to join and follow *De Quincy* to its finish.

★★ Mesrine 40 m E6 {F7c}   1990
(6b). Follow *Hell's Wall* to the point where it follows the
leftwards-rising groove. At this point move out right to a large
flake beneath a diagonal roof. Excellent climbing leads through
the roof to good jugs over the lip. Continue up the thin and
sustained wall above, crossing *Wheels of Fire* and climb directly
to the top.

Hellish 35 m E8 {F7c} ?   1992
Start at the corner at the right-hand side of *Hell's Wall*.
(6c). Climb the corner to a ledge. Move left and up (PR) until
hard moves lead to a loose undercut (poor small wires). Move
right, then back left to join *Hell's Wall* and the first good
protection. Finish as for *Hell's Wall*. Serious.

★★★ Wheels of Fire 35 m E4   1979
The awkward first corner leads to a very good top pitch above the
impressive wall. Start in the slabby corner behind a large block.
1   15 m (6a). Ascend the corner to a ledge. Climb directly up the
    steep corner and crack above to the tree belay on *Valhalla*.
2   20 m (6a). Traverse diagonally left along the lip of the overhang.
    Pull up (long reach) then finish up the short wall and groove on
    the left.

★★ Valhalla 32 m E1   1962
Climbs the obvious corner to the right of *Hell's Wall*. Start in the
slabby corner.
1   18 m (4c). Climb up the corner to a ledge. Move right across a
    slab and up steep cracked rock to a small rowan below the corner.
2   14 m (5c). Follow the corner to a square-cut overhang; pull up
    left and continue up the corner above to the top.

★★★ The Bulger 36 m E5   1971/1981
An exciting and strenuous pitch. This route free climbs the previously
aided crack up the overhang just right of *Valhalla*.
1   18 m. Pitch 1 of *Valhalla*.
2   18 m (6b). Step down right and climb the vague crack in the wall
    above, until a pull out right can be made below the roof. Pull up
    to the thin crack above and follow it rightwards to the top.

★★★ Heaven's Gate 35 m E3   1981
Climbs the arched groove right of *The Bulger*.
1   15 m. Scramble up past a holly and an oak to a large oak tree
    below the groove.

2 20 m (6a). Enter the groove above, and follow it until forced out right at the top onto the rib. Climb the wall on the right of the rib direct to a ledge on the left.

The next routes are to the left of the arête.

★★ De Quincy 30 m E7 {F7a} 1982
A mind blowing, poorly protected route, which climbs the impending wall to the right of *Lucifer* and just left of the arête. Start beneath *Hell's Wall*.
(6b). Climb thin cracks up the left side of the wall until moves round left lead to the ledge of *Hell's Wall*. Climb straight up above the ledge to a hidden peg runner. Continue in the same line, just left of the arête, passing the final crack on the left.

★★ Woden's Crack 30 m VS 1975
Start below the left arête of the wall at a wide crack.
(4c). Climb the crack and continue up the gangway, past a large flake, to a steep little corner. Climb this and the crack above on the right to a heathery finish.

★★ Lucifer 30 m E5 1981
A short but entertaining route which takes the steep groove in the wall 6 metres round the corner to the left of *Hell's Wall*.
(6a). Climb up into an open groove (or, much more easily climb rock to the right, 4a) and go up to a ledge. Climb easily up left to the next ledge. Pull up right into the slim hanging groove (peg runner) and climb it, exiting left at the top. Easy slabs lead to a tree belay.

Left of Hell's Wall

About 50 metres down and left is a small buttress fronted by a prominent pinnacle. Descent from this buttress is to the left.

The Higher the Better 38 m MS 1948
A devious, wandering route which improves only in the last 3 metres. Start 6 metres right of the pinnacle at a small cairn below broken rocks leading into a chimney, just left of the path coming down from *Hell's Wall*.
1 20 m. Climb up, then continue up the chimney on the left. Scramble 30 metres rightwards to the left of the buttress of *Hell's Wall*.

2   18 m. Traverse a ledge to its right extremity. In an airy position, move up and climb easier rocks to the belay from where an interesting view is available down *Hell's Wall*.

Needle Wall   28 m   HVS   1978
Climbs the groove and short corner, starting right of the *Pinnacle*.
(4c). Climb the groove, past a holly, to a corner above. Pull up to a small vegetated ledge on the right and finish directly up the wall above.

★ **Woden's Needle**   30 m   VD   1936
An interesting climb starting on the left of the *Pinnacle*.
Climb the fissure on the left of the *Pinnacle* to a ledge at 10 metres. Step down right, then climb up rightwards, and up to the top of the *Needle*. Finish up the wall above.

Variation   VD   1954
Climb the crack on the right of the *Needle* to the ledge at 10 metres.

The path now continues for 60 metres up and left to another small buttress. Scramble up the lower rocks to behind an oak tree below a groove with a crack sprouting a small tree.

Fleur de Lys   32 m   VD   1950
1   24 m. Ascend the groove, past the tree, then move right to an oak. Continue up the fine steep crack above.
2   8 m. Finish up a short pleasant wall and slab above.

★★ **Just and So**   26 m   E2   1988
Start 4 metres left of *Fleur de Lys*. A hidden gem.
1   12 m (5a). Follow the obvious thin crack to a large grass ledge and holly tree belay.
2   14 m (5c). Step right into the scoop and follow the thin crack for 3 metres to a hand traverse. Move 3 metres right and ascend the small overhang to the top.

Far Left Buttress

A further 50 metres left and slightly higher than *Just and So* is found an obvious 20 metre high wall of rock with a prominent arête at the right-hand end. The routes are described from right to left, although their quality and names leave much to be desired.

Schnell Dumbkopf!   25 m   VS   1991
   (5a). From the niche at the lowest point of the arête, climb up and then right and left to a ledge and tree. Finish up cracks.

Achtung Spitfire   20 m   VS   1990
Takes the centre of the slab to the left of the dirty corner. Worth doing. Start behind a large tree.
   (4c). Follow the obvious clean faultline to a steep crack which is taken direct.

Henry Heinkel   15 m   VS   1990
Start from a niche in the left of the slab.
   (4c). Pull out over the overhang and follow the crack to ledges. Climb directly to the top on good holds.

Shot Down Variation   12 m   VS   1990
   (4c). From the ledges, follow an obvious diagonal line up right and cross *Achtung Spitfire* to finish on its right.

Grot in Himmel   10 m   HVS   1991
   (5a). Make a difficult move into the right-hand of the two obvious cracks and climb it until stopped by the tree. Traverse right 2 metres and climb direct to the top on excellent holds (as for *Henry Heinkel*).

Das Ist Verboten   10 m   E2   1991
Takes the slab between the two cracks. Contrived but enjoyable.
   (5b). Climb directly onto the undercut slab using a pocket high on the right to step across left to a good foothold. Continue up on good pockets, the cracks and the tree being verboten (as if possible).

Hande Hoch   10 m   MVS   1991
   (4c). The left-hand crack is awkward to start.

Eat Lead Fritz   9 m   HVS   1991
   (5a). Climb the arête at the left end of the buttress.

The Bowderstone (254 164) Alt. 90 m

The Bowderstone has been a mecca for hard bouldering in The Lakes for several years. The challenge of the *Ladder Wall* was taken up in the early eighties and quite recently local climbers have added many new and harder problems to this remarkable boulder. To reach it, park in the National Trust car park beneath *Quayfoot Buttress* and follow the signed path past *Woden's Face* (5 minutes).

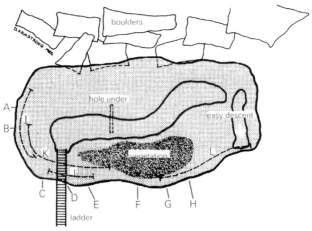

A The Crack	E Picnic Sarcastic	I On the Rebound
B The Crack Direct	F Impropa Opera	J Hot Air
C Bowderiser	G Power Pinch	K Coming up for Air
D Inaudible Vaudeville	H The Rib	L Lateral Gruntings

This is by no means an exhaustive guide; the local activists have many other variations which they will be happy to show you! What follows is a guide to the two main walls. There are more problems around the back but they are not as popular as the landings are not as good. The landings below the problems described are generally good and descent from the top is via a ladder. Many problems on the *Ladder Wall* finish at the lip of the overhang, thus leaving the vegetation above undisturbed. The overhanging nature of the boulder ensures some dry rock even in the rain. Problems are described from left to right starting at *The Crack*, which is around and to the left of the ladder. Sherman gradings are used.

As to *The Bowderstone's* origin, there is still some doubt. Some say it is an erratic carried into place by ice and others that it fell from the hillside above. As the *Bowderstone* is 19 metres long, 11 metres high and weighs in at about 2000 tonnes the latter event would have been worth watching!

Grading Guide

English	Sherman
5a/5b	V1 V2
5b/5c	V2 V3
5c/6a	V3 V4
6a/6b	V4 V5 V6
6b.6c	V7 V8 V9
6c/7a	V11 V12 V13
7b/7b+	V13 V14

The Problems

The most significant problems are described, starting from *The Crack* at the southern end and working in an anti-clockwise direction around the block.

1. **Planky's Problem** (V11, 6c) Start in the recess of *The Crack* and climb leftwards across the prow for 4 metres, most of which is footless!
2. **The Crack** (V4, 6a). The obvious crack!
3. (V9, 6c+). 1 and 2, up to 4 and up again.
4. **The Crack Direct** (V5, 6b). 3, 4, 5 and crack.
5. (V6, 6b). 3, 4, 5, 6, 7, pocket and crack.
6. (V7, 6b). 3, 8, 9, *Shelf*, 7, pocket and crack.
7. (V10, 7a). 3 to 11 (poor sloper), *Shelf* by dyno or heel hooks, finish up arete. Variation (V8) 3 to 8 then *Shelf*.
8. (V8, 6c). 3, 4, 6, 7, pocket and crack.
9. (V8, 6c). 3, 11, 9 and *Shelf* (easy version of problem 7).
10. **Coming up for Air** (V7, 6c). Start at slots below *Bowderiser*. Traverse left (low) to 3. Link to any of the above problems 3 to 8.
11. **Dave's Circuit** (V10, 7a). Start with *Coming up for Air* then 10, 12 and 13 (slopers) to the *Jugs*. Down and right via 14 and 15 (pockets) to finish up *Inaudible Vaudeville* to ladder.
12. (V9, 6c). Start on 3, slap up for sloper 12, heel hook 3 and reach *Shelf*.
13. (V8, 6c). From *Pinch* up to 10, 12 and 13, *Shelf* and then *The Crack*.
14. (V2, 5b). Jump off ground to *Shelf* and big holds to top of ladder.
15. **Bowderiser** (V6, 6b). The thin crack, painful! Finish on jugs.

THE BOWDERSTONE
South Face

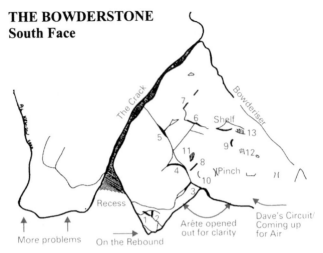

16. **Inaudible Vaudeville** (V9, 6c). From small pinch 16 and sloper 17, up to edges 18 and 19, then 20 and 21 and the ladder.

17. **Frank** (V10, 7a). Start as for *Inaudible Vaudeville* then move left to holds 14 and 15, then straight to the top.

18. **On the Rebound** (V7, 6c). Start below *The Crack*, right to 3, link into problems 3 to 8. Alternatively from 3 reverse *Coming up for Air* to the sit down start of *Picnic Sarcastic*.

19. **Picnic Sarcastic** (V9, 6c+). Up *Ramp* via *Pocket* to last edges is about 6b, then harder moves to lip via crumbling holds. To avoid the latter traverse left to sloper or finish as for *Hot Air*.

20. **Hot Air** (V9, 6c). Start of *Picnic Sarcastic* then left via pockets 14 and 15 to the jugs at the top of *Bowderiser*.

21. **Sit-Down Start** (V10, 7a). From undercuts 22 and 23 use edge 24 to gain *Ramp*, then *Picnic Sarcastic* or problem 23.

22. (V9, 6b). From 25 long reach to 26 and *Picnic Sarcastic*.

23. (V12, 7b). Problem 21 then *Picnic Sarcastic* to the large hold of *Impropa Opera* via a sharp flake and poor footholds.

24. Project. Continue problem 23 up *Impropa Opera*.

25. **Grand Opera** (V9, 6c). From large hold up left to edge and pinch and the top.

26. **Impropa Opera** (V9, 6c/7a). A classic, but nowharder due to the loss of a hold. From *Large Hold* up right to flake 30 (which is no longer there!) then edges 31, 32, 33 and 34 to larger hold and top.

THE BOWDERSTONE
East (Ladder) Face

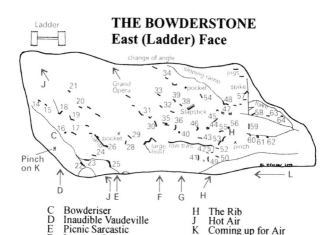

C	Bowderiser	H	The Rib
D	Inaudible Vaudeville	J	Hot Air
E	Picnic Sarcastic	K	Coming up for Air
F	Impropa Opera	L	Lateral Gruntings
G	Power Pinch		

Variation (6c+/7a). *Large Hold* to 30 then V-slot, 32, 33, 34 etc.
Variation (6c). *Large Hold* up right to 35 and use 30 for left hand to gain 32 with right hand.

27. The Sit-Down Start to *Impropa Opera* has lost a hold and awaits a repeat. It will be very hard!

28. Power Pinch (V9, 6c). From the holds on the low traverse use 36 (the *Power Pinch* – more of a layaway), then 37, 38 and 39 to pocket. Using 35 is easier.

29. Bloodsucker (V10, 7a). As previous problem but use the painful pocket 40 instead of the *Power Pinch*.

30. (V8, 6c). Use the holds on the *Low Traverse* and *Bloodsucker* pocket to gain the sloper of *Slapstick* and then edges and *Sloping Ramp*.

31. (V10, 7a). Dyno from holds on low level traverse to *Slapstick*. (Given joke grade of 6b in last guide).

32. (V7, 6c). Sit-down start 41, 42, 43, 44, 45 and *Rib*.

33. (V9, 6c+). From holds on low traverse up to sloper 44, use 46 to udge up to *Slapstick* and up.

34. Adam's Problem (V10, 7a). 35 to large slopers, then traverse left to top of *Impropa Opera*.

35. (V7, 6b+). From holds on *Low Traverse* 44 for left hand then 47 and 48.

36. (V7, 6c). Start at left end of *Low Traverse*, into 44 with left hand then 45 out to 54 and *Ramp*.

37. (V9, 6c+). Sit down start to rib. Side pull and small edges 49, 50, 51, 52, 53, and 55 to 47 and 48.
38. **The Rib** (V4, 6b). Use everything to reach traverse line right to the *Flake*.
39. (V5, 6a). Use holds on the *Rib* to gain 48 then 57 to the *Spike* and *Jugs* to the top.
40. (V8, 6c). From 53 to sloper 56, share on 47 and up to 48.
41. (V7, 6c). Start below a triangular pod. Use large side hold and scar to reach pod and the *Flake*.
42. (V7, 6c). From 61 and 62 up to small edge 63 and the *Flake*.
43. (V8, 6c). Sit-down start to 42.
44. (V4, 6a/b). Low start on slopers up and right to round hold (not flake), jump up right to below *Flake*.
45. **Lateral Gruntings** (V8, 6c). Traverse from right to *The Rib* via 62, 61, 60, 59 and a sideways lunge. Continuation (V11, 7a). Carry on to the *Low Traverse* to finish up *Impropa Opera* or *Grand Opera*.

Yew Crag (264 153) Alt. 250 m West Facing

This is the outcrop above the path from Rosthwaite to Watendlath which is composed of a mossy slab, containing some vegetated routes not meriting full description. It is bounded on the right by an overhanging wall whose routes gives limited reward for the 15 minute walk.

Incipient Arête 50 m M 1955
   Climb the broken rib bounding the left of the crag.

Panacea Ridge 45 m D 1955
   Climb the ill-defined rib some 20 metres left of and below *Serotinous*.

Serotinous 38 m S 1955
   Climb up left of *Coquette's Gully* to an oak in the gully. Break out left to finish up slabs.

Coquette's Gully 30 m D 1955
   Climb the corner on the left of the mossy slab.

Sinuate Slab 35 m S 1955
   Climb the ill-defined rib on the right of the mossy slab.

White Man Walkabout 44 m E1   1978
A deceptively steep route. Start as for *Sinuate Slab*.
1   24 m (4c). Climb the right edge of the slab to a ledge. Traverse
    right 2 metres and climb the slab, rightwards, to belay on the
    arête.
2   20 m (5a). Climb the overhanging wall rightwards on good holds.
    Pull over the overhang and climb the wall above to easier ground.

Jacko 20 m E1   1978
A steep and worrying climb up the right wall of the buttress.
    (5b). Start about half-way up the right side of the crag at a slabby
    gangway slanting up right. Climb this and block overhangs above
    to a large clump of heather. Reach high to the right and climb
    the overhanging crack to the top.

BORROWDALE SOUTH

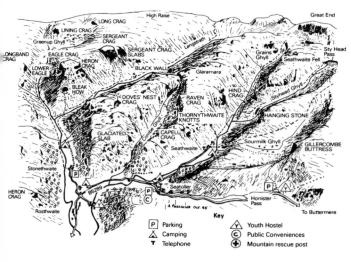

Key

P Parking   ⌂ Youth Hostel
△ Camping   © Public Conveniences
T Telephone   ⊕ Mountain rescue post

BORROWDALE SOUTH

Heron Crag (Stonethwaite) (263 143) is reached in about 20 minutes from Stonethwaite. Cross the bridge over Stonethwaite Beck, turn left and follow the path towards Rosthwaite for ½ km. The track first bends right. Where it turns sharp left go straight up the fellside, passing to the right of a small outcrop. The crag is the left-hand of two crags seen from the path.

The centre of the crag is taken by **Phil's Rib** 35 m MVS. On the slabs just to the left are **Sumo** 30 m MVS and 3 metres left again **Snake** 28 m MVS. The groove to the right of Phil's Rib is **Frank's Groove** 25 m HS, **Chapel Rib** 26 m VS starts up this then moves right and up the rib, **Watson's Way** 27 m S starts 6 metres right of the rib. All these climbs were done in 1988/1989.

Greenup Ghyll and Langstrath

These fine valleys are the feeders to Stonethwaite Beck, which joins the Derwent near Rosthwaite. The Stonethwaite valley branches south-eastwards from Borrowdale just south of Rosthwaite. One and a half kilometres above Stonethwaite, the beck branches. The direct continuation is Greenup Ghyll and the right fork is the extensive valley of Langstrath.

The crags are approached from the hamlet of Stonethwaite, where a limited amount of parking exists. A cart track leads up the valley, past a large campsite, to the point where Langstrath Beck and Greenup Ghyll join to form Stonethwaite Beck. If the crags above Greenup Ghyll are the aim, cross Langstrath Beck (normally fordable in summer) or use a footbridge a few hundred metres upstream. Cross the footbridge over Greenup Ghyll to the path on its north side and follow this up the valley. This point can also be reached by crossing the packhorse bridge at Stonethwaite and following the path to Greenup.

On the flanks of Ullscarf, high on the north-east side of Greenup Ghyll's ravine is *Long Band Crag*. Almost 1½ kilometres further up the same side of the valley is *Lining Crag*, which is out of sight from Stonethwaite. On the east side of the spur between Greenup Ghyll and Langstrath is *Eagle Crag*, facing across towards *Long Band Crag*.

The main crags of Langstrath are on the west side of this same spur. The first, *Bleak How*, lies directly up the hillside above the bridge over Langstrath Beck. Higher up to its right is *Heron Crag* and a kilometre further up the valley is *Sergeant Crag*. *Sergeant Crag Slabs* and *Blackmoss Pot Slab* are to be found a little further on from here. Opposite *Sergeant Crag*, on the west side of the valley, is *Cam Crag* with *Black Wall* up to its left.

All can be reached from Stonethwaite well within an hour.

Long Band Crag (282 125) Alt. 430 m   West Facing

Though small, this is an impressive crag of superb rock giving good quality sustained routes. It is split by a large roof at half height which is cut vertically by a fine bottomless groove. This gives the line of *The Technician*.

The usual descent is to the right.

The routes are described from left to right.

The Craftsman 35 m VS   1965
This climbs an obvious steep V-groove below the left edge of the overhang, finishing up the wall above it. Start below the groove.
1 15 m. Surmount a short wall to enter and climb the groove. Pull out right at the top, then step left across the groove to a ledge.
2 20 m. Climb the corner left of the overhang to a grass ledge at 12 metres. From its bottom edge, pull up and swing right on small holds, then move up to some small ledges. Finish up a shallow groove on the right.

⋆⋆ **The Apprentice** 30 m E4   1987
Airy and exciting climbing which starts at the foot of a groove by a large spike in the wall between *The Craftsman* and *The Technician*.
    (6a). Climb the groove making a hard move at its top onto a leftwards-rising traverse line. Climb this to the left end of the large roof – poor protection. Climb the corner of *The Craftsman* for a metre then make a hard bold traverse right, across the lip of the overhang, where a pull up onto a ledge leads to some slabs. Climb these pleasantly, keeping to the left of a large crack and loose block.

LONG BAND CRAG

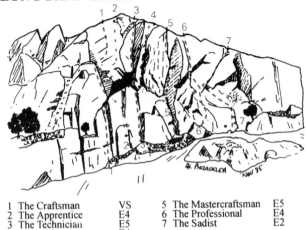

1 The Craftsman	VS	5 The Mastercraftsman	E5
2 The Apprentice	E4	6 The Professional	E4
3 The Technician	E5	7 The Sadist	E2
4 Masochist	E4		

★★★ **The Technician** 33 m E5   1965/1978
A bold route which free climbs the old aid route through the
impressive roof and blank groove above. The start of *Masochist* is
used to avoid the wet streaks below the roof. Start below the centre
of the overhang at a groove with a rowan sapling at 3 metres.

(6b). Climb the groove of *Masochist* to the overhang. Pull up left
into a short corner which is climbed over the roof into the smooth
groove above. Finish up this.

Variation **The Original Start**   1965
The second pitch, once aided, is normally wet. Start at some blocks
3 metres left of *The Craftsman*.
1   16 m. A short groove leads to a grassy ledge. Pull up to some
     small trees on the ledge above. Continue up the wall behind, step
     right to a groove and climb it to a ledge at the top of pitch 1 of
     The Craftsman.
2   26 m. Step across the groove of *The Craftsman* on the right to
     below the overhang. Cross the steep wall to rejoin the route as
     described in the short corner. Follow this over the roof and groove
     above to the top.

Masochist   34 m   E4   1976
Climbs the impressive overhanging, rightward-slanting groove to the
right of *The Technician*. It is very serious and poorly protected. Start
as for *The Technician*.
   (6a). Climb the groove to the overhang. Move up rightwards to
   a niche under the main groove (good nut runners). Gain the
   groove and follow it to the top.

★★ **The Mastercraftsman**   30 m   E5   1987
A great route, following the shallow groove right of *Masochist*. Start
at the foot of the groove at some quartz overhangs.
   (6b). Pull over the overhangs and climb the groove to the corner
   on the left. Go up this to the top of some large blocks. Move up
   rightwards to good runners in some pockets in a crack then make
   very hard moves up to some good jugs. More hard climbing leads
   past a bulge to a rest in a groove on the right. Ignore the easy
   finish right and step left to climb a difficult crack in the wall
   leading to a hard finishing move.

★★ **The Professional**   28 m   E4   1983
The grey wall at the right-hand side of the crag gives interesting
climbing. Start on a ledge 12 metres right of *Masochist*, just right of
a large pointed block.
   (6a). Climb the steep wall, moving slightly rightwards to a
   groove. Follow this up leftwards to its top. Cross the wall on the
   left to a slim groove/crack and climb this to below the obvious
   slanting overhang. Pull leftwards over the overhang to a thin crack
   and climb up to the top.

★ **The Sadist**   30 m   E2   1985
Climbs the lichenous slabby wall right of *The Professional*, starting
6 metres to its right at a pointed block.
   (5c). Climb a shallow groove to gain a slab and traverse delicately
   left up a ramp to gain the groove of *The Professional*. Go up this
   to where *The Professional* traverses left and follow the
   rightward-slanting crack to the top.

Lining Crag   (283 113)   Alt. 460 m   West Facing

This is a fine crag in a beautiful part of Borrowdale offering a quiet
break from the crowds. The excellent rock makes a visit well
worthwhile. It is situated on the west side of Greenup Edge, below
the path from Stonethwaite to Grasmere and can be reached in 45

minutes. The crag is in the form of a large open corner with easy climbing up each of the end ridges and a green-looking groove in the centre. There are fine slabs on each side of the centre.

Crucifix   50 m   S   1952
A broken route taking the ridge on the left of the grassy gully, left of *Ullscarf Edge*.
1   20 m. Gain a foothold and climb delicately up to a grass ledge with a rowan tree. Continue up the arête above with interest.
2   30 m. Climb the easy arête above.

★★ Ullscarf Edge   D   1936
Follows the obvious arête on the left of the crag.

★ Evening Wall   76 m   S   1936
A pleasant route starting 3 metres right of *Ullscarf Edge*.
1   22 m. Ascend the steep slab to a ledge. Bear right to a belay by blocks below the left end of the overhang.
2   24 m. Descend to a heather ledge on the right. Now climb up, passing an overlap on the right, to gain a ledge. After a delicate step up left, traverse left above the overlap and climb up to a ledge.
3   30 m. Traverse right and climb a short chimney. Continue up the arête on the right. Finish up the slab above.

Variation   16 m   VD
2a   Move up left and climb the corner in the arête and up to the belay.

★★ City of Love and Ashes   40 m   E1   2000
A fine route on immaculate rock throughout. Start 6 metres right of *Ullscarf Edge* just below a hanging boulder.
(5a). Climb up to the boulder and then climb the clean slab above heading up and slightly left to the open corner just right of a jagged nose. Climb up the corner until it is possible to move right to below the large overlap, pull through this and the next overlap to gain a fine slab. Go up this and left to a large ledge. Descend to the left.

★ Uncle Warren   40 m   VS   2000
A good route starting 10 metres right of *Ullscarf Edge* at a short right-facing corner.
(4b). Climb the corner for 4 metres to a ledge, step left and follow the open groove system all the way, passing the overlaps on the

right. Traverse left above these as for *Evening Wall*. (*Ullscarf Edge* makes a good finish.)

★ Solitaire   72 m   MVS   1970
A pleasant route with an exciting second pitch. Start just left of *Gorgoroth* below a rightward-slanting corner.
1   30 m (4a). Ascend the corner and the slab above, past a dead tree, to belay on the large grassy ledge below the overhangs.
2   42 m (4b). Climb the groove on the left to join *Evening Wall* at the short chimney on pitch 3. Climb the chimney for 3 metres to where it is possible to make an exposed traverse right, round the rib. Continue diagonally right over grassy ledges and the slab above to the top.

Variation   **The Weaver**   34 m   S   1960
Start just left of *Solitaire* and climb the slab above, more or less direct, to the large grassy ledge.

★ Gorgoroth   64 m   VS   1967
In its upper half this route takes the central corner which gives an impressive finale. It is well worthwhile and quite well protected where it matters. Start 10 metres left of the grassy groove in the centre of the crag.
1   30 m (4a). Ascend a faint groove in the slab to a ledge. Move right and up to the grassy ledge below the overhang. Block belays on the right.
2   34 m (4c). Traverse up right under the overhangs and enter and climb the groove to the top. (Good belays are found well back).

The Limit   72 m   HVS   1968
Start just right of the grass-filled groove in the centre of the crag.
1   30 m (5a). Climb the wall easily to a ledge at 16 metres. Trend leftwards up a steep gangway, surmount a small overhang and continue, with difficulty, to a cleaned ledge. Traverse right to a tree belay.
2   18 m (4c). Move back left along the ledge and cross the wall to gain *Gorgoroth* at the overhang. Climb *Gorgoroth* for a metre or so and move left to a ledge.
3   24 m. Climb up the wall above to the top.

★ Orthang   73 m   HVS   1966
A fine and varied outing, which takes the centre of the slab on the right of the crag. Start just right of a fallen ash.

1   45 m (5a). Climb the slab, delicately, rightwards to a small ledge. Move up a little and then go left for 6 metres. Climb straight up the wall to just below a grass ledge. Move left and up to belay at the central tree.
2   28 m (5a). Move left along the narrow ledge to the base of a short steep groove. Climb the wall on the right, with difficulty, for 6 metres. Step left into the groove. Follow this and move right, awkwardly, to finish up an arête.

Sunnyside Up 63 m S   1966
Start 6 metres right of *Orthang* below a watermarked wall.
1   24 m. Climb the wall leftwards on good flakes to the higher of two vegetated ledges.
2   24 m. Move right and climb a flake crack to a ledge on *Shemezim Grooves*. Move up right to the arête and follow this, and the slab above, to a flake belay.
3   15 m. Finish up the easy slabs above.

Variation 22 m VS   1985
2a (4c). Gain the ledge on *Shemezim Grooves* and follow it up the crack above. Instead of traversing left, continue straight up, with interest, to the flake belay above.

★ **Mr. Bad Example** 45 m E1   2000
A good route which is bold to start and finish, but is not technically hard for the grade.
    (5a). Start 4 metres right of the fallen ash tree. Climb the fine slab directly to a bilberry ledge, straight up the clean rock to the left of *Shemezin Grooves*, until level with the tree-covered ledge. Move right to finish up the arête. Belay a few metres back.

★ **Shemezim Grooves** 67 m HVS   1980
This climb follows a line of grooves parallel to the right-hand skyline of the crag. Start at the lowest point of the crag.
1   15 m. Climb up the slab to gain a grass ledge with a small tree.
2   28 m (4c). Follow the leftward-slanting gangway to a smaller grass ledge. Move left and climb the fine crack until level with the belay ledge of *Orthang*. Traverse left to gain the ledge and a fir tree belay.
3   24 m (5a). Ascend the steep wall behind the tree and continue up the groove above to the top.

★ Greenup Edge   67 m   D   1934

A good climb starting at the lowest point on the right of the crag.

1   35 m. Climb the slab for 12 metres and then ascend some ledges. Belay in a grassy gully on the right of the arête.

2   32 m. Climb up two corners. Now move left and climb up a shallow groove and slab to the top.

The Ring   112 m   VS   1968

This route girdles the crag from left to right.

1   12 m. Climb the left rib (*Ullscarf Edge*) to belay by several blocks.

2   45 m (4b). Move rightwards across the slabs to a junction with *Gorgoroth*. Follow this and belay on the large grass ledge below the overhang.

3   18 m (4c). Traverse up right under the overhang, as for *Gorgoroth*, and descend the black wall on the right to a large cleaned ledge. Tree belay on the right, as for *Orthang*.

4   22 m (4c). Continue along the ledge to its end. Descend slightly and move right. Ascend to the ridge and flake belay.

5   15 m. Climb the slabs above to the top.

Long Crag   (279 105)   Alt. 600 m   North West Facing

This crag lies on the northern slopes of Low White Stones. It is situated in a wonderfully quiet and remote part of the valley, offering excellent views over the northern fells and receiving the late afternoon sunshine. The crag is only 15 metres high but is, nevertheless, impressive. The rock, in the main, is very good and compact although the left-hand end of the main wall does take some time to dry after rain. The obvious approach is from Stonethwaite, traversing over the top of *Lining Crag*, and takes just over an hour. An alternative approach, taking slightly longer but involving less ascent, can be made from the Steel End car park at Wythburn.

To the left of the main wall area is a considerable expanse of broken rock that could probably offer some pleasant easy pitches up clean ribs. A short grassy gully separates this area from an area of slabs with a short steep headwall.

Roadside Picnic   15 m   VS   1990

(4c). Gain and climb the obvious series of right-facing grooves in the slab. Go up to the bilberry ledges and continue more dynamically using an obvious steep little flake crack. At its top step right and up to belays.

After a section of broken vegetated rock to the right you will arrive at the left-hand end of the main wall that is taken by *The Foad Factor*.

The Foad Factor 15 m HS   1990
(4b). Climb the vegetated groove to gain the obvious chimney, which proves to be not so obvious after all! Better than it looks.

A few metres further right is a prominent pointed boulder.

Double Lip Trip 20 m E3 ?   1993
Starts at the twin cracks about 3 metres left of the large pointed boulder towards the left end of the main crag.
(5c). Ascend the left-hand of the twin cracks by steep and technical climbing to the overhanging chimney. Finish up this.

Borrowdale Volcanic 15 m E6 {F6c} ?   1996
Start behind the pointed boulder.
(6b). This follows the fierce thin crackline (peg) at the left side of the main wall and gains the slanting gangway-cum-groove.

☆☆ **Rock Lobster** 20 m E7 {F7a} ?   1996
(6b). The stunning slim grooveline in the centre of the crag is both strenuous and serious. After making unprotected, tricky moves up the initial groove, a good flat hold and the first piece of gear is reached (RP 1 up and right). From here launch up the steep wall above for about 5 metres to good holds in a horizontal break and the first good gear (Friend 2). Continue up the wall above to the top.

★ **Not with a Bang** 15 m E2   1990
(5b). Towards the right end of the main wall is a right-facing, open, pinkish groove. Gain this by steep moves and climb it (PR, crux at the top) then step left to a mossy slab, which is better than it looks, and move up to a bilberry ledge. Finish through the bulges above the left end of the ledge.

Bog Drop 10 m VD   1990
The dirty chimney in the back of the recess on the right of the main wall.

To the right of this is a short vertical wall at an angle to the main wall.

The next three routes are on the small square wall orientated at right-angles to the main crag.

The Home Shoot   15 m   E1   1993
(5b). Start at the left side of the wall. Climb straight up to the flake then finish directly.

Loose Cannon on the Deck   15 m   E2   1993
(5b). Just right of centre is a flake system. Climb this and finish to the right.

★ **Paddy's Arête**   8 m   E2   1990
(6a). Climb the right arête of the short vertical wall, at an angle to the main wall. An entertaining pitch.

Eagle Crag

The bold nose of *Eagle Crag* is a familiar landmark. It is situated on the spur between Greenup and Langstrath, facing east across Greenup Ghyll towards Ullscarf.

It is best approached by following the path up Greenup Ghyll to a point where a wall runs up the fellside towards the *Lower Crag*. Cross the stream above a small waterfall. Ascend beside the wall, following it where it trends diagonally rightwards under the *Lower Crag*, then go up the gully to the left side of the main crag.

This wide grassy gully splits the *Lower Crag* from the main crag and is the usual descent route from both crags.

Lower Eagle Crag   (278 121)   Alt. 420 m   North East Facing

Ignored for many years, this smaller neighbour of *Eagle Crag*, more properly called *Pounsey Crag*, now gives a number of short sustained routes on excellent rough rock. Sadly the crag is not as clean as it used to be – more traffic would of course rectify this situation! The climbs are described from left to right.

LOWER EAGLE CRAG

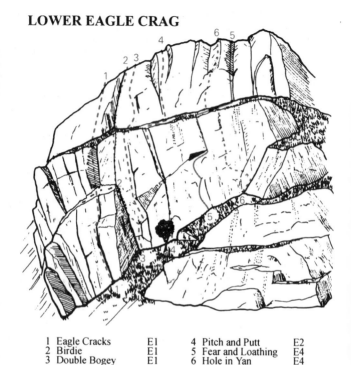

1	Eagle Cracks	E1	4	Pitch and Putt	E2
2	Birdie	E1	5	Fear and Loathing	E4
3	Double Bogey	E1	6	Hole in Yan	E4

Lucky Strike 55 m VS   1994

Sustained climbing but rather dirty. It is high in the grade and steeper than it appears from below. The route starts at a short, steep crack 5 metres left of the fence running up to the left end of the crag.

1 30 m (4c). Climb the crack which leads to a ledge, step left and then climb boldly up the arête until forced onto the right wall. Move straight up then go left to a ledge on the arête. Gain the grass ledge above.

2 25 m (4c). Around the corner to the right is a fine diagonal ramp. From the left edge, move up right, then left to pass a doubtful block. Stay in the corner and escape up the wall on the right to a subsidiary corner. Finish up this.

The Last Fairway 50 m E3   1981
An interesting route, especially for the short. Takes the corner and steep groove above at the left end of the crag, just right of the fence. Start in the tree bay below the open corner, reached by scrambling.
1   40 m (6a). Climb the left wall of the corner to below an overhang at 10 metres. Move right into the corner, then up to a ledge on the right. Go up the slab above to below the steep groove. Climb the left wall to a ledge. Go up the arête until a traverse right leads back into the groove. Pull over a bulge and go up a thin crack to the terrace.
2   10 m. Climb the middle of the slabby wall behind to the top.

The next routes start from a steep bilberry terrace running up rightwards below the main wall. This is reached by traversing along a narrow grassy ledge from the right.

Albatross 42 m E3?   1994
Start 3 metres left of *Eagle Cracks* below a hanging corner.
1   16 m (5b). Climb the corner and continue in a direct line to the heathery ledge shared by *Eagle Cracks*.
2   16 m (5c). Gain the higher sloping ledge, then step left and climb a series of shallow corners to the foot of the obvious V-crack. Swing left and up to join the final couple of metres of *The Last Fairway*. Steeper that it looks.
3   10 m. Climb the centre of the slab.

Eagle Cracks 45 m E1   1967/1981
Follows a series of cracks and grooves up the wall 10 metres right of *The Last Fairway*. Start at a large block directly below the obvious chimney/crack.
1   15 m (4c). Ascend the chimney/crack, passing a chockstone at mid-height, to a heathery ledge.
2   12 m (5b). Climb the corner crack, with continuous interest, to the terrace.
3   18 m. Go easily up blocks, then short grooves to the top.

★ **Birdie** 36 m E1   1988
A companion route to *Double Bogey* starting as for that route.
1   24 m (5b). Climb the corner crack to a grassy ledge at 10 metres. Continue up a short crack and wall above to gain an obvious layback flake. Finish up the corner crack above.
2   12 m (5a). Climb the smooth buttress on the right of the top pitch of *Eagle Cracks* trending right to finish up twin cracks.

** **Double Bogey**   36 m   E1   1981

A once popular route (though now rather dirty) starting at the obvious corner 6 metres up to the right of *Eagle Cracks*.

1   24 m (5b). Climb the corner for 8 metres, then move right and up a flake crack onto a large block. Move up the steep wall, slightly leftwards, to reach a thin crack and follow this, passing a small square overhang, to the terrace.

2   12 m. Finish up the thin crack in the slab left of the easy corner to the top.

** **Pitch and Putt**   36 m   E2   1981

A good route up the steep wall. Start 4 metres up to the right of the corner of *Double Bogey*.

1   24 m (5c). Start easily up a short wall and slab above to where the angle steepens. Move up to a thin crack and climb this and the twin cracks above to the terrace.

2   12 m (5b). Move right a couple of metres and climb a wall to reach a thin crack in a rib. Finish up this, moving right into a scoop at the top.

* **Fear and Loathing**   36 m   E4   1983

Takes the steep wall immediately right of *Pitch and Putt*. Start 6 metres up the terrace above *Pitch and Putt* at a thin crack.

1   18 m (6a). Climb the crack to a large handhold. Swing right on flakes and pull up to a small spike runner. Go up and left to a thin crack and pull round the overhang on the right. Pull up leftwards onto the terrace.

2   18 m (5b). The thin corner crack, 5 metres to the right, is followed past a small triangular overhang. Pull out at the top onto easier rock which is followed to the top.

Hole in Yan   22 m   E4   1989

A route which has a poorly protected entry. Start at the slanting slab at the right-hand end of the bilberry terrace, right of *Fear and Loathing*.

1   12 m (6a). Step onto the slab to fix protection in the crack on the main wall. Climb leftwards across the wall using a sloping edge and reach up for a good hold which is used to gain the ledge above. Continue to a second ledge (small nuts and spike) and climb directly past a large spike and up a short crack to the grass terrace.

2   10 m (5c). Ascend the vague rounded rib, 4 metres left of the top groove of *Fear and Loathing*, to a small spike. Continue slightly rightwards to gain a thin crack in the nose. Climb this awkwardly.

Eagle Crag   (277 122)   Alt. 500 m   East North East Facing

The main crag belies its image from Stonethwaite by its rectangular structure. A series of ledges divides the main cliff, which is about 50 metres high, from some very steep and unpleasant vegetated rock below.

At the right-hand end of the crag there is a prominent rib before a north-facing side wall ends in an area of deep unsavoury gullies. The most prominent feature of the main cliff is the overhanging corner-crack high on its right side; this is *Post Mortem*. To the left of this, green streaked walls are cut by a prominent south-east-facing corner which ends half-way up the crag; this is *The Cleft Direct*. The steep wall to its left is more complex. Towards its left side, a series of ledges cuts into the crag between steep walls. These ledges become more pronounced towards the end, giving the cliff a less impressive appearance.

The rock is generally good, though it tends to be rather green and lichenous and can be rather slow to dry after rain.

The routes are described from left to right.

High on the left-hand end of the crag, above the point of arrival, is a steep, smooth back wall to a large square corner, above a short slab. This is reached by 50 metres of grassy scrambling from the bottom left corner of the main crag or by climbing up rightwards from the descent gully on the left. Either approach requires great care.

Dumbo Cracks   52 m   VS   1971
Takes the cracks up the left side of the slab and back wall.
1   16 m (4c). Climb the deceptive crack to where it steepens. Move up strenuously or go through the crack to a giant perched block.
2   36 m (4b). Move left to a dead tree. Go up to the right along a ramp to the foot of the steep crack which is followed to the top.

☆☆ **The Ego Has Landed**   20 m   E8   {F7b+}   ?   2000
An extremely serious undertaking up the obvious blank wall between *Dumbo Cracks* and *Flying Circus*. Start from the narrow ledge at the top of pitch 1 of *Flying Circus*, best gained by abseil. A lone peg at 3 metres indicates the line of the route – this is the only protection.
   (6b). Make hard moves past the peg and continue with a sustained series of 6b moves to the top. Entering the shallow groove at two-thirds height is the crux.
(N.B. Informed opinion is that E9, 6c may be nearer the mark.)

EAGLE CRAG.

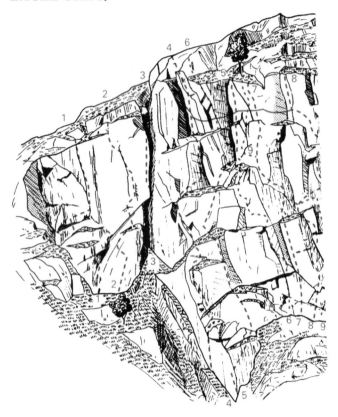

1	Dumbo Cracks	VS
2	Flying Circus	E5
3	Trapeze	VS
4	The Sprogg	HVS
5	The Great Stair	MVS
6	The Squawk	E2
7	Where Eagles Dare	E2
8	Verdict	E4
9	Falconer's Crack	VS
10	Daedalus	E3

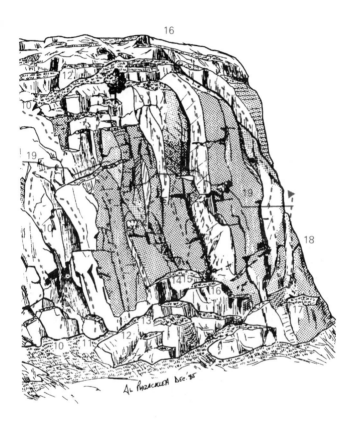

AL PHIZACKLEA DEC. '85

11	The Cleft Direct	E3
12	Icarus Direct	E2
13	Final Diagnosis	E3
14	Green Wall	VS
15	Dead on Arrival	E5
16	Post Mortem	E3
17	Inquest Direct	E2
18	Necroscopy	E2
19	Girdle Traverse	HVS

★★ **Flying Circus**   40 m   E5   1981
Fine bold climbing up the impending grey wall between *Dumbo Cracks* and *Trapeze*. Start at the foot of a slab.
1   22 m (5b). Climb the right-hand side of the slab, move left a metre or so and up a green crack, rightwards, to a good ledge. Pull up left over a slight bulge, then up to a narrow ledge and poor belay.
2   18 m (6b). Follow the thin left-trending crack and finish on the left.

Trapeze   30 m   VS   1959
Takes the dirty cleft up the right side of the wall where it abuts the main cliff. Scramble up to a ledge below the crack.
      (4c). 6 metres of steep grassy climbing lead to an overhang. The next 5 metres are overcome by strenuous laybacking. Enter and climb the cleft to a chockstone. Swing out left to escape.

At the southern end of the main crag a short rake ascends from left to right giving easy access to ledges below the crag. The next climb starts from the rake.

★★ **The Sprogg**   78 m   HVS   1965
This climb gives some varied pitches which are quite sustained. Start 10 metres up the rake below a small ash tree.
1   30 m (4c). Go easily up leftwards to an ash tree at 12 metres. Climb a short steep crack on the right, then up to a large grass ledge. Ascend the gangway-type grooves on the left and pull out right at the top. Thread belay low on the left arête behind the good ledge above.
2   15 m (5a). Move round the corner on the left, climb the steep grooves and continue to a large ledge.
3   13 m (4c). Climb up a groove on the right, past a loose block. Follow the groove on the left to a ledge.
4   20 m (5a). A few delicate moves gain a fine steep crack which is followed to the top.

Opposite: Rick Richardson on **Falconer's Crack** (VS), Eagle Crag
                                                        Nick Wharton
Overleaf: **Autopsy** (E1) – a great little route tucked away to the side of Eagle Crag. Chris King and Christine Kenyon enjoy the view; Al Davis enjoys the climb   *Ron Kenyon*

★★ **The Great Stair** 77 m MVS 1946

A series of short, awkward pitches of similar character to *The Sprogg* but somewhat easier. Start as for *The Sprogg*.

1 15 m (4b). Climb the wall, past an ash tree, to a ledge at 3 metres. Go straight up for a metre or so, then move diagonally right up a gangway to a small ledge.
2 10 m (4a). Climb diagonally left up a thin crack to a big grass ledge.
3 16 m (4b). The steep wall is climbed on small holds to a ledge. The short upper wall leads to a grass terrace with thread belay on the left arête.
4 16 m (4c). Climb up rightwards to the foot of a fine chimney.
5 20 m. Interesting, but straightforward climbing leads to the top.

★ **Needless Sports** 54 m E1 1991

Start 3 metres left of *The Squawk* at a ragged crack leading up to the right-hand end of a roof.

1 15 m (5a). Climb the crack to a ledge and belay on the right. Bold.
2 16 m (5b). Step down left and traverse delicately left along the lip of the roof to a slab. Move up right onto a small ledge (junction with *The Squawk*). Climb the wall above directly to a large niche and exit via its right rib to a belay at the foot of the chimney that forms the final pitch of *The Great Stair*.
3 23 m (5b). Climb awkwardly up the cracked wall to the left of the chimney to a good jug about a metre and a half from the top of the crag. Traverse left to the arête and finish up the groove above.

★★ **The Squawk** 54 m E2 1965/1978

A sustained route through the green walls right of *The Great Stair*, finishing up a prominent V-groove just left of its final chimney pitch. Start at the left-hand end of the ledge below the wall at a large flake.

1 15 m (5b). From the flake, ascend the hollow flakes and the thin crack above the small overhang. Enter the corner (peg runner) and go up this to a ledge and peg belay.
2 16 m (5a). From the left-hand end of the ledge climb a corner for 2 metres then move left to a ledge and quartz break. Traverse right and go up just left of *Falconer's Crack*.

Previous Page: Al Hewison gets to grips with **Supermodel** (E1), Fat Charlie's Buttress   *Gary Baum*
Opposite: **Little Corner** (E1), big muscles – Martin Armitage and Tessa Kennedy climbing at Upper Heron Crag   *Ron Kenyon*

3   23 m (5b). Move left round a corner and up doubtful blocks to a steep groove which is followed to the top.

★★★ Where Eagles Dare   51 m   E2   1975
A superb and soaring classic which takes the steep groove immediately right of *The Squawk*. Start as for *The Squawk*.
1   15 m (5c). Step right, then climb the jamming crack and the absorbing groove above moving up right to belay in the corner.
2   36 m (5b). Start up the obvious scoop, then go left to a thin crack. Pull up and swing left round a rib on good holds to gain a ledge. Follow the rib, steeply, for 5 metres to a welcome peg runner. Step right, and continue up to a ledge below the final rib of *Falconer's Crack*, which is followed to the top.

Fall of Eagles   47 m   E5   1978
Takes the big groove right of *Where Eagles Dare* finishing with a serious pitch up the wall left of *Verdict*.
1   15 m (5c). Follow pitch 1 of *Where Eagles Dare*, to belay in the corner.
2   22 m (5c). Move left and climb the big groove to a ledge at the base of a large detached flake. Climb the right side of this, then move up onto the grass ledge above and belay below the top corner of *Verdict*.
3   10 m (6b). Move to the left end of the ledge and climb the wall on very small holds to a tiny spike below a thin crack. A long reach gains the crack, then continue up easy slabs above to the top.

★★ Guns of Navarone   50 m   E6   {F7b+}   2000
An explosive route with a bold and committing first pitch up the groove that *Verdict* quits, followed by a strenuous second pitch.
1   16 m (6b). Climb the groove as for *Verdict*, but continue up the groove to gain a resting place. Further hard moves up and slightly left gain a ledge. Move up to the next ledge and an excellent peg belay. All very serious with minimal protection: on the only ascent to date a skyhook runner was used.
2   20 m (6c). Gain the arête on the right using a hidden hold in the groove, and climb the pocketed wall direct to a ledge and belay (as for *Verdict*). An excellent pitch.
3   14 m (5c). Step down and traverse right on good holds until a move can be made to jugs. Follow these rightwards to a ledge and follow the left-hand groove to the top.

★★★ Verdict   49 m   E4   1975/1976

A very good route giving steep and technical climbing with a rather serious finish up a blank groove which is easier for the tall climber. Start 5 metres right of *The Squawk* below a corner groove.

1   15 m (5b). Climb the groove to a jammed block overhang. Pull up and hand-traverse right to a ledge. Climb the crack on the left and continue over blocks to a belay in the corner at the top of pitch 2 of *Falconer's Crack*.

2   24 m (5c). Cross the wall on the right on pockets. Move up into a groove and climb it past an overhang to a small cave. Mantelshelf onto the grassy ledge on the left below the final corner.

3   10 m (6a). Enter the groove from the left and climb it (small wire runners) until a superb jug is reached just below the top. Easier climbing to finish.

★★ Falconer's Crack   58 m   VS   1946

A classic route, alternating strenuous crack and delicate and quite bold face climbing. Start at a good crack on a ledge, 5 metres right of *Verdict* and 5 metres left of the corner of *The Cleft Direct*.

1   18 m (5a). Climb the crack, passing an awkward bulge, to a ledge. Continue up the groove above, past a small sapling, and move left to belay in a corner.

2   18 m (4c). Move 5 metres left to a rib, teeter up the wall beyond and then easier ledges lead left to a belay below the chimney of *The Great Stair*.

3   22 m (4b). Move to the rib right of the chimney and climb it pleasantly to the top.

★★★ Daedalus   48 m   E3   1965

The awesome undercut chimney, then the gangway and pinkish wall above, between *Falconer's Crack* and *The Cleft* are taken by this fine strenuous climb. Start 2 metres right of *Falconer's Crack* at a short corner.

1   30 m (5c). Climb up the corner to a ledge. Gain and climb the chimney and gangway above to a tree stump. Pull over a bulge into a steep groove (peg runner). Climb this and the wall above, moving right to good holds to finish diagonally rightwards to a triangular ledge.

2   18 m (5b). Step left and climb the steep wall, leftwards, to a small ledge below a faint groove which is followed to the top.

Animotion 48 m E2   1985
Takes the wall between *Daedalus* and *The Cleft Direct*. Start as for *Daedalus*.
1   12 m (5a). Climb up to below the chimney, then rightwards to a large ledge.
2   18 m (5c). Step down left onto the wall, climb it on good holds and pull out left onto a slab. Move back right to gain a small ledge on *The Cleft Direct*. Continue straight up to easier ground and then move right to belay as for *Daedalus*.
3   18 m (5b). Pitch 2 of *Daedalus*.

★★★ **The Cleft Direct** 45 m E3   1959/1975
A good strenuous route up the obvious steep groove in the centre of the crag. Start at the foot of the steep corner below the groove, some 2 metres right of *Daedalus*.
1   12 m (5c). Climb the strenuous corner crack to a large ledge.
2   15 m (5c). Ascend the corner until moves can be made out left to a sloping ledge and large flake. Continue up the groove above, then move rightwards to a ledge at the top of pitch 1 of *Daedalus*.
3   18 m (5b). Pitch 2 of *Daedalus* to the top.

The next routes are to be found to the right of the subsidiary buttress on the right of *The Cleft Direct*.

★★★ **The Restraint of Beasts** 52 m E5   2000
An outstanding route, with good protection where it matters, tackling the prominent arête between *Cleft Direct* and *Icarus*. Start at an obvious arête about 4 metres right of *Cleft Direct* and 2 metres left of *Icarus*.
1   16 m (6b). Make precarious moves up the shallow groove (small blue Alien, Rock 2) to gain an obvious fin. Layback boldly up this to a protruding block (peg). Continue to a ledge and belay as for *Cleft Direct*.
2   36 m (5c). Gain the diagonal break running rightwards to the arête and pull steeply up this on good holds (well protected) – possible spike and nut belay as for *Icarus Direct*. Continue more easily to finish up the fine grooved arête of *Icarus Direct*.

Icarus 55 m HVS   1965
A good steep crack gives access to a rounded smooth buttress above, which provides a rather devious second pitch. Start at the steep crack in the left side of the lower wall.
1   15 m (5b). Climb the crack to a ledge. Belay as for *The Cleft Direct*.

2   20 m (5a). From the right extremity of the ledge, mantelshelf onto
    a ledge on the face. Cross to a ledge and continue rightwards to
    a shallow corner. Climb this over an overhang. Move left and up
    to belay as for *The Cleft Direct*.
3   20 m (4c). A mossy scoop leads leftwards to a ledge. Finish up
    the corner above.

★★ Icarus Direct   50 m   E2   1984

A better and more logical continuation to the good first pitch of
Icarus.
1   30 m (5b). Follow *Icarus* to the mantelshelf on pitch 2. Continue
    direct to a short steep crack. Layback moves up this lead to large
    holds above. Go easily up to a grass ledge and spike belay.
2   20 m (5c). Climb the grooved arête above directly to good holds.
    Swing rightwards onto a ledge, then up and left onto another
    ledge. Go easily up to the top.

★ Final Diagnosis   48 m   E3   1981

Good, steep and varied climbing which is quite strenuous. Start 3
metres right of *Icarus* below a slim groove/crack.
1   24 m (5c). Climb the groove/crack to ledges and move right to a
    small tree on *Green Wall*. Move up the short corner crack above
    to a sloping ledge on the right. Step up right to belay in a corner
    below a thin overhanging crack.
2   24 m (6a). Climb up leftwards to a downward-pointing spike and
    up the crack above to a large ledge. Move up the short corner
    above to another ledge. Move up right into a shallow groove
    which leads to the top.

Green Wall   47 m   VS   1955

A disappointing climb after pitch 1. Start 6 metres right of *Final
Diagnosis* on a large green platform, reached by scrambling up
rightwards from *Icarus*.
1   24 m (4c). Climb a groove past a tree to a second tree on a ledge.
    Ascend the groove above to a sloping ledge. Step left and climb
    a big overhanging crack to a good stance.
2   8 m. Move easily left to a grass ledge.
3   15 m. Finish straight up to the top of the crag.

★★ Dead on Arrival   46 m   E5   1981

A tremendous steep route giving sustained, well protected climbing
in good positions. Start just right of *Green Wall*, at some large blocks
below a short groove.

1   22 m (5c). Climb the short groove and wall on the right to reach good holds. Move up the thin crack on the left until a pull up left can be made onto a ledge above an overhang. Go easily up to the highest ledge and belay at the top of pitch 1 of *Final Diagnosis*.

2   14 m (6b). The thin overhanging crack above the belay is started on the right and followed to a sloping ledge.

3   10 m (5a). Climb up rightwards into a large open groove right of *Final Diagnosis*. Go up this, and a short groove on the left, to the top.

★ **Coroner's Crack**   42 m   E5   1981

A fine companion to *Dead on Arrival*. Pitch 2 is a very strenuous finger-wrenching crack, though unfortunately very close to *Post Mortem*.

1   24 m (5b). Climb up the short groove and wall on the right to good holds as for *Dead on Arrival*. Step right and climb the wall to the left-hand end of a small overhang. Go rightwards up a flake crack to a large ledge below pitch 2 of *Post Mortem*.

2   18 m (6b). Start off from a pedestal and climb a crack, left of *Post Mortem*, to good jams at a bulge. Climb up the very thin crack in the wall above to reach a good slot. Pull up right to finish up the final part of *Post Mortem*.

★★★ **Post Mortem**   42 m   E3   1956

A crack of unusual character provides the final decisive pitch. A classic of its type! Start on the grass ledges 3 metres right of *Green Wall*.

1   24 m (5a). A flake crack is followed diagonally rightwards to a dirty vegetated crack which leads directly to the ledge below the wide crack.

2   18 m (5c). Climb the crack over a bulge and continue to the top with less difficulty.

The next routes are at the right-hand end of the crag. These are best reached by descending rightwards from the top of the rake giving access to the crag and following the grass ledges to the gully at the right end of the crag. Scramble up this to a good grass ledge on the left.

★ **Inquest Direct**   54 m   E2   1977

An enjoyable route, taking the impressive groove near the right end of the crag. Start from the grass ledge below the groove.

1   36 m (5c). Climb a short crack to a niche. Pull over its roof into
    the steep crack above, which is followed to a resting place on
    The Girdle Traverse. Step right, move up to the overhang and
    make some hard moves into the steep groove on the right. Climb
    this past a tall spike and exit right at the top to a stance.
2   18 m (4b). Go up easily from the right end of the ledge until it
    is possible to move left for a metre or so. Continue to the top by
    a wide crack and easier ground.

Variation **Inquest** Original Start VS   1965
    (4c). Pitch 1 followed the broken rock below and right of *Post
    Mortem* to belay at its start. It then followed *Post Mortem* to the
    Girdle and reversed this to join the route as now described, below
    the overhang.

★ **Necroscopy** 45 m E2   1981
An eliminate up the slim pillar between *Inquest Direct* and *Postern
Groove* giving pleasant climbing. Start as for *Inquest Direct*.
    (5b). Climb a short crack then move up and right to an obvious
    flake crack in the nose. Follow the crack to a good ledge on the
    Girdle. Take the right edge of a white wall to gain a slim
    groove/crack leading to the belay ledge of *Inquest Direct*. Finish
    directly up the thin crack and rib above to the top.

★ **Postern Groove** 38 m VS   1960
Takes the groove at the left side of the north-facing wall at the
right-hand side of the crag. Rather vegetated. Start 8 metres right of
Inquest Direct at the first obvious groove.
1   16 m (4b). Climb the left side of the groove to a spike belay on
    the ledge on the right.
2   22 m (4c). The overhanging crack above is climbed to a ledge on
    the left. Step right and climb the overhang above using a crack
    on its left and continue to the top.

The Seams 41 m VS   1970
The obvious mossy groove right of *Postern Groove*.
1   10 m. Climb the groove to a ledge.
2   16 m (4b). Climb the groove above and move left to a stance.
3   15 m (4c). Follow the crack through the bulges, avoiding a loose
    flake on the first bulge.

★★★ **Autopsy** 30 m E1   1975
A hidden gem up the rib left of *Postern Gate*. Start on a ledge with
an ash tree below a 'Damoclean Flake', 3 metres left of *Postern Gate*.

(5b). Gain and climb the left side of the flake. At its top, move left round the rib to below a shallow groove, which is climbed until a hand-traverse can be made onto the arête. An awkward move up leads to easier climbing and the top.

★ **Postern Gate**   42 m   VS   1946
The right-hand side of the wall ends at a steep 10 metre chimney. Start at a corner 3 metres left of this and climb the wall and corner/chimney above.
1   12 m (4a). Climb the wall to a grass ledge on the left of a large silver birch.
2   30 m (4c). Step right and enter the chimney. This is followed, passing two bulges on the left wall, until a pull up leads to the upper chimney, which is followed more easily to the top.

★★ **Postern Rib**   42 m   VS   1981
Takes the rib on the right of *Postern Gate*. A good little route with immaculate rock on pitch 2.
1   12 m (4a). Pitch 1 of *Postern Gate*.
2   30 m (4c). Traverse right past a large silver birch to a ledge on the rib. Follow the rib in a fine position to the top.

★ **Girdle Traverse**   128 m   HVS   1959
A fine expedition girdling the crag from right to left. Start as for *Postern Groove*.
1   15 m (4b). Climb the left side of the groove to a spike belay on the ledge on the left (pitch 1 of *Postern Groove*).
2   22 m (5b). Move left onto a lower ledge and from the arête on the left traverse a steep open groove. Continue left, stepping across a steep open corner, towards a small tree in a groove above on the left. Move up this to belay below the corner of *Post Mortem*.
3   15 m (4c). Delicate moves lead left from the ledge for about 6 metres to a good ledge. Continue left to belay above some large blocks at the end of pitch 1 of *Green Wall*.
4   8 m. Move left and up to a grass ledge (pitch 2 of *Green Wall*).
5   18 m (5a). A very steep traverse left is made on good holds to a small cave. Higher holds and a mantelshelf lead to a good ledge on the left. Belay below the top pitch of *Verdict*.
6   12 m (4c). Traverse left to a steep rib and descend to belay below the large chimney of pitch 5 of *The Great Stair*.
7   18 m (4c). Traverse left and slightly downwards, past the steep ramp-like groove on the top pitch of *The Squawk*, until a short ascent leads to a grassy bower.

8   20 m (5a). Make a few delicate moves up a wall and climb the crack to the top (last pitch of *The Sprogg*).

To the right of the main crag several gully climbs of Moderate to Severe standard have been climbed. They do not merit detailed description. Briefly they are as follows:-

'D' Gully (1910). The gully and chimney right of *Postern Gate*.
'C' Gully (1990). The gully with a large roof – Two pitch climb on very juggy rock, passing the roof on the left and finishing up the groove left of the chimney.
'B' Gully (1910). The short gully to the right over wedged blocks and chimney above.
'A' Gully (1910). The longest gully, climbed in five pitches.

Bleak How   (273 125)   Alt. 270 m   North West Facing

This crag is situated a hundred metres up the hillside above the footbridge crossing the lower reaches of Langstrath Beck. The best approach is to bypass the lower rock and scrub on the left and follow a path rightwards below the crag.

Bleak How was excavated out of obscurity in 1984. It is a justifiably popular crag for the middle grade climber with a few harder routes in the steeper central section and on the far right. Good rock and a lovely outlook add to its attraction. Descend to the left or by abseil.

Towards the left-hand end of the main slab, 6 metres from the corner, there is a small roof near the base of the slab. The first route starts at a short rib 10 metres left of this point.

Mowgli   40 m   VS   1986
Start at the short rib.
     (4c). Climb the rib, starting on the right and making an awkward move left before moving right to a bilberry ledge. Climb the slab above.

The next two routes start at the foot of the short wall down to the left of the small roof.

★ BX Breakdown   40 m   E1   1994
     (5b). Climb the wall and slab to the right-hand end of the vegetated ledge. Traverse 1 metre left then climb up the wall to a horizontal break. Traverse 2 metres left and then climb the wall

above via the vague crackline to a ledge. From the right end of
the ledge climb the narrow slab above and finish on a stance
shared with *Brush Off*.

★★ **Rub Off**   40 m   HVS   1984
   (5a). Climb the steep wall and slab to gain the right-hand end of
   the vegetated ledge. Climb the thin crack above and swing left to
   a small niche. Continue direct past a cleaned ledge to join *Brush
   Off* at a big ledge and finish as for that climb.

★★ **Brush Off**   35 m   HVS   1984
   A featureless but extremely good route requiring a bold approach.
   Start just right of the small roof.
   (4c). Climb the slabs until forced left at 8 metres to a shallow
   triangular pocket. Move back right, away from the line of *Rub
   Off*, then go directly up to a ledge. Finish up the short wall above.

The next two eliminate routes fight to find an independent line up
the slab between *Brush Off* and *Footloose*. Both fail to do so.

Pop Goes the Asteroid   35 m   E2   1985
Start just right of *Brush Off*.
   (5a). Climb directly up the slab, over two tiny overlaps, to better
   holds. Move right and up, passing the right end of a vegetated
   ledge, to finish as for *Footloose*.

Seconds Out   35 m   HVS   1985
Start 2 metres right of *Brush Off* at a thin crack.
   (5a). Climb the crack to an overlap. Step left and pull over on
   good holds. Climb more easily (trying to keep left of *Footloose*)
   towards the vegetated ledge above. Pass the right end of this and
   finish as for *Footloose*.

Footloose   35 m   HVS   1984
A difficult start leads to easy climbing above. Start in the corner on
the right of the slabs.
   (5a). Bridge up the black corner to reach holds up on the left.
   Pull up and continue more easily to a blank groove below a grass
   ledge on the right. Step left and climb the wall to a tree belay.

★★ **Fancy Free**   30 m   E1   1984
A striking route up the curving arête right of the slabs. Start below
the right-hand side.

BLEAK HOW

A. PHEACKLER FEB '86

1	Brush Off	HVS	6	Boston Strangler	E4
2	Footloose	HVS	7	Bleak How Buttress	E2
3	Fancy Free	E1	8	The Reiver	HVS
4	Steel Pulse	E3	9	Fun Run	S
5	Breathless	E3	10	Front Runner	E1

(5a). Climb the arête, with a short deviation to the left at half height, to a small overhang. Pull over on good holds, then follow the edge of a narrow white slab up rightwards to a tree belay.

Steel Pulse 30 m E3   1984

A pulsating climb starting just right of *Fancy Free*.

(5c). Climb the slab directly to a small groove below an overhang. Traverse right to a steep corner. Bridge up to a good hold in the crack at its top. Pull up onto the left wall to some undercuts, then go up right to a good thread. Climb steeply up left on good holds to finish up the slab on *Fancy Free*.

★★ Breathless 30 m E3   1984

Fine steep climbing up the hanging groove in the back right-hand side of the central bay with initial protection where it counts. It starts at a large block below the centre of the bay.

(6a). Climb a wall and grooves above to an overhang. Pull over and ascend the groove until it steepens. Swing right and pull up onto a small ledge. Easier climbing leads to a tree belay.

Boston Strangler 28 m E4   1984
A problematic climb up the overhanging groove, just right of *Breathless*.

(6b). Follow *Breathless* for 3 metres then step right onto a grassy ledge. Climb the groove above to an overhang. A difficult move gains the groove above. Swing right onto the arête and continue up the wall above to a tree belay.

★★ **The Boj Eliminate** 36 m HVS   1985/1999
Start just to the left of the *Oval Slab* of *Bleak How Buttress* at a short corner behind some trees. This is just right of the gearing up boulder.

(5a). Climb the corner and go up to a good spike at the top left of the *Oval Slab*. Climb the groove above (as for *Bleak How Buttress*) but, instead of swinging out left, keep moving up rightwards to pull up onto a large slab in the middle of the face. Climb the slab up leftwards, under the steep headwall, to some cracks (junction with *Bleak How Buttress*). Climb 2 metres up the cracks to a good runner and make an exposed traverse horizontally rightwards on superb quartzy holds to gain good holds near the top of *The Reiver*. Step back left and climb flakes leftwards to the final break. Finish either rightwards or leftwards along the break.

Variation **Boj Direct** E1   1985
From the middle slab, climb boldly up the steep headwall direct to the quartzy holds.

★★★ **Bleak How Buttress** 36 m E2   1983
A first class route up the left-hand side of the main buttress. Start at the lowest point of the buttress below the *Oval Slab*.

(5c). A short groove gives access to the *Oval Slab*. Climb precariously up and leftwards to a spike runner at its top. Start up a short groove until a swing left can be made on a huge jug. Mantelshelf onto this and follow a series of easier grooves above to a tree belay.

★★★ **The Reiver** 36 m HVS   1984
A compelling climb taking the right-hand side of the main buttress. Interesting throughout.

(5a). Follow *Bleak How Buttress* for 6 metres. Step right and climb a rib and reddish wall to a ledge. Where the wall steepens climb slightly leftwards on good holds, then go directly to the top.

Fun Run   30 m   S   1984
Takes the slabs on the right side of the crag. It starts well but deteriorates near the top. Start below the centre of the slabs at a left slanting crack.

Follow the crack and go up to a tree. Move right over an overlap and climb up leftwards until a move left round a rib, and a further step left, gain a groove which is followed to the top.

★★ Front Runner   30 m   E1   1984
Takes the centre of the slabs. Easy except for a short section near the top which is rather bold. Start as for *Fun Run*.

(5a). Go straight up the centre of the slab, over an overlap and up to a steep wall. Move left and pull onto a ledge on the rib on the right. Gain a jug on the wall above and move right onto the arête which is followed to the top. Belay well back.

About 40 metres right of *Front Runner* is a very obvious, smooth, left-leaning slab with a groove on its right-hand side.

Psyched Out   20 m   E3   1997
Start at the bottom right-hand side of the slab.

(5b). Step onto the slab and traverse left to its centre. Climb straight up to the top of the groove and then trend left to a small tree belay.

★ Bleak How Eliminate   20 m   E5   1995
(6a). Climb the groove with difficulty, then move out right and climb the headwall above. The difficulty eases as the protection becomes more sparse.

Upper Left Buttress

This is the small buttress just above the descent path on the left of the main buttress.

First Footing   20 m   MVS   1988
Start at the foot of the leftward-slanting ramp.

(4c). Climb the ramp past the overlaps, then step right and up into a groove. Follow this to the top, finishing as for *Manuel*.

★ Amistad Con El Diablo 20 m E2   1986
Not as bad as the name implies! Start as for *First Footing*.
>   (5c). Overcome the overhung base and ascend rightwards to an
>   overlap. Surmount this with difficulty and climb up precariously
>   to an obvious thin crack. Follow this to the top.

Dago 20 m VS   1986
Start below small ledges, 2 metres to the right of the left-slanting
ramp.
>   (5a). Gain the ledges and climb the wall above to a shallow
>   groove. Climb this and the short bulge to finish.

Manuel 25 m VS   1987
Start 2 metres right of *Dago* at two distinct vertical gouges on the
wall.
>   (4b). Climb easily up to a junction with *Dago*, then move
>   diagonally left above an overlap to the left-hand skyline rib.
>   Finish up this.

Basil 25 m E1   1997
>   (5b). Start as for *Manuel*. Climb straight up to the left-hand end
>   of the higher overlap. Make a delicate move up and right into a
>   vague scoop and finish straight up.

Catching Up 25 m E1 ?   1995
>   (5b). Start up a crack on the right at a finger flake. Follow straight
>   over the overlap and the obvious crack up and leftwards to a steep
>   crack in the top bulge.

Fat Charlie's Buttress (272 124) Alt. 100 m.   West Facing

A small crag with a number of short but worthwhile routes on
excellent rock. It is just up the valley from *Bleak How*. After crossing
the footbridge, follow the riverside path until it passes through a gate.
The buttress is now 50 metres up the slope to the left and opposite
a large solitary fir tree. There is a mossy slab on the left of the crag
and a bulging undercut wall to the right.

★ Myth of Fingerprints 15 m S   1988
>   Climb the curving slabby arête on the left-hand side of the
>   buttress in a fine, delicate situation.

★★ Supermodel   15 m   E1   1996
   Thin!
      (5b). Start 2 metres right of the fence at a scoop. Climb up the
      left side of this and straight up and slightly left, avoiding the
      option of the easy finish, to end up on top of the arête.

Blubber   13 m   HVS   1996
      (4c). Start 2 metres right of *Supermodel* and climb straight up
      following a vague crack to finish below the fence.

Islay Wait   13 m   MS   1996
      Start 2 metres right of *Blubber*. Go up to below a small overlap
      then move up and diagonally left using parallel cracks. Finish as
      for *Blubber*.

★ Phantom Menace   13 m   HVS   1999
   Start on the grass ledge 2 metres right of the small overlap of *Islay
   Wait*.
      (5a). Climb up to gain the rightward-leaning diagonal crack at
      two-thirds height. Follow this to a monster jug finish.

★ Reassuringly Stocky   11 m   E1   1996
      (5c). Start 2 metres right of *Phantom Menace*. Climb the
      enjoyable slab to hard finishing moves.

Wobbly Bits   15 m   VS   1997
   Start 2 metres left of *Cholesterol Corner* at an undercut groove.
   (Friend 2.5 handy for crux.)
      (4c). Climb up and step right into the groove which leads to a
      break. Follow this left, under a boss, to the left end of a long
      grass ledge. Step up and left to a series of holds leading back
      rightwards. Make a hard move up and then either move
      rightwards to a ledge and finish via bulges, or climb directly up
      the wall above.

★★ Cholesterol Corner   12 m   E1   1996
   A good route. On the right-hand side of the crag is a rounded
   undercut buttress. Four metres in from the right edge is a short
   undercut corner.
      (5b). Climb the corner and pull out onto a rounded ledge. Move
      up to gain good holds and good (hidden) protection at the base
      of a depression. A hard move leads to better holds and the top.

★ **Cellulite** 10 m E2   2000

Takes the arête to the right of *Cholestrol Corner*.

(6a). Start just right of the arête and make strenuous moves up the undercut wall leading to better holds. Move left to the arête and continue more easily to the top.

Heron Crag (274 121) Alt. 360 m   West Facing

This crag is situated on the east side of Langstrath above and to the right of *Bleak How*. Take the footpath from Stonethwaite camp site. Cross the footbridge across Langstrath Beck and follow the good track south until below the crag. Now head directly and steeply up the fellside. The rock is generally of good quality but the cliff is broken into steps with large ledges in between. The best descent is on the left and is reached by traversing left below the *Upper Tier*. Alternatively scramble upwards for 30 metres from the terraces at the top of the climbs and traverse left across the top of the crag.

Blink 60 m VS   1973

Start 10 metres left of *Heron Crag Buttress*.

1   30 m. Climb a slabby wall and obvious mossy green groove behind a tree. Move right and climb a crack to a large heather ledge at the foot of an overhanging corner.
2   30 m. Climb the corner and a delicate slab on the left to the overhang. Move right to a small triangular ledge on the lip of the overhang. A short corner leads to easier rock to finish.

Simbolyn 72 m HVS   1973

Starts as for *Blink*, and then takes the mossy crack to the right.

1   12 m. Follow pitch 1 of *Blink* to a tree belay on the left.
2   24 m. Climb the wall and the obvious crack above, which widens into a corner. Scramble to the foot of three obvious grooves.
3   36 m. Climb the central groove and continue up the corner on the right to a block. Move left, gain a ledge and continue to the top.

★ **Heron Crag Buttress** 103 m S   1940

A rather broken and, sadly, very overgrown route, taking the ribs to the left of *Heron Crag Gully*. Start to the left of and below the *Gully*.

1   35 m. Climb the nose to gain a ledge. Continue up past a tree to belay near the *Gully*.
2   20 m. Move left and ascend the nose to a big heather ledge.

3   30 m. Go down right a couple of metres and ascend the ridge to a large flake (this point can be reached directly). Continue to a small slab and climb a short groove to a ledge on the right. Climb the awkward wall above to reach a ledge on the left.
4   18 m. Continue up the ridge, moving right off the crest to follow a crack to the top.

Heron Crag Gully   80 m   MS   1940
This is the vegetated gully just right of the centre of the crag. It is started up a steep corner crack (often wet or even a waterfall). A fin of rock at half height is avoided on the left.

Pinnacle Route   77 m   VD   1939
This climb starts 10 metres right of the *Gully* on the right of a pinnacle.
1   28 m. Climb a groove to a chimney behind the pinnacle. The top of the pinnacle can be gained, if wished, either from the chimney or the arête on its edge. Move left from the pinnacle onto a slab and continue up the groove above to a ledge in the *Gully*. Tree belay above.
2   21 m. Scramble up ledges on the right and climb a short gully to a large spike at 12 metres. Climb the corner above to gain a ledge on the left.
3   28 m. Climb the corner and wall above to an awkward landing. Move left along a ledge and climb a shallow corner and wall above to finish.

Damnation Groove (VS 1952) is a most unpleasant variation taking a line above and left of pitch 2 of *Pinnacle Route*.

Introductory Route   85 m   D   1944
Good climbing at the start which unfortunately deteriorates higher up. Start at a holly tree 10 metres right of *Pinnacle Route*.
1   18 m. Either climb the groove to the left of the holly, or the chimney to its right. Continue to below a right angled chimney. Climb the chimney using ledges on the left.
2   10 m. Traverse right to a ledge below a V-groove.
3   15 m. Climb the groove, moving up rightwards to a ledge. Move left and up to a grassy heather ledge.
4   18 m. Scramble up left and climb the nose.
5   24 m. Continue up the rocky ridge and gully on the right to the top.

Upper Heron Crag   (275 122)   Alt. 440 m

North West
Facing

A short steep wall of good quality rock, situated above and left of *Heron Crag* and just below and right of the skyline crag – *Higher Heron Crag*.

This area of rock is totally out of character with the remainder of the cliff and gives a concentration of good outcrop type climbs which are far harder than the other routes on *Heron Crag*.

The superb situation, especially in the evening sun, and the quality of the climbs make the walk up well worthwhile.

From the footbridge across Langstrath Beck follow the track south and then hike up very steeply towards the crag. Alternatively, from the footbridge, follow the track round into Greenup Ghyll and take a path by the intake wall that leads to a shoulder to the right of *Eagle Crag* and then on to *Upper* and *Higher Heron*.

A pleasant grassy ledge extends along the bottom of the crag from which the routes begin.

Descend to either the right or left of the buttress. Routes are described left to right.

★★ **Traverse of the Frogs**   30 m   E2   1996
An extremely strenuous pitch with excellent protection. Start at the very left-hand end of the crag where it is only 3 metres high.
1   15   m   (5b).   Climb   a   short   crack   to   gain   the   obvious rightward-slanting hand-traverse line and follow this to a belay at the bottom of the crack of *Heaven Knows I'm Miserable Now*!
2   15 m (5a). Finish up *Heaven Knows I'm Miserable Now*!

★★ **Heaven Knows I'm Miserable Now!**   22 m   E1   1984
The jagged rock on this route makes it easier than it looks. Start 8 metres from the left end of the crag.
(5b). Climb the left-hand groove and crack above to a ledge. Exit just left of a nose of rock at the top on the right.

★★ **Flamingo Fandango**   22 m   E1   1984
Starts 4 metres right of *Heaven Knows I'm Miserable Now*!
(5b). Climb a layback crack to a small ledge. Move up and left onto another ledge. Follow the flutings over a slight bulge to a ledge and finish up an overhanging crack in the nose above (or, more sensibly, skirt to the left of the nose).

★★ Big Foot   24 m   E2   1984

A reachy route starting 2 metres right of *Flamingo Fandango* at an obvious jam crack.

(5c). Climb the crack to a ledge. Go up to a jug, then up and left to a sinuous crack which is followed to a ledge. Finish up the nose on the left.

Little Nose   24 m   E2   1984

A pushy route up the *Central Wall*. Start 2 metres right of *Big Foot*.

(5b). Climb the shallow corner and the wall above to a hollow flake overlap. Stand on this, then move right to a good jug. Awkward moves gain the crack/groove above which is then followed more easily to the top.

★★ The Question   28 m   E2   1984

The obvious grooved arête in the centre of the crag.

(5c). Go up a short corner, then make an awkward move into the groove. Climb this and the wall above to the top.

★ Little Corner   28 m   E1   1984

Starts 10 metres right of *The Question* at a gangway slanting left into a corner.

(5b). Follow the gangway and awkward short corner to a ledge on the left. Go easily up left to the top.

★ Joie Pur   28 m   E2   1984

A deceptively steep climb up a loose, green crack above the start of *Little Corner*.

(5c). Gain the crack from the left and follow it until moves on the right enable a ledge on the left to be gained. Continue up the wall behind to a ledge. Climb a short wall above to the top.

★ Barefoot   28 m   E2   1984

A varied route starting 3 metres right of *Joie Pur* below a slightly slanting crack.

(5c). Go up a short wall to gain the crack which is followed, with interest, to a ledge on the right. Follow a crack rightwards to a ledge. Climb the pinnacle crack and groove above to a bilberry covered ledge. Finish up the short wall above.

★ Bilberry Topping   28 m   E2   1999

Start just to the right of *Barefoot*.

(5c). Climb the short wall to gain the slanting crackline. Follow the crack initially with difficulty, to where it eases. Move up rightwards to an open groove below a crackline in the upper wall. On the right is a ledge with a vital (!) block on it. Gain a good handhold to get established on the wall, overcome a small overlap and use the 'bilberry topping' to gain the large ledge above. Move left slightly and climb the obvious corner in the short wall above.

High Heron Crag

This is the conspicuous crag on the skyline above and left of the *Upper Tier* of *Heron Crag*. Approach as for *Upper Heron Crag*. Descend to the right.

Up the Khyber   25 m   HVS   1986
    Climb the steep groove near the centre of the crag.

Solar Toupee   30 m   VS   1986
    Start up the open groove just right of *Up The Khyber* and then pull up left onto the nose on good jugs. Go up steep ground to the top.

Sergeant Crag   (274 115)   Alt. 360 m   North West Facing

This prominent crag overlooks Langstrath. The main feature is the classic gully on its left. Descent should be made well to the left and involves a detour to avoid the slabby buttress to the left of the gully.

Acab   75 m   S   1957
    Climb the buttress left of *Sergeant Crag Gully* to a large sloping terrace. Climb the overhang above, or the crack on the left, and move right into the gully. Finish up the short crack on the left.

*** Sergeant Crag Gully   110 m   S   1893
A traditional gully climb of considerable merit. It is at its best in wet conditions and gives a good route in a hard winter. Start either by climbing the lower reaches of the gully or by scrambling up its left side to a steep corner, at the foot of the gully proper.
1   36 m. Climb the left wall, past a chockstone, and continue up the wall. Pass another chockstone on its right. Scramble up to the next chockstone.
2   8 m. Climb the left wall with interest (also possible on the right).
3   30m. Continue past another chockstone to below a further steepening.

4   36 m. Climb the right wall of the gully to avoid the chockstone and finish up easier ground above.

Bilko   37 m   E1   1989

A varied route on good rock taking the thin slanting crack in the wall about 5 metres right of *Sergeant Crag Gully*. Start on the grassy ledge just right of the start of the gully proper below a smooth V-groove. This is best reached by traversing in across the grass ledges on the left of the gully.

1   7 m (4c). A delightful pitch. Climb the right-hand of the twin grooves to gain a grass ledge below a fine slanting crack.
2   15 m (5b). Climb the thin crack with interest to a niche. Overcome the lip and climb up to a tree and grass ledge.
3   15 m (4a). Move 4 metres right along the ledge until it is possible to climb a groove in the wall above to gain another grassy ledge. Move right to the tree belay at the top of *Cruelty Unknown*.
    Either abseil from the tree or continue up easier rock to the top.

★ Cruelty Unknown   37 m   E3   1989

This deceptively steep route accepts the challenge of the obvious slanting crackline 10 metres to the right of *Sergeant Crag Gully*. Start to the right of *Bilko* below a slabby groove which leads to the crack.

1   7 m (4c). Climb the groove on superb rock to a belay where the wall steepens.
2   15 m (6a). Climb a short ramp on the right and gain a small ledge below the crack. Move up awkwardly to gain another ledge below a widening in the crack. Overcome this to gain another wide crack which leads (crux) to a short wall which is followed leftwards to a ledge.
3   15 m (5a). Go up easier rock rightwards to a short overlap and climb this to gain a grass ledge with a yew. Possible belay. Climb the wall behind the yew to gain good holds which lead to a grass ledge and a tree belay. Either continue up easier rock to the top or abseil from the tree.

The Redoubt   56 m   HVS   1967

This climb attacks the rounded buttress starting at a pinnacle 20 metres to the right of *Sergeant Crag Gully*.

1   16 m (4c). Climb the obvious ramp, rightwards, to poised blocks. Go rightwards to a niche and traverse back left under the overhang to a detached block.
2   40 m (5a). Traverse back right and ascend the short slabby groove to the right of the overhangs until a slab leads left between the roofs (peg runner) to a good crack above the stance. Climb this

to an eyrie. Climb the diagonal crack until a move left leads to a grass ledge. Slabs lead rightwards to a heather traverse. Either climb broken rocks to the summit of the crag or traverse left and abseil from a silver birch into the gully.

★ **Echoes of Zechariah**   40 m   E1   1993
This route weaves up the small overhanging ribs on the corner of the buttress between *The Redoubt* and *Superstar*. Start 25 metres right of *Redoubt* below an obvious detached flake, which is itself below an obvious crack with a faint crack going up right to a wider crack. The route takes the groove on its right finishing up the wider crack.
1   30 m (5b). Follow a ramp up rightwards to a point where an awkward move gains a slab between overlaps. Move left across the back of a groove. Surmount an overhang to gain the upper part of the groove. Continue with interest moving slightly left to gain the crack. Follow this to a stance.
2   10 m. Continue up easier rock to a grass ledge. Traverse left to the ledge overlooking *Cruelty Unknown*. Continue up easier rock to the top.

The following routes can be easily reached following grass ledges at a low level.

Superstar   60 m   MVS   1973
Start at the lowest point of the wall, below and to the left of *The Great Wall*.
1   18 m (4a). Climb a rib and then go leftwards to a small tree belay.
2   42 m (4b). Climb up left to a small cave below an overhang. Gain a flake on the left and move left to a ledge. Continue up the slab on the right and diagonal crack above.

Variation   **Zion**   36 m   VS   1975
2a   (4c). Traverse right to the curving corner then move back left under the overlap to a V-chimney. Climb this and the wall above, through a break in the overhangs on the left. Continue up slabs to a heather terrace. Finish up the slab on its right.

On the right of the crag is the broad broken ridge of *West Face Route*. On its left is **Two-Way Traffic Chimney** which is a gully at the top of the grassy slope below *Superstar*.

☆ **El Coronel**   40 m   HVS   ?   1998
An interesting climb weaving its way through the overhangs to the left of *Great Wall*. It forms a good approach to *The Diagonal Crack*

which starts along the ledge to the right of the top belay. Start 15 metres left of *Two-Way Traffic Chimney* just right of the lowest point of the mossy slabs.

(5a). Climb the slab, pull over the overlap and go up to loose ledges. Pull right around a rib and go up to a cleaned ledge. Move left then right through the overhangs onto pleasant slabs which lead to a heather ledge and belays.

★ Broadway   33 m   HS   1945
Start just left of the large tree at the foot of *Two-Way Traffic Chimney*. Similar to *The Great Wall*.

Climb up the wall on excellent holds, passing a small ledge. Move up slightly leftwards and follow the nose and rock above to the heather terrace. Continue up the crag above almost anywhere.

★★ The Great Wall   30 m   HS   1945
A fine climb starting just left of the foot of *Two-Way Traffic Chimney*.

Climb up past a small holly tree. Continue up the corner and the wall on the right, on superb holds, to a heather terrace. Continue up the crag above almost anywhere.

★ The Diagonal Crack   22 m   HVS   1985
An interesting and exposed pitch above *The Great Wall* starting on the heather ledge above that route.

(5b). Gain the obvious diagonal crack in the wall on the right, with some difficulty, and follow it rightwards, with no less difficulty, to its top. Finish up rocks above.

★ West Face Route   157 m   D   1945
This expedition begins at the lowest rocks on the right of the crag, 25 metres right of a large broken groove, at a small cairn. An outing for the aspirant pioneer.

1   26m. Amble up a slab and broken rocks to a wide grass terrace. Walk up leftwards for 10 metres to the crag.
2   28 m. Move upwards to a ledge system and move leftwards to the prow of the buttress.
3   36 m. Surmount short walls then traverse left to a large tree at the base of a gully (*Two-Way Traffic Chimney*).
4   18 m. Fight up the left chimney to a grass terrace. Climb over a fence (with care) and walk 10 metres up to the right.
5   14 m. Climb a wall by an irregular crack to a ledge at 6 metres. Climb the wall above to a heather ledge. Walk 10 metres to the right.

6 20 m. Climb up to a shallow corner and follow this with some difficulty to a heather ledge.

7 15 m. Continue up the pleasant wall above to a stance on a heather ledge.

Continue up the broken rocks above, trending right to more continuous rocks and up to the top.

Variation **Cheap Entertainment** 90 m D   1945

For its grade this route has some interesting positions.

Start at the top of *Two-Way Traffic Chimney* and follow a heather/grass ledge left, to above *The Great Wall*. Continue up broken climbing for about 100 metres to the top.

Doberman 30 m E1   1993

This is a pleasant route just right of *West Face Route*. Start at the foot of the vegetated chimney/ramp in the centre of the buttress, left of the route *Oak Tree Wall and The Little Pinnacle*. Rather bold.

(5a). Climb up the ramp for about 7 metres until it is possible to move out left onto a slab. Awkward. Continue up rightwards, avoiding easier rock to the left, aiming for the highest point of the buttress. A crucial runner can be placed to the left at about mid-height. Gain a traverse line just below the top of the buttress and then move left to finish. Descend down the grass/heather ramp to the left.

Oak Tree Wall and The Little Pinnacle 80 m MS   1947

This route climbs the rock to the right of *West Face Route*. There is a diagonal ledge containing an oak and much vegetation. The climb starts below this.

1 24 m. Climb straight up the wall passing a ledge at 12 metres. Now climb up leftwards to the oak.

2 24 m. Continue up the vegetated ledge (possible belay at 15 metres) and a steep open chimney to a heather ledge. Climb to the pinnacle in the wall above.

3 22 m. Climb the chimney to the left of the pinnacle and continue up the fault to the *Little Pinnacle*.

4 10 m. Ascend behind the pinnacle avoiding a loose flake. Scramble to the top.

Gash Rock (267 115)

Directly below Sergeant Crag is a large square-topped boulder – *Gash Rock* (or *Blea Rock*) which affords a few boulder problems.

Sergeant Crag Slabs (271 113) Alt. 400 m West Facing

These splendid slabs offer a wealth of superb routes for the mid-grade climber. Nearly all the routes are worth doing and some are amongst the best in the valley. The rock is excellent, the surroundings magnificent and as an added bonus they bask in the afternoon and evening sun. They are found slightly below and to the right of *Sergeant Crag* and can be reached in 45 minutes from Stonethwaite. Approach as for *Bleak How* and *Fat Charlie's Buttress* but continue along the path to *Gash Rock* (a large boulder near the beck) and then strike directly up the hillside. At the left-hand side of the slabs a short rock step gives access to an earthy terrace that runs under the routes on the main slab and provides a communal gearing up platform. Descent is usually by abseil from chains at the top left and right of the main slabs although it is possible to walk off either side of the crag. The climbs are described from left to right.

The North-West Wall

Four short routes have been done on the left-hand side wall of the crag, up and round to the left of the foot of the *The Main Slab*. This wall is bordered on its left by a wet grassy gully. Obvious features on the left-hand side of the wall are a large triangular block and two horizontal grassy cracks. Slow to dry.

★ **Mystic Knee** 20 m VS 1995
This route starts 2 metres above the top grassy crack, mentioned above, at another horizontal crack.
(4c). Follow the crack for 4 metres then go up a vertical crackline and continuation groove to a large diagonal gangway. Climb up right to ledges and belay well back.

★ **Faz's Route** 25 m E2 1995
(5b). Start at the first horizontal grassy crack. Climb boldly straight up passing the gangway/break. Belay at the tree.

★ **Hitler's Demise** 30 m E2 1995
(5c) Takes the top diagonal crackline across the wall. Traverse to the triangular block, then move up and right to gain the diagonal crackline. Follow this (using high holds near the end of the crackline) to the rib on the right. Continue more easily up the rib then go up grass ledges to belay well back.

★★ **Woodrow Wyatt's Reasoning**   30 m   E2   1995
     (5c). Starts up the centre of the crag and finishes up the rib on
     the right. Start at the base of the crag beneath the central wall.
     Climb up between a detached block and a small tree at 5 metres.
     Go up the crack behind the tree to the wall. Move up the wall
     for 6 metres (poor protection) to a horizontal crackline. Move
     round the rib on the right and then straight up to join the finishing
     slab of *Hitler's Demise*, all on good pockets.

The Main Slab

This is the obvious slab seen when approaching the crag from below.
The first two routes take the far left-hand side of *The Main Slab* and
start down and left of this ledge. The excellent *Lakeland Cragsman*
take the most obvious crack to the left of centre of the main slab.

Rockola   45 m   VS   1991
Some interesting moves but much vegetation and very poor
protection. Start at the far left side of the crag, some 3 metres left of
the rock step at a broken rib.
     (4a). Climb the rib to the overhang. Step left and climb the slabs
     above, keeping to the left until forced right near the top to join
     the upper section of *No More Motivation*.

★ **No More Motivation**   45 m   VS   1991
Start immediately below the rock step.
     (4c). Climb the short crack and shallow scoop to the overhang.
     Go over this slightly leftwards, on good holds, and follow the
     steep groove up the slab above, moving slightly left at a second,
     smaller, overhang. Easier ground leads to a broken rib just left of
     a mossy scoop.

The remaining climbs all start from the gearing up platform.

★★ **Revelation**   45 m   VS   1991
Start at the left-hand side of the main slab.
     (4c). Climb leftwards towards a block step in the overhang. Step
     up right and swing left to surmount this. Follow the crack above
     until it peters out then move right and up to a groove. Follow
     this to the tree belay.

★ **Cedric in Space**   45 m   HVS   1995
This route takes the ground between the cracks of *Revelation* and
Endurance.

(5a). Climb the seriously squeezed slab between *Revelation* and *Endurance*, finishing up the blunt rib below the belay tree. Note that if you are really strict about not using either crack, getting over the overlap is about 5c.

★★★ **Endurance** 45 m HVS   1991
A good climb that is rather slow to dry in the upper section. It takes the thin crack left of *Lakeland Cragsman*.
(5a). Follow the thin crack up the slab and through the overlap. Continue more easily to the top of the crag.

★★ **Between the Lines** 45 m E1   1995
This takes the ground between the cracks of *Endurance* and *Lakeland Cragsman*.
(5b). Start up *Lakeland Cragsman* for a few metres then step left and climb the slabs between it and *Endurance*, without recourse to either. Finish up the pebbly pillar below the tree.

★★★ **Lakeland Cragsman** 45 m HVS   1991
The slightly wider crackline 3 metres right of *Revelation*. Well protected and low in the grade.
(5a). Climb the slab and then the crack formed by large jammed blocks (easier on the left) to the overlap. Surmount this and follow the crack past two more overlaps to an easier corner and the abseil tree.

★★★ **Terminator 2** 45 m HVS   1991
Start 2 metres right of *Lakeland Cragsman*.
(5a). Climb the thin crack right of *Lakeland Cragsman* through the left-hand of three breaks in the overhang. Thin moves lead up and left until a rightward-slanting ramp/groove can be followed to a narrow ledge. Pull into a corner on the right and hand-traverse the horizontal crack leftwards to pull out left. Follow easier ground to a tree belay.

★★ **Boris in Wonderland** 45 m E2   1995
An eliminate line crossing *Terminator 2* and starting just right of that route.
(5b). Climb directly to the central of three breaks through the overlap and gain the slab above. Continue upwards until moves left lead onto the rightward-slanting rampline of *Terminator 2*. Move up, pull directly through the overlap and climb the slab leftwards to a ledge. Continue directly up the slab above to another ledge and then ascend the mossy scoop above.

★★★ **Aphasia** 45 m E2   1992
 Start at the centre of the main slab, just left of *Holly Tree Crack*. A
 fine, sustained pitch with reasonable protection. Simply brilliant!
   (5b). Climb a short steep slab to a good hold below the right-hand
   break in the overlap. Pull up right onto the slab and then go
   straight up to a bulge. A hard move over the bulge leads to a
   good hold. Continue up until moves right lead to a crack. Follow
   this to a narrow ledge. Pull up into the slight corner via a
   horizontal crack and climb the wall above directly to the top.

★★ **Hookworm** 50 m E3   1993
 A direct eliminate starting just left of *Holly Tree Crack*. Serious.
   (5c). Climb to the overlap and pull directly over this (high runner
   in crack on right) to gain a slab. Go straight up, with a hard move
   over the steepening, to reach *Aphasia* and cracks. Step right and
   then move up the slab to a ledge. Pull over the overhang and
   climb a thin crack to the right of the final crack of *Aphasia*.

★★ **Holly Tree Crack** 50 m E1   1991
 Start below a holly.
 1 35 m (5b). Climb the groove past the holly to a niche. Climb the
    crack out of the top of the niche and follow it to a ledge and
    trees.
 2 15 m (5a). Climb the corner to a ledge and gain the diagonal
    rightwards-slanting crack in the buttress above. Follow it to the
    top.

 **Warning: at the time of writing, a tree on the ledge above Holly
 Tree Ramp and The Death Stroke is in a dangerous condition.**

★★ **Holly Tree Ramp** 35 m E1   1995
 Easy for the grade. Start as for *Holly Tree Crack*.
   (5a). Follow *Holly Tree Crack* to the niche and move up right
   onto the obvious right-slanting ramp/groove line. Follow it,
   avoiding a bulge on the right, with increasing boldness to a small
   overlap containing a prominent crack. Climb this to a ledge.

★★ **Quicksilver** 35 m E1   1992
 Start 3 metres right of *Holly Tree Crack*. A bold route.
   (5b). Climb the crack moving left and up into the right-slanting
   groove. Pull over the bulge and up into a higher groove. Follow
   this awkwardly and pull out leftwards to gain the arête which is
   climbed to a ledge.

★★ **The Death Stroke** 35 m E1 1991

Start 3 metres right of *Quicksilver*.

(5b). Climb the cracks to join the right-slanting ramp which is followed to a small overlap containing a prominent crack. Climb this to a ledge.

☆ **The Blues Connection** 73 m VS ? 1991

A girdle.

1 20 m. Follow pitch 1 of *Rockola* over the roof and up the slab to a small tree.

2 33 m. Traverse right across the slab into the crack of *Revelation*. Hand-traverse right crossing *Holly Tree Crack* and belay on the tree above *Death Stroke*.

3 20 m. Move down and right and climb the slab to tree belays.

Blackmoss Pot Slab (269 112) Alt. 350 m West Facing

This is the prominent slabby buttress above Blackmoss Pot on the eastern side of Langstrath, 300 metres south off *Sergeant Crag Slabs*. An arching overlap rises from the bottom right-hand side of the slab. Although small the crag offers excellent climbing on solid, clean rock.

The first route lies at the lower left-hand side of the main buttress on a narrow buttress with a thin crack/groove running up its centre. Start directly behind a large spike.

Pebble Lane 27 m HVS 1996

1 17 m (5b). Climb the buttress mainly on pebble type holds. When a ledge is reached (delicate exit) traverse right into more prominent cracks to reach a large grass ledge with a tree belay over to the left.

2 10 m (4a). Twin cracks are followed to the top.

★ **Posidriver** 20 m E4 1996

Start at the seam/crack rising from the left-hand end of the ledge.

(5c). Follow the seam/crack to the overlap, step right and follow the slanting groove until it fades. Gain a short horizontal break to finish directly up the top wall.

★★ **Slab Happy** 15 m E2 1991

An excellent pitch. Start from the ledge just below a protection peg.

(5c). Climb the corner formed by the start of the overlap, then go directly to the apex of the slab on improving holds.

★ **Pot Luck**   15 m   HVS   1996
Start to the right of *Slab Happy* where an indefinite crack starts above
a few feet of smooth slab.
    (5a). Make boulder type moves from the ledge to reach the thin
    crack. Follow more cracks directly to the top.

The following crags and routes lie on the west side of Langstrath.

Black Wall   (258 107)   Alt. 500 m   East Facing

This is the obvious crag seen from the valley floor of Langstrath
about ½ km south of *Cam Crag Ridge*. It is approached up the steep
grass slope and is suitable for those wishing to escape the crowds. It
has a very steep white wall about 20 metres high in its centre with
an area of less steep rock to the side.

Garner Grooves   42 m   HVS   ?   1989
This route starts at the far left end of the crag, 30 metres left of the
steep white wall, just above a small pinnacle block.
1   (5a). Climb the short rightwards-slanting crack to gain a groove.
    Follow this until it is possible to break out left and up to a good
    ledge.
2   (4c). Follow the steep corners on the right to a sapling at the foot
    of a groove. Move awkwardly right round a rib into another
    groove and climb this to the top.

Upshot   10 m   E2   ?   1990
Start at the left side of the main wall.
    (5c). A ragged crack is started by climbing a rib 3 metres to its
    right and then traversing to a good hold and nut placement. Good
    holds – and steep.

☆☆ **Satan's Little Helper**   20 m   E7   {F7b+}   ?   1998
    (6b). The obvious line in the centre of the wall. There is a long
    run-out on the crux.

Peregrine Grooves   33 m   HVS   ?   1982
Start just right of the steep white wall below a short lay-back crack.
    (5a). Lay-back up the crack and follow a gangway leftwards to a
    ledge (peg runner). Move back right and climb the obvious deep
    groove.

☆☆☆ **Sheer Entertainment**   25 m   E4?   1993
  A direct line up the steep buttress at the right end of the crag. Start
below and just right of the white scoop in the right-hand buttress.
    (6a). Climb steeply to a break at 8 metres passing a couple of
    broken holds (RP 3). Stand in the break and climb the steep
    groove above. A large flat sloping hold is difficult to leave (RP
    3). Gain the first of two ledges then climb the low-angled groove
    above the second ledge which is much more difficult than it looks
    and not well protected.

Cam Crags   (263 112)   Alt. 400 m   East Facing

★★★ **Cam Crag Ridge**   M   1943
  An interesting scrambler's expedition which takes the rocky ridge
opposite *Gash Rock*, 300 metres south of the intake wall.
    The ridge is gained over a chaos of boulders and is best followed
    up its crest, which is initially narrow, then broadening towards
    the top. This ridge provides a useful approach to the crags in
    Combe Ghyll.

The crags near the base of the classic scramble are now worth the
walk for harder things on two clean solid walls. The lower, left-hand
crag is a steep wall with a prominent band of overhangs below its
right-hand side. The upper crag is a wall which lies above a
left-slanting groove taken by *Parsley the Lion*. The climbs are
sustained crack/wall climbs of excellent quality.

Lower Crag

Left of the roof are two obvious lines.

★ **'Arry 'Ardnose**   15 m   E2   1988
  (5c). This takes the twin cracks on the left which are gained by
  a layback sequence. There is a step to the right at 6 metres.

★ **Cam Crag Crack**   15 m   E4   1988
  (6b). To the right of *'Arry 'Ardnose* is a single striking crackline
  which cuts through the roof system at its left most extreme. The
  crux is overcoming the metre wide roof. The crack above is best
  laybacked and remains difficult.

Dill the Dog   10 m   E1   1988
Dirty, strenuous and thoroughly unpleasant. Start at the right-hand end of the overhang.
> (5b). Climb up the obvious ragged overhanging crack which leads to the top.

Upper Crag

★★★ **Camouflage**   25 m   E7   {F7b+}   1998
Breeches the wall left of *Camikaze*. Very bold. Start at a short overhanging groove, which is often wet at its base, left of centre of the crag.
> (6b). Climb the groove to a small ledge at its top. Step left, then back right and climb a thin crack in the slab to a halfway ledge (junction with *Parsley*) at a detached flake. Climb the wall above (very scary) directly to better holds at the top.

Parsley the Lion   25 m   VS   1988
Start in the centre of the crag.
> (4c). Easy ground leads to a ledge at 8 metres. Traverse left past a large block and go up into the obvious corner which leads to good belay on ledges on the left.

★★★ **Camikaze**   25 m   E6   {F6c}   1994
Start up *Parsley the Lion* in the centre of the crag. Serious.
> (6a). Climb straight up to a sloping ledge (peg). Make moves on hollow flakes to a horizontal break (stacked knife blades), then continue boldly straight up the wall to the left end of an overlap (Friend $^1/_2$). Pull through the bulge to the top.

★ **Teenage Kicks**   25 m   E3   1988
Start 3 metres left of a shallow groove on the right side of the crag.
> (6a). Climb the bulging wall to a large ledge and corner at 10 metres. Follow the thin crack on the left up to a horizontal crack, then up to a small ledge on the right. Continue up under the overhang to a jug. Make a long stride left onto the wall then move up to the overhang. Surmount the overhang using a hidden side-pull on the right to gain the top.

Opposite: Sergeant Crag Slabs – John Campbell gets **Between The Lines** (E1), for the first ascent   *Stephen Reid*
Overleaf: Paul James, belayed by Scott Umpleby, on the superb rock of **Aphasia** (E2), Sergeant Crag Slabs   *Stephen Reid*

★ Variation **Flexible Friend** 25 m E3   1989
Start as for *Parsley the Lion*.

(6a). Climb to the large grassy ledge. Traverse along this to the right to join *Teenage Kicks* and follow the thin crack on the left up to a horizontal crack. Continue up under the overhang to the jug, as for *Teenage Kicks*, and surmount the overhang directly (crux) to gain the top.

Camalot 30 m HVS   1996
(5a). Climb the obvious grooves and rib a few metres to the right of *Teenage Kids*. The flake at 8 metres is a bit of a lottery – be careful.

White Crag – Ivy Knott (265 118) Alt. 300 m   South-East
                                                              Facing
This is the left-hand most and lowest of a mass of small crags on the west side of Langstrath north of Cam Crag Ridge and opposite Sergeant Crag. When walking up Langstrath, pass through a gate in the drystone wall and continue south for another 300 metres before striking directly up the hillside to the crag.

★ **Langstrath Buttress** 20 m HVS   2000
A fine little climb on sound, clean, quick-drying rock. Almost worth the walk! Start below a steep groove behind a bunch of saplings 7 metres left of the large holly that grows at the lowest point of the crag.

(4c). Climb up rightwards following a slim right-slanting ramp to good holds. Traverse horizontally back left to the arête and climb this to a hand traverse line. Traverse rightwards along this, passing a dubious block with care, and make a bold and precarous bridging move into the wide groove on the right. Finish up this, or better, move onto its right arête.

Variation **Direct Finish**
(5a). Alternatively, the slim hanging groove just left of the dubious block provides a harder but better protected finish.

Previous Page: Simon Jones feeling **Slab Happy** (E2), on Blackmoss
Pot Slab   *Dave Simmonite*
Opposite: Dave Mitchell posts himself through the Letterbox on **Grey
Knotts Face** (D), Gillercombe   *Stephen Reid*

Day's End Crack   (272 128)   20 m   MS   1985
This is the obvious crack in the buttress just south of the path near
the junction of Langstrath Beck and Greenup Ghyll, on the lower
flanks of Rosthwaite Fell. Well worth the slight detour, but now
fenced off.

Stanger Ghyll Crag (265 128) lies hidden below the cobbled path
running along Stranger Ghyll, under *Alisongrass Crag* and about a
100 metres below the escarpment. A grassy scree filled gully leads
from near the top of the paved section down the left-hand side of the
crag. The crag is part of an SSSI in a sensitive area and further
development is best avoided. Two routes have been recorded, **The
Groove** (30 m, VS, 1999) climbs the wall and vegetated ledges to
gain the central corner of the crag. Finish via this and a niche above.
Chimney Crack (25 m, VS, 1999) shares the same start but follows
the wide crack 2 metres left of the corner.

Bull Crag   (266 131)   Alt. 170 m   West Facing

This hidden, low-lying crag was first explored by Bentley Beetham.
Both routes described are worth a visit and the crag could provide a
pleasant short evening's entertainment within a few minutes walk of
the Stonethwaite campsite. Take the track towards Big Stanger Ghyll
which is almost opposite the entrance gate to the campsite. After
about 100 metres bear left away from the gill over to the crag. Follow
this up until you reach an obvious large slab just right of a prominent
yew tree (10 minutes from the campsite). Descent is off to the right.

★ **Taurus**   35 m   VS   1996
   (5a). To the right of the yew, the slab rises from right to left.
   Start just left of a narrow ramp, below a birch. Climb a short
   groove to gain the ramp, move up and traverse left. Climb the
   centre of the enjoyable slab above to finish on the left. (The upper
   slab may also be reached using the start of *Mad Cow*.)

★ **Mad Cow**   35 m   VS   1996
   (4c). Start by some shattered blocks, 2 metres left of *Taurus*.
   Climb the blocks and groove above. Move right to gain the slab
   then traverse left to reach a holly. Move left and ascend the left
   side of the slab.

Paper Crag (260 136) Alt. 220 m   North East Facing

This is the obvious steep little crag above Stonethwaite Church, about 15 minutes walk from the road. By the farmer's request, do not climb over his walls but approach through Chapel House Farm and go left at the end of the woods up the spur to a sheep-crawl hole in the wall (leave this as you find it). Go through this to reach either the bottom or the top of the crag. Please contact the Farmer, Mr Richard Weir, on 017687 77 256 before visiting the crag.

The Cutting Edge 30 m E1   1992
The obvious overhanging stepped crack on the left side of the crag. Quite strenuous but well protected.

(5c). Climb up into a groove on the left side of the crag to reach the crack proper. Follow the crack up three bulges, the central one being the most difficult.

☆☆ The Borrowdale Contract 30 m E5 ?   1992
The first route climbed on *Paper Crag*. It takes the second crack system from the left-hand side of the crag, just right of *The Cutting Edge*. An excellent line with a variety of moves. Quite well protected if you can hold on to place it!

(6b). Climb to the overhanging part of the wall just left of the layback crack on the lower slab section. The first part of the crack is thin and is climbed via strenuous undercuts and side holds to where the crack opens. Continue up the overhanging crack to the top.

☆☆ Tops for Bottoms 30 m E6 {F7a+} ?   1993
(6b). Climb *The Borrowdale Contract* until the crack opens, then traverse right for 3 metres to another crack. Climb this to the top.

☆☆☆ Contract to Kill 30 m E6 {F7a+} ?   1993
Takes the central wall with excellent but bold moves.

(6c). Climb the wall to a horizontal break (peg). Thin bold moves above lead in 10 metres to gear in a left-facing groove.

☆☆☆ Paper Thin 30 m E3 ?   1993
Excellent, steep sustained face climbing up the right-hand side of the central wall.

(5c). Climb the right-hand side of the lower slabs to a line of undercut holds above a prominent flake/spike (about 5 metres left of the heather terrace). Follow the undercuts up and right passing a peg 4 metres above the flake. Move up into a shallow groove then pull out left. Above this protection improves. A short traverse left on good holds leads to the groove/crack which is followed with interest to the top.

☆ **Parchment Tigers** 30 m E1 ?   1992
The top pitch is a short but nice introduction to the crag.
1   15 m (5b). Climb the right-hand side of the lower slabs. When the flakes are reached, move right onto the heather terrace and belay on the large oak tree directly next to the face.
2   15 m (5b). From behind the tree traverse up and left passing a peg. Continue straight up passing another peg. Pull up into the steep little groove to a slab finish.

Combe Ghyll

This heavily glaciated valley abounds in outcrops of good rock. Many of these give interesting short climbs while routes of greater length are found on *Doves' Nest*, the buttresses on the east side, and on *Raven Crag* on the south-west side. The valley is accessible within an hour from the road running from Mountain View Cottages, about 1½ kilometres east of Seatoller, to Thornythwaite Farm. Parking is available about 500 metres along the road on the right on the grassy area next to the river. Follow a path over a stile, on the left, just before the parking area, which leads up into the bottom of the Combe, from where *Raven Crag* will be seen dominating the head of the Combe, with the other crags along its left side.

The Combe has traditionally been the exclusive haunt of climbers of easier grade routes but with the relatively recent addition of some harder routes it now has wider appeal.

On the lower slopes of Bessyboot, and only 15 minutes from the road, there are several small outcrops. It is possible to string together many outcrop pitches to make a long expedition of Moderate to Difficult standard to the summit of Bessyboot. The detailed route finding is left to the climber's imagination and initiative.

The Grolley 26 m VD   1972
200 metres left of the top of *Intake Ridge* is a buttress on the skyline with a prominent leftward-sloping groove near its top. Gain the groove, follow it, and finish up an awkward layback crack.

Glaciated Slab (254 128) Alt. 300 m   North West Facing

★ **Intake Ridge** 120 m D   1937
This is the hummocky ridge, 100 metres or so up the east fellside. It
is seen from the fell gate at the entrance to Combe Ghyll, rising above
the intake wall.

1   15 m. Climb the short buttress then walk 8 metres down to the
    right.
2   26 m. Climb a shallow groove followed by a gently inclined slab.
3   18 m. Broken rocks lead rightwards to below a steep wall, just
    above the *Glaciated Slab*.
4   18 m. Climb the steep rightwards-slanting crack above or, more
    easily, climb a slightly lower slab which slants right, with an
    awkward move to gain the slab above now gain the crest of the
    ridge above.
    Scramble up leftwards over an easy rock spur and then up to a
    rock buttress above.
5   23 m. Climb the heathery trough just right of the buttress, then
    escape up left on big holds. Alternatively climb the steep buttress
    on excellent rock (harder) and move up right. Climb easy rock to
    a grass platform.
6   20 m. Move right and up just left of a jutting nose and traverse
    right on a slab. Go up to the top.

Glaciated Slab

The obvious ice-planed slab on the south side of *Intake Ridge*
provides enjoyable climbs which are described from right to left.

★ **Trod Yan** 18 m M   1944
Amble up easy rock and a shallow scoop on the right of the slab.

★ **Trod Tan** 16 m D   1944
Follow the leftward-slanting crack for 3 metres then go rightwards
to the top.

★★ **Trod 'A' Tween** 18 m VD   1984
Delicately climb the slab between *Trods Tan* and *Tethera*.

★★ **Trod Tethera** 22 m D   1944
Attack the central crack with enjoyment.

★ **Trod Methera** 24 m VD   1944

Delicately climb the slab just left of *Tethera*, to finish up a twisted crack.

★ **Trod Pimp** 28 m D   1944

Climb the crack on the left to gain the ledge on *Intake Ridge*. Finish on the right.

★★ **Trod Sethera** 28 m D   1944

Climb the fissure at the left of the slab to the ledge on *Intake Ridge*. Finish on the right.

★ **Trod Lethera** 30 m M   1944

Climb the obvious chimney to the ledge on *Intake Ridge*. Finish on the right.

★ **Trod Hovera** 30 m D   1944

Climb the narrow wall, just left of *Lethera*, to the ledge on *Intake Ridge*. Finish on the right.

★ **Trod Dovera** 32 m VD   1944

Climb the overhung recess on the front of the buttress past a holly. Continue either up right or direct (much harder) to the ledge on *Intake Ridge*. Finish on the right.

West Buttress

★ **Trod Pip** 30 m MVS   1988

Start at the same point as *Trod Dovera*.
Bridge the corner behind the small holly, then pull directly over the bulge to gain easier climbing.

★ **Prodigal Sons** 25 m E3   1988

This takes the centre of the steep glaciated *West Buttress* on excellent clean rock. A very scary and poorly protected lead. Start at the foot of the buttress.

(6a). Reach a finger crack in the corner and climb this to gain a small ledge below an obvious groove (in-situ peg). Swing directly right from the ledge around the rib into an open scoop, then climb the wall directly above and pull onto a slab. Move into a small groove then up to a horizontal crack on the right. From this climb straight up to the top.

Déjà Vu   25 m   E2   1988
Steep, clean and quick drying rock. Start at the toe of the *West Buttress*.

(5b). Climb up to a flake at 6 metres, on the left edge of the buttress. Continue up using undercuts to pull awkwardly over a bulge into a shallow groove. Reach cracks to the right and follow these until they fade. Finish directly.

Twa Hummocks   (254 120)   Alt. 360 m   West Facing

Further up the east side of the valley there is a series of closely spaced outcrops. On the right are the large detached blocks which form *Doves' Nest*. To the left and higher up the fellside is the very deep gully of *Columba's Gully* and left again and lower down the fellside, to the right of a scree fan, is the broad glaciated ridge of *Twa Hummocks*.

★ **Combe Ghyll Flake**   44 m   VD   1942
An interesting route which makes a good continuation of the *Twa Hummocks* routes. Above and 50 metres left of *Twa Hummocks* is a short compact buttress. Upon close inspection, the buttress reveals its pinnacle flake.
1   22 m. Climb the rock below the pinnacle, bearing right to its base.
2   22 m. Ascend the left edge of the pinnacle, or the crack on the left, to gain its top. Step onto the wall and move up to the right arête. Belay above. Finish up the easy arête above.

Chossy   25 m   S   1989
Start 15 metres left of *Twa Hummocks North* behind a small pinnacle shaped boulder.

Climb the steep wall to an obvious V-shaped groove. Step right onto easier, loose ground and continue up this.

The Twa Hummocks North   68 m   D   1944
A pleasant route starting just right of an overturned rowan at the base of *Twa Hummocks*.
1   16 m. Climb the steep scratched slab to a heather terrace.
2   30 m. Move leftwards up the wall and go up the ridge. Climb a scoop and continue up easy rock to the top of the first hummock. Cross a saddle to the base of the second hummock.
3   22 m. Amble up slabby rocks towards the left of the second hummock, and go up easily to the top.

The Twa Hummocks South 60 m D   1944
An interesting route starting up the right arête of the crag.
1   16 m. Climb the arête, moving right at 10 metres to the ridge and
    a stance.
2   22 m. Continue up the ridge to its top, and the slabs above to the
    saddle.
3   22 m. Pitch 3 of *The Twa Hummocks North*.

Combe Ghyll Buttress 60 m D   1944
This route takes the left edge of *Columba's Gully*. Start at a detached
obelisk, made of two blocks leaning against a pinnacle.
1   18 m. Climb the obelisk onto the pinnacle. Climb over spikes
    onto the buttress behind.
2   22 m. Climb a short chimney on the left, past a perched block,
    and move right and up a large protruding block in a good
    situation.
3   20 m. Climb a short steep corner on the left and then climb easily
    to a large block. Finish up the ridge above.

Columba's Gully 30 m VS   1922
The black cleft in the centre of the crag which can give good pitches
in winter.
1   10 m. Climb up under the overhanging roof blocks to a recess
    well back in the gully.
2   20 m. Pass the large block jamming the gully and continue using
    firm chockstones to a large stance. Climb either wall of the gully,
    although the left wall gives better climbing. A large block marks
    the end of the serious climbing.

Side Exit 62 m MS   1944
Start a short way up the gully at a crack on the right wall. The crack
is unmistakable, but is hidden from view until below it.
1   14 m. The crack is difficult to enter and is followed to steep
    heather. Scramble leftwards for 16 metres to a belay.
2   12 m. Two rock steps and ledges lead left to a large platform.
3   36 m. Traverse right, using a quartz ledge at foot level. Climb
    the corner, move left and follow the slab on small holds.

Columba's Bastion 50 m VD   1944
This route takes the buttress to the right of *Columba's Gully*, starting
6 metres right of the gully below a rowan in a shallow chimney. A
scrappy climb.

1   32 m. Climb the chimney, then move right and climb the rib to a grass ledge. Traverse rightwards along the ledge and climb up to a stance beside a large projecting perched block.

2   18 m. From the foot of the corner move up left and then up right onto the top of a quartz-spangled block. Climb the steep rocks above to gain a belay. Continue up the buttress above.

Bond Street 65 m M   1945

This route more or less takes the right edge of the buttress, starting at the foot of a wall with a holly.

The next route was missed from previous guides and was submitted too late for checking. It is reported as being situated on a buttress between *Columba's Gully* and *Doves' Nest*, and starts in the middle of the face at an obvious rib.

The Hearse 70 m VS ?   1967

1   30 m. Climb the rib for 10 metres and traverse heather ledges to a block belay at the foot of the main wall.

2   25 m. Climb the groove for 18 metres. Move left up to a ledge to the left of an overhang. Block belay.

3   15 m. Step right above the overhang and climb an easy slab to the top.

Doves' Nest (253 117) Alt. 360 m   West Facing

After the track into Combe Ghyll levels you will see an obvious crag on the left, opposite *Raven Crag*. *Doves' Nest* was formed by a great rock face slipping bodily forwards and downwards. It now leans back against the rocks behind, leaving cavities of all sizes between the massive detached blocks and the main face. These passages have made *Doves' Nest* well known. It is worth emphasizing that these passages have been created by rock slippage – take care!

Three dark gashes in the crag will be seen. The *North* (left) and *Central* of these chimneys converge and terminate in a recess called the *Attic Cave*. Lower down and to the right is the *South Chimney*, which gives the easiest access to the passages. The outside routes are generally very pleasant on sound rock. A descent can be made down either side of the crag.

★ **Adam's Rib**   47 m   VD   1951
This route lies on the slab at the left of the crag. It starts at its base,
just right of the arête.
1   16 m. Climb the slab over an overlap, with difficulty. Move up
     and left to a belay near the left arête.
2   31 m. Continue up steeper rock keeping left and then move right
     to a rib. Finish up the rib overlooking the slab.

★★ **Adam's Slab**   34 m   HS   1985
Start as for *Adam's Rib*, but instead of moving leftwards take the
slab direct, passing a flake block.

★ **Meet Your Maker**   45 m   HVS   1997
Good but poorly protected climbing. Start right of *Adam's Rib*.
(4c). Climb the right-hand side of a downward-pointing block, in
the centre of the overlap, and go up the crack above to the top
left edge of the flake block. Traverse right across its top before
climbing directly to the top of the crag.

★ **Flashback**   45 m   HVS   1989
A rather scrappy start is rewarded with fine airy climbing in the upper
section taking the rib to the right of *Adam's Slab*. Start just right of
Adam's Slab below a small slanting overlap.
(5a). Climb up to the overlap and pass this on the right with some
difficulty. Continue up a crackline to a small tree. Pass this on
its left and gain a gully up to the right. Move awkwardly onto
the rib on the right and climb up in a fine position. Trend
rightwards and up to easier climbing to finish over a small overlap
and cracked corner.

★ **No Overtaking**   16 m   E1   1999
This takes the slab featuring two horizontal quartz breaks that is
found to the right of the gully bounding *Adam's Slab* area on its right.
Start below the slab a few metres right of a large rowan tree.
(5c). Step onto the steep wall and gain a large handhold. Pull onto
the slab, cross the double white lines and go straight up to the
top of the slab using a friendly flake edge. Finish up *Face Route*
or grovel back down the cave system.

★★ **Horizontal Pleasure**   80 m   HVS   1995
A very good and worthwhile route providing an entertaining variety
of moves in fine situations. A bold approach is definitely
recommended on the final pitch! Start 3 metres left of the lowest
point of the crag.

1   30 m. Climb a mossy scoop trending rightwards to the large ledge of *Face Route*. Leave the ledge via a short crack on the left and follow the left edge of the buttress to a belay on the right, at the entrance to the left-hand branch of *Central Chimney*.

2   8 m (4b). Enter the chimney 1 metre and back and foot up it to gain a jug on the left arête. From a standing position on this swing across to a jug on the right wall and climb up more easily to the pinnacle stance on *Face Route*.

3   12 m (4c). Stride across the gap to a good foothold at the base of the long narrow slab that forms the left arête of *Central Chimney* and climb it until it is possible to step onto the large chockstone on the right. Go up to a stance on the edge of the *Attic Cave*.

4   30 m (4c). A spectacular pitch, but virtually unprotected and not for the faint hearted! On the lip of the overhang on the left is a foothold. Make a very awkward move up and around the arête to stand on this. Traverse leftwards along the lip of the overhang on good footholds but with poor handholds until a small ledge on the left can be reached. Breathe a sigh of relief and trend leftwards up easier ground to the top.

Variation **The Nose**   1906

4a (4c). To avoid the horizontal pleasures of the fourth pitch climb the left-hand side of the initial arête directly to the easier ground.

★★ **Outside or Face Route** 80 m D   1944

A pleasant and varied route which starts at the lowest point of the crag.

1   30 m. Climb a crack in the slab, trending left to a large ledge. From the right end of the ledge, climb up the arête to a large ledge, below an obvious chimney (*North Chimney*). Walk 8 metres right along the ledge to below the *South Chimney*.

2   8 m. Follow the edge of the large detached block on the left to an interesting belay.

3   12 m. Drop down behind the block and disappear up the right chimney (*Central Chimney*) to just below the *Attic Cave*. Belay on top of the large chockstone.

4   30 m. Ascend the rib on the left and make a stride right across the top of *Central Chimney*. Move right a few metres. Now climb a fine crack and a wide crack above to a pinnacle on the right. Move left and up to the top.

Variation **The Inside Route** VD

An amusing route for those not suffering from claustrophobia.

2a 6 m. Instead of surmounting the block, scramble up *North Chimney* to the gap behind the block.

3a. 20 m. *The Rat Hole*. Climb the *North Chimney* for 8 metres, where a vertical black cleft will be seen on the right wall. Enter this above the chockstone (easiest done facing into the main crag). Squirm up to the right to an exit at the upper hole (the width increases after the first metre). Gain the *Central Chimney* and climb this to the *Attic Cave*.

4a 25 m. *The Rabbit Hole* – a descent of the cave behind the central block. Start at the back of the *Attic Cave* and carefully enter the blackness on the right, assisted by gravity. Descend the cleft rightwards to exit at the base of *South Chimney*. A torch is useful, but it is more exciting without one.

Variation

4b 20 m. Climb the crack above the *Attic Cave* to rejoin the ordinary route.

★★ **Clubfoot** 62 m MVS   1967

A pleasant and direct climb which starts just right of *Face Route*. The second pitch is quite bold.

1 18 m. Amble up an easy slab to a short corner. This leads to easy ground and a belay beside the *South Chimney*.

2 22 m (4a). Gain the large slab above by moving left from the foot of *South Chimney*. Follow the line of weakness up the left of the slab. Now move up and right to a stance below a small overhang.

3 16 m. Step to the right from the foot of the crack (pitch 4 *Face Route*) and climb the rib to a stance behind a large chockstone.

4 6 m. Climb the steep corner groove above.

★ **Clubfoot Variation** 35 m HVS   1999

Start as for pitch 2 of *Clubfoot*.

1 15 m (4c). Gain the large slab and climb directly up it passing a clump of heather on the left to arrive at the stance on *Clubfoot*.

2 20 m (5a). Pull directly over the overhang between *Face Route* and *Clubfoot* and then more easily direct to the top.

An ascent of the *Rabbit Hole* (reverse of 4a – *Inside Route*) starts at a gap behind a block a short way up *South Chimney*. Once inside, light will be seen high up to the left. This is the *Attic Cave* and is reached by climbing of Moderate standard. The way is obvious, though a torch is useful.

There is a small buttress on the very right of the crag. Its base is level with the ledge that leads left to the pinnacle and the foot of *Central Chimney*. It is bounded on the left by **South Chimney** (D, 1897). It contains an obvious short groove on the right.

★ **Being Done Good To** 12 m E1   1999
Start just to the right of the *South Chimney*.
  (5b). Climb up just right of the left arête of the buttress to gain and follow a crackline to the overlap. Continue up the wall above on immaculate rock.

★ **Crackerjack Groove** 18 m MVS   1998
The obvious short groove on the very right of the crag, 3 metres right of *Being Done Good To*.
  (4b). Climb up into the groove passing a dubious flake. Jam your way to an easy slab and spike belays.

Bon Temps 44 m HVS   1988
Start 50 metres left of the top of *Doves' Nest* at a broken rib with a rowan tree.
1 22 m (4c). Climb the rib and move up onto a slab. Now follow holds, zig-zagging slightly on the right, until a line of sharp edged holds is reached. Move up rightwards to belay.
2 22 m (5a). Climb up and left, then use side pulls to attain a ledge. Continue on side-pulls and step right onto a slab. Move up and then left to below an overhang (peg runner). Pull over the overhang to reach a flake, then bridge up and gain good footholds below a steep wall. Ascend this wall to the top.

Doves' Nest Slabs (254 114)

These smallish slabs lie high above and right of *Doves' Nest Crag*. Although short, the rock is excellent.

Concrete Slab

This is the last buttress before reaching the ridge.

Jackson Pollock No 5 10 m S   1999
  Follow the centre of the clean right-hand section of slab to a
  sentry box, then go diagonally left to the top.

Yakka 12 m HS   1999
  Start at the lowest point of crag. Climb the right-hand side of the
  vertical break into a crack above.

Blue Circle Buttress

This lies below *Concrete Slab*.

The Badger Parade 20 m MVS   1999
  (4a). Bridge up the right-hand of the obvious grooves at the steep
  right-hand edge of the crag, into a V-groove. Pull over using a
  hollow block and follow slabs to the top.

Precarious Block 25 m MVS   1999
  (4b). Start at the lowest point of the slab. Climb to the right-hand
  side of the scoop at one third height. Make awkward moves up
  the crack on the right to the precarious block. Surmount this and
  finish above. Awkward belay.

Sub Zero Slab (254 114) is reached by scrambling northwards from
the other slabs to a little bay. The routes are 10 metres long. ☆ **Lock,
Stock and Two Smoking Trowels** (S ?, 1999) follows the obvious
central crack, and **Silent Partner** (HS ?, 2000) climbs boldly up two
faint cracklines from the left-hand side of the slab.

Combe Door Crag (252 109) will be found (after an arduous
approach) facing north-east at 670 metres. **Shampoo a Rhinoceros**
(40 m D ?, 2000) takes an obvious easy left-slanting ramp system
starting at the centre of the crag in two pitches. **Balls Like
Spacehoppers** (10 m HVS ?, 2000) starts beneath the overhanging
promontory at the right-hand end of the crag and climbs up directly.
It is poorly protected. A variation (5b ?) trends diagonally right at
three-quarters height and surmounts the promontory.

Combe Head (249 110) is the rather dank looking crag at the head
of Combe Ghyll, which gives a number of vegetated routes starting
around the lowest point of the crag. The routes need no description
and are in the Easy grades. The rock is very greasy in wet weather.

Raven Crag (248 114) Alt. 360 m

This large broken crag lies on the south west s.
and provides long routes. The most obvious fea.
gully of *Raven Crag Gully* with a shallower gully,
its left. *Corvus*, one of the best routes of its standarc   ..ney,
takes the buttress on the left of *Tyro's Gully*.

The best descent is to the left of the crag. The routes are described
from left to right starting at the small buttress of rock to the left of
the main crag.

★★ Pedestal Wall 13 m S   1940
A pleasant little climb starting at the small flake pedestal at the foot
of the centre of the buttress.
>   Climb the centre of the face of the small buttress, trending right
>   up a crack near the top.

★ Wrinkle 13 m VS   1984
A fine little climb starting right of the flake pedestal.
>   (5a) Climb the wall direct, with a long reach to a ledge near the
>   top.

For the Record 22 m MVS ?   1987
Climb the left arête of Slug Thug to some cracks. Finish on the
right-hand side of the nose above.

Slug Thug 22 m HVS ?   1990
Takes the overhanging corner just right of *Wrinkle*.
>   (5a). Climb the overhang direct and continue up the wall bearing
>   slightly left to finish.

★ Just A Quickie 13 m MVS   1984
>   (4c) Start just right of the overhanging corner and climb the wall
>   and the cracks above.

To the right of the small pedestal buttress is a large area of slabby
rock bounded on its right side by an impressive steep wall above a
gully groove.

Cock's Comb 150 m M   1942
>   This scramble starts up the right edge of the small pedestal wall
>   then follows the broken broad ridge that bounds the slabby area
>   on its far left.

RAVEN CRAG

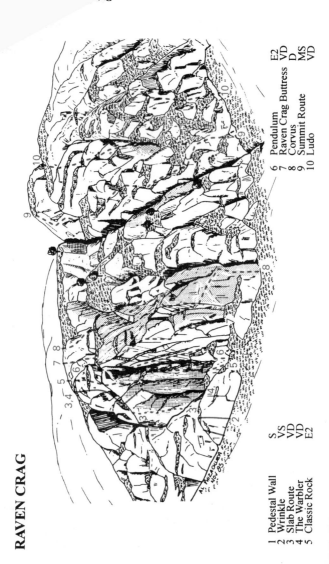

AL. MEARES '85

1	Pedestal Wall	S
2	Wrinkle	VS
3	Slab Route	VD
4	The Warbler	VD
5	Classic Rock	E2

6	Pendulum	E2
7	Raven Crag Buttress	VD
8	Corvus	D
9	Summit Route	MS
10	Ludo	VD

★★ Cock's Comb Crack 25 m E2   1989
A superb, thin crackline up the clean buttress at the top of *Cock's Comb*. The base of the crack can be reached by scrambling up left from pitch 2 of *Crystal Slab*.
(5c). From the short rib on the right climb the thin cracks leftwards to the top.

Slab Route 83 m VD   1945
A vegetated and devious climb ascending the slab right of *Cock's Comb* to the left of an obvious dark overhung recess.
1   35 m. From the bottom of the slab climb to a large projecting block, then go up left to a good stance.
2   15 m. Climb directly up then follow two parallel cracks to the left edge of the slab. Scramble up a ferny scoop to below an overhang.
3   33 m. Climb the rib on the right to the hidden chimney on the right. Climb this and finish by scrambling.

★★ Crystal Slab 94 m MVS   1985
This excellent route takes the light coloured slabby rock to the right of the dark overhung recess. Start at a groove below the slab.
1   45 m (4b). Start up a spiky groove and continue up a shallow scoop onto a light-coloured slab below a wall. Step up at the right-hand side of the wall, traverse left to a jug, move up and continue easily to the tree at the top of the slab above.
2   16 m. Climb the gangway leftwards. Go up a groove on the right to below a crack in a groove.
3   33 m. Climb the crack and the groove above.

The Warbler 89 m VD   1970
This climb takes the slabby area starting 5 metres to the left of the gully groove.
Climb the narrowing chimney and slab to below an overhanging chimney. Move up until holds lead right onto a wall, which is ascended precariously to the right-hand end of a gangway. Finish up pitches 2 and 3 of *Crystal Slab*.

★ Birds of Prey 73 m E1   1985
Start up in the gully groove below the big corner of *Pendulum* at a left-facing groove on the left wall.
1   33 m (4a). Climb the groove and slab to belay under an overhang on the gangway above *Crystal Slab*.
2   40 m (5b). Move left into a left-facing corner, 3 metres right of the tree, and swing out right onto a sloping ledge. Climb the

overhang above on good holds. Follow the crack and slab to a grass ledge and move left up the slab to the top.

★ **Classic Rock**   83 m   E2   1985

An exciting route, starting in the big corner below the gangway of *Pendulum*.

1   33 m (4c). Climb the groove directly until forced out onto the left wall. Climb on sound rock and good holds until forced back right to the corner. Bridge up until a ledge is attained. Climb the right-hand wall on doubtful flakes and traverse right 3 metres to a stance.

2   50 m (5c). Traverse back to the corner and climb it to an overhang. Traverse leftwards beneath undercut grooves to reach an open groove with a small tree. Step left into the bottom of a groove and move up to an undercut chimney. Enter and ascend the chimney with difficulty. Step left onto a small spike, then to a resting place. Step right, continue up a grooveline and bridge up to the top. Belay left of a light-coloured square-cut corner.

★ **Savage Amusement**   73 m   E3   1985

An exhilarating route taking the obvious direct continuation of *Classic Rock*.

1   33 m (4c). Climb pitch 1 of *Classic Rock*.

2   40 m (5c). Climb easily to below the overhanging corner and bridge up to a good hold on the left wall. Attain a standing position on the handhold and bridge precariously, or layback boldly onto the ledge above on the right. Follow the crack above, leftwards to another crack after the bulge. This is climbed to a large ledge and the end of the difficulties. Possible belay or continue to the top.

★ **Pendulum**   112 m   E2   1959/1977

An exciting route which ascends the big overhanging wall by a slender gangway, which runs from right to left, and finishes up the steep corner.

1   16 m. From the bottom of a grassy gully, climb a gangway on the right to a bilberry ledge.

2   21 m (4a). Continue up the gangway to its end. Move to the right to an alcove at the bottom of the gangway proper.

3   31 m (5c). Climb the left edge of the gangway, with difficulty. Pass loose blocks and continue to a belay near the end of the gangway.

4   21 m (5c). Move across into the groove and climb to below the
vertical corner. Ascend for 20 feet, avoiding the biggest overhang
on the left, and climb a smaller one to a stance.
5   23 m. Finish easily, as for *Raven Crag Buttress*.

The following routes are to the right of the prominent vertical wall
bounding the *Crystal Slab* area.

★★★ **Raven Crag Buttress** 112 m VD   1939
This pleasant and continuously interesting route starts from the left
end of the grassy shelf above the crag foot.
1   33 m. Climb the open chimney/groove and ledges above to a good
ledge.
2   26 m. Bear slightly left and climb up to a ledge overlooking the
gully on the left. Continue past a projecting flake to a ledge.
3   30 m. Climb up a groove, and either continue up the groove
above, or move left and climb the groove overlooking the gully,
until exposed moves up a short corner lead up to a large bilberry
ledge.
4   23 m. Climb the easy rocks above.

★ **Green Cormorant** 123 m VS   1970
This climb starts at the crack 3 metres right of *Raven Crag Buttress*.
Worthwhile.
1   40 m (4c). Climb the short crack to a ledge. The crack widens
and forms a pinnacle. Gain the top of the pinnacle and move
rightwards up a slab. Surmount a bulge and climb the groove
above to a grass ledge and then a tree belay on a higher ledge.
2   30 m (5a). Climb the crack just on the left of the tree until an
awkward move right leads to a ledge. Move right, and up to a
grass ledge.
3   53 m. As for the last 2 pitches of *Raven Crag Buttress*.

★ **Raven Crag Grooves** 136 m MVS   1970
Start 5 metres right of *Raven Crag Buttress* below a groove. (More
obviously seen by walking back from the crag foot.)
1   40 m (4b). Climb the right-hand crack and groove above, bearing
slightly left. Now go up to a grassy recess below a chimney/crack.
2   16 m. Climb the chimney/crack and move right to belay by an
open scoop.
3   40 m (4a). Climb a slab by means of a crack and continue to just
below a steep groove. Traverse left on good holds and mantelshelf
onto a block. Continue up on good holds to the recess at the left
end of the *Hand-Traverse* on *Corvus*.
4   40 m. Follow pitches 7 and 8 of *Corvus*.

★ Ibis   149 m   VS   1971

An interesting direct variant on *Corvus*. Start at the lowest point of the crag.

1   12 m (4b). Surmount the short wall to a big grass ledge below a steep slab.
2   20 m (4c). Climb up the wall to twin cracks which are climbed to the right-hand of two grooves. Move into the left-hand groove and climb this to the left end of the traverse ledge on *Corvus*.
3   16 m (4c). Move up right to gain the wall above the traverse on *Corvus*. Ascend this awkwardly to gain a ledge.
4   16 m. Climb vegetated rock on the left to gain the belay on *Corvus* at the end of pitch 4.
5   85 m. Follow *Corvus* to the top.

★★★ Corvus   157 m   D   1950

'A route for all seasons'. An extremely popular climb starting just left of *Tyro's Gully* on the grey slabs.

1   20 m. Start up the slabs and move right at the top to a ledge in the gully.
2   16 m. Climb the first V-cleft in the left wall of the gully to a ledge.
3   10 m. Traverse left along a series of ledges to below a corner.
4   26 m. Climb the corner, which deepens into a chimney, and a slabby scoop above to a good stance.
5   35 m. Move right for 5 metres to the foot of a rib, which is climbed to gain a steep slabby wall. Belay on the right.
6   10 m. Move up right to gain a line of flake handholds (*The Hand-Traverse*) and follow these left across the wall to a recess.
7   25 m. Climb up to a large ledge and continue up a rib to below a scoop.
8   15 m. Gain the scoop via a large flake and continue to the top.

Variation   **The Direct Start**   28 m   S   195▮

A better but harder start.

1a   15 m. Climb the slabs to the left of the normal start to a ledge below a prominent crack.
2a   13 m (4a). Climb the crack left of *The Rib* directly to belay at the top of pitch 2.

★ The Rib   93 m   MVS   197▮

This route deteriorates rapidly after pitch 1. Start at the rib to the right of *Corvus*.

1 30 m (4a). Climb the rib to a crack on the left of the rib. Go back just right of the rib, and go up to a belay on *Corvus* (above pitch 2).
2 30 m (4a). Climb the right-hand rib then move right into a groove and climb up to a block belay.
3 33 m. Climb the slab on the left into a corner. Traverse left across a wall to a ledge. Move left and up, then right, and follow a groove to the top.

★★ **Corax** 140 m S   1950
This route takes the rib just left of *Tyro's Gully* and provides a fine variation start to *Corvus*.
1 31 m. Climb the right edge of the slab, just left of *Tyro's Gully*, to join *Corvus*. Move right, into the gully, and climb its left wall to a belay below a projecting block. (Even better, instead of moving right, take the crack left of the rib to reach the same place.)
2 26 m. Climb past the block and continue up an exposed buttress above, following a crackline. Slabby rock leads to a belay.
Now move up left to join *Corvus* on pitch 5. Originally the route followed the left edge of the gully.

Tyro's Gully 110 m M   1945
This is the second gully to the left of *Raven Crag Gully*. Initially well defined, the climbing deteriorates above, staging a slight recovery at the end.

★★★ **Raven Crag Gully** 178 m VD   1893
A good route, which also provides an excellent winter climb. This is the obvious gully in the centre of the crag. Start with easy scrambling for 25 metres to a cave formed by a chockstone.
1 23 m. Climb the groove on the right side of the gully. Traverse across to the gully bed to a belay.
2 30 m. Climb the groove on the right. Avoid a cave by easy climbing on the left.
3 15 m. Scramble up the gully.
4 23 m. Climb the rib on the right and turn a cave at 12 metres on the right.
5 60 m. Continue up the gully bed to where it steepens.
6 16 m. Climb up the right of the gully past a chockstone and move right to a belay.
7 11 m. Move up a short way and traverse across the gully below the capstone. The capstone is now passed on the left.

Variation **Wet Weather Finish** 10 m S   1897
7a 10 m. Climb the steep rocks above.

★ **Summit Route** 177 m MS   1951
This pleasant mountaineering route initially follows the right edge of
Raven Crag Gully, then trends right to gain the large ledge below the
final buttress. Start just right of the gully at a grass ledge, below a
short wall.
1   16 m. Move left and climb a shallow corner to a ledge and block
     belay.
2   26 m. Move up left and climb a short steep wall. Continue up
     slabby rock to reach a belay on the right.
3   36 m. Move left to gain and climb a slabby groove overlooking
     the gully. Finish either up a short chimney or its left wall. Belay
     on a grass ledge below a corner-crack.
4   20 m. Climb the crack to a ledge on the right. Go diagonally left
     and up to a tree belay.
5   23 m. Move up a crack on the right. Climb a V-groove and crack
     up to the left to a belay below a slabby corner.
6   13 m. Climb the corner and easy rock above to gain the right-hand
     end of the large terrace.
     Walk 20 metres left to a cairn below a square scoop in the final
     buttress.
7   8 m. Climb the scoop, awkwardly, to a sloping ledge on the left.
     Thread belay.
8   10 m. Traverse left along the sloping ledge and continue at the
     same level to a belay.
9   25 m. Climb up to a small overhang on the right. Climb an
     obvious crack on its left to a rock crevasse. Continue to the top
     up a short awkward corner, in the same line.

Variation Finish MS   1959
Start 3 metres right of pitch 7.
7a 6 m. Climb round the corner.
8a 16 m. The slab is climbed on small holds to a well defined crack
     which leads to the top.

Solifidian's Route 220 m S   1953
     A low standard girdle, starting left of *Pendulum*, which follows
     a series of ledges to finish up *Summit Route*.

Raven Bastion 184 m VD   1951
This route gives similar climbing to *Corvus* but neglect has left it
very vegetated. Start as for *Summit Route*.

1   16 m. Pitch 1 of *Summit Route*.
2   35 m. Climb broken ribs above, which lead slightly right to a ledge. Continue up rounded ribs, on excellent holds, to a ledge.
3   23 m. Climb the shallow scoop just to the right, stepping left at its top to a ledge. An awkward short wall leads to a ledge with a flake belay on the right.
4   26 m. The break above leads to a short chimney/crack which finishes on a ledge. Good holds on the left lead to another ledge.
5   16 m. Above is a corner. Climb towards this to a good spike. Stand on this, move up and then step up right to a ledge. The chimney on the right leads to easier ground.
6   42 m. A series of walls and ledges now leads easily to the top. If desired a little more climbing may be added by trending diagonally left to a ledge below a prominent V-scoop.
7   16 m. Climb into the scoop, move right and climb the rib above to a stance.
8   10 m. Climb a short chimney/crack past a projecting block to the top.

Ludo   124 m   VD   1952
Scramble up to a prominent 30 metre slab, 25 metres right of *Raven Bastion*.
1   30 m. Gain the slab from the left and climb up diagonally right to a tree stump (as long as it remains). Climb up and traverse up left across the slab and round the nose to a ledge. Possible stance on the right at the point of arrival, or at the tree 6 metres higher up.
2   10 m. Just above to the left is a small projecting block. Climb the wall above this until it is possible to move left to a tree belay.
3   26 m. Step left to a groove, which leads up leftwards to join *Raven Bastion* midway up pitch 3. Climb the chimney/crack to a good ledge. Go up the wall on the left.
4   16 m. Pitch 5 of *Raven Bastion*.
5   42 m. Pitch 6 of *Raven Bastion*.

Little Stint   25 m   S   1987
Climb the short steep arête right of *Ludo* on pocket holds.

Paparazzi   55 m   HS   1988
Start up to the right of *Little Stint* at an obvious groove. Scramble up the groove and move right to a corner.
1   30 m. Climb the large corner on small pockets and follow a left-slanting crackline to a corner. Move rightwards to a corner

and continue up this to a ledge. Step to the right to below a steep wall.

2   25 m. On the right of the wall move up a rising crack and finish using layaways and side-pulls to the top.

★★ **Easy Street**   60 m   MVS   1988

This takes the obviously well-gardened area of rock on the right of the small gully 150 metres up and right of *Raven Crag Gully*.

1   30 m (4b). From blocks at the base of the groove go leftwards on good holds to a small rock ledge. Follow a gangway up leftwards then move right over a small overlap on good holds to below a slab and belay.

2   30 m (4c). Climb the slab on incuts passing an overhang on its left. Continue on good holds past a precarious flake to the top groove and finish up the rib above to gain a ledge.

Geometer   63 m   VS   1988

Start at the same point of *Easy Street*.

1   18 m. Climb to a rowan tree.

2   45 m (4c). Start up a rib on the left and move leftwards to an obvious rock boss. Pull up left onto a steep wall on good holds and climb up directly to gain a blunt arête which is followed to the top. Descent by abseil.

Thornythwaite Knotts   (248 119)   Alt. 330 m   East Facing

This is the isolated buttress on the right-hand side of the path when approaching *Raven Crag*, some 600 metres to its North. It is very vegetated in the most part and abounds with broken overhangs. It can be reached in 30 minutes from the road. Descent is to either side of the mound.

Two routes have been dug out of the central weakness in the front of the main face.

No More Heroes   37 m   HVS   ?   1985

Start at an obvious deep groove, 6 metres left of *Red Shift*.

1   25 m (4c). Climb the slab in the corner, below the overhanging back wall, to a bulge. Climb round this into a groove and up to a stance.

2   12 m (5a). Climb the overhanging groove onto slabs above and continue to the top.

Red Shift 42 m E3 ?   1985
Start behind two rowan trees, below a holly tree 6 metres up the wall.
  (5c). Climb the corner to an overhang at 10 metres, step right and
  go up the corner above. Continue until below the obvious steep
  slanting groove. Climb this, exit left, then go directly to the top.

Phantom of the Opera 30 m VS ?   1985
Start at the lowest point of the right-hand side of the crag.
  (4c). Climb a rib and left-facing groove in the arête, moving right
  to finish up a gangway.

Capell Crag (242 122) Alt. 360 m   West Facing

This broken crag, composed of a number of buttresses, lies on the
west side of Thornythwaite Fell. The route described lies on the most
southerly buttress, opposite the grass track leading east off the valley
road, midway between the hamlet and Seathwaite bridge.

Calf Close Buttress 136 m D   1952
A vegetated route with some interesting pitches, providing a useful
ascent onto Glaramara or an alternative approach to *Raven Crag*. Start
at the foot of the blunt rib at the left side of the buttress.
1   40 m. Climb a short chimney on the right. Follow ledges up to
    the left and past a ledge to two perched blocks. Scramble up and
    rightwards to a belay, with a light coloured slab on the right.
2   40 m. Climb the slab and continue up vegetation. Move left to
    the foot of a steep crooked corner crack.
3   16 m. Climb the corner with difficulty, move right, and go up
    and along a crest to a grass terrace.
4   10 m. Climb the mossy wall 6 metres to the right. Belay.
    Cross a steep fence and move up the terrace a short way.
5   30 m. Climb slabs leftwards to below a short overhanging wall.
    Climb the wall, on good but dubious holds.

Hind Crag (238 112) Alt. 350 m   West and South West Facing

The crag is on the west side of Glaramara, above the path from
Seathwaite to Stockley Bridge. It can be approached in about 25
minutes from Seathwaite. Most of the crag is very broken and
vegetated, but there is a small wall of steep rock near an old dry
stone wall at its southern extremity. Above, the wall merges into a

long pinnacled ridge overlooking the steep *South Gully* on the south side of the crag. This gully has three routes on its steep left wall but the rock is slow to dry and rather dirty. The first route starts at an area of easy-angled slabs about 60 metres left of the dry stone wall (some 150 metres up right from the toe of the buttress).

Hind Crag Buttress   123 m   VD   1924

Pleasant for 3 pitches then the climbing becomes more of a mountain scramble. Start below the left side of the slabs which are 60 metres left of the dry stone wall.

1   10 m. An easy slab leads to a small ledge.
2   15 m. The slab steepens and becomes more difficult. At 10 metres a small wall is reached and passed on the left to a grass ledge. Belay high up on the right.
3   10 m. Climb a broken crack to a ledge. From here the original route traversed left on grass for 30 metres and followed a moderate buttress 17 metres high (large cairn at the top). It is preferable to scramble direct up the fellside for 50 metres. At the level of the final cairn on the original route a rib is reached.
4   15 m. A broken rib leads to a good ledge.
5   13 m. Climb a sloping crack on the left to a ledge. Alternatively the ledge can be reached directly or by a broken crack on the right.
6   13 m. Easier climbing leads to a corner.
7   8 m. An easy slab is climbed to a grassy terrace.
8   15 m. Difficult climbing leads to a rock stance.
9   8 m. Easy rocks are climbed to a ledge.
10 16 m. Keep to the right edge on good clean rock to the finish.

Variation   **The Original Route**   D

2a 26 m. From below the small wall on pitch 2, traverse right across slabs into the gully, which is then ascended for about 10 metres. The left wall is climbed to grassy ledges and a belay, as for pitch 2.

Man Friday   70 m   S   1952

Lies on the slabs forming the left wall of the first gully on *Hind Crag*, just right of *Hind Crag Buttress*.

1   8 m. Climb first left, then up the right edge of the slab to a small ledge.
2   8 m. Go left on small holds. Climb with difficulty onto the slab above where small but good holds lead to a large block belay.
3   6 m. Go up the slab on the left to a small stance and block belay.

4 10 m. Climb the slab above the belay, and traverse right below the nose. Go left until good handholds enable the nose to be surmounted. Belay just above.
5 6 m. Go up the small crack to the top of a pinnacle.
6 22 m. Move slightly down to the right across the slab. Ascend 2 metres and traverse the slab until it drops into a corner. Go directly up the corner and a small crack on the right is then climbed to a good flake belay.
7 10 m. Climb straight up above the flake using a crack, bearing right to finish. Belay well back on the right.

Withering Height 187 m MVS   1977
A rising traverse of the left-hand wall of the gully. Start at a slim groove in the right-hand side of the steep lower wall, about 20 metres right of the old dry stone wall.
1 26 m. Climb the groove (awkward) and continue by scrambling to a block belay (end of pitch 1 of *Southern Buttress*).
2 30 m. Move right onto the arête and climb to a heathery ledge. Scramble to a block belay (end of pitch 2 of *Southern Buttress*).
3 12 m. Walk right then climb down a groove for 2 metres. Traverse beneath an overhang to a short corner. Climb it and move diagonally right to a small ledge and poor belay.
4 30 m. Move back left onto slabs. Traverse these diagonally left at the base of an overhang. Climb a shallow groove until vegetation is reached. Scramble for about 10 metres to the base of a short wall.
5 23 m. Move right to overlook the gully. Use a small gangway to traverse the wall and climb straight up to overgrown slabs.
6 30 m. Move round the corner on the right, and climb towards a large white-topped flake. Continue at the same height to a blunt arête and then drop down to a heather ledge. Belay at the foot of a large detached flake, just past a horizontal flake on the ledge.
7 20 m. Climb the crack at the left side of the detached flake. Cross the top of the flake to a corner. Climb this and continue to the right to a small grassy gully.
8 16 m. Scramble to the top.

Southern Buttress 175 m VD   1959
Takes the retaining rib of the crag overlooking *South Gully*, and gives a fairly interesting expedition. The best climbing is on pitch 1. Several variations are possible for most pitches. Start below a shallow corner 2 metres right of *Withering Height*, 6 metres left of the foot of *South Gully*.

1   15 m. Climb the corner until it is possible to step left to a mantelshelf. Traverse left and climb up to a large flake and ledge.
2   26 m. A short wall leads to a mossy slab. Steep rocks above are climbed from left to right to heathery rocks. Continue up these for about 12 metres. Traverse round a rib on the right into an open chimney which leads to a ledge.
3   8 m. Go up left, over much easier rock, to the foot of a vertical ill-defined chimney.
4   20 m. The chimney is followed to a little gully and grassy platform.
5   18 m. Climb a short wall and the arête above.
6   16 m. Climb the buttress above with an awkward finish.
7   26 m. A short wall leads to sterner rock, which can be climbed directly using a crack or groove. Easy-angled slabs lead to a belay.
8   12 m. Climb the right edge of the slabs overlooking the gully.
9   26 m. Easy climbing and scrambling. Keep to the right over slabs and a broad cracked ridge.
10 8 m. The final gendarme turns out to be a short steep wall.

The following routes start about halfway up *South Gully*, below its steep left wall.

★ **Nantucket Sleighride** 64 m   E1   1978
Start at the lower, left end of the wall, below a very slim groove with an overlap at 2 metres.
1   16 m (5a). Climb the groove directly, exiting on the left. Belay on a grass ledge at the foot of the next wall.
2   38 m (5b). The easy wall leads to a ledge on the left rib. Follow the rightward-trending rib to the block overhang. Awkward moves right on good holds lead to the obvious large groove. Climb this and exit on the right. Trend right to a thread belay at a large flat block.
3   10 m (5a). Climb the flake crack, as for *Turbulence*, but finish direct.

★ **Turbulence** 82 m   E1   1970/1978
Starts 12 metres right of *Nantucket Sleighride* at a shallow groove in the steep wall, just left of a vegetated groove with a holly tree.
1   30 m (4c). Climb up the wall left of the groove and traverse left until a step can be made into a recess. Step left into a groove. Go up this, step up right and move up to a stance. Peg belay.

2   23 m (5b). Step down and go round left into a short corner. Climb it to a ledge. Go up the next corner onto a slab below an overhanging corner. Climb this with difficulty. Pull out right into a crack and go up to a stance.
3   13 m (4a). Climb a groove above to a small ledge. Go straight up to the *Great Ledge*. Belay on the left.
4   16 m (4a). Step left and climb a flake crack. Traverse right and climb another crack. Step right and finish direct.

★★ Serenity 55 m   HVS   1978
Takes the prominent corner to the right of *Turbulence*, starting as for that route.
1   30 m (5a). Climb the wall until a rightward-leaning groove is reached. Follow this, pulling out right at the top to a peg belay.
2   12 m (4c). The cracked wall above leads to a jamming/layback corner. Go up this to a grass ledge and pinnacle belay.
3   13 m (4a). The short corner above leads to the top.

Grains Ghyll Crag   (235 093)   Alt. 360 m   North West Facing

This is a small crag high up on the true right (east) bank of Grains Ghyll. It is just visible from Stockley Bridge, within a V outlined by two ravines. The walk should ensure no crowds on some good climbs with a fine view.

Low Flyer   30 m   S   1987
Start on the grassy ledge below the smooth left-hand side of the crag. Climb the slab, past three narrow ledges, and continue up a slight corner until a gangway leads up to the right (marked by a quartz vein). Follow the gangway and traverse right onto a corner ledge. Step left onto the wall above and finish up the slab.

Slow Learner   30 m   S   1987
Start at the lowest point where a sloping grassy rake meets the horizontal ledge.
   Follow a gangway steeply up to the right until forced onto the wall on the right. Climb the wall steeply until a step left leads to the corner ledge of *Low Flyer*. Climb the crack above into a slabby scoop, avoiding a patch of vegetation on the right. Finish straight up the slab in the middle of the scoop.

Late Developer   30 m   VS   1987
The obvious rightward-slanting crack just right of the centre of the
crag.
>   (4c). Climb the crack steeply on good holds, with occasional steps
>   onto its right wall, until the angle eases and the rough rock near
>   the top of the crag is reached. A short wall is climbed delicately,
>   pulling left on small holds to gain access to the scoop. Finish up
>   the slab bounding the scoop on the right.

Gable End   26 m   VD   1987
Start near the left end of the grass ledge below the crag.
>   Climb straight up joining a shallow crack at 6 metres. Continue
>   up in the same line, crossing a slight gangway. At the top of the
>   wall walk straight across the heathery scoop and ascend the short
>   wall ahead by a narrow crack.

Garkbit Adventure   40 m   VS   1987
An extraordinary climb, strenuous and awkward. Start 3 metres right
of *Late Developer* just where the horizontal grass ledge joins the
slope of the hillside. The route follows a rather undercut line just
right of *Late Developer* before traversing rightwards near the top.
>   (4c). Climb straight up to a pedestal block, then move up on a
>   steep diagonal line to the right. After a couple of awkward moves
>   gain a stance with loose boulders. Continue up the wall above by
>   climbing a crack on the right until it becomes awkward. Traverse
>   delicately right and finish up another crack.

Aaron Crag   (232 105)   Alt. 500 m   North East to
                                                            East Facing

This is the crag which overlooks Stockley Bridge from high on the
northern slopes of Seathwaite Fell.

Three routes have been climbed on the portion of the crag above the
true left bank of Grains Ghyll – **Whit's End** (VD, 1958), **Whit's
Wall** (VD, 1959) and **Whit's Ridge** (D, 1958).

On the more extensive area of rock at the north end of the fell the
following routes have been climbed. They are approached from
Stockley Bridge by going up Sty Head Pass to the hole-in-the-wall
gate and then striking diagonally up left to the crag.

★ **The Rasp** 40 m VS   1988
Superb friction climbing. On the left of the crag is an obvious narrow
slab bounded by heather, just above a wide grassy ledge.
1   30 m (4c). Climb the slab in four sections broken by horizontal
     cracks. Follow a crack through a bulge to a belay on the left
     below the final wall.
2   10 m (4b). Climb the wall above.
     Descend either by scrambling down to the left or by continuing
     up to the top and then going down the gully on the right of the
     crag.

Maginot Line 35 m VS   1989
20 metres to the right of the dark, central gully are two obvious
cracks.
1   25 m (4c). Climb the right-hand crack. It looks fierce but a ledge
     on the left at the top makes it a paper tiger. Block belay on the
     ledge above.
2   10 m (4c). Layback up the crack above to finish with scrambling.

Black Waugh Crag (233 107) Alt. 300 m   North East Facing

This is the crag below Aaron Crag on the northern slopes of
Seathwaite Fell overlooking Stockley Bridge and is passed on the way
up Styhead Pass. The rock is good but is often damp.

Mean Streak 35 m E1   1987
Takes the slabs at the left side of the crag above some large fallen
boulders.
     (5b). Climb the slab on good incuts and side-pulls to the rowan
     sapling. Move left up a flake into a chimney. Exit right onto a
     diagonal ledge. Move to the right end and pull up on pinchgrips
     and pockets to gain the steep rib on the right. Move straight up
     using a side-pull on the right to finish with good holds.

Trisolo 25 m VD   1987
This takes the slabs on the left side of the crag, just right of the fence.
     Climb up the slabs on good incuts to a tree on a ledge. Climb
     the steep wall behind the tree and layback up the large flake to
     finish.

Recoil   27   E1   1987

This takes the obvious open-sided corner in the centre of the crag.
(5b). Climb the wall and ascend the crack, awkwardly, using an exciting but soundly wedged flake at the top.

Rebound   27 m   E2   1988

Steep climbing up the right-hand crackline in the centre of the crag.
(5c). Climb the slabs following the thin crack to delicate moves left to below the headwall. Climb the continuing crack on fair holds to a tree belay.

Strawberry Buttress (228 112) lies on the eastern slopes of Base Brown above Taylor Gill Force. The best that can be said of the routes is that they are in a lovely situation and will please lovers of solitude. Looking from the top of the falls a large wide open gully is a prominent feature. To the right is another, much smaller, narrow gully with a chockstone near the top. The area of rock to the right is *Strawberry Buttress*, which is best approached by steep zigzags from below and right of the crag.

Just to the right of the chockstone is **Route 5** (20 m HVS) which takes an obvious corner, gained from the gully via a downward-pointing spike. The rest of the routes are down and right of here on a lower tier sporting a pinnacle towards its left end. **Route 4** (13 m VD) takes the chimney to the left of the pinnacle, **Route 3** (13 m HS) takes the front of the pinnacle and **Route 2** (20 m VS) takes the wall, ledge and top wall, just to its right. Some 15 metres right of the pinnacle is **Route 1** (23 m VS) which takes the steepest and best rock on good holds to a ledge finishing up and over a bulge. All the routes were first climbed in 1988.

Seathwaite Slabs   (234 123)

The fellside to the west of Seathwaite has a number of interesting and varied features. Sourmilk Ghyll descends from the hanging valley of Gillercombe and gives an entertaining, though wet, scramble in summer and an excellent easy ice route in a hard winter. To the left of the lower part of the gill is a large boulder with a steep slab and a neighbouring smaller boulder, which give useful sport (*Lower Seathwaite Slabs*). To the right of the top of the gill is *Upper Seathwaite Slabs* a bigger, gentle-angled slab which is useful for an initiation to climbing. The view rewards the 250 metres of ascent.

Hanging Stone (228 119) Alt. 470 m   North East Facing

A small buttress, undercut at its base, and with a prominent large perched block on the top. This crag overlooks the hamlet of Seathwaite from the ridge of Base Brown on the south side of Sourmilk Ghyll.

The rock is quite clean, though rather slatey and a little loose in parts.

The climbs are described from left to right.

Puritan 20 m HVS   1985
Start 6 metres right of the tree-filled gully on the left side of the crag, at an obvious break in the overhang above a small sapling.
(5a). Pull through the break to a 'sawn-off tree stump'! Step left and over a small bulge onto a slab. Move back right and go straight up to finish just left of a large perched block.

Shake Down 20 m HVS   1985
Start as for *Puritan*.
(5a). Pull through the break and move rightwards to below a chimney/groove. Climb up this to finish over two large perched blocks at the top. Take care!

Loose Connections 26 m HVS   1985
Start 6 metres right of *Shake Down* below a loose corner above the overhangs. Care needed with rock.
(5a). Pull over the overhang and continue up the corner into a flake crack. Follow this, steeply, to a grass ledge. From this, step across the wall on the right and up a short crack to finish.

★ Joker Man 26 m E1   1985
Good climbing up the obvious rightward-slanting slabby groove. Start as for *Loose Connections*.
(5b). Pull over the overhang, keeping out of the corner. Move rightwards on sloping holds which lead into the groove. Follow this to a steep finish.

★ Skimmerhorne 26 m E2   1985
A very pleasant route which attempts to climb the obvious knife edge arête on the right of the crag. Start from an embedded rock below the arête.
(5c). Using holds on the right wall, pull up and round onto the left wall. Traverse left on small holds, then pull round onto the

slab. Trend up rightwards to good holds on the arête. Stand on these, then move up to another good hold on the arête. Finish up a short layback crack behind a flake.

Stan the Man   20 m   VS   1985
The corner at the right-hand end of the crag.
  (4c). Climb the corner directly, exiting left at the top.

Gillercombe   (223 124)   Alt. 480 m   South East to
                                                        North East Facing

This large but rather broken crag lies on the south-east face of Grey Knotts, towering above the hanging valley of Gillercombe. It is called *Raven Crag* on O.S. maps.

It can be approached from Seathwaite by following the path from the village up the hillside just left of Sourmilk Ghyll. At the entrance to the combe the crag appears to the north-west. It is best to cross the stile below *Upper Seathwaite Slabs* and contour the hillside below the crag, to avoid the marshy floor of the combe. A quicker approach is from the top of Honister, by following an indefinite path diagonally left to a col on the skyline ridge, from where the crag can be seen.

Descent can be made on either side of the crag, but that to its left (south) side, by the right-hand fork of a scree-filled gully, is rather unpleasant. It is better to cross the fence just to the right of the finish of *Gillercombe Buttress* and descend the wide gully.

★★ **Gabbro**   50 m   VD   1941
A pleasant little climb, which lies on the right of the scree gully on the left of the crag. As its name implies it is on good rock, particularly in its upper part. Start just above a large embedded boulder, above the junction of the right-hand fork.
1   20 m. Gain the top of the pinnacle on the right. Traverse right into a small V-corner which leads up to a belay in a corner.
2   10 m. Exit the corner on the right and climb up to belay under a large flake.
3   20 m. Swing round the flake on the right and continue up the slab above, on excellent rock.

Pedestal Wall

This is at the southern end of the crag about 200 metres left of and below the route *Gillercombe Buttress*. It is composed of good clean rock giving some good short, steep climbs. There is a belay block 6 metres back from the top.

South Buttress 140 m VD   1942
   This route starts up a slanting corner on the left of the *Pedestal*, then rapidly deteriorates in its ascent to the top of the crag.

Two routes **Pedestal Nose** (S) and **Pedestal Cheek** (VD), both climbed in 1942, make a way up the nose on the left of the wall.

★★ **Clara Bow** 25 m E1   1988
   Start 6 metres right of the toe of the buttress where the angle steepens.
      (5b). Climb the steep corner, then reach up left to gain another corner. A couple of thin moves lead to easier but steep climbing to the top.

★ **The Third Man** 20 m E3   1988
      (6a). Gain a crack just left of *Citizen Kane*, where difficult climbing leads straight up to a large hold at 10 metres. Move rightwards for 3 metres, then back left to the top.

Citizen Kane 20 m E4   1988
      (6a). Climb a short groove in the centre of the wall, past a peg, and pull strenuously over an overhang. Continue up a groove to finish over the final overhang.

The Wizard of Oz 20 m E5   1988
      (6b). Climb the initial bulges. Obtain a standing position on a ledge, with difficulty, then pass a peg runner to finish.

★ **Andy Warhol** 20 m HVS   1988
      (5a). Climb the obvious corner groove on the right of the wall to an awkward exit.

Louise Brooks 20 m E3   1988
      (6a). Climb the bulging crack right of *Andy Warhol* and the groove above to finish.

Gillercombe Buttress

★ **Gillercombe Bastion** 100 m MVS   1940
A good route taking the buttress to the left of *Gillercombe Gully*, starting 20 metres up the gully and 16 metres to its left, along a

grassy ledge. The first half provides pleasant and somewhat delicate climbing and the upper section is scrambling, although this can be avoided by traversing off left.

1   30 m (4a). Gain a V-opening 3 metres above and quit this on the left. Continue rightwards and follow a slab slanting up to the left to a sloping stance beside a large block belay.
2   24 m (4b). The slab above on the left is climbed on small holds, initially, to gain a niche high up. Move right and climb a short rib to grass ledges.
3   46 m. Short walls lead up to the top.

Gillercombe Gully   70 m   VD   1913
    The obvious gully to the left of the main section of buttress is followed to where it forks. The right fork is taken and a succession of chimneys leads to the top.

★★★ **Gillercombe Buttress**   195 m   S   1912
    A justly popular route, starting at the foot of the buttress just left of the rocky ramp on the right of *Gillercombe Gully*.
1   15 m. Climb up slabby rocks then move up left to a square recess on the right of the gully. Climb the recess to a stance.
2   15 m. Ascend right past a flake to the upper ramp. Follow this rightwards to a stance.
3   40 m. Move up right and traverse back left for 7 metres to an awkward exit. Go up easy rock to a possible belay. Scramble up for 25 metres and move left to a platform below a corner crack.
4   20 m. Climb the crack, or the broken groove and arête on the right. Move up right to a stance.
5   40 m. Climb a short steep scoop/corner on the right to a large ledge and possible belay and scramble up an open corner to a large ledge.
6   40 m. Step left from a flake of rock and climb a groove to a ledge (possible belay on the left). Continue up slabs passing a V-groove, on the right, to easier ground.
7   25 m. Scramble to the top.

Variation   **The Original Finish**
6a 8 m. Traverse right to a belay.
7a 10 m. Climb mossy rocks above to a ledge with a sharp pointed belay.
8a 13 m. Traverse right for about 8 metres and climb a rib to a stance (poor belay or, alternatively, use the jammed square block in the corner down to the left).

GILLERCOMBE BUTTRESS

1 Gillercombe Bastion	MVS
2 Gillercombe Gully	VD
3 Gillercombe	S
Buttress	
4 Moss Wall	HVS
5 Gillercombe	HS
Chimneys	
6 Grey Knotts Face	D
7 Peregrine Way	S
8 Tiercel Wall	HVS
9 Raven's Groove	VS
10 Patient Tigers	E2
11 The Black Knight	E1
12 The White Lady	E3
13 Eyrie	HVS

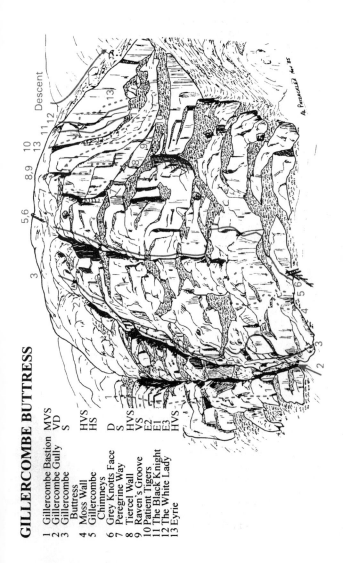

A. Phizacklea Nov '95

9a 20 m. Climb easy rocks above for a few feet. Continue up the gully to a belay on the right where the gully narrows to a chimney.

10a 18 m. Walk left round the corner and climb the loose dirty chimney.

Variation Finish   1921

6b 30 m. Climb the ordinary route to the possible belay ledge at 16 metres. Climb up left to the foot of a large detached block.

7b 15 m. Climb the wall to the right to a grassy corner. Scrambling leads to the top.

Alternative Variation Finish   1989

6c 30 m. From the middle of the ledge, climb the wall taking a line midway between the standard finish and the mottled lichen to the right, finishing by a leftward hand-traverse on doubtful flakes (poor protection).

★★ **String of Pearls** 165 m E2   1996

Takes a direct line up the steepest sections of the main buttress, on the right of *Gillercombe Buttress*. A good route on excellent rock. Start by scrambling up a rake in the path for 8 metres to the right of the start of *Gillercombe Buttress*, to a grass ledge and block thread belay.

1 23 m (5b). Enter the short slabby groove above the belay and step left to a rightwards-slanting ramp beneath a steep shallow groove. Climb the groove and pull over the small overlap onto the wall above. Move up then left to gain a slab. Ascend it to a ledge and the wall above on the left, moving rightwards to a small ledge and flake belay, below a prominent corner beside an overhang.

2 25 m (5b). Climb up onto the corner and ascend it until it is possible to pull up left. Continue directly (more easily) to a belay at the foot of the next step in the buttress.

3 25 m (4c). Climb directly up the wall towards a notch in a darker area of rock and short corner (junction with pitch 2 of *Moss Wall*). Pull up the corner/notch as for that route, then move left and up onto a ledge. Climb steeply up the short wall to gain a crack on the slab above and follow it to a good ledge and a block belay.

4 27 m (4c). Climb the wall directly behind the belay and then go more easily up the shallow rock rib to the final headwall. Move left 3 metres to belay below a prominent steep groove, 2 metres right of the start of pitch 6 of *Gillercombe Buttress*.

5   40 m (5a). Ascend the groove directly and exit right at the top. Trend rightwards and continue up the crest of the buttress on good rough rock to a good ledge and belay.
6   25 m. Scramble to the top.

Moss Wall 66 m HVS   1973
The mossy and often wet wall. Start at an obvious corner/groove 8 metres to the left of the fence.
1   40 m (4c). Climb the groove and the steep rock above. Traverse up right to a flake and make a long traverse left to climb rock bulges (sling for aid) onto a slab.
2   26 m (5a). Traverse right across a slab to a corner. Climb the corner and the rock above to the top.

Gillercombe Chimneys 140 m HS   1922
Start 6 metres left of the fence coming up to the base of the crag.
1   10 m. Climb the slabby corner and move right to below a V-groove.
2   30 m. Climb the groove to a small ledge on the right. Step back left and climb the continuation groove, with difficulty. Continue more easily rightwards to join *Grey Knotts Face* at the stance below the chimney crack of pitch 3.
3   20 m. Climb the V-groove, just right of the chimney/crack, to a grass ledge. Go up the short wall above to a ledge below pitch 4 of *Grey Knotts Face*.
4   20 m. As for *Grey Knotts Face* pitch 4.
5   60 m. As for *Grey Knotts Face* pitch 5.

★★ Grey Knotts Face 131 m D   1939
This climb more or less follows a line linking the fences below and above the crag. Not recommended for stout persons. Start just left of the fence at the base of the crag, although two additional pitches can be had on the subsidiary buttress below the main crag (1950).
1   13 m. Amble up easy rocks to a large grass ledge.
2   25 m. Climb diagonally right into a corner and move up to a square ledge (possible belay). Continue straight up the corner and through the *Letter Box* into a crevasse behind a large block. Gain the top of the block. Move left and ascend to a large ledge.
3   13 m. Rising from the left of the ledge is a chimney/crack. Climb this directly to a ledge below the continuation of the crack.
4   20 m. Climb the chimney, with a chockstone, to a grass ledge.
5   60 m. The continuation of the chimney is a shallow gully, which can be followed to the top, although it is more pleasant to use the right rib.

Variation   27 m
For those who find the *Letter Box* too exacting.
2a Traverse left above the square ledge, below a holly tree, and climb
    a prominent flake. Move left to climb a short but steep wall.
    Follow easier ground rightwards to belay on the ordinary route.

The Right Wall   (222 126)   Alt. 565 m   East Facing

High up on the northern end of the crag is a very steep wall, *The
Right Wall*. The foot of this can be reached from the main crag by
scrambling up a broken buttress on its right, and traversing the grassy
ledges leftwards. More logically it can be approached from Honister
Pass via the ridge on the right of the crag, finally traversing to the
wall. The most prominent feature of this crag is the blank wall at the
right-hand end, with the corner crack of *Eyrie* on its left. Near the
centre of the wall is the large easy angled groove of *Raven's Groove*.
Starting a short distance right of this a grassy rake ascends leftwards
to a short corner at the left end of the crag. This corner is *Peregrine
Way*.

Unfortunately the rock, which is generally quite solid, tends to be
rather dirty and can be slow to dry.

Descend to the right of the crag.

Peregrine Way   50 m   S   1939
An unsatisfactory route which takes the short corner at the left end
of the crag. Start by scrambling up the rake to below the corner.
1 20 m. Climb the corner to a stance above some huge jammed
    boulders.
2 30 m. The corner above overhangs uncompromisingly (escape
    across the steep left wall). The easier ground so reached is
    followed with no further difficulty.

Tiercel Wall   50 m   HVS   1967/1976
Takes the steep wall above the rake which is split by a narrow ledge.
Very dirty. At its right-hand end a groove fades into the lower wall.
Start 12 metres down the ramp from *Peregrine Way* below this
groove.
1 20 m (5a). Climb the wall and groove, with increasing difficulty,
    to the right end of the narrow ledge.
2 20 m (5b). 3 metres left, a thin crack runs up the steep wall.
    Climb this past a small ledge and pull out left at the top. Move
    up right to belay at the top of pitch 2 of *Raven's Groove*.

3   10 m. Go easily up the groove above to the top.

★ Raven's Groove   46 m   VS   1948
Takes the obvious central groove with a mossy left wall. Start 7 metres up the grassy rake below the groove.
1   20 m (4b). Climb the groove direct to a small stance below a short steep wall.
2   16 m (4c). The short steep wall leads to an easier angled groove which is followed to a large stance.
3   10 m. Climb easily up the continuation groove to the top.

Variation   30 m   MVS
1a (4c). The left-slanting groove, just to the right, is climbed to its top; then traverse left to join the line of the main groove.

★ Patient Tigers   52 m   E2   1975
Pleasant climbing up the slim grooves in the wall right of *Raven's Groove*. Start just right of *Raven's Groove*, as for its variation pitch 1.
1   10 m (4c). Climb a short corner and left-slanting groove to belay beneath a faint groove in the steep wall above.
2   42 m (5b). Step up right into the groove. Go up this, passing a small overhang on its left, to good holds and ledges. Move up and traverse to the right below a hanging flake. Pull up into the groove on pitch 2 of *Eyrie* and continue up this to the top.

★ The Black Knight   55 m   E1   1978
An enjoyable route up a groove system to the right of *Patient Tigers*. Start as for *Patient Tigers*.
1   13 m (4c). Climb the groove to a niche below an overhang. Pull into the crack above and step right to broken ledges.
2   42 m (5b). Climb the groove above to a bulge. Move up and trend leftwards along a steep ramp to a ledge. Go rightwards across a slab and up to join the traverse of *Eyrie* below a steep groove. Climb this groove to a ledge and continue up a layback crack formed by a huge flake to the top.

The following routes start from the grassy ledges below the blank wall at the right-hand end of the crag.

The White Lady   42 m   E3   1978
Takes the groove between *The Black Knight* and *Eyrie*, finishing up the left-slanting corner above the difficult overhang at the top. Start at the left-hand end of the ledges at a very easy angled white groove.

(6a). Climb the slabby groove and steeper continuation to a ledge on the right. Continue up the groove, passing a small overhang to join the traverse of *Eyrie*. Move up right to a ledge below the roof. Pull over into a steep groove and continue up the corner on the left to the top.

Eyrie 62 m HVS   1965
A good crack is followed by a difficult traverse in a fine situation. Start in the corner on the left of the blank wall.
1   20 m (4c). Climb the corner crack to a chockstone belay.
2   42 m (5a). Continue up the corner for 5 metres to below the large overhang. Step left to a small ledge. Swing down left and traverse left for 8 metres to a groove. Climb this (peg runner) to a ledge on the right. Move to the right along the ledge and climb the groove above to the top.

Eyrie Direct 36 m E2   1978
The logical continuation up the wide block-filled crack in the roof above pitch 1 of *Eyrie*.
(5b). Climb the crack of *Eyrie* for 22 metres to below the large overhang. Take the obvious chimney/crack slanting up right below the overhang and finish up a short groove.

The steep wall to the right of *Eyrie* now sports a stunning route.

☆☆☆ **Caution** E8 {F8a} ?   1992
Brilliant fingery climbing.
(6c). Follow an easy crack on the left-hand side of the crag for 7 metres, move right along a breakline (2 PR, the first is poor) and then climb directly to the top with hard moves to finish.

The flake crack at the right-hand end of the wall has been climbed, finishing up the rib on the left (HVS).

BORROWDALE WEST

Castle Crag   (249 159)   Alt. 175 m   West Facing

The prominent hump of *Castle Crag* overlooks the picturesque narrowing of the Borrowdale Valley about 1$^1/_2$ kilometres south of Grange. The main crag is invisible from the road and overlooks the old track from Grange to Honister. It is easily approached by the track, which starts by the Grange Cafe and leads past the Hollows Farm campsite towards Rosthwaite. Alongside the river, just past the campsite, another path strikes up a side valley. In a few hundred metres the crag can be seen on the left (20 minutes). The crag can also be approached from Rosthwaite by taking the lane opposite the Post Office. Cross the river and ascend the grassy slope over the side of Castle Crag to the crag.

There are three buttresses ascending the hillside from left to right. The left-hand and lower buttress is short, steep and unbroken with a descent to the right down a ramp under the central buttress. The central buttress is much larger and more complex, with a dirty gully dividing it from the right-hand upper buttress, which is a relatively impressive lump of rock. Descent from the central and upper buttresses is down the main path to the right. Just below the summit of the fell is a disused slate quarry which has a number of interesting boulder problems.

The rock is variable, of steeply angled slate with some loose sections that can make climbing deceptively awkward. There are, however, some good, interesting climbs. The crag dries quickly and enjoys the afternoon sun.

The climbs are described from left to right.

100 metres to the left of the *Lower Buttress* of *Castle Crag* is a small slab perched 10 metres above the scree slope just beside an old ruined sheepfold. The slab has a good ledge along its base.

★ **Mister Meaner**   13 m   E4   1989
   (6b). The finger-ripping central crackline provides a fine technical problem. Difficult to start it becomes easier, but only gradually.

The Astronaut Next Door 13 m HVS   1989
   (5c). The two cracklines on the right of the slab are climbed
   directly. The use of the right arête is not allowed!

Lower Buttress

Gardeners' World 42 m MVS   1974
This route takes the buttress to the left of *Epithet*, starting 6 metres
left of that route, at the right-hand arête.
1   30 m (4b). Ascend the right-hand side of the buttress and move
    left at 6 metres. Continue up to a ledge at 20 metres. Climb up
    the right of the wall above to a tree belay.
2   12 m (4b). Climb the slabby wall above.

Swine Trek 42 m E1   1977
An extended version of *Vortigern*, giving a mini-girdle of the *Lower
Buttress*. Start at a large pinnacle immediately left of *Epithet*.
1   12 m (4c). Ascend the pinnacle and the overhang above. Now
    follow the rib to belay on *Epithet*.
2   30 m (5b). Climb the rib on the right for 3 metres. Traverse right,
    step down into a steep groove and climb it to a ledge. Traverse
    horizontally right to join *Zoar* on the ledge below the steep crack
    and follow this to the top.

★ **Epithet** 36 m VS   1963
An interesting climb starting below the obvious V-groove to the left
of the tree at the base of the left-hand buttress.
1   16 m (4b). Climb the V-groove to the overhang at 8 metres. Pull
    out left on excellent holds and move up left to belay in the corner.
2   20 m (4b). Move up the arête on the right to gain a sapling on
    the left. Traverse to the right and climb the arête to the top.

Vortigern 36 m HVS   1963/1977
Start just right of *Epithet*.
   (5a). Climb the right wall of the groove to a ledge by a pinnacle.
   Step left off the pinnacle and ascend the continuation of the
   groove. Climb the steep wall above with difficulty. Continue up
   the groove above and finish up a short crack.

Variation **Original Finish**
   Instead of finishing up the short crack, move right, across *Zoar*,
   and traverse right to the descent path (part of *Disillusion* in
   reverse).

CASTLE CRAG

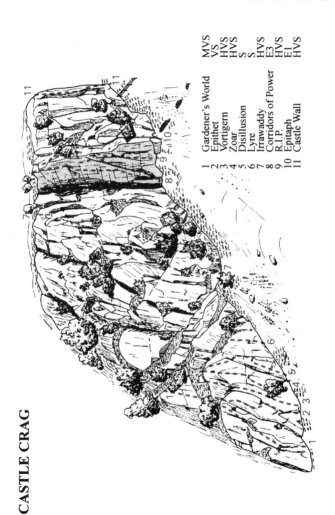

1	Gardener's World	MVS
2	Epithet	VS
3	Vortigern	HVS
4	Zoar	HVS
5	Disillusion	S
6	Lyre	S
7	Irrawaddy	HVS
8	Corridors of Power	E3
9	R.I.P.	HVS
10	Epitaph	E1
11	Castle Wall	HVS

★★ **Zoar** 36 m HVS 1970

A committing and deceptively steep route starting at the tree at the base of the buttress. A sustained effort.

(5b). Follow the grass ramp up to the left. Climb the corner above, using its right wall, until blind moves lead to the ledge on the right (peg runner and possible belay). Pull up the bulging wall, past a tiny ledge, and continue up the crack above to the top.

Direct Start (5a, 1999) starts behind the tree and goes up onto the top of the pinnacle. Follow the obvious line to join the original route.

★★ **A Face in the Crowd** 34 m E3 1989

A steep fingery route taking the wall right of *Zoar*. Start at the large block 3 metres right of that route.

(6a). Step off the pointed block and climb the short groove onto a square ledge. Indefinite cracks are followed directly until fingery moves lead to good holds on the right. Move up left to finish.

★ **Disillusion** 40 m S 1959

Start at the tree at the base of the buttress.

Follow a diagonal line up rightwards to a ledge at 12 metres. Move right, and step down awkwardly. Make a high step right and follow broken ledges up until moves left across the smooth face lead to a broken crack. Climb up this to the top.

Lyre 32 m S 1962

Start below the slabby rocks on the right of *Disillusion*.

1 22 m. Climb the pock-marked wall to a heather ledge and block belay.
2 10 m (5a). Climb the smooth corner on the left, with a sting in its tail.

Central Buttress

★★ **Irrawaddy** 80 m HVS 1955

This is a fine route up the *Central Buttress* which starts at the yew tree, just right of the base of the grass rake descent from the left-hand buttress.

1 30 m (5a). Climb the steep wall behind the yew until moves right lead to the arête and a ledge.
2 20 m (5a). Move right and climb the steep wall on good holds to a tree covered ledge.

3 30 m (4c). Traverse up rightwards to the top of a large leaning pinnacle, below a steep stepped crack. Climb the crack to easier ground and the top.

Variation **Vortex** 30 m HVS   1968
Start 3 metres right of *Irrawaddy*, below a hanging groove.
1a (5b). Pull into the groove with difficulty and climb to the small overhang. Pass this on the right. Step left and climb the wall above to the overhang. Overcome this on the left and gain the ledge above.

Castle of Fire 60 m HVS   1979
This takes the broken rib, starting 5 metres left of the dirty gully separating *Central* and *Upper Buttresses*.
1 16 m (4b). Follow the rib to a tree belay.
2 24 m (4c). Climb a V-chimney to loose blocks and a tree belay.
3 20 m (5a). Ascend the steep V-groove with difficulty. Move left to a tree belay.

Upper Buttress

Corridors of Power 53 m E3   1979
A steep and strenuous route up the big wall to the right of the gully. The protection is rather dubious in parts. Start below the gully on the left side of the buttress.
1 23 m (5b). Scramble up dirty, slabby rock for 12 metres to where the gully steepens. Climb the very steep groove on its right side, and the easier groove above, until it is possible to step left to a grass ledge. Poor belays.
2 30 m (5c). Step back into the groove and traverse the slab on the right to below a small overlap. Surmount this, and follow the thin crack to a steep open groove. Climb this to a spike, pull up leftwards (peg runner) over a small overhang and move up to a ledge. Finish up the groove and wall above.

★★ **The Blue Max** 42 m HVS   1969
A spectacular route, starting as for *Libido*.
1 26 m (5a). Climb the crack of *Libido* to a possible stance at 10 metres. Move left and up a short wall to a doubtful flake. Traverse left and climb a thin crack to an awkward stance.
2 16 m (5a). Climb the overhanging wall above on good holds.

Libido   42 m   VS   1955
The main issue of this climb is the large diagonal crack in the right
wall of the gully on the left of the buttress. Scramble up to below
the crack.
1   26 m (4c). Ascend the crack to a ledge. Several steep steps then
    lead to a steep vegetated ledge below a short wall. Belay at the
    tree on the ledge above.
2   16 m. Climb the wall above, past a large embedded flake, and go
    up the slab on the left.

★★ **R.I.P.**   53 m   HVS   1963
An intriguing route, with an exciting first pitch and an airy top pitch.
Start below and right of *Libido*, below an obvious groove, on the left
front of the buttress.
1   30 m (5a). Ascend the groove to a peg runner. Bridge up
    awkwardly until it is possible to pull out left and precariously
    enter a narrow groove. Move up, awkwardly, past a small tree,
    into a corner (*Libido*), and follow this to a belay ledge on the
    right.
2   23 m (4c). Step back down the corner and traverse left a little.
    Ascend past a sapling and go diagonally right to the arête, which
    is followed to the top.

Epitaph   46 m   E1   1963
This route has an interesting first pitch and an airy finish. Following
a rock fall the original pitch 1 has gone. Start on the right of the
huge block, just right of *R.I.P.*, and scramble up to a tree on the top
of the block below a steep groove.
1   16 m (5b). Climb the groove and ascend to the overhang. Pass
    the overhang, using a hidden side-hold on the left, and the block
    above, cautiously, to a yew tree belay.
2   30 m (4c). Traverse left onto *Libido*, then climb the rib behind
    the tree, directly in an exposed position, to join and follow *R.I.P.*

Variation   **Original Finish**   23 m   S
2a Scramble up rightwards to a ledge and climb the short wall, just
    left of the loose overhanging corner, to a heather ledge on the
    left. Finish up easy rock.

Jigsaw (VS, 1961) takes the rocks just right of *Epitaph* but is
unworthy of detailed description.

Opposite: Jilly Reid in glorious Borrowdale sunshine on **Gillercombe
Buttress** (S)
                                                        Stephen Reid

Castle Wall   36 m   HVS   1961
A varied route. Some of the rock appears to be of doubtful stability.
Start at the ash tree to the right of the fence, on the right of the crag.
   (5a). Scramble up leftwards, then climb steeply rightwards and
   fight past an old yew tree, with difficulty. Climb the flake crack
   above, moving right and continue up an awkward crack. Move
   left and finish up an overhanging wall on the right of a slanting
   crack.

Hows Crag   (250 160)   Alt. 195 m   East Facing

This crag lies on the tree covered eastern slopes of *Castle Crag*. It
is generally vegetated although the right-hand end is quite clean. It
would be worth waiting for a spell of dry weather before making a
visit. It is a crag for the Borrowdale aficionado but it has been
claimed that *The Fortress* offers one of the best crack pitches in the
valley!

It is best approached by following the track to the quarry on the top
of the hill, then descending a ridge on the east which leads round the
south side of the crag. It takes about 40 minutes from Grange.

Castle Crag Gully   25 m   VD   1944
   The disgusting gully at the left end of the crag.

Green Wall   46 m   HVS   ?   1981
The lower half of the pitch is obvious, but the line taken by the upper
half could not be ascertained. The description as recorded is included
for the connoisseur to further investigate. Start 6 metres right of
Castle Crag Gully, just left of a large elm tree.
   Climb the green groove, move right into a crack and climb it until
   a traverse left across a steep wall leads to a ledge. The groove
   above leads to tree belays.

The Shock of the New   55 m   E2   ?   1983
A shocking route up the centre of the crag. The rock is rather poor
and protection mediocre. Start about 3 metres right of the large tree
near the lowest point of the crag.
1   10 m. Climb the easy groove to a grassy ledge.

Opposite: Joe Wilson looking relaxed on the second pitch of
Tumbleweed Connection (E2), Goat Crag
                                        Dave Hinton – Joe Wilson Collection

2   45 m. Climb up from the left end of the ledge and then go diagonally leftwards across the wall past a short groove and steep slab to a small ledge below a groove. Move up and step right to a ledge. Go up the grooves above to a tree belay at the top.

Castle in the Air   45 m   HVS   ?   1978
Start as for *The Shock of the New*.
   Climb the groove to a ledge and small tree. Continue up the steep wall to a small overhang. Pull over this and continue to a crack in a corner on the right. Climb this and slabs above to the top.

Castillion   45 m   HVS   ?   1978
A very mossy, dirty route which starts 5 metres right of *Castle in the Air*.
1   30 m. Climb the wall to a ledge below a shallow groove which leads to a tree belay.
2   15 m. The crack on the left leads to a shallow groove. Follow the slab above to the top.

★ **The Fortress**   43 m   HVS   1995
An alternative start for *Castillion*.
1   28 m (4b). Start on the front of a clean buttress. Pull up the wall. Move round some blocks into the right-facing groove. Good climbing up the groove and rib above leads on to an awkward landing on the large ledge and tree belay.
2   15 m (5a). Move up and left across the ledge to a small cave with a crack in the back. Climb the fine crack of *Castillion*. Tree belay.

Vicious Vicky from Barrow   43 m   E1   ?   1995
Start to the right of *The Fortress*.
1   28 m (5b). Climb the corner. Make hard moves to gain the sloping ledge. Move up and right over a short bulge. Traverse left and climb the last few feet of *The Fortress* to a tree belay.
2   15 m. Move to the right-hand end of the ledge below the steep wall and climb the groove to a tree belay.

★ **Tomb Raider**   45 m   E5   1997
1   29 m. Follow pitch 1 of *Vicious Vicky* to the terrace then scramble up to the steep wall.
2   16 m (6b). Starting behind the oak tree, 5 metres right of *Castillion*, pull easily into the V-groove. Follow the natural curving line of overlaps using underclings and sidepulls to a downward-pointing spike. Use this to reach some good pockets

on the wall above. Climb past an in-situ wire to a jug. Gain the ledge above and then the top. Sustained!

Dreamscape 16 m E6 {F7a+} ?   1999
Start 2 metres left of the top pitch of *Tomb Raider*. A serious route.
(6b). Climb the groove to undercuts, where a move past pockets and an obvious one finger undercut leads to a hidden jug. Hard moves using underclings lead to good holds and reasonable gear. Hand-traverse left for 1 metre and climb the thin wall (crux).

Suspended Animation 16 m E4   1998
Start 4 metres down and right of *Tomb Raider*, behind a tree.
(6a). Climb cracks and pockets for 6 metres until the left end of the small overhang is reached. Using two finger slots just above the overhang, swing rightwards to a committing mantelshelf onto the obvious flat ledge. A high step onto sloping holds on the left enable the upper wall to be gained. This leads to a tree belay.

Mac's Wall (249 163) Alt. 150 m   North West Facing

This small wall is situated in the wood on the north flank of *Castle Crag* to the east of the track leading from Hollows Farm campsite to *Castle Crag*. Situated about 50 metres south east of the bridge on the stream.

★ **Big Business** 10 m E3   1988
(6b). Just left of the centre of the clean, steep wall is a faint crack. Immediately left of this, it is possible to climb directly up a dark streak to the top. A hard boulder problem which becomes progressively easier.

Zombie in the Dark 10 m E3   1992
Start just right of *Big Business*.
(6c). Follow a faint crack line direct to a peg runner then move up to some jugs and finish up *Big Business*.

Strange Brew 10 m E3 ?   1993
Start at a niche 1 metre right of *Zombie in the Dark*. Climb to a layaway and then climb directly up the wall.

Mac's Crack   10 m   VS   1974
   (4c). Climb the crack on the right of the wall, moving left slightly
   to finish up a short crack.

One Across   12 m   E1   1989
Start at the extreme right of the wall.
   (5c). This takes the high level traverse of the wall by
   hand-traversing a ragged break to finish up *Big Business*.

Two Down   12 m
   (6a). This boulder problem takes the lower traverse line starting
   on the right and finishes at a block on the left of the wall.

Waterslide Slab (254 158); approaching from Rosthwaite, this small
aptly named crag lies in a hollow to the west of the path a few
hundred metres short of where it branches to Millican Dalton's Cave.
The lines are more or less obvious starting from the left, **Route 1**
(S), **Route 2** (VS), **Route 3** (VS), and **Cascade** (VS). All are under
10 metres high and all were climbed in 1994. Less obvious is why
anyone should want to climb them.

Millican's Buttress   (252 159)   Alt. 160 m   North East Facing

This is a steep crag 24 metres high, situated 100 metres left of
Millican Dalton's Cave. Follow the road and track south from Grange
past Hollows Farm campsite. At the wooden bridge, keep left and
continue along the side of the river. Follow the main path as it veers
right, going up to and through a break in a wall and then up over a
small col where it turns up towards the slate screes below *Millican's
Cave*. The crag lies 50 metres to the left of the first cave you come
to as you follow the path up. An easy descent can be made down the
left-hand side of the crag. The tree belays are well back. The routes
are described from right to left.

The Crystal Maze   25 m   S   1990
Start at the right-hand end of the crag. Climb the steep wall on good
holds for 6 metres. Now climb up and left on large quartz holds
crossing the top of *Karaoke* to a tree belay.

Crystal Gazer 25 m VS   1994
Start as for *The Crystal Maze*. Climb the steep wall for 6 metres.
Move up and follow the arête to a small overhang. Move left steeply
to join the top of the *Dark Crystal*.

The Dark Crystal 27 m HVS   1994
   (5b). This is the longest route on the buttress. The climb starts
behind the tree at the right-hand end of the impressive
overhanging wall. Make some hard moves on small holds onto
the gangway above. Go up the wall above on good jugs to the
foot of the steep crack. Climb to its top, traverse a few feet right
and move up and left to an awkward landing.

Green Death 25 m E2   1999
Start behind the tree just left of The *Dark Crystal*.
   (5b). Climb the disgusting groove. Make an awkward hard move
left and climb the chimney to a small tree which you pass on the
left. Traverse the almost certainly slimy wall for 3 metres. Climb
up and right onto the last few moves of *Crystal Maze*.

Karaoke 25 m VS   1994
Start below the large tree overlooking the overhanging wall. Follow
a ledge system right to a chimney and exit left.

★★ **Sheriff of Nottingham** 23 m E6 {F7b}   1994
   (6b). The arête up the left-hand side of the overhanging streaked
wall is hard to start and even harder to finish. Move right past 2
pegs and then into a groove at the top.

In the Blood 23 m E6 {F7b+}   1997
   (6c). Follow *Sheriff of Nottingham* to the break. Now, instead of
moving right, attack the wall directly making intimidating moves
to a crucial Wallnut 6 placement. Moving up and right from this
is the crux.

The next routes start on the high grassy ledge up to the left.

★★ **Liquid Morphine** 15 m E2   1994
   (5c). Mantelshelf onto a ledge on the right and finish up the steep
groove above.

★ **Cold Lazarus** 15 m E3   1994
   (6a). One metre left, a finger-hold is used to pass a peg to reach
a fantastic jug. Finish straight up with no deviation left.

To the left of the ledge there is a series of grooves and arêtes.

** **Pennies from Heaven**   15 m   E1   1994
A pleasant route.
   (5b). Start just right of the first obvious groove using a dubious
   flake. Follow sloping holds rightwards to a good jug. Finish on
   good holds straight above.

* **Black Eyes**   15 m   E1   1994
   (5b). Start left of the first groove and climb the wall directly.

Goodbye Dennis   15 m   E2   1994
   (5c). Start up the groove sporting an obvious roof. Move right at
   the roof then follow the gangway to finish as for the previous
   route.

Dennis the Menace   12 m   MVS   1994
   Climb the arête to the left of *Goodbye Dennis*.

* **Singing Detective**   12 m   E2   1994
   (5b). To the left of the arête of *Dennis the Menace* is a wide open
   corner. The groove on the left-hand side is climbed to the top
   where moves rightwards can be made onto the rib. Make awkward
   moves to finish straight above. It can be made easier by stepping
   right from the rib.

The Crack   12 m   HVS   1994
   Start at the arête on the left of the wide corner. Climb the crack
   on the right side of the arête.

Millican's Arête   12 m   E1   1994
This route follows the left side of the arête on the left of *The Crack*.
   (5b). Start at the foot of the arête and climb to an undercling.
   Finish up the crack on the left.

The Groove   10 m   HVS   1994
This follows the corner left of *Millican's Arête*.
   (5a). Climb the groove to a small ledge on the right wall. Make
   hard moves up the groove then step left (moving right may be an
   easier and safer option).

Dalt Quarry (249 165) Alt. 120 m

North and South Facing

A very small slate quarry in the trees below *Goat Crag*, giving short but often pleasant sport routes in a sheltered setting. The rock is sound and all bolts and lower-offs are in place. Four tie-offs should suffice. Park in Grange and approach via the track to Hollows Farm Campsite, go past the campsite car park (campers only!) and head up rightwards over a wooden bridge; the quarry is 125 metres further up the track on the right. There is a pool (*The Dalt Loch*) in the quarry floor – please do not disturb it for conservation reasons. The climbs are on the *South* and *North* sides.

South Side

1.	**Dark Angel**	F7b+	1995
2.	**Shadow Warrior**	F7c	1994
3.	**Bat Out of Hell**	HVS, 5a (trad)	1993
	(aka Mac's Crack)		
4.	**Skegness is so Bracing**	F6a+	1990
5.	**Hothouse**	F6b+	1990
6.	**Backfire**	F6b	1990
7.	**Nameless**	F5	1990
8.	**Zima Junction**	F6a+	1990
9.	**Valdez is Coming**	F6b+	1990

DALT QUARRY
South (Left-hand) Side

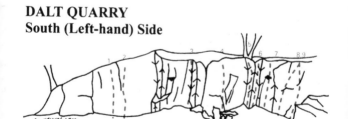

AL HEWISON 2000

North Side

10. **Al's Slab**	F5+	1990
11. **Panzerfaust**	F6c+	1990
12. **Heart of Glass**	F6b	1990
13. **Better Red Than Dead**	F5+	1990
14. **Laguna Verde**	F5	1990
15. **Blue Oyster Cult**	F6a	1990

(can be started on the R and finished more directly 6b)

16. **Zipcode**	F5	1990
17. **Chickenhawk**	F5+	1990
18. **The Seam**	F4	1990
19. **Dalt Loch Monster**	F6a	
20. **Dalt Loch Chimney**	F5	1990
21. **Wounded Knee**	F3+	1990
22. **Ian's Day Off**	HVS, 5a (trad)	1995
23. **Bury My Heart**	F3+	1990
24. **Legless in Gaza**	F6b	1990
25. **Baywatch**	F5+	1990
26. **Little Sydney**	F5	1990

DALT QUARRY
North (Right-hand) Side

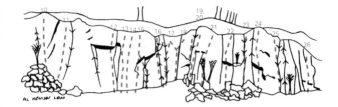

AL HEWISON 2000

Goat Crag

Goat Crag is obvious from Grange as the large scattered crag on the west side of the valley near the hump of *Castle Crag* and opposite *Bowderstone Crag*. The cliff is very extensive but can hardly be regarded as a unity. For ease of identification and description it has been divided into various sections. They differ enormously in character and are further described under their respective headings.

A track from Grange village ends at Hollows Farm Campsite after a little over a kilometre. From the campsite the *Southern Buttresses* can be reached by following the old Honister track to a gate at the end of the woods. Continue for a hundred metres then strike directly up the fellside on the right, keeping well to the left of the prominent outcrop of *Steel Knotts*. If either *Steel Knotts*, *The Northern Crag*, *Knitting Needle Gully Wall* or *Upper Crag* is the destination, go through the campsite, over a stile and up the hillside until it is possible to skirt the top edge of the woods below the crag. Continue to a shoulder below the left end of the *North Crag*. *Steel Knotts* is immediately to the left, round the corner. The other crags are reached by following the track which slants rightwards up the hillside below the main crag. Both *Southern* and *Northern* areas can be reached in ten to fifteen minutes from the campsite.

Note that the traditionally used parking spot below the campsite has been rendered out of bounds by the placement of some large boulders and the nearest parking is now in Grange.

At the time of writing, the National Trust have applied for planning permission to place stepping stones in the River Derwent so as to enable a quick approach from Bowderstone Quarry car park, but it is not certain that this will be approved.

The Southern Buttresses   (245 163)   Alt. 300 m   East Facing

The *Southern Buttresses*, well to the left of *Steel Knotts* are quite broken. In fact, some effort of imagination is required to think of them as true crags at all, so retiring are they among the screes, streams and old workings on the fellside. *Perched Block Buttress* is the most prominent, as it is characterized by a large overhang on its right side. To its left, there are some broken rocks which give a little climbing, and to the right further broken rocks provide even more indifferent scrambles.

The rock on these buttresses can be pleasant, sometimes steep, quit
difficult and usually interesting.

Lobstone Buttress

Lobstone Buttress   86 m   S   194
This is the buttress almost opposite the corner in the wall to the le
of *Castle Crag* and just right of the obvious stream/gully. Start by
small needle of rock, below a holly, on the left of the buttress.
1   26 m. Mount the little pinnacle and climb past the holly, up th
    wide crack, to the top of a pinnacle.
2   25 m. Move left and ascend a corner and rocks above. Move bac
    right and up past unstable blocks to the top of the outcro
    Scramble leftwards up the buttress to where the rocks regain thei
    verticality. To the left of the centre is a steep flake chimney.
3   20 m. Climb the flake chimney, passing several chockstones, t
    the great pinnacle flake summit.
4   15 m. Step across the chasm and follow slabs to a large ledg
    Easy rocks lead to the top.

Variation Start   18 m   VS
1a (5a). The steep strenuous crack on the left of the pinnacle i
    climbed to its top.

Perched Block Buttress

This is the buttress 100 metres right of *Lobstone Buttress*. Th
Perched Block is a large detached slab standing on a terrace abov
the steep lower wall.

★ **Perched Block**   78 m   VS   1940/19.
A disjointed route, with a fine first pitch, which starts 6 metres t
the left and just above the base of the crag, below a shallow corne
1   30 m (4c). Ascend the corner to its top with difficulty. Scrambl
    to below *The Perched Block*.
2   18 m. Climb the edge of the block and move down left to a dee
    chimney.
3   30 m (4c). Climb the groove on the left or, with more difficult
    climb the imposing chimney past a rock pinnacle to the easi
    rocks above. Scramble to the top.

Variation   **The Original Start**   28 m   19
1a (4b). Start higher up to the left and climb up to just right of
    yew. Walk up to *The Perched Block*.

Black Crack   30 m   HVS   199•

Start 3 metres higher up the gully than the original start of *Perched Block* at an obvious right-slanting fault line.

(4c). Traverse right until a deep crack appears. Climb this to a small shelf. Traverse right delicately until easier rock leads to a spike belay.

★ **Random Choice**   36 m   HVS   198•

Start at the base of the lower buttress down to the right of the start of *The Perched Block* on the right of the arête below an obvious corner crack.

(5a). Climb the crack to about 3 metres below a large roof. Move left onto the arête and up to a ledge. Move 3 metres left under the roof to a groove. Gain the groove, using a juniper, and continue up the groove above rightwards to finish.

Upper Buttress

At the left-hand side of the upper buttress is a deep chimney (pitch 3 of *The Perched Block*) that has a pillar forming its left side. The following route takes the crackline on the front of this pillar.

★ **Azania**   30 m   HVS   1994

(5b). Follow the obvious crack to a sloping ledge. Step left to follow a flake crack continuation and a groove leading to a twin spike. Climb the fine wall above on good holds.

★★ **Brass Monkey**   20 m   E1   1988

Just to the left of *The Perched Block* itself is a clean steep wall with an obvious groove/crack, immediately above the hole beneath the block.

(5b). Laybacking the flake crack leads to a definite crux at the overlap. Finish up an easy groove.

Peregrine Wall   23 m   HVS   1955

Start just right of *The Perched Block* below a very dirty green wall.

(5a). Climb the wall for 3 metres, using a crack, and continue into a steep crack, just right of the top of *The Perched Block*. Go up via a jammed flake to the top.

★★ **African Skies**   43 m   E1   1988

An airy and enjoyable traverse above the large roof on the right of *The Perched Block*. Start at the left end of the roof by a detached pinnacle, just right of *Peregrine Wall*.

(5b). Step off the pinnacle and gain the groove above. Follow the diagonal crack right and gain the groove of *Well Heeled*. Climb the groove a couple of metres until it is possible to swing right on pockets to gain an easier-angled gangway. Step down and right to the lip of the overhang, then climb the steep wall until it is possible to step right across the overhanging groove of *Cry Freedom*. Step down and traverse right to a good pocket in the middle of the wall. Climb straight up finishing in a shallow corner right of the grass ledge and tree. Well protected but beware of rope drag.

★ **Well Heeled**   30 m   E2   1988
Takes the roof and groove directly from the yellow shield of rock below the left side of the large roof. Start at a small tree 6 metres right and below the start of *African Skies*.
    (5b). Climb a groove left of the yellow shield of rock until excellent jams lead out right under the roof (good 3.5 Friend). At its narrowest point surmount the roof on good holds and climb the groove above leading left. Gain a good ledge and scramble to the top.

★ **Cry Freedom**   52 m   E3   1963/1988
This route takes the obvious challenge of the large roof at its widest point following the overhanging groove of the old aid route *Via Roof Route*. Wild and airy positions!
1   26 m (4a). Scramble up the grassy ledges directly below the roof to belay on a large pinnacle and a holly tree below the right-hand side of the roof.
2   26 m (6b). Step off the pinnacle and climb up to the roof. Make a hard move to gain good holds leading left across the wall of the overhanging groove, until it is possible to gain a resting place on the left at the lip (4 peg runners). Step back right into the groove and climb it on good pockets to an exit left at the top. Climb straight up keeping just left of a crack and passing left of a grass ledge and holly tree.

Steel Knotts   (246 164)   Alt. 240 m   South East Facing

To the right of the *Southern Buttress* of *Goat Crag*, low down on the hillside, is the short clean buttress of *Steel Knotts*. It is composed of excellent rock and gives some pleasant routes. Descent is down the scree to the left of the crag.

The climbs are described from left to right.

Skid Row 63 m HVS   196.
A girdle traverse starting just right of the holly near the left end of
the crag.
1 25 m (5a). Climb the wall, using two cracks slanting left, to a
   holly. Move right past a holly and a sapling to gain a niche
   beneath an overhang. Continue at the same level to a stance on
   Route 1.
2 18 m (4b). Move right and down to a ledge to *Ambling Ant*. Climb
   down this and right into a corner. Belay at the holly on *Route 2*.
3 20 m (4c). Finish up *Route 2*, by the wall on the right and the
   slabs above.

★★ The Sting 23 m E2   197.
A fine little route giving good jamming. Start below a thin vertical
crackline, 5 metres right of a large holly, near the left end of the
crag.
    (5c). Climb the crack, past a holly and a small ledge at
    half-height, to finish up the short rib on the left.

Meandering Maggot 36 m HVS   1984
A contrived route. Start just left of *Route 1*.
    (5b). Ascend a crack until a move right onto *Route 1* gains the
    niche on the left, below an overhang. Climb up, avoiding the
    overhang on its left, to follow pleasant cracks rightwards to the
    top.

★ Route 1 30 m HVS   196.
A deceptively awkward climb. Start at a large detached block at the
centre of the crag.
    (5a). Ascend the crack above to a corner. Finish up the final wide
    crack with interest.

★★ Ambling Ant 30 m MVS   198.
A pleasant open climb starting on a block 6 metres down and right
of *Route 1*.
    (4b). Step off the block, then go up a corner/crack to a ledge, just
    left of a holly. Pass the corner above by moves on the left to gain
    a ledge. Continue up the wall above, passing a large detached
    block, to easier rock and the top.

★ **Route 2**   30 m   MVS

A pleasant route starting at an obvious crack.

(4b). Climb the crack to a holly, then climb up the wall on the right and finish up slabs.

★ **Tottering Tortoise**   40 m   VS   1965

Where the crag turns the corner on the left, start below the obvious snaking corner crack.

(5a). Ascend the crack with interest to join *Route 2*. Pass a holly and go up the wall on the right. Finish up the slabs above.

Paint it Black   30 m   E2   1982

Start at a short corner, just right of *Tottering Tortoise*.

(5c). Climb the corner onto a large ledge on the right. Climb the obvious black crack until it becomes thin. Move left onto the wall and make a hard move right, and go up to a large hold. Stand on this and then continue to a large ledge. Climb the wall and crack, right of a holly, to finish up the slabs above.

★ **The Lost Boys**   30 m   HVS   1995

Start in the corner as for *Paint it Black*.

(5a). Climb the arête to step out onto the pinnacle. Continue up the arête from the pinnacle and finish by climbing the cracks to the left of the holly tree up a steep wall.

★ **Free Falling**   28 m   E3   1995

Start in the centre of the steep wall on the front of the crag 3 metres left of *B.M.C. 1*.

(6a). Climb the broken ribs to a small niche at around 4 metres. Make some awkward moves up and continue through the left-hand side of the shallow scoop to a ledge. Finish up the easy slabs to the top.

B.M.C. 1   30 m   MVS   1986

This takes the groove bounding the right-hand side of the steep east face and the centre of the upper wall.

1   20 m (4b). Climb the dirty groove to a ledge on the right and move left onto the large terrace. Traverse to a small holly.

2   10 m (4b). Move right 2 metres to a vague weakness. Climb this and the wall above.

The Northern Crag   (245 165)   Alt. 350 m   North East Facing

The *Northern Crag* is the crag that local climbers usually refer to as *Goat Crag*.

It slants up the fellside 50 metres to the right of *Steel Knotts* and is quite different from its smaller neighbours. Its aspect, together with the amount of moss and vegetation, particularly on the left-hand end, mean that it is rather slow to dry after wet weather.

The cliff layout is fairly complicated. A long slanting area of rock is prominent from the approach. A rocky diagonal rake, up which the foot-path wanders, cuts in below it, just above some lower subsidiary rocks. The cliff is terminated on the left by a grassy gully, which is in turn guarded by a lone tower on its left. This is taken by *The Kremlin*. The vegetated slabs of the lower left end of the crag become cleaner and steeper, as one moves right and eventually merge into a much more impressive area of excellent steep rock on the right, topped by some 'beetling yellow overhangs'. The rock then fades away indecisively into extremely steep heather ledges and short walls.

Only two of the climbs on this crag are of easier standard than Very Severe. Some still present the hazards of vegetation and loose rock, though routes on the right of the main crag are among the best in the area.

Descent, by walking, from the top of routes is a long arduous trek. It first involves a scramble up and leftwards over the steep tree and heather covered slopes to the ridge above the crag. A long loose descent down the gully and hillside to its south is made until it is possible to contour below *Steel Knotts*, then back up the path below the *North Crag*. A quicker and more convenient means of descent is by abseil from one of the numerous trees along the top of the crag. Care should be taken to ensure a suitable second abseil point is reached as single rope lengths are inadequate in many places. Suitable trees are available on ledges at half height for this purpose.

The routes are described from left to right.

Silly Billy   23 m   VD   1985
Start at the foot of the smooth rib, 20 metres left of *The Kremlin*, and just above the approach path.
    Follow a crack to gain and climb short corner/grooves above. Finish up short slabs and easier rock to gain the obvious tree. Abseil descent.

Billy Goat Bluff   23 m   E1   1985
An easily accessible little climb taking the obvious smooth rib of *Silly Billy*. Poorly protected.

   (5a). Start below the right side of the rib and climb this with a slight excursion on the right. The crux is a faint groove at mid-height. Continue up easier rock to an obvious tree. Abseil descent.

★ **The Kremlin**   50 m   VS   1965
Left of the main crag is a tree-filled gully, with a slanting tower on its left side. Though contrived, this route ascends the tower, giving interesting climbing on excellent rock. Start below a groove to the left of the tower, just above the point where the approach path comes up to the crag.
1   30 m (4b). Climb the groove for 12 metres and move right to a scoop. Continue rightwards up to the roof and into a scoop capped by a second overhang.
2   20 m (5a). Ascend the overhang above and move right to the arête. Continue up the slabs above.

Variation   16 m   VS   1967
2a Traverse 5 metres left, between the overhangs, to where a long stride gains slabs which lead to the top.

On the right of the tree-filled gully (useful for descent) there is a large area of slabs which contains a number of now rather vegetated routes.

★ **Dwarf's Divorce**   77 m   E2   1980
This climbs up the short upper walls above the dirty slabs near the left end of the crag. Poorly protected on pitch 3. Start as for *The Gnome*.
1   45 m (4a). Climb straight up the slabs then diagonally leftwards to a tree and grassy ledges below a steep wall.
2   16 m (5b). Move to the right edge of the wall and ascend to a small overhang. Step right and climb the right edge of the wall, past a sloping hold, to a large sloping ledge.
3   16 m (5c). Step right round a rib past a hanging block, and climb the rib and wall above, trending leftwards to the left-hand of two thin cracks. Climb this to a tree belay at the top.

★ **The Gnome** 72 m VS   1966

An interesting climb, starting to the right of the foot of the gully, below a vegetated groove in the slab. It takes the slabby area just left of a prominent crack in a pinnacle rib taken by *The Bridal Suite*.

1 16 m (4a). Climb the slab and pass a prominent tree to a grass ledge above.

2 30 m (4c). Climb slabs and ledges on the right, until a higher ledge is attained. Traverse 5 metres left and follow a line of good holds up a steep wall to a peg runner. Pull over the overlap into a slabby recess and make a few delicate moves left to a slab above. Peg belay. Alternatively, from the slabby recess, a move leads right to a junction with *The Bridal Suite*.

3 26 m (4a). Step left and follow the deep vegetated groove to the top.

The Bridal Suite 96 m VS   1966

An interesting climb starting 3 metres right of the tree-filled gully and 5 metres left of a tree at the lowest point of the slab. The second pitch takes the obvious crack in a pinnacle rib.

1 40 m (4a). Ascend the slabs rightwards. Go up indefinite grooves to a chockstone belay on the left, below and right of the pinnacle rib.

2 40 m (4b). Move left and up to a groove on the right of the pinnacle rib. After a metre or so, move up leftwards and climb the obvious crack to the top of the pinnacle.

3 16 m (4a). Go left to a groove. Follow this, and the rib on the left, to the top.

★★ **April Fool** 65 m VS   1966

An excellent second pitch makes this route well worthwhile. Start just right of *The Bridal Suite* and just left of a large tree at the base of the slab.

1 40 m (4b). Ascend an awkward slab and follow slabs rightwards to a tree belay below a crack in a rib.

2 25 m (4c). Follow the crack to a point 3 metres below the spike at its top then traverse left 3 metres. Climb some indefinite cracks and pleasant slabs above to below a steep wall. Step down left to a stance. Scrambling on the left leads to the top. Alternatively, climb *The Direct Finish*.

★ Variation **The Direct Finish** 10 m HVS   1967

3a (5a). Climb the steep wall above by a shallow groove. A lassoed tree was used to finish originally – not now though!!

The path along the crag foot begins to ascend a rocky ramp below a very vegetated area of the crag. About 50 metres up the ramp there is a groove on the left, above a levelling.

Tarkus   84 m   VS   1971
A vague and vegetated line to the left of *The Queer Thing*. Not recommended.

The Queer Thing   92 m   VS   1966
A now very vegetated climb starting at the levelling in the ramp.
1   26 m (4a). Climb the slab, a shallow groove and a rib above to a yew belay.
2   16 m. The corner behind the yew leads to a large ledge.
3   40 m (4c). An easy groove leads to the top of a pinnacle. Continue up slabs to a larger groove, which leads to a stance and tree belay.
4   10 m. Finish up the groove above.

A step in the path, then a scramble up a rocky rake leads to a shoulder abutting the foot of the crag. This is used as an assembly point for climbers on this area of the crag. About 20 metres to the left is a large embedded flake with an obvious yew tree on its left.

★★ **The Peeler**   83 m   VS   1965
A popular climb which takes the crack and its continuation groove starting behind the yew tree.
1   30 m (4b). Move left from the tree and climb the crack in its entirety to a good stance and oak stump belay.
2   23 m (4c). Ascend the corner groove on the left and step left to gain an arête which leads to a holly. Purists may wish to continue to the original finish by following pitch 3. They may then learn why most people abseil from the end of pitch 2!
3   30 m. Climb a corner, over perched blocks, to a large flake. Ascend this, then easy climbing and scrambling lead to the top.

★ **High Flyer**   52 m   E1   1978
An enjoyable route which ascends the thin slab right of *The Peeler* and the awkward groove above. Start directly behind the yew tree, just left of a thin crack. The second pitch is poorly protected
1   26 m (5a). Go straight up the steep slab, exiting leftwards at the top to an oak stump and good ledge.
2   26 m (5b). Ascend the grooved arête above the belay. Pull out right at the top, below a blank wall. Traverse right to a corner

and move up to a ledge and belay on *Deadly Nightshade*. Easy scrambling above leads to the top.

★ **Deadly Nightshade** 112 m HVS   1965
Start at a thin crack behind the embedded flake, just right of *High Flyer*. Rather mossy and vegetated.
1   30 m (4c). Climb the crack, past some saplings, to a small ledge. Follow a flake crack right to a rib and go up this to a small tree. Continue up the dirty groove above to a ledge.
2   42 m (5a). Go diagonally left to a corner-groove and move up this to a heather ledge. Ascend a short groove above, step right and go up a shallow scoop to a good ledge.
3   20 m (4c). Move right to a diagonal ramp and follow it to a V-corner, which leads to a ledge below a steep corner.
4   20 m (4b). Climb the corner, then go diagonally left across mossy slabs and up to a tree.

Teva Fever 80 m E1   1992
Start at the crack behind the embedded flake.
1   40 m (5a). Climb the crack, stepping right at the top onto the arête left of *Manpower*. Follow this to finish up a groove, swinging right to belay on a ledge as for *Manpower*.
2   40 m (5b). Climb directly onto the slab, trending slightly right to the cracked arête. Climb the crack directly to finish up *Alone in Space*.

★★ **Manpower** 75 m E2   1983
An excellent route with bold thin climbing. Protection on pitch 1 is only as good as the state of the in-situ peg. Start 5 metres right of the embedded flake, below a crack leading to a corner/groove below the left side of some overhangs.
1   36 m (5c). Climb the crack, over a bulge, and follow a narrow ramp up the corner to below the overhangs at its top. Pull left across the overhangs, and go up a short groove to a corner. Climb this and pull up to a grassy ledge and thread belay.
2   26 m (5b). Follow the slab above to a steep headwall. Move right and climb the wall to a ledge.
3   13 m (5a). Cross the wall on the right, firstly up a little bit, then back left into a corner. Follow this to a ledge and tree belays.

★★ **The Rat Race** 101 m E2   1966/1975
Steep climbing on sloping holds through the overhangs right of *Manpower*. Start as for *Manpower*.

GOAT CRAG

1	The Peeler	VS
2	High Flyer	E1
3	Manpower	E2
4	The Rat Race	E2
5	Alone in Space	E1
6	The Cursing Caterpillar	HVS
7	The Blaspheming Butterfly	HVS
8	The Big Curver	E2
9	Fear of Flying	E3
10	Wild Times	E5
11	D.D.T.	HVS
12	Praying Mantis	E1
13	Bitter Oasis	E4
14	Blind Faith	E2
15	Heretic	E2

1   42 m (5c). Climb the crack, over a bulge, and move right to some
    ledges. Ascend the luminous green slab to below the steep right
    wall. Step left into the corner and go up this to a good hold on
    the right at the top. Immediately go back left round a bulge to a
    groove. Climb up this, and the corner above, pulling out right at
    the top, and move up to a small ledge.
2   26 m (5a). Go up left, across the mossy slab, to a crack which
    leads to a short steep wall, just right of an undercut rib. Go up
    and left to a small ledge on the arête and follow this up leftwards
    to a junction with *Deadly Nightshade*.
3   13 m. The corner above is followed to a ledge.
4   20 m (4c). Descend slightly to the right and traverse diagonally
    right across a steep wall to the arête. Good holds lead to the top.

★★ The Cursing Caterpillar   116 m   HVS   1965
A good climb weaving up the crag which starts about 12 metres right
of *The Rat Race* at a small flake below a slab, just left of a large
perched flake.
1   23 m (4b). Climb the flake and slab above. Move right to a
    groove and go up this, past a holly, to a large ledge and tree
    belay.
2   30 m (5a). Move left round a bulge into a scoop below an
    overhanging wall. Traverse left to a small overhang at its left end.
    Pull over this and climb up steeply to a resting place. Traverse
    left, then go up the ramp on the right to an excellent thread belay.
3   13 m (4a). Follow the overlap rightwards, step down onto a slab
    and traverse to a stalwart tree.
4   30 m. A groove in the slab above leads to heather ledges. Move
    up right to a large yew tree.
5   20 m (4c). Climb the line of the jamming crack which has now
    collapsed.

★ Solid Air   110 m   E1   1978
An interesting line starting as for *The Cursing Caterpillar*.
1   26 m (5a). Pitch 1 of *Alone in Space*.
2   20 m (5a). Traverse left to a peg runner under a small overhang.
    Pull left over this and move up steeply to a resting place, as for
    The Cursing Caterpillar; then traverse left to a ledge beside a
    small ash.
3   26 m (4c). Climb the corner on the left until below a corner in
    an overlap. Gain the slab above and follow a crackline rightwards
    for 6 metres. Move right and ascend another crack until near the
    top of the slab. Move right and up a corner to a ledge.

4   16 m (5b). Traverse 5 metres left to two good footholds below a
    ledge. Move left to below a V-groove, gain a niche, then ascend
    to a mossy ledge.
5   22 m (4c). Ascend rightwards to a flake. Gain and climb a
    slanting corner and groove above to the top.

★★★ **Alone in Space**   100 m   E1   1977
This excellent route has a well protected crux but do not
underestimate pitch 1, which can feel distinctly exciting. Start as for
The Cursing Caterpillar.
1   26 m (5a). Climb the flake and slab, as for *The Cursing
    Caterpillar*, until it is possible to move left to gain a short crack
    in a bulge. Go up this, then move right to a ledge and peg belay.
2   28 m (5b). Step up right to a thin crack below a break in the
    bulge above. Pull up, step left and ascend the slab and corner to
    a thread belay below an overhang.
3   15 m (5a). Climb the overhang and continuation groove. Step
    right to a grass ledge below a green wall. An escape right is often
    made here but the climbing on pitch 4 is better than it looks.
4   31 m (5a). From the right side of the ledge, make an ascending
    traverse left to a tree. Climb the jamming crack above and swing
    left onto an arête. Easier climbing leads to tree belays.

Chrysalis   87 m   VS   1966
A contrived route, finding the easiest line up the crag. Start below
broken rocks, 5 metres right of a hanging flake, where the shoulder
abuts the crag base.
1   16 m. Climb broken vegetated rocks past a yew tree to an oak
    tree belay.
2   28 m (4c). Ascend a grassy groove above until a step left can be
    made onto a slab. Ascend the slab and continuation groove to an
    overlap, then step down left to a thread belay. (Top of pitch 2 of
    The Cursing Caterpillar).
3   13 m (4b). Go right to an overlap and climb the weakness in it.
    Step left, climb a slab, then move right to a stance.
4   30 m (4c). Move right for about 6 metres and attain a small slab
    above, just right of a steep wall. Traverse left across the wall to
    the left edge and ascend to an oak tree. The rib above is followed
    to the top.

The Blaspheming Butterfly   80 m   HVS   1962
Once a good climb with a pleasant first pitch and more difficult
second pitch, both becoming somewhat overgrown. Start at the right

side of a large flake, 10 metres up to the right of the shoulder below the crag.

1 40 m (5a). Ascend the flake to a ledge below a line of cracks. Climb the cracks, laybacking a bulge at 5 metres, and continue to a ledge on the left. Follow the continuation crack, over a bulge, to a yew tree belay on the left.

2 40 m (5a). Climb a short steep corner on the right. Ascend ledges to a steep diedre which is climbed to the top.

Variation **The Original Finish** VS   1965

An easier alternative but not as interesting.

2a 33 m (4b). Climb a short steep corner, then step left and ascend slabs to a tree belay on *The Cursing Caterpillar*.

3a 20 m (4b). Pitch 5 of *The Cursing Caterpillar*.

★★ **The Big Curver** 90 m E2   1965/1966

A long, wandering route but with some pleasant climbing and a steep and strenuous final pitch. Start as for *The Blaspheming Butterfly*, just right of a large flake.

1 42 m (5a). Climb *The Blaspheming Butterfly* to a ledge and traverse a break rightwards to a niche after about 20 metres. Mantelshelf onto a flake on the right and ascend the slabs above to a grass ledge and tree belay.

2 26 m (4c). Ascend to a ledge on the right. A groove on the left leads to a tree. Climb the slab above for 3 metres, traverse right to a groove, and step up right to a small stance. (Top of pitch 2 of *Praying Mantis*.)

3 22 m (5c). Climb a shallow groove in the overhangs above, pulling up right onto the slabs above. The slabs are followed to a tree belay on the left at the top.

★★ **Fear of Flying** 62 m E3   1978

Thin and rather serious climbing up the left side of the undercut buttress. Start 3 metres right of *The Blaspheming Butterfly*, below a jamming crack, just left of a large ash tree.

1 36 m (6a). Climb the crack and step left at its top to a tiny ledge. Step up onto the wall and climb to a small overhang. Pull over, with difficulty, to a small ledge and continue up the grooves above to a ledge and tree belay on the left.

2 26 m. Climb the easier slabs above, just right of the final pitches of *The Blaspheming Butterfly*, to the top.

★★ Wild Times   34 m   E5   1983

A very strenuous and sustained route up the overhangs and steep wall above. Protection is difficult to arrange. Start behind a prominent yew tree on a ledge below the left end of the overhangs.

(6b). Climb a wall and short V-groove to the overhangs. Gain a standing position on a block, above on the left. Climb the steep wall, using three vertical slots, to the traverse of *The Big Curver*. Climb the right rib of a short groove on the left and continue up the wall above, avoiding vegetation on the left, to a ledge and tree belay. Continue up the easy slabs above, or abseil off.

★ Day of the Jackals   60 m   E4   1981

A steep, strenuous start, with easier climbing above. Start below the right-hand end of the overhangs.

1   30 m (6b). Climb a short wall to a horizontal break, pull over a bulge into a small niche and follow the crack above to a ledge (junction with *Point Blank*). Step up leftwards and climb the arête to a ledge and tree belay.

2   30 m. (5c). Climb a short wall and groove above, as for pitch 2 of *D.D.T.*, to below a steep groove, where *D.D.T.* traverses left. Make an awkward move up the groove to a jug. Stand on this and swing right, round the arête, onto a slab. Follow the left side of the slab to a tree belay at the top.

★★ Point Blank   66 m   HVS   1977

A pleasant route. Start on a ledge on the right of the overhangs, at a groove behind a holly tree.

1   30 m (5a). Climb the groove to an overhang and traverse left to a ledge below a crack. Climb the crack and continuation groove to a ledge and tree belay.

2   36 m (4c). A short wall leads to another ledge. Climb the pleasant slabs above to a junction with *D.D.T.*, where it traverses off left. Follow the corner crack above to a tree belay.

★★★ D.D.T.   70 m   HVS   1965

The obvious, impressive corner to the right of the undercut buttress yields a climb of considerable character. It has a bold start but protection is good where it is needed. Start just right of the holly tree below *Point Blank*.

1   40 m (5a). Climb the corner avoiding a bulge on its right wall. Step back left into the corner and climb it, and the crack above, to a ledge and tree belay.

2 30 m (4c). A short wall on the right leads to a V-groove (*Praying Mantis* shares this groove for 5 metres). Climb the groove, past an awkward steepening, onto an upper slab. Traverse off diagonally leftwards to a tree belay.

★★ Lithuania 64 m E4   1990

A contrived route up the wall to the right of *D.D.T.* So named because it struggles for independence. Start up *D.D.T.*

1 42 m (6b). Climb *D.D.T.* to the first small bulge at 6 metres. Traverse right on pockets to gain a shallow scoop and climb this to join the lower traverse of *Tumbleweed*. Step left and follow a small groove (just right of the good crack on *D.D.T.*) to a sloping hold and continue up a short jamming crack to reach a good slot out on the right (on *Altered Images*). Trend left on tiny holds to gain an obvious round pocket, then climb directly up to the base of the large groove on pitch 2 of *D.D.T.* Step right here, and climb the right-hand side of the arête of this groove to the second belay of *Praying Mantis*.

2 22 m (5c). Pitch 3 of *The Big Curver*.

★★★ The Voyage 83 m E3   1976

A magnificent trip, being a rising traverse of the impressive *North Buttress*. Sustained and always interesting. Start as for *D.D.T.*

1 30 m (5c). Climb D.D.T. for 10 metres, then step right to a junction with *Tumbleweed Connection* below a bulge. Go straight up to a peg runner, traverse right to a groove in the arête and follow this to a tree belay at the top of pitch 1 of *Praying Mantis* (as for *Tumbleweed Connection*).

2 30 m (5c). Step down and traverse right below an overlap (*Athanor* in reverse). Step up right to a junction with *Footless Crow*. Follow this, first right, then up a ramp above, rightwards, to its bolt and peg cluster. Traverse down rightwards onto *Bitter Oasis* and follow this, up an easy slab to a ledge.

3 23 m (5c). Go up left as for *Bitter Oasis*. Move right and follow a flake crack over a bulge to a foothold below a corner. Climb the corner and wall above to a tree belay at the top.

☆☆ The Ruptured Duck 35 m E3 ?   1991

A direct line up the wall to the right of *Tumbleweed Connection*. Start 3 metres right of *D.D.T.* at two parallel cracks.

(6a). Climb the cracks to an old peg at the bottom of a groove. Hand traverse right to an arête. Climb the arête directly and go up the wall to a junction with *Tumbleweed*. Step left and climb the wall to the bottom of an open groove. Make an awkward

GOAT CRAG
Praying Mantis Area

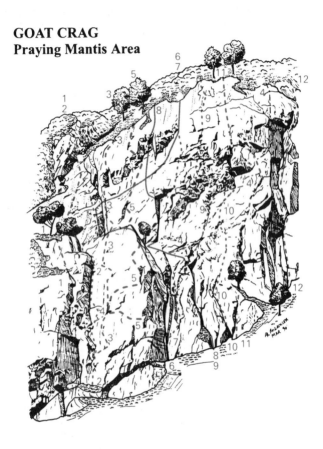

1	Point Blank	HVS	7	The Thieving	E3
2	D.D.T.	HVS		Magpie	
3	Lithuania	E4	8	Athanor	E3
4	The Voyage	E3	9	Footless Crow	E5
5	Tumbleweed	E2	10	Mirage	E5
	Connection		11	Bitter Oasis	E4
6	Praying Mantis	E1	12	Monsoon	HVS

move right past an obvious undercut to the arête. Climb up to the bottom of a groove (junction with *Tumbleweed*). Step left and climb the shallow scoop to a diagonal break. Traverse right to the tree (*Praying Mantis*) or climb the slabby wall to the obvious V-groove above.

★★ **Altered Images**   71 m   E3   1983
A conglomerate of variation pitches of other routes providing an interesting and enjoyable route. Start below the arête, 6 metres right of *D.D.T.*
1   13 m (5c). Climb the arête direct to the hand traverse of *Tumbleweed Connection*. Move up, then go up right to a large flake.
2   28 m (5c). Traverse left to the arête, step left onto the front, and move up to join *Tumbleweed Connection* at the end of its traverse. Reverse this to a peg runner and climb the wall above. Descend the ramp rightward to a tree belay. (Top of pitch 1 of *Praying Mantis*).
3   30 m (5b). Follow the rightward leading scoop above the tree to a peg runner (*Praying Mantis Direct*). Step left, and climb straight up the wall to join *Tumbleweed Connection*, where it swings left across the overhangs. Continue in the same line up the wall until a swing left can be made onto the slab, which is followed to a tree belay at the top.

★★★ **Tumbleweed Connection**   56 m   E2   1976
A tremendous route with varied and interesting climbing up the buttress between *D.D.T.* and *Praying Mantis*. Start on a ledge at the foot of the corner of *Praying Mantis*.
1   26 m (5c). Follow the prominent hand traverse line left to the arête. Pull up into a slight scoop. Traverse left to the foot of twin, thin cracks. Continue traversing leftwards for 3 metres. Move up to a bulge and straight up to a peg runner. Traverse delicately right for 3 metres to a groove in the arête, which is followed to the tree belay at the top of pitch 1 of *Praying Mantis*.
2   30 m (5b). Follow the ramp on the left to a steep wall and climb the prominent groove above. Continue in the same line, crossing the traverse of pitch 3 of *Praying Mantis*, until a pull up left can be made across the undercut arête onto the slab above. Climb more easily up the slab to the top.

Variation   **Tumbleweed By-Pass**   E2   1979
1a   35 m (5c). Climb *Tumbleweed Connection* to the peg and continue straight up the wall above to the crack on pitch 2.

★★★ **Praying Mantis**   85 m   E1   1965

The original and classic route of the *Northern Crag*, which weaves a way up the frowning buttress right of *D.D.T.* It is one of the best routes of its grade in the valley. Start below the prominent large corner, 15 metres right of *D.D.T.*, and left of the 'beetling, yellow overhangs'.

1   25 m (5b). Climb the square-cut groove, past a large flake, then the rather polished crack to a niche. Step left to a slabby wall, attain the groove above by stepping up to the right, and move up to a tree belay.

2   16 m (4c). Follow a ramp up to the left and then traverse left across a smooth wall to a V-groove. Climb the groove for 5 metres until a step up right leads to a small stance below block overhangs.

3   8 m (4c). Traverse horizontally right to a small stance in a very exposed position.

4   36 m (4c). Ascend the wall on the right to a depression in the buttress above. Climb this, until a step left gains a final slab leading to a heathery finish.

★ Variation   **The Direct Pitch**   10 m   E2   1965

A pleasing direct, but more difficult line linking the first and last pitches.

2a   10 m (5b). Follow the rightward-leading scoop from above and left of the tree belay to a peg runner. Go straight up to the tiny exposed stance at the end of pitch 3 of *Praying Mantis*.

★★ **The Thieving Magpie**   65 m   E3   1979

An interesting eliminate, with a fine first pitch and a strenuous and exposed top section. Start below the shallow V-groove, just right of *Praying Mantis*.

1   25 m (5c). Climb the groove, until forced into the curving right-hand groove, and follow this up to a roof. Climb flakes up and leftwards to the tree belay at the top of pitch 1 of *Praying Mantis*.

2   40 m (6a). Go up and right to the foot of a V-groove and climb this to an overhang (as for pitch 2 of *Athanor*). Traverse right on undercuts for about 6 metres to reach a layaway in the bulge above. Climb the bulge to a slab and then go directly up the bulge above to finish up the final slab.

★★★ Athanor   73 m   E3   1968/1974

An excellent route giving varied and sustained climbing of both a strenuous and delicate nature. Start 6 metres right of *Praying Mantis* below a vegetated groove.

1   28 m (6a). Climb the rib on the left to a large flake. Go up the blank-looking groove above, then a short steep crack, until it is possible to pull up left to a traverse line under a small overlap. Traverse left and up to the tree belay at the top of pitch 1 of *Praying Mantis*.

2   15 m (5c). Go up and right from the tree to the foot of a prominent V-groove. Climb this to the overhangs at its top, pull up left to a peg runner on *Praying Mantis Direct*, and then go straight up to a small stance.

3   30 m (5c). Climb directly up to the groove above the stance and continue towards the overhangs, until it is possible to pull up the right wall to gain the slabs above. These are climbed easily to the top.

Variation   **Original Start**   10 m

Rather dirty, wandering and pointless. Start just right of *The Thieving Magpie*.

(5a). Climb the right-hand groove for a couple of metres, step into the left-hand groove and climb it for 5 metres until it is possible to traverse right to belay below the blank-looking groove.

★ Trojan Horse   60 m   E6   {F7b+}   1990

An enjoyable eliminate.

1   30 m (6b). Follow *Athanor* for about 6 metres to where it steps left to a big flake. Continue up the scoop above and then climb the wall trending slightly rightwards to arrive at a smooth groove (*Mirage* pulls into the base of this groove from below). Gain undercuts in the bulge above, then a tricky sequence up and right round the rib regains *Mirage* at the good slot. Follow *Mirage* straight up the slab to the bolt belay.

2   30 m (6b). Climb directly up the undercuts of *Footless* (PR) and continue up directly (poor PR) to the undercut fang. (Climb over this using a detached spike.) Continue up directly until a move right leads to the steep little wall of *Bitter Oasis*. Finish up this.

★★ Legless Lizard   56 m   E5   1985

A link pitch from *Athanor* to *The Thieving Magpie*, which climbs the wall and twisting crack through the orange bulges 5 metres left of *Footless Crow*.

1 30 m (6b). Climb *Footless Crow* to the niche, step up left to a
   good foothold, then go straight up the wall to a small ledge, just
   right of a crack. Climb the wall and bulge right of the crack to
   gain a good flake hold. Climb up leftwards over the bulge to a
   chockstone. Move right and go up a flake crack to a small ledge.
   (Just right of the belay at the top of pitch 3 of *Praying Mantis*).
2 26 m (5b). Finish directly over the bulge and up the slab above,
   as for *The Thieving Magpie*.

★★★ **Footless Crow**   56 m   E5   1974
A superb route, giving incredible climbing directly up the steep
buttress right of *Athanor*. The disappearance of the crucial undercut
increased its technical difficulty slightly and also reduced the
protection previously available. The route has been repeated with
protection from the peg on the *Direct Variation*. This however seems
only possible for the tall climber using superior reach to clip the peg.
For those unable to make the reach, or the purist not wishing to clip
the peg, the pitch would present a long runout which would appear
to push the grade up to E6. Start as for *Athanor*.
1 6 m. Climb the rib on the left to below the blank-looking groove.
2 50 m (6c). Climb the groove above to below a steep crack, as for
   Athanor. Pull up into the niche above, then go up right to gain a
   rightward-trending ramp above. Follow this to a bolt and pegs
   below the roof (possible belay, but very poor stance). Step up and
   left below the overhangs to the obvious angle peg. For those able
   and willing, the peg on the *Direct Variation* is clipped. Then
   make either a l-o-n-g reach, lunge, or slap up left to gain the
   obvious long crack. Step left round the rib to a little green wall
   and climb up to the overhangs. Pull straight up, and step left
   above the overhang. Continue straight up the slabby wall,
   avoiding the heather on the left. Climb a short corner crack on
   the right which leads to a ledge and belay below two birch trees.

Footless Crow – Direct Variation   13 m   E6   {F7b+}   1986
A variation climbed before the demise of the undercut flake. Sparsely
protected.
   (6b). Move left from the ramp of *Footless Crow* and up leftwards
   to a poor peg runner (R.P. placements under the roof). Climb
   rightwards up the open corner to a peg runner. Pull up past a peg
   to gain a Friend placement on the original route, just after the
   crux.

★★★ **Mirage**   60 m   E5   1981

At first delicate and bold, then very steep and strenuous, this route gives climbing comparable in quality to *Footless Crow*. Start below a groove 3 metres right of *Athanor*.

1   30 m (6b). Climb the groove and go up to the obvious undercuts. Follow these up leftwards, then climb a thin crack to an awkward pull up right. Pull straight up to a large flat hold, stand on it, and step right, round a rib. Go up rightwards to a pocket, level with the peg runner on *Bitter Oasis*, which is some 2 metres to the right. Traverse left from the pocket to a slight rib and then go straight up to gain *Footless Crow*, a couple of metres below the bolt and peg belay.

2   30 m (6a). Climb up rightwards, past an old bolt runner and move straight up to beneath a bulge (old bolt runner on the left). Step left, and climb the weakness through the bulges to a thread. Pull into the scoop above, beneath the down-pointing spike of *Bitter Oasis*, which is then followed to the top.

★★★ **Bitter Oasis**   54 m   E4   1974

Another magnificent route with two fine pitches on this superb section of crag. More serious now the peg has gone. Start at a birch tree 5 metres up a vegetated crack, about 10 metres right of *Praying Mantis*. This is reached by scrambling from the right.

1   28 m (5c). Climb up leftwards from the tree, then step right into the groove and climb it to a bulge. Pull over this to a slab (the oasis), and follow this diagonally rightwards. Move up to a ledge.

2   26 m (5c). Step up left to a pedestal, gain the wall above and traverse leftwards, to a small foothold below a hanging spike. Climb the left side of the spike, then move left to where an old bolt runner used to be. Go straight up the wall on finger pockets to a ledge and climb more easily up leftwards to twin birch trees.

☆☆ **Unnamed**   54 m   E5   ?   1990

Very enjoyable, challenging climbing. Bold until you find the hidden runners. Start as for *Bitter Oasis*.

1   28 m (6a). Climb the short wall on the right to the overhang. Pull over this then climb the wall above first right to a niche then up left slightly to the traverse on *Bitter Oasis*. Go straight up to the belay on *Bitter Oasis*.

2   26 m (6a). Follow *Bitter Oasis* until halfway across the traverse then go up to the sharp overhang. Pull over this in a hurry to good runners and a rest. Go right slightly then pull over the bulge leftwards to a good ledge and belay.

☆☆ **Midsummer at the Oasis**   55 m   E4   ?   1995
Start as for *Bitter Oasis*.

  (6a). Move right from the initial holds of *Bitter Oasis* and
  continue to the overlap above. A hard pull over this leads to good
  layaways just right of *Bitter Oasis*. Continue up and slightly
  rightwards on better holds to join *Bitter Oasis* halfway across the
  rising traverse. Continue up and right past the stance to gain the
  arête. Difficult moves past a peg lead to the final sequence of
  Voyage and a tree belay.

Monsoon   68 m   HVS   1966
Takes the hidden grooves up the right side of the wall, right of *Bitter
Oasis*. Start below a dirty groove 6 metres right of *Bitter Oasis*.
1   26 m (4b). Climb the dirty grooves and scramble to a large ledge
    and tree belay.
2   42 m (5a). Climb the corner with increasing difficulty, until it is
    possible to escape right, below a small holly, to a rib. Ascend
    this, then step back left to finish up a narrow slab.

The following routes start in a grassy bay just right of the second
pitch of *Monsoon*. This can be reached by either climbing pitch 1 of
Monsoon or, better, by scrambling up the short walls and ledges on
its right to the same point. This grassy bay is directly below the tree
used for abseil descent from the top of routes on the right side of the
crag.

★ **Vitas Dancer**   36 m   HVS   1979
Takes the rib on the right of the second pitch of *Monsoon*. Start up
to the right of the belay, at the top of pitch 1 of *Monsoon* in the
centre of the bay.

  (5a). Climb the wall, leftwards, to the rib, and follow it to an
  overlap. Climb up leftwards to join *Monsoon* and follow this to
  the top.

The Urn (33 m VS, 1968) takes the dirty, unpleasant crack at the
back of the bay.

Blind Faith   26 m   E2   1982
Takes the steep wall and arête to the right of *The Urn*. Start below
the groove in the left side of the wall.

Opposite: Goat Crag – Brian Davison works out the crux moves of
Bitter Oasis (E3), belayed by Neil Stabbs   *Nick Wharton*

(5c). Climb the groove to a hanging flake. Layback its right side then cross the wall, rightwards, to a good handhold below a thin crack. Go up this then swing right to gain the arête and follow this to a tree belay at the top.

Variation Start **Second Sight** E3   1984
Start just right of *Blind Faith*, below a crack line.
 (6a). Climb the crack, which is strenuous and sustained, to a junction with *Blind Faith* where it crosses the wall.

★★ **Heretic** 25 m E2   1978
Fine fingery climbing up the steep slabby wall, right of the arête of *Blind Faith*. Well worth seeking out. Start at an embedded flake on a ledge, behind a small oak tree, round the arête right of *Blind Faith*.
 (5b). Climb the scoop in the wall for 6 metres and step right onto a large grassy ledge. Climb the wall above directly to a tree belay.

Mousetrap 30 m S   1966
A rather insignificant route. Start about 15 metres right of *Heretic* below a shallow groove.
 Ascend the slabby groove to a ledge. Continue up the grooves and cracks above to the top.

★★ **The Girdle Traverse** 195 m HVS   1966
A wandering route with some good climbing particularly in its second half, but little that is independent of other routes. Start as for *The Peeler*.
1 40 m (4c). Climb the crack of *The Peeler* until, at 6 metres from its top, a swing out onto the right wall can be made. Traverse right to a small tree belay at the top of pitch 1 of *Deadly Nightshade*.
2 23 m. Move right to a groove, and continue diagonally right up a ramp to a thread belay at the top of pitch 2 of *The Cursing Caterpillar*.
3 30 m (5a). Reverse pitch 2 of *The Cursing Caterpillar* to a large ledge and tree belay.
4 40 m (5a). Traverse right to a ledge and junction with pitch 1 of *The Big Curver* which is then followed to a ledge and tree belay.
5 18 m (4c). Pitch 2 of *The Big Curver* to a stance at the top of pitch 2 of *Praying Mantis*.

Opposite: Chris Gore and Pete Kirton on **Footless Crow** (E5), Goat Crag (prior to the demise of the undercut)   *Al Phizacklea*

6   8 m (4b). Traverse right, as for pitch 3 of *Praying Mantis*, to a small stance.
7   36 m (4c). Follow pitch 4 of *Praying Mantis* to the top.

Knitting Needle Gully Wall   (245 165)   Alt. 325 m

North North East Facing

An area where one can get away from the crowds. To the right of the main *North Crag*, steep vegetation bars entry to a steep gully. On the right of the gully is an obvious white coloured wall, against which used to be a prominent needle. This has now gone, taking two routes with it and leaving a rather precariously perched flake. Despite widespread belief, this needle was not the *Knitting Needle* as originally described, which is an obscure spike lower down and right of the gully which is best left to its obscurity. The steep left wall of the gully contains a number of now somewhat neglected and vegetated routes. The gully can be reached either by scrambling up from the main crag or by following the *Via Vegetata* across the hillside from *Knitting How* on the right.

Crag Rat   72 m   HVS   1966
Start by a rib to the right of the dirty gully, at the lower end of the wall, about 6 metres above the gully bed at a tree.
1   30 m (5a). Ascend a groove on the right of the rib to a sloping ledge. Continue up a leaning crack, with difficulty, to a small oak. Move up to a large flake.
2   12 m (4c). Climb the obvious groove to a large grass ledge. Tree belay as for *King Rat*.
3   30 m (4c). Follow a series of grooves out left, passing several loose flakes with care. Climb steeply on dubious flakes more or less direct to the top. Alternatively, from a ledge 20 metres from the belay, a step leads into a deep groove which leads to the top. Both ways are loose!!

★ **King Rat**   60 m   VS   1966
A good climb starting 6 metres up the gully from *Crag Rat* at a steep wall below a groove-crack.
1   30 m (4c). Climb the wall to the crack and groove above. This leads, more easily, to a tree belay on the grass terrace.
2   30 m (4c). Follow the open groove on the right until it is possible to move left across a mossy slab. The impending corner above is climbed to an awkward finish. Go right then left up easier rock to the top.

Glenmorangie 78 m VS   1966

This route initially follows the groove slanting up right in the middle of the crag then breaks through the upper steep wall to finish.

1   26 m (4c). Climb a short groove to a ledge. Ascend the steep crack on the right to a birch tree on a grass ledge.

2   12 m (4b). Move up left past some large loose flakes. Step left below a small V-corner to an oak tree belay.

3   30 m (4c). Climb the groove above to a small overhang. Avoid this on the right and ascend diagonally left to a tree belay.

4   10 m. Easy rocks follow.

Variation **Direct Start** 40 m HVS   1967

Start just left of the ordinary start, below a thin crack running up a steep wall.

1a (5a). Climb the crack to a grass ledge. Move slightly right into a groove and climb this, and another one above, to a large ledge. Oak tree belay on the right.

The Great Ape 62 m HVS   1966

A steep route starting 8 metres left of the chimney/gully, on the front of a small buttress at a steep thin crack.

1   20 m (4c). Follow the steep fault, with difficulty, past a small oak tree and easy ledges to a birch tree belay (top of pitch 1 of *Glenmorangie*).

2   42 m (5b). Trend slightly right and up a series of grooves to a small ledge. (Possible belay on the right). Ascend directly and attack the bulge on the left to attain a small niche. A short steep crack and overhanging wall lead, with difficulty, to the top.

Rodine 52 m VS   1966

This route starts 3 metres left of the chimney/gully and climbs up just left of *Trad*.

1   20 m (4b). A short gangway leads left until it is possible to move right and climb a groove to a large flake and belay.

2   12 m (4b). Climb the groove above and go through trees to a stance.

3   20 m (4c). Step left and climb a short groove. Surmount an overhang on good holds. Climb a very steep wall on excellent holds and finish up heather.

Trad   45 m   VS   1966
A loose climb starting in the chimney/gully.
1   30 m (4c). Climb the chimney for about 20 metres, with difficulty
    in places. Move left to some trees and a ledge above below a
    small steep wall.
2   15 m. A crack on the right is strenuous to start. Above,
    scrambling leads to a tree belay.

Upper Crag   (244 166)   Alt. 335 m   North East Facing

The upper part of the crag is a large area of extremely vegetated rock.
Almost everywhere the crag is shrouded in trees and heather ledges.
Towards the summit, however, there are steep and attractive areas of
rock. The routes here do not really reward the tedious approach. There
is a gully, which forks to the right, and beyond it there is a vegetated
ridge of rock, with a bold clean pate near its summit, which is taken
by the following route.

★ **The Nab**   85 m   HVS   1966
The ridge, which gives a surprisingly good climb starting on the right
bounding wall of the gully.
1   16 m. Climb the wall by a crack, breaking out right at the top.
    Tree belay.
2   26 m. Climb directly up bulging rock to a second tree and traverse
    right past a prominent rib to below a fine corner.
3   13 m. Follow the corner on excellent holds to a ledge and thread
    belay on the left.
4   30 m. Step right and traverse, spectacularly, up to the right, until
    an awkward move leads to a peg runner. Move right again, and
    climb direct to the top.

Ragnorak   66 m   VS   1966
This climb starts up a groove in the centre of the upper buttress. It
is unpleasantly vegetated in its lower reaches.
1   30 m. Climb the corner and step right into a shallow groove
    which leads to an oak. Continue directly to a ledge and tree belay.
2   16 m. Move diagonally left for 6 metres. Now break right, up a
    gangway, to a birch belay below a large mossy streak.
3   20 m. Step left and ascend a steep groove. Pass a small insecure
    tree and continue until progress can be made by bridging (peg
    runner). A few metres on small holds lead to good holds on the
    left and the top.

Rat Trap 100 m VS   1966

Towards the right edge of the crag, there is another cleaned line amongst heavily vegetated slabs. It leads towards a big groove in the upper steep wall, via a steep crack.

1   30 m. Ascend a cleaned groove until a short traverse left can be made to the base of a wide crack. Climb the crack.
2   20 m. Follow a cleaned break through the vegetation.
3   16 m. A diagonal traverse up to the left is made to the foot of the steep corner. Tree belay.
4   16 m. Climb the groove and surmount the overhang, using the left wall, to a large ledge. (Peg belay). The right wall of the groove remains loose, despite the removal of large blocks.
5   18 m. From the right edge of the ledge, ascend diagonally left to the top of the crag.

Knitting How (or Nitting Haws)

This is the long broken, broad ridge ascending the fellside a kilometre north of *Goat Crag*. It gives an easy scramble together with a number of rock climbs.

The short buttress at the foot of the ridge has a number of easy routes, including **Grey Wolf** (VD). This starts strenuously up a short rib in the centre of the buttress, just right of a holly tree, then finishes up the slab and short rib above.

Upper Knitting How   (244 168) Alt. 305 m   South East Facing

This crag is high up on the ridge and is composed of two tiers. The upper tier is clean with some interesting short problems. The lower tier is longer and gives the following routes, which are described from right to left.

Hogmanay Climb 40 m VD   1956

A rather broken but interesting climb which starts where two massive boulders lean against the main crag, towards the right of the crag.

1   10 m. Climb the slab on the first boulder, then the right edge of the second boulder and along its crest to a ledge.
2   20 m. Climb up leftwards (usually wet) and follow a groove slanting up to the left to a bent tree.
3   10 m. Climb the stepped wall above, in an impressive position.

Amenable Slab 40 m   D   1956
Start 10 metres left of *Hogmanay Climb*.
1   30 m. Climb an awkward slab, on the left of a rib, past a holly
     tree. Go up a vegetated corner to the tree on *Hogmanay Climb*.
2   10 m. Climb the stepped wall as for *Hogmanay Climb*.

Atavistic Chimney 28 m   D   1956
Start 5 metres left of *Amenable Slab*.
1   18 m. Climb a rib and crack on the left to a ledge.
2   10 m. The chimney above is climbed to and through a stout old
     juniper to a broad ledge.

Variation   **Flake Finish** HS   1985
Not so much of a fight as the original way.
2a   13 m. Move up a crack on the right to an overlap. Move right
     and use a flake and crack to gain the top.

★ **Easter Monday** 25 m   E1   1981
A good little climb with a steep, classic jamming crack. Well worth
the walk! It is situated in the centre of the crag, hidden by trees, and
just left of *Atavistic Chimney*.
     (5c). Climb up easy rocks to a yew tree and continue up the
     obvious crack and groove directly to the top.

Lower Knitting How   (245 169)   Alt. 255 m   North East
                                                                  Facing

A line of broken outcrops slants down the hillside 200 metres
north-east of *Knitting How*. Near the lower left-hand end and just
above and right of a levelling in the ridge is a prominent corner with
an impressively steep, clean cut, right wall. The rock is of good
quality but lacking in friction. Descent is down the hillside to the left.

★ **Ripping Yarn** 33 m   E3   1984
The steep delicate corner gives a good sustained route. Start from the
grassy ledge below the corner.
     (5c). Go up the corner to a ledge just below the top. Pull up right
     into a slanting slabby groove which is followed to a tree belay
     on the rib at the top.

★ **Woolly Jumper**   26 m   E5   1985
An excellent sustained pitch up the right-hand crack in the smooth impending wall.
>   (6b). Gain and follow the crack past two peg runners, pulling up rightwards at the top. Scramble to a tree belay.

Happy Herdwick   10 m   HVS   1999
Start on the wall around the corner from *Woolly Jumper*, down and right of the large triangular roof.
>   (5a). Climb the slim mossy groove to a large flake right of the roof. Now climb the right-slanting groove and step left to the tree.

The following two routes are on the small wall 25 metres to the right of *Woolly Jumper*.

Knitting Nicola   20 m   E2   1993
Start at the left edge of the wall.
>   (5b). Climb up on good holds to a right-trending diagonal crack. Climb this to an obvious layaway in the wall and then climb directly to the top of the edge.

Bucking the Ram   20 m   E5   1999
A line up the middle of the small wall. Start on the right.
>   (6b). Move up and left to the leftward-slanting crack (small RP), then go up and left to some small holds.

Stitch in Time   20 m   E3   1993
Start below a groove on the right side of the wall.
>   (5b). Using small holds on the left, make hard moves to gain the break, avoiding the bush. Use a layaway hold to get the small holds on *Knitting Nicola* and finish up this.

Blea Crag   (238 172)   Alt. 420 m   North East Facing

This dank crag is situated on the slopes overlooking the hanging valley of Greenup above Swanesty How. It is mentioned for historical reasons since it was popular at the turn of the century. The source of this popularity is no longer apparent.

The crag boasts a number of routes but detailed descriptions are not given.

Mouse Ghyll Grooves 76 m   MVS   1968
   This ascends the groove system on the left of *Mouse Ghyll*.

Mouse Ghyll 42 m   D   1897
   This ascends the left-hand of the three gullies.

Mouse Ghyll – Abraham's Finish 50 m   MVS   1897
   This variation ascends the right wall of the gully, by a crack, just
   above the second chockstone. It was the valley's first VS.

Bridge Gully 45 m   VD   1895
   The central gully on the crag.

Gully to Right 25 m   VD   1924
   The right-hand gully.

Cat Bells Quarry (248 197)   Alt. 150 m   North Facing

A very accessible quarry wall, adjacent to the road skirting round Cat
Bells. The wall is about 10 metres high and provides a number of
short routes up thin cracks.

BOULDERING AREAS

Apart from **The Bowderstone** (254 164) which is famous for its hard problems, and is fully described in the text, Borrowdale has revealed little in the way of good bouldering (so far!).

Quayfoot Boulder   (254 169)
This small cubic boulder located in a damp meadow just north of Quayfoot car park, offers a few short problems but the often boggy landing is discouraging.

Gash Rock   (267 115)
A large boulder lying below *Sergeant Crag Slabs* in Langstrath. Two problems, up the North and South side respectively, were described here in the early part of the last century and it is believed to have been first climbed by Owen Glynne Jones in 1893. The landings are unpleasant, the rock is lichenous, and it is hardly a venue in the modern idiom.

Much better bouldering can be found just outside the valley:

Honister Boulders   (217 144)
Several large boulders can be seen either side of the road after crossing the bridge when descending from Honister Pass into Buttermere. One is marked on the 1:25000 OS Map as the Maidenstone. These afford some excellent evening bouldering with generally good landings, though a bouldering mat is useful.

Mungrisdale Boulders   (355 328)
Numerous problems have been developed recently on the excellent gabbro boulders that can be found scattered on the fellside between the road and Carrock Fell. Some of the landings are a bit gnarly and a bouldering mat is desirable.

CRAGS SUITABLE FOR GROUPS

There has been an increasing use by groups of some of the more popular crags. The following list of crags suitable for groups is given to spread the load and help stop congestion and wear and tear on these popular crags.

Borrowdale

Castlehead (269 227) — Easily accessible with a number of short climbs.

Glaciated Slab — Combe Ghyll (254 128) — A pleasant slab with a number of routes of varying grades.

Seathwaite Slabs (234 123) — The lower boulders are handy for small groups and the upper slabs with their easy angle give suitable initiation and mountain atmosphere.

Shepherd's Crag, Brown Slabs (263 187) — A now overused and worn introductory area of rock.

Wodens Face (253 167) — A useful crag, though possibly rather long and now suffering from overuse.

Outside the valley but still easily accessible are:

Eastern Crags Guide

Castle Rock, South Crag (322 197) — A number of routes of varied grades.

Carrock Fell (355 324) — Numerous outcrops giving plenty of suitable choice.

CLIMBING WALLS

There is now a good range of climbing walls available to those living in or visiting the Lake District of which the best, or most readily accessible, are described here for use on those occasional rainy days and dank evenings:

Ambleside: St. Martin's College (ex-Charlotte Mason's College).
Recently revamped bouldering wall at the college. Low cost with good bouldering but limited leading. Open 18:00 to 22:00, Monday to Thursday, but there have been difficulties with access and the wall may not be open as stated. Tickets available at the wall.
Access check; Tel: 015394 30300

Barrow: Park Leisure Centre.
Good access, low cost but limited climbing – rather compact with a tall narrow wall and a bouldering area. Excellent other facilities. Open all day until 21:45 weekdays, 10:00 to 18:00 weekends.
Access check; Tel: 01229 871146

Carlisle: The Sands Centre.
Reasonable, low cost, climbing facility in a large sports centre. Good bouldering and leading. Very good access and excellent general facilities. Open 09:30 to 22:30, seven days a week.
Access check; Tel: 01228 625222

Cockermouth: Leisure Links.
Varied bouldering with natural stonework and Bendcrete. Low cost and good access. Other sports facilities available. Open 08:00 to 22:00 weekdays, weekends 09:00 to 17:00.
Access check; Tel: 01900 823596

Egremont: Wyndham Sports Centre.
A good facility located in the centre of Egremont on the west coast, only half an hour from Wasdale Head. There are practice areas, bouldering, leading walls and a huge roof. Open 09:00 to 22:00 Monday to Friday, 09:30 to 16:30 Saturday, and 10:00 to 14:00 Sunday.
Access check; Tel: 01946 821038

Ingleton: Inglesport Climbing Barn.
Best of the small walls. Very good use of space with leading and
bouldering. Regular innovations. Relaxed friendly atmosphere. Cafe
and shop nearby. Open 09:00 to 22:00 Monday to Thursday, 09:00
to 17:30 Friday, 08:30 to 18:00 weekends.
Access check; Tel: 015242 41146

Kendal: The Lakeland Climbing Centre.
A magnificent indoor climbing facility with excellent bouldering and
leading. Includes a very impressive 18 metre main wall (with fixed
gear) and a huge roof. Located on the Lake District Business Park,
across the A6 from Morrisons supermarket. Changing and shower
facilities. Open 10:00 to 22:00 weekdays, 10:00 to 19:00 weekends,
except June to August, 10:00 to 17:00. Closed Mondays, except Bank
Holidays.
Access check; Tel: 01539 721766

Keswick: Keswick Climbing Wall and Activity Centre.
Located on Southey Hill Industrial Estate, at the western end of the
town. There is quite extensive bouldering, some leading and
top-roping walls. Good cafe and friendly atmosphere. Open 10:00 to
22:00 Monday to Thursday, 10:00 to 21:00 weekends and Friday.
Access check; Tel: 017687 72000

Penrith: Penrith Leisure Centre – Eden Climbing Wall.
An excellent wall adjoining the town's swimming pool. Practice area,
good bouldering and recently extended leading walls. Open 10:00 to
21:30 weekdays, 10:00 to 21:00 weekends.
Access check; Tel: 01768 863450

GRADED LIST OF CLIMBS

There are those that like to believe that it is possible to rank the 1250 or so routes that now exist in the valley in some meaningful order! We have asked a large number of climbers to express their opinions on the grades allocated to all Borrowdale routes, old and new, and have made a great effort to combine the many and often varied responses. Taking these into account we have decided to rank the routes as low, medium or high examples of a given grade. Within these rankings the routes are listed in the order that the crags appear in the guide. Hopefully this list will be used as a way of quickly identifying routes of a similar grade on geographically close crags. Routes that display a ? symbol are listed first for completeness, but their grade should be treated with some caution. Note that a ? symbol does not necessarily indicate a poor route, merely one about which we have insufficient evidence to confirm the grade. Happy complaining!

Further ascents required for confirmation of grading

E8

	Hellish (6c) {F7c}	Bowderstone Crag
☆☆	The Ego has Landed (6b) {7b+}	Eagle Crag
☆☆☆	Caution (6c) {F8a}	Gillercombe Crag

E7

☆☆	Rock Lobster (6b) {F7a}	Long Crag
☆☆	Satan's Little Helper (6b) {F7b+}	Black Wall

E6

☆☆	Last Request (7a) {F7c}	Reecastle Crag
☆	Borrowdale Volcanic (6b) {F6c}	Long Crag
☆☆☆	Contract to Kill (6c) {F7a+}	Paper Crag
☆☆	Tops for Bottoms (6b) {F7a+}	Paper Crag
	Dreamscape (6b) {F7a+}	Hows Crag

E5

☆☆	High Anxiety (–,6a)	Walla Crag
☆	Joyrider (4c,6a)	Walla Crag
☆☆	Breakin' in Space (6b)	Lower Falcon Crag
	Defy Gravity (6b)	Lower Falcon Crag
	Nothing by Chance (4a,6b)	Lower Falcon Crag
☆	Vicky (6b,6a)	Lower Falcon Crag
	Direct start to Penal Servitude (6c)	Reecastle Crag
	Progeny (6b)	Aard Crag
☆☆	Dark Angel (6b)	Quayfoot Buttress
☆☆	Unnamed (6a,6a)	Goat Crag

E4

☆☆☆ Magical Mystery Tour (5a,5b,6a,5b)	Walla Crag
☆☆ On a Mission from God (–, 6a)	Walla Crag
☆☆ Over The Top (4b,6a)	Walla Crag
Return Ticket (4b,6a)	Walla Crag
☆ Canna Do It? (5c,6a)	Lower Falcon Crag
☆☆ Terrierman (6a)	Lower Falcon Crag
Ishmael (5c)	Black Crag Far Right Hand
☆☆☆ Sheer Entertainment (6a)	Black Wall
☆☆ Midsummer at the Oasis (6a)	Goat Crag

E3

☆ Dangerous Corner (4c,5c)	Walla Crag
Serious Omission (–,5c)	Walla Crag
☆ Sex Bomb Boogie (4a,5c)	Walla Crag
☆ Ugly Sister (4c,5c)	Walla Crag
☆ Vanishing Act (4b,5c)	Lower Falcon Crag
Off The Cuff (5c)	Reecastle Crag
Lucky Luke (6a)	Goats Grag
Bodybag Variation (5b)	Cat Ghyll Bluffs
Excalibur (free) (–,–,5c,–)	Lodore Crag
☆ Jenny Wren (6a)	Shepherd's Crag
The Kiss (6a)	Ladder Brow Crag
The Touch (6a)	Ladder Brow Crag
Spawn (5c)	Black Crag Far Right Hand
Ad-Lib (5c)	Grange Crags
Double Decker (6a)	Grange Crags
Graveyard Fiend (6b)	Quayfoot Quarry
Double Lip Trip (5c)	Long Crag
Albatross (5b,5c,–)	Lower Eagle Crag
Strange Brew	Mac's Wall
☆☆ The Ruptured Duck (6a)	Goat Crag

E2

Brutally Handsome (4c,5c)	Walla Crag
☆ Shadow Lands (4a,5b)	Walla Crag
Spruce the Bedworm Rides Again (4a,5b)	Walla Crag
☆☆ Way Out Yonder (–, 5c)	Walla Crag
In the Neck (5c)	Reecastle Crag
Dicing with Death (5c)	Cat Ghyll Bluffs
Speed Kills (4c,5c,4c)	Cat Ghyll Bluffs
Dangerous Assignment (5c)	Gowder Crag
Scare the Tourist (6a)	Shepherd's Crag
Heartbreaker (5c)	Green Bank Crags
Upshot (5c)	Black Wall
The Shock of the New	Hows Crag

E1

The Who (5b)	Castle Head
My Mam's Rockery	Cat Ghyll Bluffs
Rave Night at the Mortuary (5a)	Cat Ghyll Bluffs

El contd.

Cold Sweat (–,5b)	Gowder Crag
Lancelot Start (5b)	Lodore Crag
Angel in the Wood (5b,–)	Black Crag
☆ Dust to Dust (5b,–)	Black Crag
Traffic Warden (5a)	Grange Crags
Cleavage {F6a}	Quayfoot Quarry
☆ Parchment Tigers (5b,5b)	Paper Crag
Vicious Vicky from Barrow (5b,–)	Hows Crag

HVS

Beneath Nightmare Castle (5a)	Rakefoot Buttress
Phantoms of Fear (5a)	Rakefoot Buttress
The Walk on the Wild Side (4c,5a)	Upper Falcon Crag
The Hemp Road (–,5a)	Cat Ghyll Bluffs
Merlin	Lodore Crag
Waiting for God (5a)	Black Crag
☆ El Coronel (5a)	Sergeant Crag
Garner Grooves (5a,4c)	Black Wall
Peregrine Grooves (5a)	Black Wall
Balls Like Spacehoppers (5a)	Dove's Nest Slabs
Castillion	Hows Crag
Castle in the Air	Hows Crag
Green Wall	Hows Crag

VS

Age Concern	Black Crag
Death Bed (4c,4c)	Black Crag
Hazard Warning (4c)	Black Crag
Tombstone	Black Crag
Horn Control (4c)	Black Crag Far Right Hand
Ignition Switch (4b)	Black Crag Far Right Hand
Short Slab	Little Black Crag
The Hearse	Twa Hummocks
Slug Thug (4c)	Raven Crag

MVS

For The Record	Raven Crag

HS

Silent Partner	Dove's Nest Slabs

S

☆ Lock, Stock and Two Smoking Trowels	Dove's Nest Slabs

VD

Easy Ridge	Christmas Crag

D

Shampoo a Rhinoceros	Dove's Nest Slabs

Graded List

E8
★★★ Bleed in Hell (6c) {F8a+}   Bowderstone Crag
 ★★ Disorderly Conduct (6c) {F7b}   Reecastle Crag

E7
  ★ Breach of the Peace (6b) {F7b+}   Reecastle Crag
★★★ Burn at the Stake (7a) {F8a}   Reecastle Crag
 ★★ Grievous Bodily Arm (6c) {F7c}   Reecastle Crag
 ★★ Remission (6c) {F8a}   Reecastle Crag
 ★★ The Torture Board (6c) {F7c+}   Reecastle Crag
 ★★ The Whipping Post (7a) {F8a}   Reecastle Crag
 ★★ De Quincy (6b) {F7a}   Bowderstone Crag
 ★★ Inferno (6c) {F8a}   Bowderstone Crag
★★★ Camouflage (6b) {F7b+}   Cam Crags

E6 (High)
 ★★ Geronimo (6c) {F7c+}   Shepherd's Crag
    The Bodycount (6c) {F7b+}   Grange Crags
 ★★ Guns of Navarone (6b,6c,5c) {F7b+}   Eagle Crag

E6 (Medium)
★★★ Daylight Robbery (6c) {F7b+}   Reecastle Crag
  ★ Short Sharp Shock (6c) {F7b+}   Reecastle Crag
  ★ The Devil's Alternative (6b) {F7a+}   Shepherd's Crag
★★★ Hell's Wall (6c) {F7c+}   Bowderstone Crag
 ★★ Mesrine (6b) {F7c}   Bowderstone Crag
    In the Blood (6c) {F7b+}   Millican's Buttress
 ★★ Sheriff of Nottingham (6b) {F7b}   Millican's Buttress
  ★ Trojan Horse (6b,6b) {F7b+}   Goat Crag

E6 (Low)
  ★ Exclamation (6b) {F7b+}   Shepherd's Crag
    The Witness (6b)   Shepherd's Crag
★★★ Camikaze (6a) {F6c}   Cam Crags
    Footless Crow Direct Variation (6b) {F7b+}   Goat Crag

E5 (High)
    Sentenced to Hang (6b)   Reecastle Crag
  ★ Ker Plunk (6a)   Shepherd's Crag
    The Dissident (6b)   Greatend Crag
  ★ Coroner's Crack (5b,6b)   Eagle Crag
★★★ Footless Crow (–,6c)   Goat Crag
 ★★ Wild Times (6b)   Goat Crag
  ★ Woolly Jumper (6b)   Lower Knitting How

E5 (Medium)
★★★ Penal Servitude (6b)   Reecastle Crag
    Rough Boys, Right-Hand (6c)   Shepherd's Crag

E5 (Medium) contd.

★★ The Mastercraftsman (6b)	Long Band Crag
★★ Dead on Arrival (5c,6b,5a)	Eagle Crag
★★ Flying Circus (5b,6b)	Eagle Crag
★★★ The Restraint of Beasts (6b,5c)	Eagle Crag
★★ The Borrowdale Contract (6b)	Paper Crag
The Wizard of Oz (6b)	Gillercombe Crag
★ Tomb Raider (6b)	Hows Crag
★★ Legless Lizard (6b,5b)	Goat Crag
★★★ Mirage (6b,6a)	Goat Crag
Bucking The Ram (6b)	Knitting How

E5 (Low)

★★ Squashed Raquet (6a)	Reecastle Crag
American Beauty (6b)	Shepherd's Crag
Rough Boys, Left-Hand (6b)	Shepherd's Crag
Perestroika (6a)	Greatend Crag
★★★ The Bulger (–,6b)	Bowderstone Crag
★★ Lucifer (6a)	Bowderstone Crag
★★★ The Technician (6b)	Long Band Crag
Fall of Eagles (5c,5c,6b)	Eagle Crag
★ Bleak How Eliminate (6a)	Bleak How

E4 (High)

Drybum (6a)	Upper Falcon Crag
★ Inarticulate Speech (4a,6a,6a)	Lower Falcon Crag
★ Sunset Cruise (6b)	Lower Falcon Crag
★★★ Wheels of Fire (6a,6a)	Bowderstone Crag
★★ Inclination (6b)	Shepherd's Crag
Wack (–,4c,6b)	Black Crag
Hiroshima (6b)	Greatend Crag
★ Trouble Shooter (5b,6a,6a)	Greatend Crag
Masochist (6a)	Long Band Crag
★ Cam Crag Crack (6b)	Cam Crags
★ Mister Meaner (6b)	Castle Crag

E4 (Medium)

★ Cyclotron (4a,6a)	Lower Falcon Crag
Extrapolation Right Hand (5c)	Lower Falcon Crag
★ Lamplighter Eliminate (6a,6b,5a)	Lower Falcon Crag
★★ Premonition (4b,6a)	Lower Falcon Crag
★ Twittering Height (5c)	Shepherd's Crag
The Emigrant (6a)	Powterhow Buttress
Blonde Ambition (6a)	Reecastle South Crag
The Colour of Magic (6a)	Goats Crag
The Sheep's Apprentice (6a)	Cat Ghyll Bluffs
★ Tristar (5b,6a,–)	Black Crag
Cithaeron (6a)	Aard Crag
★★★ Nagasaki Grooves (5b,6b,–)	Greatend Crag
★ Brain Stain (6a)	Quayfoot Buttress

E4 (Medium) contd.

Loitering with Intent (5c)	Quayfoot Buttress
★★ The Professional (6a)	Long Band Crag
★ Fear and Loathing (6a,5b)	Lower Eagle Crag
Hole in Yan (6a,5c)	Lower Eagle Crag
Boston Strangler (6b)	Bleak How
★ Posidriver (5c)	Blackmoss Pot Slab
★ Suspended Animation (6a)	Hows Crag
★ Day of the Jackals (6b,5c)	Goat Crag
★★ Lithuania (6b,5a)	Goat Crag

E4 (Low)

★★★ Dry Grasp (4a,5b,6a)	Upper Falcon Crag
★ Stumble Bum (4c,6a,6a)	Upper Falcon Crag
★ The Niche, The Left Exit (6a,4c)	Lower Falcon Crag
★★★ Inquisition (6a)	Reecastle Crag
The Executioner (6a)	Reecastle Crag
★ Rogue Herries (6a)	Goats Crag
★★★ Grand Alliance (4c,5b,6a,–)	Black Crag
Glasnost (5c)	Greatend Crag
★ Greatend Pillar (4b,6b,5a,5a)	Greatend Crag
★★ The Apprentice (6a)	Long Band Crag
★★★ Verdict (5b,5c,6a)	Eagle Crag
Citizen Kane (6a)	Gillercombe Crag
★★★ Bitter Oasis (5c,5c)	Goat Crag

E3 (High)

Miracle Cure (5c)	Castle Head Quarry
Qantas (6a)	Upper Falcon Crag
Atomiser (6a)	Lower Falcon Crag
Meccano Man (6a)	Lower Falcon Crag
The Raging Bull (6b)	Lower Falcon Crag
Brown Crag Grooves, Direct Start (6a)	Shepherd's Crag
P.S., Direct Finish (6a)	Shepherd's Crag
★ Savage Messiah (–,6a)	Shepherd's Crag
The Last Fairway (6a,–)	Lower Eagle Crag
★ Final Diagnosis (5c,6a)	Eagle Crag
★ Prodigal Sons (6a)	Glaciated Slab
★ Savage Amusement (4c,5c)	Raven Crag
Louise Brooks (6a)	Gillercombe Crag
The White Lady (6a)	Gillercombe Crag
★★ A Face in the Crowd (6a)	Castle Crag
★ Cry Freedom (5c)	Perched Block Buttress
★★ The Thieving Magpie (5c,6a)	Goat Crag
★★★ The Voyage (5c,5c,5c)	Goat Crag

E3 (Medium)

★★ Burning Bridges (5c,5c)	Walla Crag
Wild Thing (4c,5c)	Walla Crag
★★ Joke (5b,6a)	Lower Falcon Crag

E3 (Medium) contd.

★★★ Plagiarism – Direct Finish (5c)	Lower Falcon Crag
★★★ White Noise (5c)	Reecastle Crag
★ Crime and Punishment (5c,5c)	Reecastle Crag
★★★ Single to Cemetary Gates (5c)	Cat Ghyll Bluffs
First Offence (4c,6a,4b)	Gowder Crag
★ Dire Straits (6a)	Shepherd's Crag
Exasperation (5b,–,6a)	Shepherd's Crag
★★ Porcupine (5a,6a)	Shepherd's Crag
★ Saturday Night Beaver (6a)	Shepherd's Crag
Scallywag (6a)	Shepherd's Crag
Shepherd's Pie (6a)	Shepherd's Crag
★ Astral Weeks (4b,6a,5b,–)	Black Crag
★★★ Prana (4b,5c,–)	Black Crag
★★ Up for Grabs (5b,6b)	Black Crag
Lead Free (6a)	Grange Crags
Rolling Thunder (6a)	Grange Crags
★★★ Heaven's Gate (–,6a)	Bowderstone Crag
★★★ The Cleft Direct (5c,5c,5b)	Eagle Crag
★★★ Daedalus (5c,5b)	Eagle Crag
★★ Breathless (6a)	Bleak How
Steel Pulse (5c)	Bleak How
Cruelty Unknown (4c,6a,5a)	Sergeant Crag
★★ Hookworm (5c)	Sergeant Crag Slabs
★ Paper Thin (5c)	Paper Crag
★ The Third Man (6a)	Gillercombe Crag
★ Big Business (6b)	Mac's Wall
Zombie in the Dark (6c)	Mac's Wall
★ Free Falling (6a)	Steel Knotts
★★ Altered Images (5c,5c,5b)	Goat Crag
★★★ Athanor (6a,5c,5c)	Goat Crag
★★ Fear of Flying (6a,–)	Goat Crag
Second Sight (6a)	Goat Crag
Stitch in Time (5b)	Knitting How

E3 (Low)

Beyond Redemption (–, 5c)	Walla Crag
★★★ Route 1 (4a,5b,5c)	Upper Falcon Crag
★★ Close Encounters (6a,5c)	Lower Falcon Crag
★★ Five Nations of the Iroquois (4b,5b,5b,5c,5a,5c,5a)	Lower Falcon Crag
★★ Star Wars (5c,5c)	Lower Falcon Crag
★★★ Guillotine (5c)	Reecastle Crag
★★★ Thumbscrew (5c)	Reecastle Crag
Stranger to the Ground (5c)	Goats Crag
Everard (5c)	Caffell Side Crag
★★ Battering Ram (5c,5c)	Shepherd's Crag
Human Racing (5c)	Shepherd's Crag
Missing Link (5c)	Shepherd's Crag
Rob's Cafe (6a)	Shepherd's Crag
Rob's Route (6a,5c,5c)	Shepherd's Crag

E3 (Low) contd.

★★ Stone Tape (6a,5b) — Shepherd's Crag
★★ Straight and Narrow (6a) — Shepherd's Crag
★ Wild Side (6a) — Shepherd's Crag
★ Track of a Tear (5c) — Ladder Brow Crag
★ The Promise (5c) — Green Bank Crags
★★ Fender Bender (5c) — Grange Crags
Reliant Robin (6a) — Grange Crags
★ The In Between (5c) — Quayfoot Buttress
★ The Punchline (6a) — Bowderstone Crag
★★★ Post Mortem (5a,5c) — Eagle Crag
Psyched Out (5b) — Bleak How
★ Flexible Friend (6a) — Cam Crags
★ Teenage Kicks (6a) — Cam Crags
Red Shift (5c) — Thornythwaite Knotts
Corridors of Power (5b,5c) — Castle Crag
★ Ripping Yarn (5c) — Lower Knitting How

E2 (High)

Unforseen Danger (6a) — Castle Head
★ Blazing Apostles (5c,5b) — Walla Crag
★★★ Kidnapped (5c) — Lower Falcon Crag
★★ Masquerade (5b,5c) — Lower Falcon Crag
★ Wuthering Heights (–,5c) — Lower Falcon Crag
★ Water Torture (5c) — Reecastle Crag
Hairy Mary (5c) — Caffell Side Crag
Slack Alice (5b) — Caffell Side Crag
Street Walker (5c) — Caffell Side Crag
★★ Black Sheep (5b) — Shepherd's Crag
★ Entertainment Traverse (5c) — Shepherd's Crag
Milk (5c) — Shepherd's Crag
Mule Train (5c) — Shepherd's Crag
Poop and Clutch (5c) — Shepherd's Crag
★★★ Wild Sheep (5b) — Shepherd's Crag
The Look (5c) — Ladder Brow Crag
★ Desmond Decker (5c) — Grange Crags
★★ Fuel Crisis (5c) — Grange Crags
★★ Exclusion Zone (5b,5c,5a,5a) — Greatend Crag
Japanese Connection (5c) — Greatend Crag
★★ Manhattan Project (5b,5b,4c,5b) — Greatend Crag
★★ Sidewinder (5b) — Quayfoot Buttress
Wodentops (6a) — Woden's Face
Das ist Verboten (5b) — Bowderstone Crag
★ Not with a Bang (5b) — Long Crag
★ Paddy's Arete (6a) — Long Crag
★★ Big Foot (5c) — Heron Crag
★ Faz's Route (5b) — Sergeant Crag Slabs
Rebound (5c) — Black Waugh Crag
★ Cold Lazarus (6a) — Millican's Buttress

E2 (High) contd.
★ Well Heeled (5b)   Perched Block Buttress
★ Dwarf's Divorce (4a,5b,5c)   Goat Crag
★★ The Rat Race (5c,5a,–,4c)   Goat Crag
★★★ Tumbleweed Connection (5c,5b)   Goat Crag

E2 (Medium)
Life Guard (5b)   Rakefoot Buttress
★ Muscular Delinquent (5c,5b)   Walla Crag
★★ Extrapolation (5c,–)   Lower Falcon Crag
★★★ Plagiarism (4b,5c,–)   Lower Falcon Crag
★★★ The Dangler (5a,5c)   Lower Falcon Crag
★★★ The Niche (5c,5b,4c)   Lower Falcon Crag
★★ Rack Direct (5b)   Reecastle Crag
★★★ The Rack – Finger Flake Finish (5c)   Reecastle Crag
Lost Boys (5c)   Reecastle South Crag
Light Fantastic (5c)   Goats Crag
★★ Pussy Galore (5c)   Goats Crag
★ The Witch (5c)   Lower Goats Crag
★ Apricot Lil (5b)   Caffell Side Crag
Miss O'Gynist (5c)   Caffell Side Crag
★ Charlie the Chicken Farmer (5c)   Cat Ghyll Bluffs
The Naked Edge (5b)   Cat Ghyll Bluffs
★ This Little Piggy (5c)   Cat Ghyll Bluffs
★ Bob Martins (4c,5b)   Shepherd's Crag
Evolution (5c)   Shepherd's Crag
Final Act (5c)   Shepherd's Crag
Golden Delicious (5c)   Shepherd's Crag
Parlophone (5c,–)   Shepherd's Crag
Shanna (5c)   Shepherd's Crag
Tarzan (5c)   Shepherd's Crag
The Fou (5c,5a)   Shepherd's Crag
★ Bush Doctor (5c,5a,4c,5c)   Black Crag
Cloudburst Finish (5c)   Black Crag
Romeo Error (5c,5a,5a)   Black Crag
★ Silent Sun (5b,5b)   Black Crag
★★ Vertigo (–,4c,5c,–)   Black Crag
★ Nepotism (5c)   Aard Crag
Cross Ply (5c)   Grange Crags
★★ Pressure Drop (6a)   Grange Crags
★★ Pressure Drop Direct (5c)   Grange Crags
★★ Rough Justice (5c)   Grange Crags
Rush Hour (5c)   Grange Crags
Aragorn (5c,4b)   Greatend Crag
★ Freak Power (6a)   Quayfoot Buttress
★★★ The Go Between (5b,5c)   Quayfoot Buttress
★★ Just and So (5a,5c)   Bowderstone Crag
★ The Sadist (5c)   Long Band Crag
★★ Pitch and Putt (5c,5b)   Lower Eagle Crag
Animotion (5a,5c,5b)   Eagle Crag

E2 (Medium) contd.

★ Inquest Direct (5c,4b)	Eagle Crag
★ Necroscopy (5b)	Eagle Crag
★★★ Where Eagles Dare (5c,5b)	Eagle Crag
★ Barefoot (5c)	Heron Crag
★ Joie Pur (5c)	Heron Crag
Little Nose (5b)	Heron Crag
★★ The Question (5c)	Heron Crag
★★ Traverse of the Frogs (5b,5a)	Heron Crag
★ Cellulite (6a)	Fat Charlie's Buttress
★★★ Aphasia (5b)	Sergeant Crag Slabs
★ Hitler's Demise (5c)	Sergeant Crag Slabs
★★ Woodrow Wyatt's Reasoning (5c)	Sergeant Crag Slabs
★★ Slab Happy (5c)	Blackmoss Pot Slab
★ 'Arry 'Ardnose (5c)	Cam Crags
Deja Vu (5b)	Glaciated Slab
★ Classic Rock (4c,5c)	Raven Crag
★★ Cock's Comb Crack (5c)	Raven Crag
★ Pendulum (–,4a,5c,5c,–)	Raven Crag
★ Skimmerhorne (5c)	Hanging Stone
Goodbye Dennis (5c)	Millican's Buttress
Green Death (5b)	Millican's Buttress
★★ Liquid Morphine (5c)	Millican's Buttress
Paint it Black (5c)	Steel Knotts
Blind Faith (5c)	Goat Crag
★★ Manpower (5c,5b,5a)	Goat Crag
★★ The Big Curver (5a,4c,5c)	Goat Crag
Knitting Nicola (5b)	Knitting How

E2 (Low)

★ Total Mass Retain (5b,4a)	Walla Crag
★★ Stretch – Direct Finish (5c)	Lower Falcon Crag
Gyves (5b)	Reecastle Crag
★★ The Gibbet Direct (5c)	Reecastle Crag
★★ Ricochet (5c)	Reecastle South Crag
★★ Widowmaker (5b)	Reecastle South Crag
★ Berlin Wall (5b)	Goats Crag
Bat Out of Hell (5b)	Cat Ghyll Bluffs
★★ M.G.C.(5c)	Shepherd's Crag
★★ True North (5b)	Shepherd's Crag
Odds 'n' Sods (5c)	Shepherd's Crag
P.P.S. (5c)	Shepherd's Crag
Wasp (4b,5b,5a,5a,5c)	Black Crag
High Plains Drifter (4c,4c,–,5c,5b,4c,4c,4b)	Black Crag
★ Tumbling Dice (4b,5b,5c,5a,4c)	Black Crag
★★ Red Neck (5b)	Grange Crags
★ Sudden Impact (5c)	Grange Crags
★★★ No Holds Barred (5b,5a)	Greatend Crag

E2 (Low) contd.

The Lion Heart (5c,5a)	King's How
★ Woden's Wotsit (5b)	Woden's Face
Loose Cannon on the Deck (5b)	Long Crag
★★ The Squawk (5b,5a,5b)	Eagle Crag
★★ Icarus Direct (5b,5c)	Eagle Crag
★ Amistad Con El Diablo (5c)	Bleak How
★★★ Bleak How Buttress (5c)	Bleak How
Pop Goes the Asteroid (5a)	Bleak How
★ Bilberry Topping (5c)	Heron Crag
★★ Boris in Wonderland (5b)	Sergeant Crag Slabs
Eyrie Direct (5b)	Gillercombe Crag
★ Patient Tigers (4c,5b)	Gillercombe Crag
★★ String of Pearls (5b,5b,4c,4c,5a,–)	Gillercombe Crag
★ Singing Detective (5b)	Millican's Buttress
★★ The Sting (5c)	Steel Knotts
★★ Heretic (5b)	Goat Crag
★ Praying Mantis, Var. Direct Pitch (5b)	Goat Crag

E1 (High)

Amazing Journey (5b)	Castle Head Quarry
Walla's Nose (5b,4b)	Walla Crag
★★ Interloper (5c,4c)	Lower Falcon Crag
★ The Gibbet (5c)	Reecastle Crag
Beer and Sex and Chips and Gravy (5c)	Cat Ghyll Bluffs
I Need a Hero (5b)	Cat Ghyll Bluffs
One-In-Six (5b)	Cat Ghyll Bluffs
★ Polymer (5b,4c,5b)	Gowder Crag
★★ Brown Crag Grooves (5b,4b)	Shepherd's Crag
Could be the Last (5b)	Shepherd's Crag
Downer's Delight (5b)	Shepherd's Crag
Imago (5c,5a)	Shepherd's Crag
★★ Jaws (5b,–)	Shepherd's Crag
★★ Magnetic North (–,5b)	Shepherd's Crag
★ North Buttress Girdle (–,5a,5a,4b,5b,5b)	Shepherd's Crag
★★★ The Bludgeon (4c,5b)	Shepherd's Crag
Theseus (5b,5a)	Shepherd's Crag
★★ North Buttress (4c,5b)	Shepherd's Crag
Frenzy (4b,5a)	Black Crag
Plastic Pig (5b)	Grange Crags
The 'A' Team (5c)	Grange Crags
Jacko (5b)	Yew Crag
Bilko (4c,5b,4a)	Sergeant Crag
★ No Overtaking (5c)	Doves' Nest Crag
★ Nantucket Sleighride (5a,5b,5a)	Hind Crag
Mean Streak (5b)	Black Waugh Crag
Recoil (5b)	Black Waugh Crag
★★ Pennies From Heaven (5b)	Millican's Buttress
★★ Brass Monkey (5b)	Perched Block Buttress
★ High Flyer (5a,5b)	Goat Crag

E1 (Medium)

Iron Warriors (5a)	Rakefoot Buttress
Space Wolves (5a)	Rakefoot Buttress
Unknown Warriors (5b)	Rakefoot Buttress
★★ Route 2 (4c,5a,5b)	Upper Falcon Crag
★★ Girdle Traverse (4c,4c,5a,4b,5b,–)	Lower Falcon Crag
Good Times Bad Times (5a)	Lower Falcon Crag
★★★ Usurper (4b,5a,–)	Lower Falcon Crag
★ Bold Warrior (5b)	Reecastle Crag
★ The Gauntlet (5b)	Reecastle Crag
Balancing Act (5b)	Goats Crag
★★ Mackanory (5b)	Lower Goats Crag
The Trick (5c)	Lower Goats Crag
Anyone for Tennis (5b)	Brown Dodd
Hawkwing (5b)	Brown Dodd
Anthill (4c,5b,4a)	Gowder Crag
Last of the Summer Wine (4c,5b,4c)	Gowder Crag
★★★ Aaros (5b)	Shepherd's Crag
★ Hippos Might Fly (5a)	Shepherd's Crag
Plug (5b)	Shepherd's Crag
★★ The Grasp (5b)	Shepherd's Crag
Auguries of Eternity (5c,–)	Green Bank Crags
★ The Jaws of Sheitan (5c,4b)	Green Bank Crags
Anaconda (5b)	Black Crag
★ Ashes to Ashes (5b,–)	Black Crag
★★★ Raindrop (5b,5a,5b,4c)	Black Crag
Parricide (5b)	Aard Crag
Crime Wave (5b)	Grange Crags
★ Driving Ambition (5b)	Grange Crags
★ Low Profile (5b)	Grange Crags
The 'B' Team (5b)	Grange Crags
The Shield (5b)	Grange Crags
★★★ Banzai Pipeline (5a,5b,5a,5a)	Greatend Crag
The Black Prince (5b)	King's How
★★ The Crypt Direct (4a,5b)	Quayfoot Buttress
The Girdle Traverse Var. (5b)	Quayfoot Buttress
★★ Valhalla (4c,5c)	Bowderstone Crag
The Home Shoot (5b)	Long Crag
★ Birdie (5b,5a)	Lower Eagle Crag
★★ Double Bogey (5b,–)	Lower Eagle Crag
★★★ Autopsy (5b)	Eagle Crag
★ Needless Sports (5a,5b,5b)	Eagle Crag
Basil (5b)	Bleak How
Catching Up (5b)	Bleak How
★ Reassuringly Stocky (5c)	Fat Charlie's Buttress
★★ Supermodel (5b)	Fat Charlie's Buttress
★ Echoes of Zechariah (5b,–)	Sergeant Crag
★★ Holly Tree Crack (5b,5a)	Sergeant Crag Slabs
★★ Quicksilver (5b)	Sergeant Crag Slabs
★★ The Death Stroke (5b)	Sergeant Crag Slabs

E1 (Medium) contd.

Dill the Dog (5b)	Cam Crags
The Cutting Edge (5c)	Paper Crag
★ Being Done Good To (5b)	Doves' Nest Crag
★ Turbulence (4c,5b,4a,4a)	Hind Crag
★★ Clara Bow (5b)	Gillercombe Crag
Swine Trek (4c,5b)	Castle Crag
One Across (5c)	Mac's Wall
★ Black Eyes (5b)	Millican's Buttress
Millican's Arete (5b)	Millican's Buttress
★★ African Skies (5b)	Perched Block Buttress
★★★ Alone in Space (5a,5b,5a,5a)	Goat Crag
Billy Goat Bluff (5a)	Goat Crag
★ Solid Air (5a,5a,4c,5b,4c)	Goat Crag
Teva Fever (5a,5b)	Goat Crag
★ Easter Monday (5c)	Knitting How

E1 (Low)

★★★ Dedication (4a,5a)	Lower Falcon Crag
★ Mort (5b)	Goats Crag
★ Munich Agreement (5b)	Goats Crag
★ Nightmare Zone (5b)	Goats Crag
★ Optional Omission (5a)	Goats Crag
★ Supercrack (5b)	Garotte Buttress
Bird Brain (5b)	Brown Dodd
Bird's Nest Buttress (5b)	Brown Dodd
★ Wild Boys (5b)	Cat Ghyll Bluffs
★★ Gosh (5a,5b,5a)	Gowder Crag
★★ Conclusion (5b,–)	Shepherd's Crag
★ Cream (5a)	Shepherd's Crag
★★ Ovation (5b)	Shepherd's Crag
★★ P.S. (5a,5b)	Shepherd's Crag
★★ The Black Icicle (5b,5a)	Shepherd's Crag
★★ Black Crag Eliminate (4b,5b,4a,5b)	Black Crag
★★ Jubilee Grooves (5a,4c,5b,4a)	Black Crag
★ The Mortuary (5a,5a,5a,4c)	Black Crag
★ Triptych (–,5a,5b,4a,–)	Black Crag
Wring Out the Old (5b)	Troutdale Gully Wall
★ Hatchback (5a)	Grange Crags
★ Impulse (5b)	Grange Crags
North America Wall (5b)	Grange Crags
Ponticum (5a)	Grange Crags
Stir (5a)	Grange Crags
Soxon (5a)	Woden's Face
White Man Walkabout (4c,5a)	Yew Crag
★★ City of Love and Ashes (5a)	Lining Crag
★ Mr Bad Example (5a)	Lining Crag
Eagle Cracks (4c,5b,–)	Lower Eagle Crag
★ BX Breakdown (5b)	Bleak How
★★ Fancy Free (5a)	Bleak How

E1 (Low) contd.

★★ Front Runner (5a)	Bleak How
★★ Cholesterol Corner (5b)	Fat Charlie's Buttress
★★ Flamingo Fandango (5b)	Heron Crag
★★ Heaven Knows I'm Miserable Now (5b)	Heron Crag
★ Little Corner (5b)	Heron Crag
Doberman (5a)	Sergeant Crag
★★ Between the Lines (5b)	Sergeant Crag Slabs
★ Holly Tree Ramp (5a)	Sergeant Crag Slabs
★ Birds of Prey (4a,5b)	Raven Crag
★ Joker Man (5b)	Hanging Stone
★ The Black Knight (4c,5b)	Gillercombe Crag
Epitaph (5b,4c)	Castle Crag
★★★ Praying Mantis (5b,4c,4c,4c)	Goat Crag

HVS (High)

★ Pinball Wizard (5a)	Castle Head
Ichor (5a,4c)	Walla Crag
Girdle Traverse (4c,–,5a,4c)	Upper Falcon Crag
Plastic Happiness (4c,5b,5b)	Upper Falcon Crag
★ Stretch (5a,4c,4c)	Lower Falcon Crag
★ The Push (5a)	Lower Falcon Crag
★★★ The Rack (5a)	Reecastle Crag
★ Blondin (5a)	Caffell Side Crag
The Rift (5b)	Brown Dodd
★★ Chamonix Girdle (4c,4b,–,4b,4a)	Shepherd's Crag
★★ Creeping Jesus (5a)	Shepherd's Crag
★★ Crunchy Frog (5a)	Shepherd's Crag
★★ Devil's Wedge (5a,5a)	Shepherd's Crag
★★ Encore (5a)	Shepherd's Crag
Ethelred (5a)	Shepherd's Crag
★★ Evel Kneivel (5a,4a)	Shepherd's Crag
★★★ Finale (5a,4a)	Shepherd's Crag
★ Frontline (5a,5a,4b)	Shepherd's Crag
★ Gibbon Variation (5b)	Shepherd's Crag
★ Seamus (5b,4c)	Shepherd's Crag
Roach Clip (5a,5b)	Black Crag
★★★ The Mortician (4b,5a,4c,–)	Black Crag
Regardless (5a)	Grange Crags
Big Sur (5b)	Greatend Crag
Sauron (5a,5a)	Greatend Crag
★★ Girdle Traverse (5c,5a,5a)	Quayfoot Buttress
★★ Morceau (5a,5a,–)	Quayfoot Buttress
★★ The Creep (5b,5a)	Quayfoot Buttress
★ Orthang (5a,5a)	Lining Crag
Girdle Traverse (4b,5b,4c,–,5a,4c,4c,5a)	Eagle Crag
★★ The Boj Eliminate (5a)	Bleak How
★ Phantom Menace (5a)	Fat Charlie's Buttress
The Redoubt (4c,5a)	Sergeant Crag
★ Meet Your Maker (4c)	Doves' Nest Crag

HVS (High) contd.

★ Andy Warhol (5a)	Gillercombe Crag
★ Eyrie (4c,5a)	Gillercombe Crag
The Astronaut Next Door (5c)	Castle Crag
★★ The Blue Max (5a,5a)	Castle Crag
Vortex (5b)	Castle Crag
Vortigern (5a)	Castle Crag
★★ Zoar (5b)	Castle Crag
Meandering Maggot (5b)	Steel Knotts
★ April Fool – Direct Finish (5a)	Goat Crag
★★★ D.D.T. (5a,4c)	Goat Crag
★★ Point Blank (5a,4c)	Goat Crag

HVS (Medium)

Stubble (4c)	Castle Head
Dark Angels (5a)	Rakefoot Buttress
Lunar Wolves (5a)	Rakefoot Buttress
The Straits of Despair (5a)	Rakefoot Buttress
White Dwarf (5a)	Rakefoot Buttress
White Scars (5a)	Rakefoot Buttress
Thanks (5a,4b)	Walla Crag
★ Autobahn (4c,5a)	Lower Falcon Crag
★★★ Illusion (4b,5a,–)	Lower Falcon Crag
Who is this Lakeland Activist? (5a)	Lower Falcon Crag
Route 8 (5a)	Goats Crag
★ The Niche (5a)	Lower Goats Crag
★ The Garrotte (4c,5a,5a)	Garrotte Buttress
Juicy Lucy (5a)	Caffell Side Crag
Boiling Point (4c)	Brown Dodd
★ Spiderman (5a)	Cat Ghyll Bluffs
★ Paradise Lost (4c,5a,4b)	Gowder Crag
★★ The Neb (5a,5a)	Gowder Crag
★ The Rib (4c)	Gowder Crag
★ Voodoo (4c,4c,–,5a)	Gowder Crag
★ Gemma (5b)	Shepherd's Crag
★★ Just Another Expedition	Shepherd's Crag
★ Katherine (4c,5a)	Shepherd's Crag
★★ Kransic Crack Direct (5a)	Shepherd's Crag
Meet on the Ledge	Shepherd's Crag
Stoned Again (5b)	Shepherd's Crag
Symbiosis (5a,4b,–,5b)	Shepherd's Crag
★ Thin Air (4b,5a)	Shepherd's Crag
Fight with a Beech Tree (5a)	Ladder Brow Crag
Moral Narcosis (4c)	Ladder Brow Crag
The Smile (5a)	Ladder Brow Crag
★ The Dice Man (–,4a,5a,–)	Black Crag
★ The Lastest (4b,5a,5a,–)	Black Crag
★★★ Troutdale Pinnacle Superdirect (4b,4c,5a,5a,–)	Black Crag
Holly Tree Climb	Troutdale Gully Wall
★ Family Tree (5a)	Aard Crag

HVS (Medium) contd.

Black Crack (4c)	Perched Block Buttress
★ Random Choice (5a)	Perched Block Buttress
★ The Lost Boys (5a)	Steel Knotts
Crag Rat (5a,4c,4c)	Goat Crag
★ Deadly Nightshade (4c,5a,4c,4b)	Goat Crag
Monsoon (4b,5a)	Goat Crag
The Blaspheming Butterfly (5a,5a)	Goat Crag
Happy Herdwick (5a)	Lower Knitting How

HVS (Low)

Girdle Traverse (4a,5a,4b,4c,4c)	Walla Crag
★ Funeral Way (5a,4c)	Lower Falcon Crag
★★ The Noose (4c)	Reecastle Crag
★★ Emma Line (5a)	Goats Crag
★ Inner Limits (5a)	Goats Crag
Kes (5a)	Brown Dodd
Holly Tree Corner (5a)	Cat Ghyll Bluffs
★★ Kaleidoscope (–,5a,4b,4b)	Gowder Crag
★★ Delight Maker (4c,5a)	Shepherd's Crag
★★ Monolith Crack (4c,4b)	Shepherd's Crag
Stony Silence (5b)	Shepherd's Crag
TDM (5a)	Shepherd's Crag
Grip Factor (5a,–)	Black Crag
★ 1993 (4c)	Christmas Crag
The Nose (5a)	Grange Crags
The Sorcerer	Greatend Crag
Catafalque (–,5a,4c)	Quayfoot Buttress
★★ Irony (4c,4c,5a)	Quayfoot Buttress
Needle Wall (4c)	Bowderstone Crag
Thor's Wrath (5a)	Bowderstone Crag
Trundle (4c,5a)	Bowderstone Crag
★ Shemezim Grooves (–,4c,5a)	Lining Crag
The Limit (5a,4c,–)	Lining Crag
★★ Rub Off (5a)	Bleak How
Simbolyn	Heron Crag
★★★ Lakeland Cragsman (5a)	Sergeant Crag Slabs
Pebble Lane (5b,4a)	Blackmoss Pot Slab
★ Langstrath Buttress (4c)	White Crag
★ Langstrath Buttress Direct (5a)	White Crag
Bon Temps (4c,5a)	Doves' Nest Crag
★ Clubfoot Variation (4c,5a)	Doves' Nest Crag
★ Flashback (5a)	Doves' Nest Crag
No More Heroes (4c,5a)	Thornythwaite Knotts
Puritan (5a)	Hanging Stone
Shake Down (5a)	Hanging Stone
Moss Wall (4c,5a)	Gillercombe Crag
Tiercel Wall (5a,5b,–)	Gillercombe Crag
★ The Fortress (4b,5a)	Hows Crag
Castle of Fire (4b,4c,5a)	Castle Crag

HVS (Low) contd.

Castle Wall (5a)	Castle Crag
★ Route 1 (5a)	Steel Knotts
Skid Row (5a,4b,4c)	Steel Knotts
★★ Girdle Traverse (4c,–,5a,5a,4c,4b,4c)	Goat Crag
Peregrine Wall (5a)	Goat Crag
★★ The Cursing Caterpillar (4b,5a,4a,–,4c)	Goat Crag
The Great Ape (4c,5b)	Goat Crag
★ The Nab	Goat Crag
★ Vitas Dancer (5a)	Goat Crag

VS (High)

Snow Storm (5a,4b)	Walla Crag
★ Alternator (4c,4c)	Lower Falcon Crag
Deruptus (5a,4c)	Lower Falcon Crag
★★ Lamplighter (4b,4c,–)	Lower Falcon Crag
★★ Spinup (4c,4c)	Lower Falcon Crag
Ivor The Boneless (4c)	Cat Ghyll Bluffs
Marijuana (4b,–,4c)	Cat Ghyll Bluffs
Strawberry Fields (4c)	Cat Ghyll Bluffs
Vicissitude Regained (4c)	Cat Ghyll Bluffs
★★★ Adam (4c,5a)	Shepherd's Crag
★ A Fistful of Dollars (4c,4c)	Shepherd's Crag
★ Bits 'n' Pieces (4c)	Shepherd's Crag
★ Brown Crag Traverse (4c,4b,–,4a,–)	Shepherd's Crag
★★ Central Girdle (4b,4c,–,4a)	Shepherd's Crag
Hee Haw (5a)	Shepherd's Crag
P.T.O. (4c)	Shepherd's Crag
★ Rogues' Gallery (4c,5a,4b,–,4b)	Shepherd's Crag
★ Sin (–,4c)	Shepherd's Crag
★★ True Cross (4c)	Shepherd's Crag
★★ Vesper (4c,4b)	Shepherd's Crag
★★ Girdle Traverse (4b,4c,4b,4c,5a,4a,–,–,–)	Black Crag
★★ Obituary Grooves (4b,4c,4c)	Black Crag
The Groan	Black Crag
The Mole (5a,4c)	Black Crag
Intrusion (4c)	Grange Crags
★★ Mercedes (4c)	Grange Crags
Meshach (5c)	Quayfoot Buttress
Shadrach (5c)	Quayfoot Buttress
Girdle Traverse (4a,5a)	Woden's Face
★ Tantalus (4c)	Woden's Face
★★ Woden's Crack (4c)	Bowderstone Crag
The Craftsman	Long Band Crag
★ Gorgoroth (4a,4c)	Lining Crag
Roadside Picnic (4c)	Long Crag
★★ Falconer's Crack (5a,4c,4b)	Eagle Crag
★ Dago (5a)	Bleak How
Manuel (4b)	Bleak How
★ Wrinkle (5a)	Raven Crag

VS (High) contd.

★ Epithet (4b,4b)	Castle Crag
★ Mac's Crack (4c)	Mac's Wall
★ Tottering Tortoise (5a)	Steel Knotts
★★ April Fool (4b,4c)	Goat Crag
★ King Rat (4c,4c)	Goat Crag
★ The Kremlin (4b,5a)	Goat Crag

VS (Medium)

Death Guard (4c)	Rakefoot Buttress
Night Lords (4c)	Rakefoot Buttress
Salamanders (4c)	Rakefoot Buttress
Ultramarines (4c)	Rakefoot Buttress
World Eaters (4c)	Rakefoot Buttress
Crumble	Walla Crag
Necrosis (4c,4c)	Walla Crag
Obsession (–,5a)	Walla Crag
★★ White Buttress (–,4b,4b)	Walla Crag
Graviter (–,4a,4c)	Lower Falcon Crag
Black Moss Groove (4c)	Lower Goats Crag
Littlejohn (5a)	Goats Crag
The Rib (4c)	Brown Dodd
Cat Ghyll Grooves (–,4c)	Cat Ghyll Bluffs
Spider Wall (4c)	Cat Ghyll Bluffs
Horrible Arete (4c)	Surprise View Buttress
Gowder Face (4b,4a,4b)	Gowder Crag
★ Little Pig (4c,4b)	Gowder Crag
★★ Lodore Buttress (4c,4a,4b)	Gowder Crag
Masochism	Gowder Crag
★★ Revenge of the Giant Climbing Ants (–,4c,4c,–,4a)	Gowder Crag
★ The New Girdle Traverse	Gowder Crag
Warlock (–,4a,4c,4b)	Gowder Crag
A Few Dollars More (4c,4c)	Shepherd's Crag
★★ Ardus – Direct Finish (4c)	Shepherd's Crag
★★ Brown Slabs Crack (4c)	Shepherd's Crag
★★★ Eve(4b,4c,4b)	Shepherd's Crag
★★★ Fisher's Folly (4c,4c)	Shepherd's Crag
★★ Kransic Crack (4c)	Shepherd's Crag
★ Scorpion (–,–,4b)	Shepherd's Crag
Cosmetic Artifice (4c)	Ladder Brow Crag
Reckless Ecstasy (5a)	Ladder Brow Crag
Renaissance of the Retired (4b,5a)	Ladder Brow Crag
The Late Remorse of Love (4b,–)	Green Bank Crags
The Perishing Pleasure of Apes (4c)	Green Bank Crags
★ Gleaned Groove (–,–,4c,4c)	Black Crag
★ Moonraker (4c,4c)	Black Crag
One Foot in the Grave (4b)	Black Crag
★★ The Coffin (–,4b,4b)	Black Crag
The Gravestone (4b)	Black Crag
★★ The Shroud (4b,4c,4c,4a)	Black Crag

VS (Medium) contd.

★★★ Troutdale Pinnacle Direct (4b,4c,4a,–)	Black Crag
Karakoram Experience	Troutdale Gully Wall
Kit Kat	Troutdale Gully Wall
Poor Man's Utah (4c)	Aard Crag
Christmas Decoration	Christmas Crag
★ Christmas Pudding (4c)	Christmas Crag
Jingle Bells	Christmas Crag
First Contact (4c)	Grange Crags
★ A Confected Persona (–,4c)	Quayfoot Buttress
Achtung Spitfire (4c)	Bowderstone Crag
Rib Pitch (4c)	Bowderstone Crag
Schnell Dumbkopf (5a)	Bowderstone Crag
★ Uncle Warren (4b)	Lining Crag
Lucky Strike (4c,4c)	Lower Eagle Crag
★★ Postern Rib (4a,4c)	Eagle Crag
The Seams (–,4b,4c)	Eagle Crag
Mowgli (4c)	Bleak How
Wobbly Bits (4c)	Fat Charlie's Buttress
Blink	Heron Crag
Solar Toupee	High Heron Crag
★ Mystic Knee (4c)	Sergeant Crag Slabs
★ No More Motivation (4c)	Sergeant Crag Slabs
★ The Blues Connection	Sergeant Crag Slabs
Parsley the Lion (4c)	Cam Crags
★ Mad Cow (4c)	Bull Crag
★ Taurus (5a)	Bull Crag
Columba's Gully	Twa Hummocks
★ Green Cormorant (4c,5a,–)	Raven Crag
★ Ibis (4b,4c,4c,–)	Raven Crag
Garkbit Adventure (4c)	Grains Gill Crag
Late Developer (4c)	Grains Gill Crag
Maginot Line (4c,4c)	Aaron Crag
★ The Rasp (4c,4b)	Aaron Crag
Libido (4c,–)	Castle Crag
Crystal Gazer	Millican's Buttress
Karaoke	Millican's Buttress
Chrysalis (–,4c,4b,4c)	Goat Crag
Glenmorangie (4c,4b,4c,–)	Goat Crag
★ Perched Block (4c,–,4c)	Goat Crag
Ragnarok	Goat Crag
Rat Trap	Goat Crag
★ The Gnome (4a,4c,4a)	Goat Crag
★★ The Peeler (4b,4c,–)	Goat Crag

VS (Low)

Dionysius	Walla Crag
★ Southern Rib (4c)	Walla Crag
The Beast	Walla Crag
Ador (4c)	Reecastle Crag

VS (Low) contd.	
Skewered (4c)	Reecastle Crag
Gone for a Pizza (4c)	Lower Goats Crag
The Buzzard (4b,4b)	Brown Dodd
★★★ Fool's Paradise (–,4c,4c,4b,–,4b)	Gowder Crag
Gowder Buttress (4c,–,4c)	Gowder Crag
Heather Groove (4b)	Gowder Crag
★ Hog's Earth (4b,–,4b)	Gowder Crag
Slab Start (4b,4a)	Gowder Crag
The Antiman	Gowder Crag
★★ Brown Crag Wall (4b,4a,4a)	Shepherd's Crag
★★ C.D.M. (4c)	Shepherd's Crag
Groove and Crack (4b,4a)	Shepherd's Crag
★★ Shepherd's Chimney (4a,–,5a,4a)	Shepherd's Crag
★ Short Notice (4b)	Shepherd's Crag
★ Slings (4b,4a,4a)	Shepherd's Crag
★★ Holly Tree Corner (–,4b,–,–,4a)	Black Crag
★ Happy Christmas (4b)	Christmas Crag
★ Cavalier (4c)	Grange Crags
Porridge (4c)	Grange Crags
Super Cool (4c,4b)	Grange Crags
★ Short Circuit (4b)	Quayfoot Buttress
Henry Heinkel (4c)	Bowderstone Crag
Shot Down Variation (4c)	Bowderstone Crag
The Ring (–,4b,4c,4c,–)	Lining Crag
Dumbo Cracks (4c,4b)	Eagle Crag
Green Wall (4c,–,–)	Eagle Crag
★ Postern Gate (4a,4c)	Eagle Crag
★ Postern Groove (4b,4c)	Eagle Crag
Trapeze (4c)	Eagle Crag
Zion (4c)	Sergeant Crag
★★ Revelation (4c)	Sergeant Crag Slabs
Rockola (4a)	Sergeant Crag Slabs
Geometer (–,4c)	Raven Crag
Phantom of the Opera (4c)	Thornythwaite Knotts
Stan the Man (4c)	Hanging Stone
★ Raven's Groove (4b,4c,–)	Gillercombe Crag
Rodine (4b,4b,4c)	Goat Crag
Tarkus	Goat Crag
The Bridal Suite (4a,4b,4a)	Goat Crag
The Queer Thing (4a,–,4c,–)	Goat Crag
Trad (4c,–)	Goat Crag
MVS (High)	
Crucified (4b)	Reecastle Crag
Poland (4b)	Goats Crag
★★ Derision Groove (4a,4b)	Shepherd's Crag
Why Not (4b)	Shepherd's Crag
The Crack (4b)	Grange Crags
★★ Aberration (4b,4c)	Quayfoot Buttress

MVS (High) contd.

★★ The Great Stair (4b,4a,4b,4c,–)	Eagle Crag
★ Just a Quickie (4c)	Raven Crag
★ The Rib (4a,4a,–)	Raven Crag
★ Gillercombe Bastion (4a,4b,–)	Gillercombe Crag
Gardeners' World (4b,4b)	Castle Crag
B.M.C. 1 (4b,4b)	Steel Knotts

MVS (Medium)

★★ Hedera Groove (4a,4b)	Lower Falcon Crag
The Riddler (4b,4c)	Lower Falcon Crag
★★★ Ardus (4a,4a,4b)	Shepherd's Crag
Lower Girdle of Fisher's Folly Buttress	Shepherd's Crag
Rattle	Shepherd's Crag
The Wreath (–,4a,4a)	Black Crag
Stingray (4b)	Grange Crags
★★ The Mound (4b)	Quayfoot Buttress
Wembley (4a)	Quayfoot Quarry
Hande Hoch (4c)	Bowderstone Crag
★ Solitaire (4a,4b)	Lining Crag
First Footing (4c)	Bleak How
Superstar (4a,4b)	Sergeant Crag
★ Crackerjack Groove (4b)	Doves' Nest Crag
Precarious Block (4b)	Doves' Nest Slabs
The Badger Parade (4a)	Doves' Nest Slabs
★★ Crystal Slab (4b,–,–)	Raven Crag
★★ Easy Street (4b,4c)	Raven Crag
Withering Height	Hind Crag
Dennis The Menace	Millican's Buttress
★★ Ambling Ant (4b)	Steel Knotts
★ Route 2 (4b)	Steel Knotts

MVS (Low)

I'm Free (4b)	Castle Head
The Adze	Gowder Crag
★ Ant Highway (4b,–)	Shepherd's Crag
★★ Shepherd's Gully (–,4b)	Shepherd's Crag
★ Troutdale Ridge (–,4b,–,–)	Black Crag
★ Custard Cream (4c)	Woden's Face
★ Trod Pip	Glaciated Slab
★ Raven Crag Grooves (4b,–,4a,–)	Raven Crag
Mouse Ghyll – Abraham's Finish	Blea Crag
Mouse Ghyll Grooves	Blea Crag
★★ Clubfoot (–,4a,–)	Doves' Nest Crag

HS

Kid Gloves	Goats Crag
Batman	Cat Ghyll Bluffs
Blood Axe	Cat Ghyll Bluffs
★★ Chamonix	Shepherd's Crag

HS contd.

★ Crescendo	Shepherd's Crag
Free 'n' Easy	Shepherd's Crag
Christmas Tree Groove	Christmas Crag
Blue Riband	Woden's Face
★ Woden's Cheek	Woden's Face
★ Balder's Crack	Bowderstone Crag
The Foad Factor (4b)	Long Crag
★ Broadway	Sergeant Crag
★★ The Great Wall	Sergeant Crag
★★ Adam's Slab	Doves' Nest Crag
Yakka	Doves' Nest Slabs
Paparazzi	Raven Crag
Gillercombe Chimneys	Gillercombe Crag

S

The Axe	Reecastle Crag
★★ Scratch	Reecastle South Crag
Everybody's Dream	Goats Crag
Left Hand Route	Lower Goats Crag
★ Mull Wait	Goats Crag
★ Son of Oz	Goats Crag
Poxy Brown Crows	Brown Dodd
Vicissitude	Cat Ghyll Bluffs
Jennipod	Gowder Crag
Tempo	Gowder Crag
The Groove	Gowder Crag
★ Desperation	Shepherd's Crag
★★ Donkey's Ears	Shepherd's Crag
Countermure	Ladder Brow Crag
Farewell to the Fifties	Green Bank Crags
The Chest of Ozymandias	Green Bank Crags
Arthur Scargill	Black Crag
★★★ Troutdale Pinnacle	Black Crag
Ring in the New	Troutdale Gully Wall
Christmas Groove	Christmas Crag
Sleigh Ride	Christmas Crag
Alvis	Grange Crags
Mini Minor	Grange Crags
The Crack	Grange Crags
Freak Brothers	Quayfoot Buttress
Twin Peaks	Quayfoot Quarry
Jaffa Cake	Woden's Face
★★ Wimpey Way	Woden's Face
★ Woden's Face Direct	Woden's Face
The Right Wall	Bowderstone Crag
Thor's Entrance	Bowderstone Crag
Serotinous	Yew Crag
Sinuate Slab	Yew Crag
Crucifix	Lining Crag

S contd.

★ Evening Wall	Lining Crag
Sunnyside Up	Lining Crag
The Weaver	Lining Crag
Fun Run	Bleak How
★ Myth of Fingerprints	Fat Charlie's Buttress
★ Heron Crag Buttress	Heron Crag
Acab	Sergeant Crag
★★★ Sergeant Crag Gully	Sergeant Crag
Chossy	Twa Hummocks
Jackson Pollock No. 5	Doves' Nest Slabs
★★ Corax	Raven Crag
Little Stint	Raven Crag
★★ Pedestal Wall	Raven Crag
Solifidian's Route	Raven Crag
Man Friday	Hind Crag
Low Flyer	Grains Gill Crag
Slow Learner	Grains Gill Crag
★★★ Gillercombe Buttress	Gillercombe Crag
Peregrine Way	Gillercombe Crag
★ Disillusion	Castle Crag
Lyre (5a)	Castle Crag
The Crystal Maze	Millican's Buttress
Lobstone Buttress	Goat Crag
Mousetrap	Goat Crag

MS

Fiddle About	Castle Head
Scrape	Reecastle South Crag
★ Tina Turner	Cat Ghyll Bluffs
Shepherd's Delight	Shepherd's Crag
Sylvan Way	Shepherd's Crag
Revenant's Groove	Ladder Brow Crag
The Cyclostome	Quayfoot Buttress
★ Family Outing	Woden's Face
The Higher the Better	Bowderstone Crag
Thor's Exit	Bowderstone Crag
Islay Wait	Fat Charlie's Buttress
Heron Crag Gully	Heron Crag
Oak Tree Wall and The Little Pinnacle	Sergeant Crag
Day's End Crack	Cam Crags
Side Exit	Twa Hummocks
★ Summit Route	Raven Crag

VD

Tommy's Crack	Castle Head
★ Walla Crag Gully	Walla Crag
★ Lodore Groove	Gowder Crag
The Gardener	Gowder Crag
The Old Girdle Traverse	Gowder Crag

	VD contd.	
	Bluebell Wall	Shepherd's Crag
★★★	Brown Slabs Direct	Shepherd's Crag
★★	Brown Slabs Face	Shepherd's Crag
	Hollow Stones	Shepherd's Crag
	Jackdaw Promenade	Shepherd's Crag
★★	Jackdaw Ridge Direct	Shepherd's Crag
★★★	Little Chamonix	Shepherd's Crag
	North Ridge	Shepherd's Crag
	Shepherd's Warning	Shepherd's Crag
★	Turning The North	Shepherd's Crag
	Flamboyant Decay	Ladder Brow Crag
	Troutdale Gully	Black Crag
	Ashley Slab	Little Black Crag
	Phoenix Ridge	Greatend Crag
★★	Quayfoot Buttress	Quayfoot Buttress
★★	Woden's Face	Woden's Face
	Fleur de Lys	Bowderstone Crag
	Thor's Ridge	Bowderstone Crag
★	Woden's Needle	Bowderstone Crag
	Bog Drop	Long Crag
	Pinnacle Route	Heron Crag
	The Grolley	Combe Ghyll
★★	Trod A' Tween	Glaciated Slab
★	Trod Dovera	Glaciated Slab
★	Trod Methera	Glaciated Slab
	Columba's Bastion	Twa Hummocks
★	Combe Ghyll Flake	Twa Hummocks
★	Adam's Rib	Doves' Nest Crag
	The Inside Route	Doves' Nest Crag
	Ludo	Raven Crag
★★★	Raven Crag Buttress	Raven Crag
★★★	Raven Crag Gully	Raven Crag
	Raven Bastion	Raven Crag
	Slab Route	Raven Crag
	The Warbler	Raven Crag
	Hind Crag Buttress	Hind Crag
	Southern Buttress	Hind Crag
	Gable End	Grains Gill Crag
	Trisolo	Black Waugh Crag
★★	Gabbro	Gillercombe Crag
	Gillercombe Gully	Gillercombe Crag
	South Buttress	Gillercombe Crag
	Castle Crag Gully	Hows Crag
	Silly Billy	Goat Crag
	Hogmanay Climb	Knitting How
	Bridge Gully	Blea Crag
	Gully to Right	Blea Crag

D

Falcon Pinnacle	Lower Falcon Crag Left
★★ Ashness Ghyll	Ashness
The Slab	Goats Crag
Fool's Gambol	Gowder Crag
★ The Hog's Back	Gowder Crag
★★ Brown Slabs	Shepherd's Crag
★★★ Brown Slabs Arete	Shepherd's Crag
★ Jackdaw Ridge	Shepherd's Crag
Ashley Rib	Little Black Crag
Open Cast	Greatend Crag
★ Balder's Buttress	Bowderstone Crag
★★ Bowderstone Pinnacle	Bowderstone Crag
Woden's Way	Bowderstone Crag
Coquette's Gully	Yew Crag
Panacea Ridge	Yew Crag
★ Greenup Edge	Lining Crag
★★ Ullscarf Edge	Lining Crag
Introductory Route	Heron Crag
Cheap Entertainment	Sergeant Crag
★ West Face Route	Sergeant Crag
★ Intake Ridge	Glaciated Slab
★ Trod Hovera	Glaciated Slab
★ Trod Pimp	Glaciated Slab
★ Trod Tan	Glaciated Slab
★★ Trod Tethera	Glaciated Slab
★★ Trod Sethera	Glaciated Slab
Combe Ghyll Buttress	Twa Hummocks
The Twa Hummocks North	Twa Hummocks
The Twa Hummocks South	Twa Hummocks
★★ Outside or Face Route	Doves' Nest Crag
★★★ Corvus	Raven Crag
Calf Close Buttress	Capell Crag
★★ Grey Knotts Face	Gillercombe Crag
Amenable Slab	Knitting How
Atavistic Chimney	Knitting How
Mouse Ghyll	Blea Crag

M

Copperhead	Lower Goats Crag
100 – Foot Slab	Shepherd's Crag
Attic Stairs	Shepherd's Crag
Troutdale Introductory	Black Crag
Frigga's Staircase	Bowderstone Crag
Walking the Plank	Bowderstone Crag
Incipient Arete	Yew Crag
★★★ Cam Crag Ridge	Cam Crags
★ Trod Yan/Lethera	Glaciated Slab
Bond Street	Twa Hummocks
Cock's Combe	Raven Crag
Tyro's Gully	Raven Crag

FIRST ASCENTS

Alternate and Varied leads are indicated respectively by (alt) and (var).

1892	**Walla Crag Gully**	G D Abraham, A P Abraham
1893 Sept 1	**Raven Crag Gully**	W A Wilson, J W Robinson

"It was certainly the worst-looking pitch in the whole ascent. A large cave was formed by two massive boulders jammed between the narrow walls seventy feet above our heads. The first floor of the gully was fifty feet up, and from its roof dripped the inevitable water supply to damp our daring ardour. The walls of the Gully were close together and covered in wet moss. Holds were very scarce..."

> Owen Glynne Jones, Rock Climbing in the English Lake
> District, 1897

"Under fairly dry conditions the first 80-foot obstacle can be climbed more or less directly, making use at times of the long buttress that really splits the gully in two at the start. Most parties avoid this pitch and its waterfall. The latter seems especially moist and enervating when the climber is standing with uncertain handhold on a slowly disintegrating foothold with no further prospect in life than a downward one."

> George Abraham, British Mountain Climbs, 1909
> 28 April 1897. Top pitch direct O G Jones, C W Patchell,
> H C Bowen.

1893 Sept 6	**Sergeant Crag Gully**	O G Jones, J W Robinson

"The retaining walls of the gully form the sides of the cave, and the ascent is to be affected on the left. From a short distance this appears to be a smooth vertical slab: even on close inspection the holds it offers appear to be of the most minute dimensions."

> Owen Glynne Jones, Rock Climbing in the
> English Lake District, 1897

1895	**Bridge Gully**	G D Abraham, A P Abraham
1897 Sept 27	**Mouse Ghyll**	W C Slingsby, A G Topham

"When the first party were here, a startled mouse sprang from the grassy ledge over the leader's head, and dropped safely at the bottom of the staircase ninety feet below. May it live long enough to learn that the ghyll has been named in its honour"

> Owen Glynne Jones, Rock Climbing in the
> English Lake District, 1897
> October 1897. Abraham's Finish. G D Abraham, A P Abraham,
> W Phillipson.

1897	**South Chimney, Dove's Nest**	M Dalton, A Thomson, 'E.R.'
1910 May	**A,B & D Gullies** Eagle Crag	W A Bowdler

1912 May 28   **Gillercombe Buttress**   H B Lyon, W A Woodsend
*"Immediately above our heads the overhang was very
pronounced, whilst about 15 feet up on the left, a narrow
sloping "mantelshelf" appeared to be the only means of exit, as
a very folorn sort of hope. A good belay would have been
acceptable here, but a leaf of rock behind which we tried to
pass the rope was not sufficiently split from the main mass.
How we longed for a narrow strip of iron to insert behind the
leaf as a belaying pin! On a future occasion I tried this
somewhat unorthodox method when making the ascent with a
large party and found a large nail or cold chisel, picked up in
the farmyard at Thorneythwaite, to answer the purpose
admirably."*

Harry Lyon, F&RCC Journal 1914

*17 May 1921. By the Modern Finish. J Ray, H Harland,
G A Solly, G Wilson.
18 May, 1921. By Variation Finish. R S T Chorley,
O E Harland, J C Appleyard.
27 August, 1989. Alternative Variation Finish. D Craig, P J
Greenwood.*

1913 Sept   **Gillercombe Gully**   H B Lyon, A S Walker
1914 May 4   **Troutdale Pinnacle**   F Mallinson, R Mayson
*"The neck between the Pinnacle and the perpendicular rock
behind is a boulder which rocks slightly. Taking off from this
loose boulder you have a 40 feet straight run up to finish. It is
a grand and sensational exit which is sure to prove exceedingly
popular with all who make its acquaintance"*

Ralph Mayson, F&RCC Journal 1914

*Also known as Black Crag Buttress.
Early photographs show that the pinnacle once boasted a
detached spike which rested upon the present narrow-backed
ridge.
23 August 1959. Variation Finish. P Ross, E Rocher
Variation Finish. Anaconda, A Hocking, W Hunter 20 May 1997.*

1914 May   **Bowderstone Pinnacle**   F Mallinson, R Mayson
*20 September 1933. Direct Start. C J A Cooper,
E Wood-Johnson.
Variation. Bowderstone Pinnacle Superdirect M Przygrodski
(unseconded) 18 October 1977*

1921   **Woden's Face Original Route**   B Beetham, C D Frankland
1921   **Woden's Face Direct**   C D Frankland, B Beetham
1921   **Troutdale Ridge**   C D Frankland, B Beetham
1922   **Brown Slabs Arête**   C D Frankland, B Beetham
1922 June   **Gillercombe Chimneys**   H S Cross, J Wray, O E Harland,
E F Harland
1922   **Columba's Gully**   B Beetham, W V Brown
1924   **Ashness Ghyll**   A Dibona, A R Thomson
1924   **Gully to Right**   A Dibona, A R Thompson

1924	**Hind Crag Buttress** A Dibona, A R Thompson
	20 April 1935. Direct Route. A Wood-Johnson, Mabel M Barker, E Wood-Johnson.
1934	**Greenup Edge** W Heaton Cooper
1935 Sept 12	**Woden's Cheek** B Beetham

"Then came the first series of the Fell and Rock Club's climbing guides, and to many, finality, so far as Cumberland was concerned, seemed to have been reached. I remember venturing the remark that these guides would soon be out of date. The idea was hotly scouted as most disrespectful, and I was plainly informed that what few climbs had been left undone before the war, had all now been cleaned up, that there were no others of importance left to do."

Bentley Beetham, F&RCC Journal 1942

1936 Aug 26	**Woden's Needle** B Beetham
	29 March 1954. Variation. A P Rossiter, N S Brook.
1936	**Evening Wall** J Cameron, W Heaton Cooper
1936	**Ullscarf Edge** D J Cameron, W Heaton Cooper
1937 Sept 5	**Intake Ridge** B Beetham
1939 June 18	**Grey Knotts Face** B Beetham
	12 September 1950. Grey Knotts Outcrop, below the main crag, provides 2 additional pitches up to the start. Variation details unknown.
1939 Sept 6	**Raven Crag Buttress** B Beetham and members of the Goldsborough Club
1939 Sept 11	**Pinnacle Route** B Beetham
1939 Sept 23	**Peregrine Way** B Beetham
1940 April 20	**Perched Block** B Beetham
	This ascent avoided the issue of the lower buttress.
	11 April 1955. Pitch 1, R Jackson (prior top rope inspection).
1940 May 19	**Gillercombe Bastion** W Peascod, D G Conner, S B Beck, J H Conner
1940 Aug 6	**Pedestal Wall** B Beetham
1940 Sept 9	**Heron Crag Gully** B Beetham and members of the Goldsborough Club
1940 Sept 18	**Heron Crag Buttress** B Beetham
1941 April 14	**Gabbro** B Beetham
1942 April 10	**South Buttress** Gillercombe B Beetham
1942 April 15	**Cock's Comb** B Beetham
1942 April 22	**Combe Ghyll Flake** B Beetham
1942 April 23	**Lobstone Buttress** B Beetham
	Variation details unknown.
1942 April 24	**Pedestal Nose** B Beetham
1942 April 24	**Pedestal Cheek** B Beetham
1943	**Cam Crag Ridge** B Beetham, J B Meldrum and members of the Goldsborough Club
1944 April 13	**Introductory Route** S Cross, B Beetham
1944 April 15	**Thor's Exit** B Beetham

1944 April 16	**Thor's Ridge** B Beetham
	4 December 1985. Variation. Thor's Wrath, R Kenyon, C Eckersall.
1944 Whit	**Face Route** R S T Chorley, B Beetham, R W Somervell
	Climbed previously. Variation details unknown.
	Many problems and variations were described by Millican Dalton in the FRCC Journal 1914.
1994 June 23	**Gunner's Climb** A Verity, A Dobson, J Tebbutt
1944 July 23	**Castle Crag Gully** B Beetham
1944 July 31	**Combe Ghyll Buttress** B Beetham
1944 Aug 24	**Columba's Bastion** B Beetham
1944 Aug 25	**Twa Hummocks, North and South** B Beetham
1944 Aug 30	**Balder's Crack** B Beetham
1944 Sept 1	**Side Exit** B Beetham
1944 Sept 4	**Trods Yan, Tan, Tethera, Pimp, Lethera, Hovera** B Beetham
1944 Sept 6	**Trods Methera, Sethera, Dovera** B Beetham
1945 April 12	**Balder's Buttress** B Beetham
1945 April 13	**Frigga's Staircase** B Beetham
1945 April 24	**Bond Street** B Beetham P Bond
1945 Aug 24	**Woden's Way** B Beetham
1945 Aug 28	**West Face Route** B Beetham, T H Somervill, T B Meldrum, T R Burnett, L W Somervell
	7 September 1945. Variation. Cheap Entertainment, B Beetham.
1945 Sept 3	**Slab Route** B Beetham, W Priestley-Phillips
1945 Sept 6	**The Great Wall** B Beetham
1945 Sept 6	**Broadway** B Beetham
1945 Oct 20	**Tyro's Gully** B Beetham, H Westmorland
1946 April 5	**Quayfoot Buttress** B Beetham
1946 April 7	**Brown Slabs** B Beetham
1946 April 10	**Chamonix** B Beetham
1946 April 15	**North Ridge** B Beetham
1946 April 17	**Hollow Stones** B Beetham
1946 May 15	**Ardus** V Veevers, H Westmorland, P Holt
	1956. Direct Finish. P J Greenwood, F Travis.
	Francois Travis climbed barefoot. She had employed Greenwood as a guide.
	11 August 1960. Variation. Short Notice, D W English, W O'Hare.
1946 May 19	**Bluebell Wall** B Beetham
1946 May 26	**Little Chamonix** B Beetham
1946 June 1	**Falconer's Crack** W Peascod, S B Beck
1946 June 15	**The Great Stair** W Peascod, S B Beck
1946 June 16	**Postern Gate** W Peascod, S B Beck
	(However!): "The main buttress of Eagle Crag can be climbed starting from "D" Gully on a level with the terrace. After climbing about twenty feet of broken rock is turned to the left on to a good ledge, distinguishable by a split block which offers safe anchorage. The writer has not yet had the opportunity of following this route through, but believes that

G.D. Abraham and his brother climbed up over the top of the buttress from the ledge some years ago".

William Bowdler, F&RCC Journal 1910

1946 July 29	**Shepherd's Delight** B Beetham
	14 June 1947. Variation. Shepherd's Warning., B Beetham.
1946 July 31	**Shepherd's Chimney** B Beetham
1946 Aug 1	**Turning the North** B Beetham
1946 Aug 4	**100-Foot Slab** B Beetham
1946 Aug 27	**Jackdaw Ridge** B Beetham
	4 September 1946. Variation Starts. Jackdaw Ridge Direct and Jackdaw Promenade, B Beetham.
1946 Sept 12	**Sylvan Way** B Beetham, J B Meldrum
1947 April 1	**Donkey's Ears** B Beetham
1947 April 19	**Brown Slabs Crack** B Beetham
1947 May 24	**Attic Stairs** B Beetham
1947 July 20	**Oaktree Wall** G N Sissons, J T Kas
1947 July 20	**The Little Pinnacle** G N Sissons
1947 July 28	**Monolith Crack** B Beetham
	30 July 1948. Variation. Monolith Chimney, B Beetham.
1947 Aug 30	**Gowder Buttress** B Beetham
1947 Sept 1	**Brown Slabs Face** B Beetham
1947 Sept 7	**Ant Highway** B Beetham
1947 Sept 10	**Shepherd's Gully** B Beetham
1947 Nov 8	**Lodore Groove** B Beetham, F H Colley
1948 Feb 22	**The Hog's Back** B Beetham
	11 May 1974. Variation. The Antiman, D Johnson, K Rudd (alt).
	2 April 1951. Variation. Fool's Gamble, R Scott, S Dirkin.
	11 July 1976. Variation. Masochism, S Lewis, B Dixon.
	Easter 1958. Variation. Slab Start, J A Austin, J Ruffe.
1948 April 7	**Brown Slabs Direct** B Beetham
1948 May 16	**Raven's Groove** L Muscroft, R J Birkett
1948 June 5	**The Higher the Better** B Beetham
1948 July 30	**Devil's Wedge** B Beetham
1948 Aug 14	**Crescendo** B Beetham
1948 Oct 17	**Desperation** V Veevers, G B Fisher
1948 Oct 24	**Slings** V Veevers, G B Fisher
1948 Nov 14/15	**Gowder Face** B Beetham
	A combination of the best of two routes Gowder Face North and South.
1949 April 8	**Vulcan's Buttress** B Beetham
1949 May 8	**Vicissitude** D N Greenop, W A Lannaghan
	17 November 1985. Variation. Vicisstude Regained, P Hirst, R McHaffie, G Spensley
1949 June 19	**Gowder Old Girdle** B Beetham
	Not a true girdle of the cliff.
1949 Aug 6	**Walking the Plank** B Beetham
1950 March 9	**Fleur de Lys** G B Fisher, G B Withington
1950 March 29	**Phoenix Ridge** B Beetham
1950 April 22	**Brown Crag Wall** R Wilkinson, K C Ogilvie, J D Wildridge

1950 April 29	**Open Cast** B Beetham
1950 June 10	**Corvus** B Beetham
	Variation climbed in 1951, details unknown.
1950 May 9	**Styx** B Beetham
1950 July 1	**Corax** B Beetham
1950 July 9	**Troutdale Introductory** B Beetham
1950 Aug 19	**Falcon Front** P R J Harding, E S Williams
	An impressive loose expedition whose line was lost for some time.
1951 April 13	**Fool's Paradise** P W Vaughan, J D J Wildridge
	Variation pitches 1a and 2a are often used being a quicker way of getting to the meat of the climb, by avoiding the arête pitch. Variation 2b was ascended on the original ascent.
	Pitch 2 was climbed in 1985 by R Kenyon, though probably climbed before, and incorporated in the main description as it utilizes the whole of the arête.
1951 May 13	**Summit Route** B Beetham, J Foyle
	"Some distance to our right a hand holding a brush appeared over the edge, daintily swept it clear of earth and moss and withdrew, to be followed by two hands and then by Bentley's cheerful though somewhat grubby countenance. He was engaged in 'gardening' a new route, equipped with the brush, a saw and other implements."
	Frank Monkhouse and Joe Williams, Climber and Fellwalker in Lakeland, David and Charles, 1972
	3 October 1959. Variation Finish. D Murray, D A Crawford.
1951 May 31	**Raven Bastion** B Beetham
1951 Aug 11	**Eve** W Peascod, B Blake
	Named after the barmaid in the Borrowdale Hotel.
1951 Aug	**Adam's Rib** G B Fisher, G B Withington
1952 May 15	**Calf Close Buttress** B Beetham
1952 May 22	**Scorpion** G B Fisher, R Richardson
1952 June 4	**Damnation Groove** J D J Wildridge
1952 June 10	**Man Friday** G B Fisher, F Bantock, F Newall
1952 July 6	**Kransic Crack** G B Fisher, D Oliver, F Bantock
	1956. Variation. Direct Finish. D Peel. Soloed on sight as the result of a dare.
	1978. Right-Hand, details unknown.
1952 July 27	**Troutdale Pinnacle Direct** J D Oliver, M Nixon, K Pepper
1952 July	**Crucifix** J D J Wildridge, H Hall
1952 July	**Ludo** G B Fisher, F Bantock
1952	**Lodore Buttress** H Drasdo, A Beanland
1953 Dec 6	**Thor's Entrance** R Miller, A C Cain
	Variation. Rib Pitch, details not known but prior to 1968
1953 April 25	**Solifidians's Route** D N Greenop, W A Lanaghan (alt)
1954 June 6	**North Buttress** P J Greenwood, E Mallinson
	Climbed by the Slab Finish. Now described as a variation.

The Direct Finish, as now described was added soon afterwards with 1 point of aid. P J Greenwood, D Whillans, P Whitwell. Now free.

It is rumoured that on an early solo first ascent attempt on this route, Bentley Beetham became stuck and eventually leapt off into a tree!

1954 Aug 26   **Troutdale Pinnacle Superdirect**   P Ross, D Oliver

"On its third pitch he was seriously committed, with the second badly belayed. When Ross announced that he was coming off, the second screamed, 'You'll kill us both.' Ross's immediate thoughts were, Bloody hell, it's Saturday. That was the first thing that came to me. I'm going to miss the dance. Even if I survived the fall, I wasn't going to be in any shape to dance."

        Paul Ross, quoted in Cumbrian Rock, Trevor Jones 1988

15 May 1959. Variation Finish. P Ross, E Rosher.

Ross's first new route in the valley.

1954 Sept   **Rogues' Gallery**   P Ross, G B Fisher, E Ray, D Oliver
1955 Feb 9   **Libido**   P J Greenwood, C Drake
1955 Feb 27   **Derision Groove**   J Wood, P Ross (alt)
1955 Easter   **Green Wall**, Eagle Crag   M Thompson, P Lockey
1955 Easter   **Fisher's Folly**   M Thompson, P Nichol

Direct Finish added by P Ross later that year.

1955 April 11   **Peregrine Wall**, Goat Crag   R Jackson, A R Barlett
1955 April 30   **The Fou**   P Ross, R Wilkinson

One peg, for aid, on pitch 1. Now free.

10 June 1958. Variation. Entertainment Traverse, by P Ross, P Lockey. Sling and etrier used for aid. Now free.

1955 June 9   **Vesper**   P Ross, P J Greenwood (alt)
1955 June   **Troutdale Gully**   C Wilson, B Furmston
1955 July 2   **Porcupine**   P Ross, E Ray

2 pegs for aid on pitch 2. Climbed free by P Whillance, February 1977.

1955 July 16   **Girdle Traverse**, Black Crag   P J Greenwood, D English, P Ross (alt)
1955 July 29   **Irrawaddy**   P J Greenwood, I Smeaton

Variation. Vortex, climbed by C Read, J Adams (alt) 15 April 1968. 1 peg for aid.

Climbed free by T Marr.

1955 July 30   **Obituary Groves**   P J Greenwood, P Ross (alt)

"1955 could be said to belong jointly to Ross and Greenwood. Ross did his first two Extremes in Borrowdale, The Fou and Porcupine, then Greenwood during an active weekend in July, produced Irrawaddy, Hard Very Severe 5a, on Castle Crag, then stayed sufficiently abstemious on the Saturday night to produce Obituary Grooves with Ross on Black Crag. Both said separately that the other was a better climber, but the important thing was their excellent tally of new routes and their equality as a team"

        Trevor Jones, Cumbrian Rock, 1988

1955 Aug 4	**Brown Crag Traverse** P J Greenwood, K Pearce, T Marsden
1955 Aug 23	**Central Girdle** T Marsden, J Dowsett
1955 Aug 30	**Adam** P Ross, B Wilkinson
1955 Oct 2	**Conclusion** P Ross, P Whitwell
1955 Nov 28	**Panacea Ridge** D N Greenop, J Miller
1955 Nov 28	**Incipient Arête** D N Greenop, J Miller
1955 Dec 11	**Coquette's Gully** D N Greenop
1955 Dec 18	**Serotinuous** D N Greenop, G Benn (alt)
1955 Dec 18	**Sinuate Slabs** D N Greenop, G Benn

The previous five routes had all been climbed before but not recorded.

1956 Jan 2	**Hogmanay Climb** D N Greenop
1956 Jan 2	**Amenable Slab** D N Greenop
1956 Jan 2	**Atavistic Chimney** D N Greenop

Variation. Flake Finish, 1985.

1956 May 19   **Post Mortem** P Ross, P Lockey (var)

"On the first pitch, as Lockey followed up a steep flake crack, a large six-foot pinnacle slid out of it and started to grate its way downwards. Fortunately Lockey made a grab for a handhold and swung his feet off as the stone monolith plunged down in a shower of sparks and sulphurous smells. On the main pitch Ross climbed up to a jammed chockstone in a wide awkward crack, then came down for a rest after attaching a sling. Lockey climbed past it, knocked a piton in the right wall, for protection only, then he too retreated. Ross took a rest at the chockstone and the led the rest of the pitch, with just two pieces of protection."

Trevor Jones, Cumbrian Rock, 1988

1956 May 29   **Funeral Way** P Ross, P J Greenwood (alt)

The Direct Start added by P Allison, J J S Allison in 1963 is now used as the start to Stretch.

1956 June 10	**Graviter** P Lockey, P Ross (alt)
1956 June 10	**Illusion** P Lockey, P Ross (alt)

Variation Start. Good Times Bad Times, by D Knighton, B Conlon, 27 August 1978.

1956 Aug 10   **Hedera Grooves** P Ross, P Lockey

1956 Sep 1   **Deruptus** P Ross, D Sewell

Variation Finish. J Taylor, 26 April 1978.

1956   **Kransic Crack Direct** D Peel

Soloed on sight as the result of a dare.

1957 March 31   **Acab** K Jones, E S Graves, S M Redmond

1957 April 14   **The Bludgeon** P Ross, P Lockey

Variation finish. Missing Link, climbed in February 1982 by A Jones, D Hellier. This free climbed an old route called Apollo climbed by C Laverty and G Leech on 10 August 1960. This route finished up what is now the top metre or so, of Stone Tape, and used 11 points of aid.

Variation finish. Shepherds Pie, climbed on 9 September 1984 by R Curley, D Williamson, N Stansfield, C Thwaites. Top-roped prior to leading.

1957 May 22   **Spinup**   P Ross, D Sewell
1975 Variation finish. D Nicol, R Wilson.

1957 May 25   **White Buttress**   P Ross, D Sewell

1957 May 28   **Southern Rib**   P Ross, D Sewell

1957 May   **Dedication**   P Ross, E Metcalf

1958 May 4   **Route 1**, Upper Falcon Crag   P Ross, P Lockey (var)
4 pegs for aid on pitch 3. Climbed free by A Parkin, P Clarke, May 1975.

1958 May 25   **Whit's Ridge**   C R Wilson, T P Loftus

1958 May 25   **Whit's End**   C R Wilson, T P Loftus

1958 June 1   **The Shroud**   P Ross, P Lockey

1958 Aug 23   **Obsession**   P Ross, W Aughton

1958 Oct 18   **Vertigo**   P Ross, W Aughton
Much aid used on pitch 3. Climbed with 1 peg for aid by P Livesey and re-named Austentatious, June 1976. Climbed free by P Whillance, D Armstrong June 12 1977. Original name re-used.

1958 Nov   **Redberry Wall**   J Austin, B Fuller

1958   **Black Icicle**   D Fielding
Claimed and named by R McHaffie June 1973.

1958   **MGC**   B Robert, G West of the Manchester Gritstone Club
The pegs from the aided ascent were removed, no doubt for use on Derbyshire Limestone.
Previously climbed with aid in 1957 by R McHaffie, L Kendall, A Liddell and P Ross. Ross finished the climb by what is now the direct finish to Fisher's Folly.

1959 Feb 20   **Southern Buttress**   D N Greenop, J P Greenop, E Brown

1959 March 7   **Slime Corner**   J Austin, B Fuller

1959 March 15   **Wack**   P Ross, G Woodhouse, F Carroll
Climbed with 6-7 pegs for aid. Lower pitch added and roof climbed with tension from a high runner. P Livesey, P Gomersall July 1977. Re-named Scrutineer. Climbed free by J Lamb and original name re-used 12 July 1981. Variation. High Explosion, details unknown.

1959 March 21   **Disillusion**   P Ross, W Aughton

1959 April 19   **P.S.**   P Ross, W Aughton
Direct finish added by J Lamb, P Botterill 20 June 1981.

1959 May   **P.T.O.**   P Ross, R Marshall

1959 May 31   **Trapeze**   P Ross, G Woodhouse

1959 May 31   **Girdle Traverse**, Eagle Crag   P Ross, G Woodhouse, F Carroll

1959 Aug 16   **Pendulum**   F Crosby, D A Elliott
7 pegs used on first ascent. Climbed free by J Eastham, G Myers, J Myers June 1977.

1959 Sept 19   **Brown Crag Grooves**   F Crosby, P Muscroft
Direct Start. P Botterill, J Lamb July 1979.

1959 Oct 4	**Whit's Wall** D A Elliott
1960 April 24	**Postern Groove** D Miller, P Moffat
1960 June 10	**Marijuana** C Laverty, M Reay, A Richardson, G Leech

Direct finish. A Liddell, M Burbage 14 November 1965.
Variation. Strawberry Fields, by K Rudd, M Lomas December
1970 using some aid on pitch 1. Climbed free by T W Birkett.

1960 Aug 10	**Theseus** C Laverty, G Leech, A Richardson (1st pitch)

3 pegs used for aid. Climbed with 1 peg for aid by G Oliver,
P Ross Now free. P Ross, G Oliver added pitch 2.

1960	**Inclination** F Crosby, D Byrne-Peare

An artificial aided finish to Shepherd's Chimney, climbed free
by J Lamb, P Botterill July 1979.

1961	**Irony** R Belden

Climbed with aid. Aid reduced by L Kendal, J J S Allison, 1961.
Freed by A Liddell, R McHaffie, 1961.

1961 June	**Hallucination** O Woolcock, N J Soper (alt)
1961 Sept 18	**Jigsaw** J J S Allison, L Kendall
1961 Oct 18	**Castle Wall** J J S Allison, L Kendall
1962 March 11	**Voodoo** R McHaffie, A Kew, L Kendall

2 pegs used on pitch 1. Now free.

1962 April 29	**Girdle Traverse,** Walla Crag P Ross, A Campbell

The original girdle finished up Obsession. The final pitches
were added by P Ross, P Lockey (alt) 21 July 1966.

1962 May 27	**Thanks** R Blain, P Ross (alt)
1962 July 8	**Interloper** A Liddell, R McHaffie (alt)

1 sling and 3 pegs for aid. Climbed free by C Read and
J Adams. 12 June 1971.
Variation. Defy Gravity, A Jones, T Daley, W Hannah 31
August 1986.

1962 Aug 20	**The Niche** A Liddell, R McHaffie (alt)

" We wondered why this line had not been climbed by Paul
Ross. We spun a coin to see who was going to lead the first
pitch. Adrian won the toss and set of up the steep wall. About
fifteen feet below the niche he had no runners on and decided
to put a peg in, then he climbed up a few feet and made the
very difficult traverse into the Niche. He belayed on a piton. I
set off to climb the pitch which I found to be very difficult. I left
the piton in place. I came off the traverse into the Niche. I set
off on the second pitch and put two more pitons under the roof."
    Ray McHaffie, quoted in Cumbrian Rock, Trevor Jones 1988
Pitch 1 led with rope drag off a peg on the left of the niche.
Two pegs were used for aid whilst removing loose blocks on
pitch 2. Now free.
Variation. The Left Exit. B Robertson, P Ross. 24 September
1966 using 4 points of aid. All now free.

1962 Aug	**Plagiarism** P Nunn, O Woolcock

1 peg and sling for aid. Now free. The original ascent utilized
Dedication to start, though L Brown and G Oliver had climbed
the start described on an abortive attempt.

Direct Finish, R Graham, P Ingham 2 June 1986.

1962 Sept 15   **Girdle Traverse,** Lower Falcon Crag   R McHaffie, L Kendall
The first complete traverse, using the earlier Selection Traverse climbed 8 February 1959 by P Ross and B Aughton which finished up Deruptus. On this ascent the abseil onto Dedication was taken. A direct and more difficult connection has since been made, avoiding the abseil.
Extension from pitch 6. Summer 1975. D Nicol and M Hardiman. With 1 point of aid. Now free.

1962 Sept 22   **Valhalla**   W Barnes, D A Elliott
1 sling for aid. Now free.

1962 Sept 25   **Lyre**   D A Elliott, W Young

1962 Dec 22   **Exclamation**   S Clark, W A Barnes, T Martin, D A Elliott
An artificial aided finish to Shepherd's Chimney. Climbed free by B Berzins, M Berzins 22 September 1979, using a pre-placed wire runner and high side runner in the adjacent Shepherd's Chimney.

1963 March 6   **R.I.P.**   R McHaffie and party
Pitch 2 added by N J Soper, P Nunn, A Wright 2 April 1963.

1963 May 11   **Charon**   J Allison, G Arkless

1963 May 25   **Cat Ghyll Grooves**   J J S Allison, D Moy
1 peg for aid. Now free.

1963 May   **The Dangler**   S Clark, T Martin
First ascent made using a considerable amount of aid. The bolt had been placed by Mick Burke prior to this ascent. Climbed free by R Fawcett, C Gibb 1976. Pitch 1 as described climbed by J Anderson, R McHaffie 1962.

1963 July 11   **Route 2,** Upper Falcon Crag   J J Allison, D Hadlum, A Liddell
One peg used for aid on the top pitch. Now free.
Variation finish. Qantas, climbed by J Peel, G Peel September 1979.

1963 Aug   **Vortigern**   J Roper, P Shackleton (alt)
3 pegs for aid. Climbed free by T Stephenson, R Parker, C Sice 22 October 1977.

1963   **The Girdle Traverse,** Upper Falcon Crag   R McHaffie, A Liddell (alt)
2 pegs for aid on pitch 3. Now free.

1963   **The New Girdle,** Gowder Crag   C Spacey, R Hill

1963 Nov 19   **Epitaph**   A N Boydell, T Taylor
2 pegs for aid. Now free.

1963 Dec 2   **Epithet**   A N Boydell, T Taylor

1964 Feb   **Hell's Wall**   S Clarke, B Henderson
An artificial aided route. Climbed free by R Fawcett, C Gibb 1979
"Fawcett had to resort to seige tactics over several days before its thin, tendon-tearing cracks were forced into submission"
                                      Trevor Jones, Cumbrian Rock, 1988

1964 May   **Black Crag Eliminate**   R McHaffie, J Eastwood

Variation Finish. Roach Clip, climbed by S Miller, D Bowen 10 July 1980.

1964 May 29   **Lamplighter**   L Hewitt, S Glass
Pitch 1 as described climbed May 1964. Original pitch 1 used 2 pegs for aid. This is now free and forms part of Lamplighter Eliminate.

1964 June 22   **Rattle**   M Thompson, W A Barnes

1964 July   **Mandrake**   A Liddell, M Burbage
1 point of aid. Now free.

1964 Aug 13   **The Gibbet**   P Ross, A N Boydell
2 pegs used for aid. Climbed free by D Armstrong, R Parker 29 August, 1978.

1964 Aug 14   **Scrape**   P Ross, B Callaghan

1964 Aug 16   **Scratch**   W Barnes, P Ross

1964   **Stone Tape**   L Ainsworth
Pitch 2 only. Pitch 1 added by J Lamb, R Cowells 17 August, 1978.

1965 March 20   **Snow Storm**   M A Toole, D Byrne-Peare
Climbed in mistake for Southern Rib.

1965 May 1   **Eyrie**   P Nunn, O Woolcock (alt)
The first pitch had been climbed previously.

1965 May 2   **Aberration**   O Woolcock, P Nunn (alt)

1965 May 28   **Daedalus**   P Nunn, B Griffiths, P Ross
Finishing up Falconer's Crack. 2 nuts and 1 sling for aid in the chimney and 2 pegs for aid on the bulge on pitch 1. Pitch 2 as now described added by P Nunn, M Richardson October 1965 with 1 peg for aid. All now free.

1965 May 30   **Praying Mantis**   L Brown, S Bradshaw
This was the first route on Goat Crag and only new route by Les Brown on the crag.
Chockstone recommended for resting on pitch 1. Now climbed free.
Direct pitch L Brown, K Jackson using 1 point of aid May 1965. Now free.

1965 June 2   **The Technician**   P Ross, D Byrne-Peare
Much aid used. Climbed free by P Botterill, P Whillance, D Armstrong 18 June 1978 utilizing the start of Masochist to avoid seepage on the lower wall.

1965 June 9   **The Sprogg**   P Ross, P Nunn (var)
Sling for aid on pitch 2 and nut and sling for aid on pitch 4. Now free.

1965 June 10   **Icarus**   P Nunn, P Ross (var)
2 slings for aid on pitch 1 and a peg and sling on pitch 2. Now free.

1965 June 10   **The Squawk**   B Henderson, K Moseley (alt)
Peg and sling used for aid on pitches 1 and 3. Climbed free by R Bennett, G Edwards, 9 April 1978.

1965 June 12   **The Craftsman**   I Singleton, M Salkeld

1965 June   **The Creep**   C J S Bonington, R Lawson, I Lawson

Pitch 1 climbed with several nuts for aid. Now free.

1965 July 16   **Finale**   T Savage, P Ross
Nut and sling for aid. Now free.

1965 July 18   **The Lastest**   P Ross, T Savage
Peg for aid on pitch 3. Now free.

1965 July 18   **Dionysius**   A G Cram, W Young, R J Schipper

1965 Aug 14   **The Cursing Caterpillar**   B Henderson, P Ross (var)
Peg for aid on pitch 2. Now free.

1965 Aug 14   **Deadly Nightshade**   O Woolcock, P Nunn (alt)

1965 Aug 22   **The Kremlin**   J Cook, C Spacey (alt)
2 pegs used for aid. Now free.
Variation by J Duff, D Mitchell 28 July 1967.

1965 Aug 23   **Route 1**, Steel Knotts   K Leech, T Taylor
Claimed and named as Lurching Leech but probably done before.

1965 Aug 23   **Tottering Tortoise**   T Taylor, K Leech
Variation. Route 2. Details unknown though probably climbed earlier than Tottering Tortoise.

1965 Sept 10   **The Blaspheming Butterfly**   P Ross, M Thompson, B Henderson
Variation finish climbed on the original ascent.
Diedre finish as now described, climbed by B Henderson and Party.

1965 Sept 19   **Stretch**   M A Toole, J Cook (var)
1 point of aid. Now free. Pitch 1 was originally climbed as a direct start to Funeral Way by P Allison, J J S Allison 1963. Direct finish climbed by D McDonald, B Wilson 27 May 1980.

1965 Oct 6   **Joke**   P Ross, W White (alt)
Climbed with much aid. Climbed free by R Fawcett, C Gibb 1976.

1965 Oct 13   **The Big Curver**   P Ross, I Wilson, J Lee
7 pegs used on the final pitch. Climbed free by A Liddell, J Cook 30 April 1966.

1965 Oct 17   **D.D.T.**   J Lee, A Jackman, P Ross
3 pegs used on the first pitch and 1 point on the second pitch. Climbed free by A Liddell.

1965 Nov 7   **Skid Row**   D McDonald, C T Leech (alt)

1965 Nov 13   **The Peeler**   B Henderson, D McDonald, J Cook

1965   **Ichor**   R McHaffie, A Liddell

1965   **Angelus**   B Thompson, W A Barnes

1966 April 11   **The Rat Race** (Pitch 1)   B Henderson, J Cook, R McHaffie
Pitches 2,3 & 4. M A Toole, B Henderson, B Robertson. A large number of pegs were used on pitch 1. First ascent with 3 points of aid B Robertson. Climbed free by P Botterill, S Clegg 15 June 1975.

1966 April 17   **The Bridal Suite**   J Cook, B Eldred

1966 April 20   **April Fool**   M Thompson, T Lewis, P Ross (var)
Direct finish climbed using a lassoed tree to finish by R McHaffie, P Copeland April 1976. Now free.

1966 April 23	**The Queer Thing** B Henderson, J Cook, M Thompson
1966 April 23	**Monsoon** G Oliver, C Griffiths
1966 April 24	**The Girdle Traverse**, Goat Crag P Ross, M Thompson
	Much of this had been done before by B Henderson, P Ross
	8 September 1965 with 1 point of aid. Now free.
1966 May 15	**Ragnarok** G Oliver, C Griffiths
1966 May 30	**Holly Tree Corner**, Black Crag A Marr, P Bean
	Holly Tree Direct was combined with the Holly Tree Corner
	climbed by G Ward, C R Wilson on 17 July 1937, to give an
	independent climb.
1966 May	**Rat Trap** B Henderson, T Nichols, P Macloughlin
1966 June 5	**Chrysalis** P Ross, J Cook (alt)
	2 pegs for aid on pitch 2, 1 tape on pitch 3 and 1 peg on pitch
	4. Now free.
1966 June	**Glenmorangie** B Henderson, P Nunn (alt)
	Direct Start by B Henderson, B Freelands April 1967.
1966 June	**King Rat** B Henderson, P Nunn (alt) N J Soper
1966 June	**Crag Rat**, (Pitch 1) B Henderson, H Sommer
	Pitch 2 and 3 B Henderson, N J Soper (var).
1966 July 2	**Rodine** B Henderson, A Toole (var)
1966 July 9	**Trad** B Henderson, P Ross
1966 July 16	**Mousetrap** B Henderson, H Sommer
1966 July 16	**The Gnome** R J Schipper, P Semple, W Young
	1 peg for aid. Now free.
1966 July 27	**The Riddler** P Copeland, R McHaffie (alt)
1966 Aug	**The Nab** M Thompson, R G Schipper
	3 points of aid. Now free.
1966 Sept 25	**Orthang** A Toole, B Henderson, P Nunn
1966 Sept	**The Great Ape** B Henderson, B W Robertson, G Oliver
	1 point of aid. Now free.
1966	**Sunnyside Up** Details unknown
	Variation Direct Finish by R Kenyon, T Price, L Jordan, 16
	June 1985.
1967 Jan 28	**Hog's Earth** P Nunn, O Woolcock (alt) N Campbell-Bannerman
	Only the first pitch was new.
1967 Feb 12	**The Coffin** R McHaffie, D Brownlee
1967 Feb 12	**Gorgoroth** M A Toole, B Henderson (alt) N Wilson
1967 April 14	**The Undertaker** R McHaffie, B Benson, D Martin
1967 May	**Tiercel Wall** P Nunn, O Woolcock
	The first pitch had been climbed previously. Several points of
	aid on pitch 2. Climbed free by E Cleasby, M Lynch 1976.
1967 June 10	**The Hearse** R McHaffie, M Cavendish
1967 June 14	**The Gravestone** R McHaffie, M Cavendish
1967 July 22	**Eagle Cracks** J J S Allison, J P Allison (alt) J Baldock
	Peg and sling used for aid, Climbed free by D Armstrong,
	P Whillance 2 August 1981.
1967 July 23	**The Redoubt** P Nunn, B Henderson
1967 Aug 7	**The Wreath** R McHaffie, M Cavendish
1967 Sept 16	**Alternator** T Martin, D Mills

	Variation Finish. F Wilkinson, M Hopson 30 April 1995.
1967 Sept	**Clubfoot** O Woolcock, R Woolcock
1967	**Seamus** J Rafferty, E Forster (alt) T Dixon, R Eastwood
	1 peg used for aid. Now free.
1968 April 4	**Mouse Ghyll Grooves** N J Soper, J Harris (alt)
1968 Sept 14	**Athanor** J Adams, C Read (alt)
	6 pegs for aid. Climbed free J Lamb, K Rudd 19 August 1974.
1968 Sept 29	**The Mole** R McHaffie, P Phillips, L Heinemann
	1 peg for aid. Now free.
1968 Sept	**The Ring** B Henderson, T Toole
1968 Sept	**The Limit** R McHaffie, W Freelands
	Pitch 2 by B Henderson, P Owens.
1968	**The Urn** R McHaffie, M Wingrove
1969 April 13	**The Mound** R McHaffie, P Phillips
1969 April 19	**Greatend Pillar** J Adams, C Read (alt) B Henderson, R McHaffie
	2 points of aid. Climbed free by C Sice, R Parker 18 September 1977.
1969 April 27	**The Girdle Traverse**, Quayfoot Buttress R McHaffie, P Phillips
	1 peg and sling for aid. Now free.
	Variation finish by W Freelands, R McHaffie 9 July 1969.
1969 May 10	**Tantalus** K Jones, W Baddet
1969 July 21	**The Blue Max** W Freelands, R McHaffie
1969 July 24	**Masquerade** W Freelands, R McHaffie
	1 point of aid. Now free. More direct line of pitch 2, as described, climbed by J Taylor, C Downer 26 April 1978.
1969 July	**The Buzzard** B Henderson, R McHaffie, B Owens
1969 Aug 7	**The Mortician** B Thompson, W A Barnes (alt)
1969 Aug 13	**Plastic Happiness** W Freelands, R Allen
1970 Jan 25	**Raven Crag Grooves** R McHaffie, J J S Allison
1970 Jan	**The Warbler** R McHaffie (solo)
1970 May 2	**Zoar** W L Robinson, C Read (var)
	Climbed previously with aid. Now free.
	Direct Start. D Bodecott, G Widdowson, 5 June 1999.
1970 May 16	**The Seams** C Read, J Adams (alt) W Young, W L Robinson.
1970 May 30	**Solitaire** M A Toole
	Variation. The Weaver, by R McHaffie, P Phillips September 1960.
1970 June	**Autobahn** W Freelands, R McHaffie
1970 June	**The Right Wall** R McHaffie B Sutton
1970 July 5	**Turbulence** C Read, J Adams, W L Robinson (var)
	3 points of aid. Climbed free by T Stephenson, C Sice 8 April 1978.
1970 July	**Excalibur** W Freelands, R McHaffie, B Bull
	11 points of aid on first ascent. Reduced to 5 points of aid by S Clark. Climbed free by S Miller, K Murphy, K Farkas, 17 June 1992.
	Variation. Lancelot Start, K Murphy, K Farkas, S Miller, 17 June 1992.

1970 July	**The Sorcerer** R McHaffie, B Bull	

1970 July | **The Sorcerer**   R McHaffie, B Bull
4 points of aid on pitch 2.

1970 July | **Tingler**   R McHaffie, J Douglas

1970 July | **Merlin**   R McHaffie, J Douglas

1970 July | **The Groove**   R McHaffie, J Douglas

1970 Aug 23 | **Trundle**   M Burbage, G Oliver

1970 Aug 30 | **Shadrach**   R McHaffie, J Glen
1 peg and sling for aid. Climbed free by K Rudd, M Lomas.

1970 Sept 12 | **Green Cormorant**   R McHaffie, B Sutton, T Poole
1 peg for aid on pitch 1 and 1 peg on pitch 2. Climbed free by A Greig, R McHaffie.

1970 Sept | **Meshach**   R McHaffie

1971 April 11 | **Ibis**   R McHaffie, J Glen, P Denning

1971 April 15 | **Groove and Crack**   R McHaffie

1971 April 17 | **The Crypt Direct**   K Rudd
1 peg used for aid. Now free.
This supercedes a route called The Crypt by R McHaffie, J G Alderson 1 May 1969 which escaped leftwards below the crucial top section; now a variation finish.
Variation. The In Between, by C Downer, C Bacon 30 July 1985.

1971 April 22 | **Gosh**   P Maughan, R McHaffie
2 pegs used for aid. Climbed free by J Lamb Summer 1972.

1971 April 30 | **Ragged Crow**   A Greig, R McHaffie (alt)

1971 May 14 | **Sauron**   A Greig, R McHaffie
1 peg for aid. Now free.

1971 May | **Parlophone**   P Downie, R McHaffie
1 peg for aid. Climbed free by P Botterill, J Lamb 28 June 1979.

1971 May | **Aragorn**   R McHaffie
3 points of aid. Climbed free by J Lamb.

1971 June | **North Buttress Girdle**   R McHaffie, P Phillips, G Barton

1971 Aug | **Dumbo Cracks**   P Downie, P Maughan (alt)

1971 Aug | **Crack and Chimney**   R McHaffie, C Spool

1971 Sept 4 | **The Bulger**   S Clark, R McHaffie
An artificial aided route. Climbed free by P Botterill, J Lamb 30 May 1981.

1971 Sept | **Warlock**   R McHaffie, J Laidlow
Variation. Side Line, by R McHaffie, B Sutton 11 June 1981.

1971 Sept 30 | **Abednego**   R McHaffie, P Downes

1971 Summer | **Moonraker**   R McHaffie, R Allen (alt)

1971 Autumn | **Tarkus**   K Rudd, R McHaffie

1971 Nov 27 | **Sin**   R McHaffie, P Tinning, J Glen

1971 Dec 23 | **Kaleidoscope**   R McHaffie, C McCormick

1972 Feb 16 | **The Beast**   R McHaffie

1972 April | **The Axe**   R McHaffie

1972 April | **The Noose**   R McHaffie and party
Variation Finish. In the Neck, S Crowe, K Magog 24 June 1995.

1972 May	**The Groan** R McHaffie, K I Meldrum
	1 point of aid. Now free.
1972 June 28	**Paradise Lost** M R Myers, T W Birkett (alt)
1972 July 24	**Nagasaki Grooves** C Read, J Adams
	5 pegs for aid. Climbed free by P Livesey 22 June 1974 (solo with a back rope).
	Variation. Hiroshima, climbed by P Livesey, P Gomersall May 1978.
1972 Aug 22	**The Grolley** P Shorter, P Mayers, P Shorter
1972 Oct 14	**Chamonix Girdle** T Dale, R Kenyon (alt)
	2 points of aid were used on the original finish which is now free at 5b (pitch 2 of Bob Martins).
1973 April 22	**Crumble** T W Birkett, C Brown
	Pitch 2 climbed by P Lockey about 1965.
1973 May 29	**Superstar** R McHaffie, L Kendall
	Variation. Zion, climbed in 1975 details unknown.
1973 June 22	**Simbolyn** R McHaffie, L Kendall
1973 June 26	**Blink** R McHaffie, L Kendall
1973 June	**Raindrop** P Livesey, J Sheard
	Variation. Cloudburst Finish, by C Downer, C Bacon 1 August 1981.
1973 Aug 6	**Necrosis** M Philips, D Elsby
1973 Aug	**Moss Wall** R McHaffie, D Durkin
	Sling used for aid.
1973 Oct 7	**The Rack** R McHaffie, B Mallaghan
1973 Oct	**Iron Maiden** R McHaffie
1973 Nov	**The Rift** R McHaffie
	Attempted previously with much aid.
1973	**The Sting** R T Marsden, T E Dunsby
1974 April 19	**Footless Crow** P Livesey
	Based on the old aided route Great Buttress climbed by A Liddell and P Ross 10 November 1965, using 8 points of aid. "The man who transforms The Great Buttress from a peg route to a free route is sure of his niche in climbing history"

Mike Thompson, Borrowdale – A Climber's Guide, 1966

"Mac was sending up John Adams and Colin Read, telling them there were lots of routes – like Nagasaki Grooves on Greatend Crag – which they thought they'd done but they hadn't done free. 'Why don't you go and do it properly?' he said. 'And while you're at it, you should sort out the Central Buttress on Goat Crag as well.' He was serious about Nagasaki Grooves but I don't think he really meant it about Central Buttress – he didn't think that was on for free climbing. But that's what gave me the impulse. On my way to have a proper look at the route I passed a band of Dutch hippies camping in the valley and they had a van with a big crow painted on one side, with its feet chopped off. Then I inspected the route – no resting place, you've got to keep flying... We'd done a day's work and went out in the evening. It was nice

weather and the rock was reasonably dry. And I just did it. I can't remember much about it... All I had were a few nut runners – there were no micro-nuts in those days – and the rusty old bolts and pegs the others had left in place. I wore E.B.s and a Whillans harness. Soon I was getting a lot of drag on the rope. The sailor lad, Robin Witham, was perched as high as he could get, on a little ledge about 20 feet above ground. I ran out of rope when I still had some 30-odd feet to go. There was nowhere to belay – no protection points at all. The rock was dirty and dusty – I hadn't bothered to clean up the top part because it looked easier than lower down, though it was still about Hard V.S. standard. There was only one thing for it. I told Witham to untie himself and then soloed to the top, dragging 160 feet of rope through the runners behind me"

Pete Livesey, quoted in A Century on the Crags,
Alan Hankinson, 1988

The Direct Variation was climbed by D Dinwoodie, G Livingston on 19 August 1986.
The crucial undercut flake became detached in the hands of T Prentice in July 1989. The route as now described was climbed by B Wardley, M Glaister shortly afterwards at a slightly harder grade.

1974 May 12	**Bitter Oasis**	P Livesey, J Sheard

"Virtually led on sight, I climbed the very steep groove, all the time making for what I thought was a gently sloping ledge. But when I got there the 'oasis' I'd hoped for turned out to be an overlapping, vertical wall, and the climbing went on being very hard with nowhere to rest. I had to push on for another 30 feet before I found a belay ledge".

Pete Livesey, quoted in A Century on the Crags, Alan
Hankinson, 1988

Variation. Mirage Finish, by P Botterill, M Berzins 22 June 1977 is now incorporated in Mirage 15 April 1981.

1974 May	**Torquemada Buttress**	R McHaffie, T Nixon
1974 June 22	**Dry Grasp**	P Livesey (solo with a back rope)

The top pitch was originally an aided finish (including the use of 4 bolts) to Route 2 and was called Fiery Cross, climbed by P Ross, B Henderson.
Variation Finish. Dry Bum, A Hocking, J Howe September 1996.
Variation. Climbed in mistake for Qantas by P Whillance 1980.

1974	**Imago**	R McHaffie, C Gibson, N Robinson
1974	**Mac's Crack**	R McHaffie, D Johnson, R Priestley and three others (The Manpower Services Team)
1974	**Gardener's World**, Castle Crag	R McHaffie, D Brownlee
1975 March 29	**Blondin**	S Clegg, J Lamb
1975 March 30	**Slack Alice**	J Lamb, P Botterill

Variation. Dogma, climbed by D Greenald, S Lewis, B Dixon 18 July 1976.

1975 April 26	**Earthstrip**	C Downer, D Hellier (alt), I Conway, D Nicol

"Downer started his campaign on Greatend Crag with a team of fellow enthusiasts. There was so much vegetation that they had to work as a team in an entirely novel manner. Four of them, suspended from separate ropes, synchronised their leg-leverage to dislodge areas of connected vegetation which eventually unrolled like a vast green carpet, and thudded to the ground, leaving hundreds of square feet of untouched rock."

Trevor Jones, Cumbrian Rock, 1988

1975 April 26	**Greatend Grooves**	I Conway, D Nicol, D Hellier, C Downer
1975 April 28	**Greatend Corner**	D Nicol, C Downer, I Conway, D Hellier
1975 May 4	**The Neb**	T W Birkett, M R Myers
1975 May 8	**The Garrotte**	R McHaffie, M Wingrove

Climbed free on this date by S Clark, B Wilson. Original ascent by R McHaffie employed 3 points of aid.

1975 May 15	**Juicy Luicy**	P Whillance, M Hetherington
1975 June 1	**The Cleft Direct**	P Botterill, R Clegg

No aid used. Supersedes a route called The Cleft, which used 4 pegs and 1 sling for aid on pitch 2 climbed by P Ross, A Rocher 22 August 1959. Pitch 1 climbed by J Lamb, P Whillance 17 May 1975.

1975 June 6	**Patient Tigers**	S Clegg, J Lamb, M Hetherington, P Whillance
1975 June	**Evil Kneivel**	R McHaffie, H Rainer

Variation. Encore, by I Dunn, C Dunn Summer 1983.
Variation. Long Notice, S J H Reid, W Phipps, 3 April 1996.
(Probably climbed before).

1975 June	**C.D.M.**	D Armstrong

Certainly done before.

1975 June 20	**Usurper**	P Gomersall, N Bulmer
1975 July	**Extrapolation**	D Nicol, I Conway, R Wilson

1 peg for aid. Climbed free and direct by J Lamb, P Botterill 29 July 1975.
Right-Hand Variation. J McHaffie, C Downer 2 May 1999.

1975 July	**Woden's Crack**	D Armstrong

Probably done before.

1975 Aug 4	**Where Eagles Dare**	P Whillance, S Clegg
1975 Aug 17	**Autopsy**	S Clegg, P Botterill
1975 Aug 27	**Verdict**	S Clegg, P Botterill (var)

Top-roped, then 1 nut used for aid on pitch 3. Climbed free by M Berzins, R Berzins 8 August 1976.

1975 Aug 28	**Crunchy Frog**	T W Birkett, R McHaffie

A free version of an old aid route called Snake climbed by C Leverty, R McHaffie, A Clarkson 23 May 1960.

1975 Aug 28	**Gleaned Grooves**	T W Birkett, R McHaffie
1975 Sept 7	**Savage Messiah**	T W Birkett, R McHaffie

1 sling for aid. Climbed free by M Berzins, S Clegg 20 September 1975.

1975 Sept 20	**Jaws**	M Lynch, E Cleasby
1976 Easter	**The Gardener**	R McHaffie, J Glen

1976 Easter	**The Groove** R McHaffie, J Glen
1976 Easter	**Catafalque** R McHaffie
	Variation. Loitering with Intent, by P Botterill, J Lamb 2 July 198█
1976 June 4	**Heather Groove** R McHaffie, W Glass
1976 June 7	**The Rib** Gowder Crag R McHaffie, W Glass
1976 June 9	**Tempo** R McHaffie, W Glass
1976 June	**Big Sur** C Downer, D Nicol
	The crack in the slab below the stance was climbed direct by R Wilson 18 June 1977.
1976 June	**Endless Summer** C Downer, D Nicol (alt)
1976 July 24/25	**Tumbleweed Connection** P Botterill, D Rawcliffe
	Variation. Tumbleweed Bypass, B Wayman, C Downer 10th June 1979.
	A direct start and finish to pitch 1 are included in a route called Altered Images climbed on 29 May 1983.
1976 July 26	**The Voyage** S Clegg, P Botterill
1976 July 28	**Grand Alliance** R Matheson, E Cleasby
	Pitch 1 climbed previously by a route called D.T.'s.
1976 July	**Mule Train** D Armstrong
	Variation. D Armstrong 1976.
1976 Aug 26	**Masochist** P Botterill
1976 Oct 10	**The Adze** R McHaffie, W Glass
1976 Oct 11	**Jennipod** R McHaffie, W Glass
1976	**Bits 'n' Pieces** D Armstrong
	Certainly done before.
1977 May 10	**Black Sheep** P Botterill, D Hopkins
	Variation. Wild Side, by J Dunne, D Savage 15 April 1985.
	Variation. Wild Sheep, by K Wilkinson, D Booth, A Morris, 31 March 1989. Probably climbed previously
1977 June 7	**Jubilee Grooves** W Freelands, R McHaffie
1977 June	**Point Blank** C Downer, H Cobb (alt) D Nicol
1977 June 26	**High Plains Drifter** W Freelands, J Lamb, S Clark
1977 June 26	**Banzai Pipeline** D Nicol, C Downer (alt) H Cobb, C Bacon
	Variation. The Japanese Connection, climbed by P Whillance, R Parker 11 May 1980.
	Banzai Pipeline shares some climbing with the old route Redberry Wall put up by J Austin and B Fuller in November 1958.
1977 July 8	**Inquest Direct** J Lamb, W Freelands
	Climbed free and with the Direct Start.
	Original route called Inquest climbed by P Nunn, P Ross 10 June 1965, utilizing what is now given as the variation start for pitch 1.
	Climbed free by J A Austin 1975.
1977 Aug 28	**Grip Factor** K Neal, J Hume, M Trowbridge
	Previously climbed in part by R McHaffie.
1977 Sept 4	**Prana** P Gomersall
1977 Sept 17	**Punk Rock** C Downer, D Nicol (alt)
1977 Sept 19	**Rack Direct** S Miller, R Parker

1977 Sept 24	**Alone in Space** T Stephenson, C Sice (var) R Parker
	Named after a falling climber.
1977 Sept	**Tristar** P Livesey, R Fawcett, P Gomersall
	Pitch 1 climbed previously by D.T.'s with aid.
1977 Oct 15	**New Wave** C Downer, C Bacon, D Nicol
1977 Oct 22	**Withering Height** K Neal, C Oswald
1977 Oct 22	**Swine Trek** T Stephenson, C Sice, R Parker
1978 April 8	**Star Wars** T W Birkett, R Graham (alt)
	1 point for resting. Now free. Pitch 1 by T W Birkett, R McHaffie, A Hyslop 1977.
1978 April 8	**Serenity** T Stephenson, C Sice (alt) J Lamb, R Parker
1978 April 9	**Wuthering Heights** A Hyslop, R McHaffie, R Graham
1978 April 15/16	**Close Encounters** R Graham, T W Birkett (alt) R McHaffie
1978 April 16	**Romeo Error** E Cleasby, B Rodgers, I Williamson
1978 April 25	**Kidnapped** P Botterill, J Lamb
	Links the direct start to Dedication climbed by C Bacon, J Cook in 1965 and the variation finish to Plagiarism.
1978 April 26	**Cyclotron** K Forsythe, T W Birkett
	Variation. Atomiser 1979 by R Fawcett, B Swales, I Dobson 1978.
1978 April 26	**Meet on the Ledge** D J Hellier
1978 April 29	**Solid Air** R J Kenyon, A Hewison
	Pitches 1 to 3 climbed earlier by R Kenyon, R Bennett.
1978 May 8	**Fear of Flying** C Downer, A Hunter, C Bacon, D Nicol
	1 nut for aid. Climbed free May 1978. D Mullen, J Lamb.
1978 May 8	**Fall of Eagles** R G Hutchinson, J W Earl
1978 May 17	**Trouble Shooter** P Whillance, D Armstrong
1978 May 18	**Castle in the Air** R McHaffie, P Poole, K Telfer
1978 May 26	**Castillion** R McHaffie, N Mathews
1978 Spring	**Bob Martins** P Livesey, R Berzins, M Berzins
	The Traverse from Shepherd's Chimney was climbed with aid by A Kew, R McHaffie. Later led free by A Liddell.
1978 June 9	**High Flyer** C Downer, C Bacon
1978 June 17	**The Black Knight** P Whillance, D Armstrong (alt)
1978 June 17	**The White Lady** P Whillance, D Armstrong
1978 June 17	**Eyrie Direct** P Whillance, D Armstrong
1978 June 24	**The Rib**, Raven Crag R McHaffie, C Bashforth
1978 July 8	**Apricot Lil** P Whillance, D Armstrong, M Berzins
1978 July 8	**Everard** P Whillance, D Armstrong, M Berzins
1978 July 15	**Nantucket Sleighride** C Sice, T Stephenson, R Parker (alt)
1978 July 22	**Creeping Jesus** J Healey, A Mitchell
	Certainly climbed before.
1978 July	**Needle Wall** D Armstrong
1978 July 30	**Heretic** B Wayman, G Landless
	Inspected for years by climbers abseiling down the line of the route.
1978 Aug 9	**White Noise** J Lamb, R McHaffie
	Variation. J Arnold, T Mawer, 1999.
1978 Aug 12	**Anthill** R McHaffie, P Denny

1978 Aug 19	**First Offence** M Doyle, K Telfer, D Barr
1978 Aug 24	**Thumbscrew** J Lamb, D Cherry
1978 Aug 26	**White Man Walkabout** N Gibbons, B Rushton
1978 Aug 27	**Jacko** N Gibbons, B Rushton
1978 Aug 30	**Silent Sun** P Botterill, R Parker
1978 Sept 5	**Guillotine** J Lamb
1978 Sept 14	**Thin Air** R McHaffie, N Robinson (alt)
	Final groove climbed previously by R McHaffie.
1978 Sept 23	**The Mortuary** M G Mortimer, M G Allen
1978 Oct 5	**The Grasp** D McDonald, R McHaffie, N Robinson
1978 Oct 7	**Five Nations of the Iroquois** R Graham, E Cleasby (alt)
	Variation to pitch 5 climbed by D Armstrong, P Botterill
	29 June 1980.
1978 Oct 22	**Aaros** R Graham, R McHaffie, T W Birkett, K Forsythe
1978 Oct 22	**P.P.S.** K Forsythe, T W Birkett, R McHaffie, R Graham
1978 Nov 26	**Widowmaker** D Mullen, H Walmley
	Originally an aided finish to Scratch. Climbed on the day after
	the Carlisle M C dinner and graded E3. Quite an achievement.
1978 Dec 1	**Could be the Last** R McHaffie, B Dobson, J Baxter
	Some hope! Top roped 2 days earlier by R McHaffie.
1979 March 31	**Ricochet** J Lamb, R Parker
1979 April 8	**Dire Straits** D Armstrong, P Whillance
1979 April 18	**Why Not** F W Crosby, S Thompson
1979 April 22	**Wheels of Fire** P Whillance, D Armstrong (alt)
1979 April 27	**Ador** R McHaffie, M Wingrove
1979 April 27	**Bold Warrior** R McHaffie, M Wingrove
1979 April 28	**The Executioner** P Whillance, D Armstrong
1979 May 6	**Blazing Apostles** D Cronshaw, D Knighton
1979 May 7	**Total Mass Retain** D Knighton, D Cronshaw
1979 May	**Muscular Delinquent** D Knighton, D Cronshaw
1979 May 14	**Castle of Fire** R McHaffie, M Wingrove
1979 May 16	**The Rib**, Brown Dodd R McHaffie
1979 May 16	**Boiling Point** R McHaffie
1979 May 27	**Corridors of Power** T W Birkett, R McHaffie, S Scott
1979 June 8	**The Thieving Magpie** R Berzins, M Berzins (alt) J Lamb
1979 July 14	**Vitas Dancer** R Kenyon, D Stewart
1979 Aug 11	**Triptych** C Downer, N Halls (alt)
1979 Aug 12	**The Black Prince** P Whillance (solo)
1979 Aug 19	**The Lion Heart** P Whillance, D Armstrong (alt)
1979 Summer	**Veil of Tears** I Williamson, A Tilney
1979 Summer	**Frenzy** R McHaffie, W Webb
	1 sling for aid. Climbed free, K Telfer, S Kennedy 1979.
1979	**Frontline** N Robinson, R McHaffie, M Gates
1980 April 7	**Odds 'n' Sods** K Telfer, G Telfer
1980 May 28	**Free 'n' Easy** P Poole, K Telfer
1980 May 30	**Shemezim Grooves** S Miller, R Allen
1980 June 26	**Bush Doctor** S Miller, R Kenyon
1980 Summer	**Dwarf's Divorce** P Dickens, K Telfer (var)
1981 Feb 1	**The Raging Bull** J Lamb, P Botterill (var)

1981 Feb 8	**Lamplighter Eliminate** J Lamb, P Botterill (var)
	Pitches 2 and 3 added on 4 April 1981.
	Pitch 1 originally climbed with 2 points of aid as the start to Lamplighter.
	Variation. Breakin' in Space, climbed by R Curley, C Thwaites 2 to 5 June 1985.
1981 Feb 14	**Premonition** P Botterill, J Lamb
	The final groove is the direct finish to Dedication by S Halliwell, J Lothian 5 March 1967.
1981 Feb 14	**Polymer** D McDonald, D Rawcliffe, B Wilson
1981 March 29	**Exasperation** I Dunn, R McHaffie
1981 April 5	**The Dice Man** C Downer, A Brown (alt) S Kysow
1981 April 8	**Tumbling Dice** C Downer, A Brown (alt)
1981 April 10	**Water Torture** P Botterill, P Whillance
1981 April 15	**Mirage** R Graham, D Lyle
	Climbed pitch 1 only.
	Pitch 2 climbed on 22 June as The Mirage Finish to Bitter Oasis by P Botterill, M Berzins. This follows the approximate line of The Great Buttress Direct which was climbed with 17 points of aid by W Freelands, G Sims on 12 December 1971.
1981 April 20	**Easter Monday** I Whittaker, D Airey
1981 May 7	**The Devil's Alternative** J Lamb, P Whillance (var)
	Variation. Woody's Alternative, S Wood 4 July 1999.
1981 May 12	**Penal Servitude** D Armstrong, P Whillance (var)
	Direct Start. A Hocking, R Cheetham 1994.
1981 May 14	**Poxy Brown Cows** P Whillance (solo)
1981 May 16	**Kes** D Armstrong, P Whillance
1981 May 16	**Hawkwing** P Whillance, D Armstrong
1981 May 19	**Lucifer** P Whillance, D Armstrong (var)
	Originally an aid route of the same name.
1981 June 1	**Heaven's Gate** J Lamb, P Botterill
1981 June 20	**The Go Between** J Lamb, P Botterill
1981 June	**Green Wall**, Hows Crag R McHaffie, M Taylor
1981 July 9	**The Rack – Finger Flake Finish** P Whillance, D Armstrong
1981 July 13	**Rough Boys** M Wilford, K Lindhorne
	Climbed using the Right-Hand Finish. Left-Hand Finish climbed some time later. Possible first ascentionist P Whillance 1983.
1981 July 13	**Shanna** M Wilford, K Lindhorne, C Downer
1981 July 14	**Day of the Jackals** M Wilford, K Lindhorne, C Downer
	Pitch 2 added by C Downer on 5 August 1981.
1981 July 15	**American Beauty** M Wilford, C Downer, J Lamb
1981 July 29	**Flying Circus** P Whillance, D Armstrong (var)
1981 July 29	**Final Diagnosis** D Armstrong, P Whillance (alt)
1981 July 29	**Postern Rib** P Whillance (solo)
1981 Aug 2	**Necroscopy** D Armstrong, P Whillance
1981 Aug 2	**Double Bogey** P Whillance, D Armstrong
1981 Aug 17	**Dead on Arrival** P Whillance, D Armstrong (var)
1981 Aug 18	**Coroner's Crack** P Whillance, D Armstrong

1981 Aug 20	**Parting Shot** J Lamb

Climbed with a runner pre-placed very high in an adjacent tree.

1981 Aug 23	**The Last Fairway** D Armstrong, P Whillance
1981 Aug 23	**Pitch and Putt** P Whillance, D Armstrong
1981 Summer	**True North** J Lamb, R Allen
1981 Sept 6	**Stumble Bum** R Graham, D Lyle

Pitch 2 climbed as a variation to Dry Grasp by M Browell, B Bradley in May 1981. Pitch 3 climbed up to its junction with Dry Grasp by J Lamb, P Botterill in February 1975.

1982 May 6	**Exclusion Zone** C Downer, S Kysow
1982 May 13	**No Holds Barred** C Downer, S Kysow
1982 May	**Delight Maker** R McHaffie, B Johnson
1982 Spring	**Little Pig** K Telfer
1982 June 18	**Blind Faith** C Downer, S Kysow

Variation Start. Second Sight, climbed by S Howe, C Dale 12 May 1984.

1982 June	**De Quincy** J Moffatt, P Kirton
1982 July 24	**Paint it Black** B Davison, D Smart
1982 Aug 10	**Brain Stain** N Dixon, S Walker, P Whitfield
1982 Sept 19	**Astral Weeks** C Downer, S Kysow
1982	**Peregrine Grooves** R McHaffie, J Glen
1983 May 15	**Ethelred** T Dale, D Bowen
1983 May 20	**Manpower** C Downer, A Hall
1983 May 20	**Merlin** R McHaffie, W Sutton
1983 May 29	**Altered Images** C Downer, A Hall, R Graham

Pitch 1 climbed by M Berzins, P Botterill in 1977 as a direct start to Tumbleweed Connection. The section of pitch 2 above the peg on Tumbleweed Connection to the stance had been climbed as a direct variation to that route by B Wayman, C Downer 10 June 1979.

1983 May 29	**The Professional** D Armstrong, P Whillance
1983 June 12	**The Shock of the New** P Denny R McHaffie
1983 July 10	**Fear and Loathing** T Stephenson, H Sterling
1983 July 16	**Hippos Might Fly** A Brown, J Geeson
1983 July 30	**Wild Times** P Botterill, P Rigby
1983 Aug 20	**Straight and Narrow** T W Birkett, D Lyle

An eliminate on a line climbed, using the start and finish but which stepped further right at half height, by R McHaffie many years previously.

1983 Sept 17	**Golden Delicious** M Duff, C Bolton
1983 Nov	**Inarticulate Speech** C Dale (self belaying)
1983 Nov 15	**Bleak How Buttress** D Hellier

A superb route which indicated the potential of the crag.

1983 Nov 20	**Red Neck** C Downer, C Bacon

The start of the rush for new routes on these buttresses. Two old routes which have been long lost were recorded on the crags on 16 September 1972 by R McHaffie, S Thompson, called Sid's Route (VS) and Sting (S). Sid's Route could not be located but Sting is now taken by the route Stingray.

Variation. The Skinhead Finish, R Curley 18 August 1984.

1983 Nov	**Gibbon Variation** R Kenyon	
	Certainly done before.	
1983	**Hee-Haw** R Kenyon, C Eckersall	
	Certainly done before.	
1983 Dec 5	**Sudden Impact** C Downer, T Watts	
1983 Dec 15	**Intrusion** C Downer, C Bacon	
1984 Feb 26	**Driving Ambition** C Downer, C Bacon	
1984 March 2	**Traffic Warden** R McHaffie, P Taylor	
1984 March 10	**Desmond Decker** C Downer, C Bacon, R McHaffie, P Taylor	
1984 March 10	**Mercedes** R McHaffie, C Downer, P Taylor	
1984 March 10	**The Crack** Veteran's Buttress R McHaffie, P Taylor	
1984 March 10	**Cavalier** C Downer, C Bacon, R McHaffie, P Taylor	
1984 March 10	**Alvis** R McHaffie, P Taylor	
1984 March 15	**First Contact** R McHaffie, P Taylor	
1984 March 15	**Rough Justice** C Downer, P Lee	
1984 March 23	**Crime Wave** C Downer, C Bacon	
1984 March 25	**Pressure Drop** C Downer, C Bacon	

Variation. Direct Start, C Downer, A Hall 9 May 1986.

1984 April 1	**Fender Bender** C Downer, R McHaffie	
1984 April 1	**Hatch Back** C Downer, C Bacon, R McHaffie	
1984 April 2	**Sleeping Partner** C Downer, C Bacon	
1984 April 3	**Fuel Economy** C Downer, R McHaffie	
1984 April 3	**Fuel Crisis** C Downer, R McHaffie	
1984 April 5	**Regardless** C Downer, C Bacon	
1984 April 8	**Lost Boys** P Whillance, D Armstrong	
1984 April 12	**Joining Forces** C Downer, C Bacon, S Kysow	

Variation. Climbed on first ascent but easier alternative subsequently followed.

1984 April 13	**Cross Ply** C Downer, I Dunn, C Dunn	
1984 April	**Green Fingers** R McHaffie	
1984 April	**Gardener's World** R McHaffie, J I Meldrum	
1984 April	**Mini Minor** R McHaffie	
1984 May 3	**Ripping Yarn** D Armstrong, P Whillance	
1984 May 6	**Daylight Robbery** C Sowden, M Berzin (var)	
1984 May 6	**Wrinkle** R Kenyon	
1984 May 6	**Just a Quickie** R Kenyon	
1984 May 24	**Fancy Free** C Downer, S Kysow, C Bacon	
1984 May 24	**Brush Off** C Downer, C Bacon, S Kysow	

The start of a rush for routes on this excellent buttress.

1984 May 25	**Breathless** C Downer, S Kysow	
1984 May 25	**Footloose** C Downer, C Bacon, S Kysow	

Evidence of old pegs indicated that this had probably been climbed or attempted previously.

1984 May 27	**Battering Ram** R Smith, J Earl (alt)	
1984 May 28	**Fun Run** A Hall, H Bingham	
1984 May 28	**Front Runner** C Downer, C Bacon	
1984 June 2	**Boston Strangler** A Murray, R Parker	
1984 June 5	**The Reiver** C Downer (solo)	

1984 June 15	**Steel Pulse**	C Downer, J Waters
1984 June 15	**Low Profile**	C Downer, C Bacon, P Lee
1984 June 17	**The Question**	R Kenyon, C King
1984 June 17	**Flamingo Fandango**	R Kenyon, C King
1984 June 17	**Big Foot**	C Dale, R Curley
1984 June 17	**Little Nose**	C Dale R Curley
1984 June 17	**Heaven Knows I'm Miserable Now**	C Dale, R Curley
1984 June 17	**Joie Pur**	C Dale, C King, R Kenyon, R Curley
1984 June 17	**Barefoot**	C Dale, C King, R Kenyon, R Curley

Led in barefeet.
A day of frenzied activity on an isolated but excellent outcrop.

1984 June 19	**Roger Radish**	R McHaffie, C Downer
1984 June 23	**Squashed Racquet**	C Downer, M Berzins

The original start was as for The Rack. The Direct Start
incorporated in the main description was by P Ingham,
R Graham 27 June 1986.

1984 June 23	**Percival Pea**	R McHaffie, P Taylor
1984 June 24	**Rhubarb Patch**	P Lince, M Taylor
1984 June 24	**Millesimus**	M Lynch, R Wightman, B Rogers
1984 June 24	**Ponticum**	B Rogers, T Walkington
1984 June 24	**Rush Hour**	M Taylor, P Lince
1984 June 26	**Rolling Thunder**	C Downer, A Hall, S Howe
1984 July 4	**Woden's Wotsit**	R Kenyon, C Eckersall
1984 July 9	**Impulse**	C Downer, S Kysow, J Cameron, P Bingham
1984 July 12	**Colin Cucumber**	R McHaffie, P Denny
1984 July 19	**Rub Off**	M Armitage, D Falcon
1984 July 24	**The Gibbet Direct**	C Downer, R McHaffie
1984 July 26	**Icarus Direct**	C Downer, R McHaffie
1984 July 29	**Crime and Punishment**	C Downer, R McHaffie, S Howe
1984 Aug 5	**Inquisition**	C Downer, R McHaffie
1984 Aug 5	**The Gauntlet**	C Downer, R McHaffie

Direct Start. Off the Cuff, S Crowe, K Magog, 26 June 1995.

1984 Aug 7	**Plastic Pig**	R Curley, A Jack
1984 Aug 9	**Reliant Robin**	R Curley
1984 Aug 11	**Little Corner**	D Armstrong
1984 Aug 18	**'A' Team**	C Brooks, D Scott
1984 Aug 18	**'B' Team**	C Brooks, D Scott, R McHaffie
1984 Aug 19	**'G' Force**	P Hirst, R McHaffie
1984 Aug 20	**Gyves**	P Hirst, R McHaffie
1984 Aug 20	**Crucified**	R McHaffie, P Hirst
1984 Aug 20	**Skewered**	R McHaffie, P Hirst
1984 Aug 24	**Arthur Scargill**	R McHaffie (solo)
1984 Sept 8	**The Crack** Car Park Crag	R McHaffie, P Hirst
1984 Sept 8	**Porridge**	P Hirst, R McHaffie
1984 Sept 8	**Stir**	P Hirst, R McHaffie
1984 Sept 9	**Rob's Route**	R Curley, D Williamson, N Stansfield, C Thwaite

Top roped prior to leading.
Variation start. Rob's Cafe, added same day by same party.
Also top roped prior to leading.

1984 Sept 23	**Human Racing**	R Curley, D Williamson, N Stansfield, C Thwaites

Top roped prior to leading.

1984 Oct 31	**Casper Carrot**	R McHaffie, P Hirst, W Peascod
1984 Oct 31	**Trod 'A' Tween**	R Kenyon

Probably done before.

1984 Nov 4	**Oliver Onion**	R McHaffie, P Hirst
1984 Nov 4	**Lilly Leek**	P Hirst, R McHaffie
1984 Nov 4	**Super Cool**	R McHaffie, P Hirst (alt)
1984 Nov 10	**Emma Apple**	W Peascod, R McHaffie, P Hirst (alt)

Named after Bill Peascod's daughter.

1984 Nov 17	**Spiderman**	R McHaffie, P Hirst
1984 Nov 17	**Holly Tree Corner**, National Trust Crag	P Hirst, R McHaffie
1984 Nov 17	**Wild Boys**	R McHaffie, P Hirst (alt)
1984 Nov 25	**Batman**	R McHaffie, P Hirst
1984 Nov	**Stingray**	D Craig, W Peascod

Climbs the line called Sting climbed 16 September 1972 by R McHaffie, S Thompson, which had returned to vegetation.

1984	**Meandering Maggot**	R Kenyon, T Price
1985 April 16	**Ker Plunk**	J Dunne, J Jack

Mysteriously missed from the previous two editions of this guide. Adam Hocking climbed this arête in 1996 believing it to be unclimbed and called the route Superstructure. He subsequently soloed it in 1997 at the age of 17, prompting a concerned Ray McHaffie to say that "You can kill yourself after a life of climbing, but not at the start"!

1985 April	**Pop Goes the Asteroid**	C Dale (solo)
1985 May 6	**Shake Down**	C Downer, J White
1985 May 6	**Puritan**	C Downer, J White
1985 May 7	**Stan the Man**	A Hall, C Downer

Definitely done before.

1985 May 7	**Joker Man**	C Downer, A Hall
1985 May 7	**The Naked Edge**	P Hirst, R McHaffie
1985 May 9	**Skimmerhorne**	C Downer, A Hall
1985 May 9	**Loose Connections**	C Downer, A Hall
1985 May 11	**Classic Rock**	R McHaffie, P Hirst (alt)
1985 May 12	**The Diagonal Crack**	R Kenyon
1985 May 18	**Bird Brain**	R Cassidy, R Gerrish
1985 May 18	**Bird's Nest Buttress**	R Gerrish, R Cassidy
1985 May 29	**Seconds Out**	C Downer (solo)
1985 May 31	**Birds of Prey**	R McHaffie, P Hirst
1985 May	**Bat Out of Hell**	R McHaffie, P Hirst
1985 June 1	**Crystal Slab**	P Hirst, E Hirst
1985 June 2	**Hairy Mary**	D McDonald, M Moran
1985 June 4	**Anyone for Tennis**	R Cassidy
1985 June 6	**Woolly Jumper**	D Armstrong, A Murray
1985 June 8	**Street Walker**	D David, J Waters
1985 June 8	**One-in-Six**	R McHaffie, P Hirst
1985 June 8	**Adam's Slab**	R Kenyon

1985 June 13	**Animotion** C Downer, D Scott, A Hall
1985 June 16	**Day's End Crack** R Kenyon
	Certainly done before.
1985 June 18	**The Nose** S Miller, R Allen
1985 June 19	**North America Wall** S Miller, R Allen
1985 June 19	**Dihedral Wall** S Miller, R Allen
1985 June 20	**The Boj Eliminate** S J H Reid, L Steer
	Easier alternative found by S J H Reid, S Pollington, 1st June 1999.
1985 June 29	**Fight with a Beech Tree** T Robinson, S Banks
1985 June 30	**Savage Amusement** C Downer, P Hirst
1985 July 3	**Red Shift** P Hirst, R McHaffie
1985 July 3	**The Shield** S Miller, T Stephenson
1985 July 10	**No More Heros** R McHaffie, P Hirst (alt)
1985 July	**Spider Wall** R Kenyon
1985 Aug 9	**Legless Lizard** D Dinwoodie, D Hawthorn
1985 Sept 29	**Billy Goat Bluff** R Kenyon
1985 Oct 19	**Silly Billy** D Armstrong (solo)
1985 Oct 20	**Ambling Ant** R Kenyon, T Price, L Jordan
1985 Oct 26	**I Need a Hero** R McHaffie, P Hirst
1985 Oct 26	**Blood Axe** P Hirst, R McHaffie
1985 Oct 26	**Ivor the Boneless** P Hirst, R McHaffie, M Trickett
1985 Oct 26	**The Sadist** R Wightman, K Long, A Phizacklea
1985 Nov 23	**Tina Turner** R McHaffie
1985 Nov 24	**Phantom of the Opera** R McHaffie
1986 June 2	**Geronimo** P Ingham, R Parker
	First lead of the top rope problem of Father Ape by J Moffatt (1982).
1986 June	**Mowgli** T Price, A Davis
	So called because the route involved a "stupid little prat messing about in the jungle".
1986 July 5	**Dago** S Sena, R Kenyon, D Smith, C Kenyon
1986 July 5	**Amistad Con El Diablo** S Sena, R Kenyon, D Smith
1986 July 27	**Ad-Lib** D Armstrong, J Williams
1986 Sept 5	**Canna Do It?** A Jones, T Daley, W Hannah
1986 Sept 6	**B.M.C.1** M Armitage, J Unsworth
1986 Oct 10	**Sunset Cruise** A Jones, T Daley
1986	**Up the Kyber** J Fotheringham, C Bonington
1986	**Solar Toupee** C Bonington, J Fotheringham
1986	**Walla's Nose** C Bonington, C G Bonington
1986 Oct 12	**On Edge** R McHaffie, J Garner
1986 Oct 12	**Slide Show** R McHaffie, J Garner
1987 April 11	**The Witness** K Telfer, J Telfer
	First lead of the top rope problem Alaskan Wolf climbed by R Brooks Aug 1983.
1987 April 23	**Little Stint** P Hirst, J Wood
1987 April 25	**Mean Streak** R McHaffie, P Hirst
1987 April 26	**Manuel** M Park, A Irving, P Osliff
1987 May 16	**Recoil** R McHaffie, P Hirst

1987 May 16	**Breach of the Peace** P Ingham, P Cornforth, P McVey	

The first of a series of desperates on Reecastle by the Ingham/Cornforth team.

1987 May 17	**Horrible Arête** R McHaffie, P Hirst

A new low in Mac's climbing career.

1987 May 24	**The Torture Board** P Cornforth
1987 May 24	**Short Sharp Shock** P Ingham
1987 May 31	**Remission** P Ingham
1987 May	**The Apprentice** A Jones, S Mackay
1987 May	**Trisolo** P Hirst, R Mchaffie, R Jenkinson
1987 June 18	**Grievous Bodily Arm** P Ingham
1987 June	**The Mastercraftsman** A Jones, W Hannah
1987 July 4	**My Mam's Rockery** S Harper, N Ball
1987 July 10	**Low Flyer** H Beanland, R Smithson
1987 July 10	**Slow Learner** H Beanland, R Smithson
1987 Aug 14	**Late Developer** R Smithson, H Beanland
1987 Aug 27	**Gable End** H Beanland, R Smithson
1987 Aug 27	**Garkbit Adventure** R Smithson, H Beanland
1988 Feb 26	**Myth of Fingerprints** M Boniface, N Wallis, C Phillips

Llanberis slate-heads hit Lakeland choss!

1988 April 28	**Beer and Sex and Chips and Gravy** S Miller, K Wilkinson
1988 April 28	**This Little Piggy** K Wilkinson, S Miller
1988 April 29	**First Footing** M Naftalin, R Henderson
1988 May 6	**Evolution** R Parker, G Brown

Probably climbed before.

1988 May 6	**Charlie the Chickenfarmer** K Wilkinson, S Holmes
1988 May 8	**Phil's Rib** O Ross, F Walker
1988 May 8	**Frank's Groove** F Walker, O Ross
1988 May 10	**Parsley the Lion** S Holmes, D Ferguson
1988 May 14	**African Skies** S Miller, W Young
1988 May 14	**Route 1** P Hirst, G Spensley
1988 May 14	**Route 2** P Hirst, G Spensley
1988 May 14	**Route 3** P Hirst, G Spensley
1988 May 14	**Route 4** P Hirst, G Spensley
1988 May 14	**Route 5** P Hirst, G Spensley

Inspiring names!

1988 May 15	**Rebound** R McHaffie, P Hirst, G Spensley
1988 May 15	**Cry Freedom** S Miller, J Beveridge, D Johnson

Originally climbed with several pegs for aid by J J S Allison, D Moy in 1963 and named Via Roof Route.

1988 May 15	**The Sheep's Apprentice** K Wilkinson
1988 May 20	**Andy Warhol** T Walkington, A Cammack

Tom Walkington saw mention of Pedestal Wall in the 1986 guide and went to investigate – this was the start of his series of routes.

1988 May 20	**The Wizard of Oz** T Walkington

Second did not follow.

1988 May 21	**Well Heeled** S Miller, D Johnson
1988 May 21	**Dill the Dog** D Ferguson, B Barker

1988 May 23	**'Arry 'Ardnose** K Wilkinson
1988 May 28	**Cam Crag Crack** K Wilkinson
1988 May 28	**Paparazzi** P Hirst, G Spensley
1988 May 28	**Geometer** P Hirst, G Spensley
1988 May 31	**Just and So** P Norman, R Henderson
1988 May	**Teenage Kicks** D Cronshaw, J Ryden, I Vickers

*Variation, Flexible Friend, S Holmes, K Wilkinson 3 June 1989.
Unknown to this team Teenage Kicks, which takes the better
line, had been climbed a few weeks earlier.
Protection peg at crux used on first ascent. Peg removed and
led by I Vickers 1 July 1989.*

1988 June 4	**The Dissident** J Earl, B Smith
1988 June 4	**Perestroika** B Smith, J Earl
1988 June 4	**Glasnost** B Smith, J Earl
1988 June 4	**Inferno** P Ingham, I Cummins

*The hardest route in the valley at the time, tentatively given the
E7 grade by Paul Ingham.*

1988 June 5	**Snake** O Ross, F Walker
1988 June 8	**Citizen Kane** T Walkington, S Hubball
1988 June 10	**Louise Brooks** T Walkington, S Hubball
1988 June 10	**The Third Man** T Walkington, S Hubball
1988 June 11	**Clara Bow** T Walkington, D Robinson
1988 June 16	**The Rasp** G Oliver, C Mitchell
1988 June 26	**Easy Street** P Hirst, G Spensley, R McHaffie (alt)
1988 July 13	**Sumo** O Ross, A Watson
1988 Aug 3	**Watson's Way** A Watson, F Walker, O Ross
1988 Aug 4	**Up for Grabs** K Wilkinson, S Miller

*Free version of an old aid route D.T.s, J Lee, S Clark (var),
13th October 1965.*

| 1988 Aug 7 | **Birdie**   R Kenyon, C Kenyon |
| 1988 Oct | **Prodigal Sons**   P Ross, D Byrne-Peare |

*A necky route heralding Paul Ross's return from the States to
live in Keswick – his first new route in the valley since 1966.*

1988 Oct	**Trod Pip** D Byrne-Peare, P Ross
1988 Oct	**Déjà Vu** P Ross, D Byrne-Peare, R McHaffie
1988 Nov 5	**Bon Temps** P Hirst, G Spensley, K Wilkinson
1988 Nov 23	**Brass Monkey** K Wilkinson, S Holmes

Climbed on a cold wet day.

1988 Dec 3	**Big Business** K Wilkinson
1988	**Stoned Again** P Smith (solo after abseil inspection)
1989 Jan 1	**One Across** K Wilkinson, R McHaffie, P Hirst
1989 Jan 1	**Wring Out the Old** K Wilkinson, P Hirst, R McHaffie
1989 Jan	**Ring in the New** R McHaffie
1989 Jan	**Holly Tree Climb** R McHaffie
1989 Jan	**Karakorum Experience** R McHaffie
1989 Jan	**Kit Kat** R McHaffie
1989 March 23	**The Astronaut Nextdoor** K Wilkinson, A Stainforth
1989 March 30	**Mister Meaner** K Wilkinson, I Turnbull
1989 May 26	**Just Another Expedition** P Ross, C Bonington

1989 May 29	**Lead Free** T Mawer, D Absalom
	Wire preplaced in the top wall.
1989 May	**Pussy Galore** K Wilkinson, P Hirst
1989 June 1	**Random Choice** R Kenyon
1989 June 4	**Flashback** R Kenyon, C Meikle
1989 June 4	**Blue Riband, Jaffa Cake, Custard Cream, Woden's Face Girdle Traverse** R McHaffie (solo)
1989 June 7	**Family Outing** R McHaffie, J M McHaffie, J R McHaffie
1989 June 26	**Maginot Line** G Oliver, D Craig
1989 June	**Cruelty Unknown** J Beveridge, R Kenyon, J Grinbergs (Team effort)
	Named after the effect of the resident population of midges.
1989 July 29	**Wodentops** P Carling
	Probably done before.
1989 July	**Bilko** J Grinbergs, J Beveridge
1989 July 16	**Hole in Yan** A Phizacklea, W Hannah
1989 Aug 1	**Garner Grooves** N Kekus, S Hubball
1989 Aug 2	**Speed Kills** R McHaffie, J Bosher (alt)
1989 Aug 12	**Cold Sweat** R McHaffie, J Bosher
1989 Aug 13	**Dangerous Assignment** R McHaffie, J Bosher
1989 Aug 17	**The Hemp Road** R McHaffie, B Brown
1989 Aug 19	**Dicing with Death** R McHaffie, J Bosher
1989 Aug 27	**Meccano Man** K Telfer, J Gilhespy
1989 Aug 27	**The Push** J Gilhespy, K Telfer
1989 Sept 3	**Light Fantastic** R Davies, K Telfer
1989 Sept 3	**Mort** R Davies
1989 Sept 3	**Munich Agreement** N Brunger, J Gilhespy
1989 Sept 3	**Optional Omission** J Gilhespy, N Brunger
1989 Sept 3	**The Slab** R Davies
1989 Sept 3	**Poland** N Brunger, K Telfer
1989 Sept 3	**Emma Line** J Gilhespy, N Brunger, R Davies, K Telfer
1989 Sept 3	**Son of Oz** S Telfer, R Sharpe
1989 Sept 3	**Rogue Herries** K Telfer, R Davies, N Brunger, J Gilhespy
1989 Sept 3	**The Colour of Magic** R Davies, K Telfer, N Brunger, J Gilhespy
1989 Sept 3	**Stranger to the Ground** K Telfer, R Davies, N Brunger
1989 Sept 9	**A Face in the Crowd** S Miller, T Stephenson, G Rowley
1989 Sept 10	**Chossy** S Hodgson, D Robinson
	Climbed before but not claimed.
1989 Sept 16	**Who is this Lakeland Activist?** Ron Kenyon
1989 Sept 30	**Last of the Summer Wine** D Byrne-Peare, P J Greenwood, P Ross, C Bonington (alt)
1989 Sept 31	**Inner Limits** R Kenyon, C Kenyon
1989 Oct 1	**Nightmare Zone** R McHaffie, J Bosher
1989 Oct 1	**Everybody's Dream** J Bosher
1989 Oct	**Chapel Rib** R Kenyon, C Kenyon
1989 Nov	**Top Rope** R McHaffie, C Blake
1989 Dec 18	**1990** R McHaffie, C Blake
1989	**Cock's Comb Crack** E Rogers, M Biden

1989	**Nothing by Chance** K Telfer, J Gilhespy
1989	**Stoney Silence** R Kenyon
1990 Feb	**Nervous Shakedown** R McHaffie, J Bosher
1990 April 23	**C Gully**, Eagle Crag S J H Reid, J Grinbergs
	A route very much not in the modern idiom.
	The only previous recorded attempt was in 1910.
1990 April 29	**Lithuania** A Phizacklea, D Kells, S Wood, J Holden
1990 May 1	**Sentenced to Hang** P Cornforth
1990 May 6	**Roadside Picnic** J Sparks, M Walsh
1990 May 6	**The Foad Factor** J Sparks, M Walsh
1990 May 6	**Bog Drop** J Wesaway, T Stevens
1990 May 20	**Dream Warriors** R McHaffie, J Bosher
1990 May 26	**Trojan Horse** N Foster, M Berzins
1990 May 27	**Not With a Bang** J Clay, J Sparks, M Walsh
1990 May 27	**Paddy's Arête** J Clay
1990 June 1	**Serious Omission** M Lowerson, N Steen
1990 June 16	**Unnamed** A Jones, D Kirby
1990 June 20	**Black Moss Groove** R McHaffie, J Bosher
1990 June 20	**Left-Hand Route** R McHaffie, J Bosher
1990 June 20	**The Niche** R McHaffie, J Bosher
1990 July 30	**Slug Thug** R Stone, D Stokes
1990 Summer	**Upshot** K Wilkinson, R McHaffie
1990 Sept	**Achtung Spitfire** A Slattery, M Fanning
1990 Sept 15	**Henry Heinkel** A Slattery, M Fanning
1990 Sept 15	**Shot Down Variation** A Slatterly, M Fanning
1990 Sept 23	**Miss O'gynist** S Crowe, S Gee, R Bennett
1990 Sept 26	**Blonde Ambition** K Wilkinson, D Booth
1990 Sept	**The Emigrant** K Telfer, J Gilhespy
1990	**Mesrine** D Booth
1990	**Vicky** A Jones, R Graham
1990/93	**Skegness is so Bracing, Hothouse, Backfire, Nameless, Zima Junction, Valdez is Coming, Al's Slab, Panzerfaust, Heart of Glass, Better Red than Dead, Laguna Verde, Blue Oyster Cult, Zipcode, Chickenhawk, The Seam, Dalt Loch Monster, Dalt Loch Chimney, Wounded Knee, Bury My Heart, Legless in Gaza, Baywatch, Little Sydney** Dalt Quarry A Nichol, D Nichol
1991 April 16	**Schnell Dumbkopf** R Henderson, S Henderson
1991 April 20	**Das ist Verboten** A Slattery, S J H Reid
1991 April 20	**Grot in Himmel** A Slattery, S J H Reid
1991 April 20	**Hande Hoch** A Slattery, S J H Reid
1991 May 5	**Vanishing Act** K Telfer, J Gilhespy
1991 May 7	**Copperhead** S J H Reid (solo)
	Probably done before. An in-situ copperhead was found at the top of the route.
1991 May 7	**Gone for a Pizza** S J H Reid, A Slattery
1991 June 15	**The Ruptured Duck** P Rigby, A Greig
1991 June 20	**The Bodycount** D Booth (unseconded)
1991 July 7	**Endurance** R McHaffie, J Bosher

1991 July 7	**Lakeland Cragsman** R McHaffie, J Bosher
1991 July 7	**No More Motivation** R McHaffie, J Bosher
1991 July 7	**Revelation** R McHaffie, J Bosher
1991 July 17	**Holly Tree Crack** R McHaffie, J Bosher
1991 July 17	**The Death Stroke** R McHaffie, J Bosher
1991 July 24	**Eat Lead Fritz** A Slatterly, R 'Eddie' Davidson
1991 Aug 1	**Needless Sports** S J H Reid, K Kenyon
	Straightened out by S J H Reid, S A Clark 25th May 1992.
1991 Aug 3	**Burning Bridges** M Lowerson, N Steen
1991 Aug 3	**High Anxiety** M Lowerson, N Steen
1991 Aug 4	**Sex Bomb Boogie** N Steen, M Lowerson
1991 Aug 4	**Way Out Yonder** M Lowerson, N Steen
1991 Aug 11	**Beyond Redemption** M Lowerson, N Steen
1991 Aug 11	**Spruce the Bedworm Rides Again** N Steen, M Lowerson
1991 Aug 18	**Slab Happy** K Wilkinson, R McHaffie
1991 Aug 18	**On a Mission from God** M Lowerson, N Steen
1991 Aug 18	**Shaddow Lands** N Steen, M Lowerson
1991 Aug 26	**Magical Mystery Tour** M Lowerson, R Smith (alt)
1991 Sept 1	**Brutally Handsome** M Lowerson, R Bennett
1991 Sept 1	**Over the Top** M Lowerson, S Crowe
1991 Sept 3	**Rockola** J Bosher, R McHaffie
1991 Sept 3	**The Blues Connection** R McHaffie, J Bosher
1991 Sept 8	**Terminator 2** R McHaffie, J Bosher
1991 Sept 16	**Cosmetic Artifice** D N Greenop
	Similar line climbed by D N Greenop in May 1978
1991 Sept 17	**Countermure** D N Greenop, P Rudd
	Similar line climbed by D N Greenop in May 1978
1991 Sept 17	**Renaissance of the Retired** D N Greenop, P Rudd
1991 Sept 17	**Revenant's Groove** D N Greenop, P Rudd
	Similar line climbed by D N Greenop in May 1978
1991 Sept 22	**Dangerous Corner** M Lowerson (unseconded)
1991 Sept 22	**Wild Thing** M Lowerson, J Breen, T Iceton
1991 Sept 25	**Flamboyant Decay** D N Greenop
1991 Oct 3	**Auguries of Eternity** D N Greenop, C Greenop (alt)
1991 Oct 3	**The Jaws of Sheitan** D N Greenop, C Greenop (alt), B J Porter
1991 Oct 3	**The Late Remorse of Love** D N Greenop, C Greenop (alt), B J Porter
1991 Oct 4	**Farewell to the Fifties** D N Greenop (solo with back rope)
1991 Oct 5	**The Chest of Ozymandias** D N Greenop (solo with back rope)
1991 Oct 5	**The Perishing Pleasure of Apes** D N Greenop (solo with back rope)
1991 Oct 6	**Joyrider** M Lowerson, N Steen
1991 Oct 6	**Ugly Sister** M Lowerson, N Steen
1991 Dec 30	**A Few Dollars More** R McHaffie, T Richardson
1992 Jan 1	**A Fistful of Dollars** R McHaffie, T Richardson
1992 Feb 23	**The Punchline** K Wilkinson, R McHaffie
1992 April 14	**The Whipping Post** D Birkett
1992 May 5	**Bleed in Hell** D Birkett

A stunning achievement. Did not receive a second ascent until 1999 when A Hocking eventually suceeded after several attempts

1992 May 25	**Stubble** B Stacey, M Cousins	
1992 May 28	**Soxon** D Johnson, P Andrews	
1992 June 8	**Aphasia** C Downer, C Bacon, R McHaffie	
1992 June 11	**Quicksilver** C Downer, R McHaffie	
1992 June	**Die-Hard** R McHaffie, T Richardson	
1992 July 2	**Caution** D Birkett	

An amazing lead – still unrepeated.

1992 July 5 **The Borrowdale Contract** P Lockey, P Lockey, P Ross, M Brotherton

Paul Lockey led on sight.

1992 July 7	**Teva Fever** D Morrison, C Downer
1992 July 10	**A Confected Persona** D N Greenop, P Rudd
1992 July 10	**The Cyclostome** D N Greenop, P Rudd
1992 July 13	**Revenge of the Giant Climbing Ants** M Gainey, P Newman
1992 July 14	**Hellish** D Birkett

RP3, RP1 and Rock 2 pre-placed.

1992 July 27	**The Cutting Edge** P Ross, P Lockey
1992 Summer	**Burn at the Stake** P Cornforth

D Birkett and N Conway repeated it and graded it F8a "the hardest route in the Lakes at the time".

1992 Aug 6	**Single to Cemetary Gates** D Johnson, M Johnson
1992 Aug 8	**Ashley Rib** R McHaffie
1992 Aug 8	**Short Slab** R McHaffie

"This will be the last new route I do in Borrowdale – it's too hard to find anything good...!"

1992 Aug 8	**Zombie in the Dark** M Johnson, G Atkinson
1992 Aug 16	**Ashley Slab** R McHaffie, P Buttle
1992 Aug 18	**Ovation** D Bodecott, P Absalom, P Arkle
1992 Oct 20	**Parchment Tigers** P Ross, P Lockey
1992 Nov	**Falcon Pinnacle** A Slattery
1992 Dec 25	**Christmas Decoration** R McHaffie
1992 Dec 25	**Christmas Rib** R McHaffie (solo)
1992 Dec 25	**Easy Ridge** R McHaffie
1992 Dec 25	**Happy Christmas** R McHaffie
1992 Dec 25	**Jingle Bells** R McHaffie (solo)
1992 Dec 25	**Sleigh Ride** R McHaffie
1993 Jan 2	**Christmas Groove** R McHaffie, T Richardson

Variation. Christmas Tree Groove, R McHaffie 9 January 1993

1993 Jan 3	**1993** R McHaffie, T Richardson
1993 Jan 3	**Christmas Pudding** R McHaffie, T Richardson
1993 Jan 3	**Gargoyle Groove** R McHaffie, T Richardson
1993 Feb 5	**Cleavage** A Slattery
1993 Feb	**Black Crack** N Gilbourne, A Cannon
1993 March	**Strange Brew** M Johnson, G Atkinson
1993 April 3	**Paper Thin** P Ross, P Lockey
1993 April 27	**Twittering Heights** C Bainbridge, P J Kane

1993 May 12	**Mackanory** A Slattery, H Henderson
	Possibly climbed by R McHaffie and J Bosher in 1990.
1993 May 18	**Gemma** P J Kane, C Bainbridge
1993 June 10	**The Keek**
	This climb was written up but first ascenscionists' names were not given – not surprisingly!
1993 June 12	**Return Ticket** M Lowerson, N Steen
1993 June 13	**Plug** A Cannon, N Gilbourne
1993 June 29	**Doberman** R Kenyon, B Barnard, S J H Reid, D Scott, S Prahbu
1993 June	**Quay West** A Slattery, R Davidson
1993 June	**Twin Peaks** A Slattery
1993 June	**Mosquito Coast** D Nichol, A Nichol, A Nichol
1993 June	**Wombley** A Slattery (solo)
1993 July 2	**Echoes of Zechariah** S Prior, R Kenyon
1993 July 5	**Smear Today – Gone Tomorrow** D Nichol, C Downer
1993 July 25	**Graveyard Fiend** M Johnson (unseconded)
1993 July	**Hookworm** D Nichol, A Nichol
1993 Summer	**Bodybag Variation** M Johnson
1993 Summer	**Rave Night at the Mortuary** M Johnson
1993 Summer	**Lucky Luke** T Ralph, M Charlton
1993 Aug 28	**Double Lip Trip** J Clay, J Davidson
1993 Aug 28	**Loose Cannon on the Deck** J Clay, J Davidson
1993 Aug 28	**The Home Shoot** J Clay, J Davidson
1993 Sept 4	**Knitting Nicola** G Atkinson
1993 Sept 4	**Stitch in Time** M Johnson
1993 Sept 11	**World Eaters** R McHaffie (solo)
1993 Sept 14	**Death Guard** R McHaffie
1993 Sept 14	**Night Lords** R McHaffie (solo)
1993 Sept 14	**Ultramarines** R McHaffie (solo)
1993 Oct 24	**Iron Warriors** R McHaffie, P Hirst
1993 Oct 24	**Salamanders** R McHaffie, P Hirst
1993 Oct 24	**White Scars** R McHaffie, P Hirst
1993 Oct 26	**Dark Angels** R McHaffie, G Wright
1993 Oct 26	**Lunar Wolves** R McHaffie, G Wright
1993 Oct 26	**Space Wolves** R McHaffie, G Wright
1993 Oct 26	**White Dwarf** R McHaffie, G Wright
1993 Oct 31	**The Trick** K Telfer, J Gilhespy
1993 Oct 31	**The Witch** K Telfer, J Gilhespy
1993 Oct 31	**The Straits of Despair** R McHaffie, G Wright
1993 Nov 18	**Life Guard** R McHaffie, P Hirst
1993 Nov 21	**Bat Out of Hell** Dalt Quarry R McHaffie, J Bosher
	aka Mac's Crack
1993 Nov 21	**Unknown Warriors** R McHaffie, B Cook
1993 Dec 31	**Phantoms of Fear** R McHaffie, (solo with back rope)
1993	**Sheer Entertainment** K Wilkinson, A Scott
1993	**Tops for Bottoms** P Cornforth
1993	**Contract to Kill** P Cornforth
1994 Jan 1	**Beneath Nightmare Castle** R McHaffie (solo with back rope)

1994 May 94	**Liquid Morphine** C Downer, R McHaffie
1994 May 21	**Pennies From Heaven** C Downer, R McHaffie
1994 May 23	**Cold Lazarus** C Downer, R McHaffie
1994 May 25	**Camikaze** P Cornforth, G Cornforth
1994 May 26	**Dennis the Menace** C Downer, R McHaffie, M Osbourne
1994 May 26	**Goodbye Dennis** C Downer, R McHaffie, M Osbourne
1994 June 5	**Black Eyes** C Downer, R McHaffie
1994 June 13	**Karaoke** R McHaffie, C Downer
1994 June 13	**Singing Detective** C Downer, R McHaffie, A Stockord
1994 July 5	**Shadow Warrior** M Johnson
1994 July 9	**BX Breakdown** C Bennett, P Chapman, C Chapman
1994 July 13	**Lucky Strike** T Marr, M Tooke
1994 July 17	**Albatross** T Marr, M Tooke
1994 July	**Azania** S Prior, A Davis
1994 Aug 20	**Cithaeron** A Ross, P Ross
1994 Aug 20	**Nepotism** P Ross, A Ross
1994 Aug 21	**Family Tree** P Ross, A Ross
1994 Aug 21	**Parricide** A Ross, P Ross
1994 Aug 21	**Progeny** A Ross, P Ross
1994 Sept 16	**Poor Man's Utah** P Ross (solo)
1994 Oct	**Cascade** R McHaffie (solo)
1994 Oct	**Route 1** R McHaffie (solo)
1994 Oct	**Route 2** R McHaffie (solo)
1994 Oct	**Route 3** R McHaffie (solo)
1994 Nov 12	**The Crystal Maze** R McHaffie, P Hardy
1994 Nov 13	**Crytal Gazer** R McHaffie, P Hardy
1994 Nov 13	**The Dark Crystal** R McHaffie, P Hardy
1994 Nov 20	**Millican's Arête** R McHaffie, P Hardy
1994 Nov 20	**The Crack** R McHaffie, P Hardy
1994 Nov 20	**The Groove** R McHaffie, P Hardy
1994	**Sheriff of Nottingham** P Cornforth
1995 Feb 15	**One Foot in the Grave** R McHaffie, "Buffalo Bill"
1995 March 5	**Waiting for God** R McHaffie, P Hardy
1995 March 20	**Tombstone** R McHaffie, P Hardy
1995 April 9	**Magnetic North** D Bodecott, D Absalom (alt)
1995 April 19	**Freak Power** S Purdy, P Hill
1995 May 2	**Catching Up** F Dooley, C Scammel
1995 May 3	**Bleak How Eliminate** D Birkett, P Ross
1995 May 6	**Faz's Route** Faz Faraday, J Cooper
1995 May 6	**Hitler's Demise** T Walkington, Faz Faraday
1995 May 14	**The Fortress** R McHaffie, T Richardson
1995 May 15	**Between the Lines** J Campbell, S J H Reid
1995 May 15	**Holly Tree Ramp** S J H Reid, J Campbell
1995 May 21	**Boris in Wonderland** R Kenyon, C King
1995 May 21	**The Lost Boys** D Messenger, J Sharpe
1995 May 28	**Vicious Vicky from Barrow** R McHaffie, T Richardson
1995 June 10	**TDM** S J H Reid, J Campbell
1995 June 23	**Mystic Knee** E Barnes
1995 June 24	**Woodrow Wyatt's Reasoning** T Walkington, E Barnes

1995 June 26	**Midsummer at the Oasis**	S Crowe, K Magog
1995 July 8	**Freak Brothers**	A Lywood, A Harper
1995 July 13	**Cedric in Space**	R Kenyon, S Prior
1995 July 18	**Morceau**	D Bodecott, T Knowles
1995 July 19	**Moral Narcosis**	C Greenop, D N Greenop
1995 July 19	**Reckless Ectasy**	D N Greenop, C Greenop
1995 Aug 4	**The Walk on the Wild Side**	P Ross, P Armstrong
1995 Aug 12	**Symbiosis**	C Greenop, D N Greenop
1995 Aug 13	**Dark Angel**	M Johnson, A Hocking
1995 Aug 13	**Ian's Day Off**	M Johnson, A Hocking
1995 Sept 17	**Free Falling**	D Messenger, J Sharpe
1995 Sept 20	**Horizontal Pleasure**	S J H Reid, J E Reid

Climbed on their wedding anniversary!

Variation. The Nose P Salter, T Rennison 1906 – the first HVS in Borrowdale.

"The stiffest problem is the Nose, at the top of North Gully. It has only been done by one party, about 8 years ago, Percy Salter and the late Tom Rennison. Being more difficult than the Pillar Nose direct, with very minute and insecure holds, almost as hazardous for follower as for leader. A second ascent is not recommended."

Millican Dalton, F&RCC Journal 1914

1995 Sept	**Double Decker**	A Hocking, A Wilde
1995 Oct 19	**Age Concern**	R McHaffie (solo)
1995 Oct	**Dust to Dust**	D Patey, R McHaffie
1995 Nov 5	**Ashes to Ashes**	D Patey, R McHaffie, T Richardson
1995 Nov 14	**Death Bed**	R McHaffie, J Ward
1995	**Angel in the Wood**	R McHaffie, A Becket, J Palmer
1996 April 3	**True Cross**	S J H Reid, W Phipps

Quite probably done before.

1996 April 23	**Lower Girdle of Fisher's Folly Buttress**	S J H Reid, W Phipps

Quite probably done before.

1996 May 15	**Pot Luck**	P Ross, P Armstrong
1996 May 15	**Pebble Lane**	P Ross, P Armstrong
1996 May 16	**Taurus**	N Dowie, J Robinson
1996 May 29	**Balancing Act**	M Turner, A Blyth
1996 June 2	**Final Act**	R McHaffie, J McHaffie

Mac's "last new Borrowdale route"... until more followed.

1996 June 17	**Mad Cow**	N Dowie, A Cammack
1996 June 19	**Blubber**	G Baum, A Hewison
1996 June 19	**Cholesterol Corner**	A Hewison, G Baum
1996 June 19	**Islay Waits**	G Baum, A Hewison
1996 June 19	**Supermodel**	A Hewison, G Baum
1996 June 26	**Traverse of the Frogs**	J 'Frog' Hughes, S J H Reid (alt)
1996 July	**Borrowdale Volcanic**	M Greenbank, P Cornforth (both led)
1996 July	**Rock Lobster**	P Cornforth, M Greenbank (both led)

The RP1 – the only gear in 17 metres – was pre-placed.

1996 July11	**Reassuringly Stocky**	A Hewison, G Baum, J Meeks
1996 July 21	**Posidriver**	S Jones, D Simmonite

1996 July 22	**String of Pearls** C Read, G Swainbank (alt)
1996 Sept 19	**Camelot** R Graham, T Rogers
1996 Sept 20	**Manhattan Project** G Swainbank, C Read (alt)
	D & F McDonald may have climbed some of this as Singing Hinny in the 1970's.
1996	**Kid Gloves** EVMC assault
1996	**Littlejohn** A Hocking (solo)
1996	**Route 8** A Hocking (solo)
1997 April 14	**Basil** C King, A Hewison
1997 April 16	**Wobbly Bits** S J H Reid, A Hewison
1997 April 17	**Tomb Raider** J McHaffie, R McHaffie
1997 May 14	**Meet Your Maker** D Johnson, E Ostell
1997 Easter	**Jenny Wren** J Ibbotson, T Calder, M Taylor
1997 July 8	**Disorderly Conduct** A Hocking
1997 July 29	**In the Blood** A Hyslop, S Wood
	Gear pre-placed.
1997 Aug 3	**Milk** M Przygrodzki, F Przygrodzki
1997 Oct 19	**Dark Angel** M Przygrodzki, R McHaffie
1997 Nov	**Saturday Night Beaver** C Downer, R McHaffie
1997 Nov	**Scallywag** C Downer, R McHaffie
	Side runners used on first ascent eliminated by S Hubbard.
1997	**Psyched Out** M Morton, J Church
1997	**The Jolly Joker** A Hocking, J McHaffie
1997	**Cream** R Graham
	May well have been done before.
1998 March 22	**Sidewinder** J McHaffie, R McHaffie
	First of the year's crop.
1998 March 22	**Short Circuit** R McHaffie
1998 May 22	**Last Request** A Hocking, W Hunter
1998 May	**Satan's Little Helper** D Booth, I Turnbull
1998 July 31	**Poop and Scoop** S Ringrose, A Cannon
	Quite probably done before.
1998 July 31	**Thrutch and Clutch** S Ringrose, A Cannon
	Quite probably done before.
1998 July	**Hazard Warning** R McHaffie (solo)
1998 July	**Horn Control** R McHaffie (solo)
1998 July	**Ignition Switch** R McHaffie (solo)
1998 Aug 19	**Camouflage** M Dale
	Originally led with a peg for protection.
	M Lovatt then led the route without the peg. The third ascent was led on sight without the peg by J McHaffie 19 April 2000.
1998 Sept 4	**Ishmael** J McHaffie, R McHaffie
1998 Sept 4	**Spawn** J McHaffie, R McHaffie
1998 Sept 20	**Crackerjack Groove** S J H Reid, C A J Reid, I J W Reid, J E Reid
	May have been done before.
1998 Sept 27	**Tarzan** A Cannon, D Crompton
1998 Sept 27	**El Coronel** M Armitage, T Kennedy
1998 Oct 3	**Suspended Animation** J McHaffie, R McHaffie, W Hunter

1999 Jan 10	**The Touch** K Telfer, J Gilhespy
1999 Jan 24	**Track of a Tear** K Telfer, J Gilhespy
1999 Jan 24	**The Kiss** K Telfer, J Gilhespy, P Morgan
1999 Feb 5	**Green Death** J McHaffie, R McHaffie
1999 Feb 7	**The Look** K Telfer, S Lynch
1999 Feb 7	**The Smile** K Telfer, S Lynch
1999 Feb 7	**Heartbreaker** K Telfer, J Gilhespy, P Morgan
1999 April 18	**The Promise** K Telfer, S Lynch
1999 April 25	**Phantom Menace** M Lynch, D Kay
1999 May 2	**Bucking the Ram** A Hocking, J Kirkbride
1999 May 3	**No Overtaking** A Hewison, A Davis
1999 May 15	**Dreamscape** J McHaffie, R McHaffie
1999 June 6	**Being Done Good To** R Kenyon, C Kenyon
1999 July 8	**Mull Wait** G Baum, J Meeks
	Surely climbed before.
1999 July 9	**Bilberry Topping** R Kenyon, M Armitage
	Originally aided onto the bilberry ledge. R Kenyon led cleanly 28th July 1999.
1999 July 17	**Chimney Crack** R McHaffie
1999 July 17	**The Groove** R McHaffie
1999 July 27	**The Who** N Snowball, C Cooper
1999 July 30	**Scare the Tourist** N Tudor, A Cannon
1999 Aug 10	**Supercrack** D Bodecott, P Bunting
1999 Aug 17	**Katherine** A Lywood, R Patey (alt)
1999 Sept 4	**Jackson Pollock No. 5** D Harris, J Moore
1999 Sept 4	**Yakka** J Moore, D Harris
1999 Sept 4	**The Badger Parade** D Harris, J Moore
1999 Sept 4	**Precarious Block** J Moore, D Harris
1999 Sept 9	**Happy Herdwick** A Hocking, W Hunter
1999 Sept 9	**Clubfoot Variation** A Hewison, A C Robinson
1999 Sept 17	**Downer's Delight** R Patey, R McHaffie
1999 Sept 26	**Terrierman** P Rigby, J Williams
1999 Nov 20	**Lock, Stock and Two Smoking Trowels** D Harris, J Moore, G Pattison
2000 April 5	**Cellulite** A Hewison, G Baum
2000 April 19	**Langstrath Buttress** S J H Reid, A Hewison
	Both finishes were climbed on the same day.
2000 May 1	**City of Love and Ashes** A Hewison, J Meeks, G Baum
2000 May 1	**Balls Like Spacehoppers** D Harris, J Roberts
	Variation climbed by same team.
2000 May 1	**Shampoo a Rhinoceros** D Harris, J Roberts
2000 May 1	**Silent Partner** J Roberts, D Harris
2000 May 6	**Guns of Navarone** A Hocking, A Wilson (alt), C Downer
2000 May 6	**Uncle Warren** A Davis, A Hewison
2000 May 6	**Mr. Bad Example** A Hewison, A Davis

2000 June 17   **The Ego Has Landed**   J McHaffie, S Wood

An outstanding lead, after minimal top-rope inspection, and a possible contender for the most serious climb in the Lakes. "The biggest lead in the Lakes. You're going to die all the way".

Adam Hocking, having top-roped the line
shortly after the first ascent.

2000 July 6   **The Restraint of Beasts**   W Hunter, C Downer

The name was chosen in memory of the late Chris Bacon who made many contributions to Borrowdale climbing and was a fencing contractor by profession.

2000 July 22   **Wasp**   C Read, G L Swainbank

Pitch 4 was originally climbed as a variation to Troutdale Pinnacle Superdirect by P Ross, E Rosher 15 May 1959.

Note

Some details of the first ascents of the following routes are not known: Amazing Journey, Berlin Wall, Fiddle About, High Explosion, I'm Free, Miracle Cure, Pinball Wizard, Route 2 – Steel Knotts, The Keek, Tommy's Crack, Two Down, Unforeseen Danger, Wimpey Way, Woden's Groove, Zion.

MOUNTAIN ACCIDENTS

Procedure for Climbers in the Lake District

There has recently been considerable change in the procedures for mountain rescue in the Lake District. This change has been brought about by many factors, including the increase in the number and availability of rescue teams, the developments and improvements in equipment and techniques, and the increased availability (thanks to the R.A.F.) of helicopters for mountain rescue purposes.

Consequently, only minor casualties should come within the scope of treatment and evacuation by the climber's companions. The rule for all other cases is to make the casualty safe, to initiate the treatment, and to send expeditiously for a Mountain Rescue Team.

Sending for Help

A reliable member of the party should be sent for the Rescue Team, with full information about the nature of the injuries and the position of the incident (including, if possible, the map reference). **He should then find the nearest telephone, dial 999, and ask for the Police**, who will notify the most readily available team. The sender of the message should stay by the telephone until he receives instructions from the Team Leader, who may want further information or may want his help to guide the team to the incident.

General Treatment

Pending the arrival of the rescue team, basic first-aid treatment should be given. The patient should be examined as far as is possible without unduly exposing him. Wounds should be covered and external bleeding controlled by pressure on dressings. Application of tourniquets can be very dangerous and often make haemorrhage worse; they should only be used by experts and then only in extreme cases. Fractures should be immobilised by the most simple method available. The patient, if shocked, or suffering from actual or potential exposure, should then be put in a sheltered place, protected from the rain and wind, wrapped in as many layers of clothing as possible, encased in a 'poly bag' or other impermeable material, and, if conscious and not suffering from abdominal injuries, given warm drinks containing glucose. If available a tent should be erected around him.

The majority of cases will respond to this treatment and their condition should have improved by the time the team arrives. The more serious cases, where such an improvement may not occur, include head injuries, spinal fractures, chest and abdominal injuries with possible internal haemorrhage, and multiple injuries with consequent severe shock. They require urgent expert treatment, and every effort should be made to stress the urgency and the nature of the injuries when the 999 call is made. The use of a helicopter, by courtesy of the R.A.F., can be quickly obtained through the Mountain Rescue Team Leader and the Police.

Treatment of special cases

Fractures of the limbs are usually best treated, in the case of the arm, by padding it and bandaging it to the chest, and in the case of the leg, by padding it and bandaging it to the other leg.

Severe head injuries run the risk of death from asphyxia with deepening unconsciousness. The position of the patient, his head and tongue should be adjusted to facilitate breathing. Apparently less severe head injuries should be continually and carefully observed as the condition of the patient can rapidly deteriorate.

Fracture of the spine, if suspected, means that the patient should not be moved and should be made to keep still. If he is in a dangerous position, a difficult decision will have to be made as to whether or not to move him. If he has to be moved to save his life, then obviously every care should be taken to prevent movement of the spine.

Internal haemorrhage should be suspected if the patient has sustained blows to the chest or abdomen. It is confirmed if, despite the measures adopted for the treatment and prevention of shock, his condition progressively deteriorates. All steps should be taken to facilitate the rapid arrival of a doctor, team and, if possible, a helicopter. A record should be kept of pulse rate to facilitate subsequent diagnosis.

Lack of help. The most difficult decision has to be made when the patient is severely injured, possibly unconscious, and there is only one climbing companion present. He should try to summon help from nearby climbers or walkers by shouting, giving the distress call on his whistle, flashing a torch, or sending up a red flare. If there is no response then he has to assess the relative dangers of leaving the patient, or of failing to get help, and should act decisively in the interest of the patient.

Index

Guidebooks to Climbing i

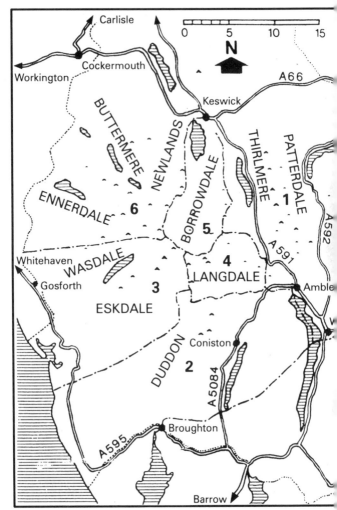